WITHDRAWN
UTSA Libraries

DISCLOSURE BY
AUSTRALIAN COMPANIES

Disclosure by Australian Companies

R. W. GIBSON

Senior Lecturer in Accounting
University of Melbourne

MELBOURNE UNIVERSITY PRESS

First published 1971
Printed in Australia by
Halstead Press Pty Ltd, Kingsgrove, N.S.W. 2208 for
Melbourne University Press, Carlton, Victoria 3053
Great Britain and Europe: ISBS Inc., London
U.S.A. and Canada: ISBS Inc., Zion, Illinois 60099
Registered in Australia for transmission by post as a book

This book is copyright. Apart from any fair dealing for the purposes of private study, research, criticism or review, as permitted under the Copyright Act, no part may be reproduced by any process without written permission. Enquiries should be made to the publishers.

© Robert William Gibson 1971

ISBN 0 522 83996 7
Dewey Decimal Classification Number 657.3

To my wife,

Wendy

Preface

The Australian nation moves into the seventies on a surge of unprecedented development of its natural resources, with continued economic prosperity and full employment. The future promises a continuation of this prosperity and development which will undoubtedly create new problems in company financial affairs which will in turn demand further developments in disclosure by companies. The accounting profession is awakened to the need to define more adequately the process of accounting measurement and the reporting of the results of that process of measurement. It is therefore highly relevant to understand the way in which companies have responded to the influences which have shaped *Disclosure by Australian Companies* over the century or so in which companies have been readily incorporated and accepted as part of our social and economic framework.

I would like to acknowledge the particular contributions made by some of the people who have assisted me in the course of the research which has culminated in this book. The editor of the *Australian Accountant* has readily agreed to the use of certain material dealing with interim reports which was originally published in that journal and which with suitable modification has been incorporated in this work. Without the resources of the library of Messrs J. B. Were & Son, Members of the Stock Exchange of Melbourne, and the gracious assistance of the librarian, Miss C. Edwards, and her staff I do not believe it would have been possible to establish the empirical basis of many of my conclusions. This library was able to provide records of selected company reports extending back more than fifty years in some cases. Mr R. E. Anderson of the State Library of Victoria and Miss P. Reynolds of the La Trobe Library facilitated my access to the official papers which were relevant to my enquiries.

I am especially indebted to Mrs Peg Dell who efficiently and expertly typed the manuscript both in its original form as a thesis for the Degree of Master of Commerce and in this rewritten form. My wife Wendy has acted as a sounding board for many of the ideas developed in the text and has assisted as an unofficial literary editor. She has also spent many late nights reading over copy. My position as a member of the academic staff of the University of Melbourne has helped in making available the time necessary to complete this work as it is in the nature of a University for staff to devote a part of their time to the search for knowledge and a better understanding of the society in which we live.

My wife and children have tolerated the devotion of much of my attention to this work rather than to them over a considerable period of time. To each of them and to each of those mentioned above and to those whose lives created the events which are the subject of this book I express my sincere thanks and appreciation.

I also wish to acknowledge the financial support of this and related research by the Australian Research Grants Commission and the Australian Society of Accountants and assistance in publication from the Publications Fund of the University of Melbourne.

I appreciate the assistance of Melbourne University Press.

R.G.

Contents

	Preface	vii
	Abbreviations	xi
1	Introduction	1
2	Why Disclosure?	5
3	Disclosure to Whom?	9
4	Attitudes to Disclosure	17
5	The Formative Years	24
6	Developing Concepts	34
7	Mr Isaacs's Bill	39
8	Mr Isaacs's Bill—Postscript	48
9	Disclosure as a Safeguard	52
10	'Towards Uniformity'	57
11	Disclosure c. 1928–1936	67
12	The Stock Exchanges—Official List Requirements	74
13	Reserves and Provisions	86
14	The Royal Mail Case	100
15	Victorian Companies Act 1938	104
16	The Profit and Loss Statement	111
17	Directors' Remuneration	124
18	Holding Companies	132
19	Verification of Stock	147
20	Format of Statements	153
21	Classification in the Balance Sheet	161
22	Western Australia	169
23	I.C.A.A. Recommendations	172

24	The Valuation of Stock	181
25	Depreciation	190
26	A.I.M. Award and Report Production	202
27	Operating Account Details	212
28	Taxation	223
29	Group Accounts	232
30	Subsidiaries and Divisions	250
31	Value in the Balance Sheet	255
32	Victoria and Tasmania 1958	263
33	The Uniform Acts	268
34	Public Borrowings Acts	275
35	Interim Reports	280
36	Additional Information	291
37	Conclusion	300
	Appendixes	304
	1 Details of 'Forty-two Leaders Sample'	304
	2 Companies included in Stock Exchange Fifty Leaders excluded from 'Forty-two Leaders Sample'	306
	3 Empirical Surveys of Company Reporting	307
	4 Comparative Table of Disclosure Required by Companies Acts, 1931–1936	310
	5 Presentation of Group Accounts by 'Forty-two Leaders Sample'	312
	6 Report on Treatment of Profits and/or Losses of Subsidiaries by 'Forty-two Leaders Sample'	314
	7 Description of Reserve or Goodwill on Consolidation, Selected Cases from 'Forty-two Leaders Sample'	316
	References	317
	Bibliography	333
	Index	349

Abbreviations

A.W.A.	Amalgamated Wireless (Australasia) Ltd
Ampol	Ampol Petroleum Ltd
Ansett	Ansett Transport Industries Ltd
APPM	Associated Pulp and Paper Mills Ltd
A. & K.	Australian and Kandos Cement Holdings Ltd
A.C.I.	Australian Consolidated Industries Ltd
A.G.C.	Australian Guarantee Corporation Ltd
A. Gypsum	Australian Gypsum Industries Ltd
A.P.M.	Australian Paper Manufacturers Ltd
B.M.I.	Blue Metal Industries Ltd
Bradford	Bradmill Industries Ltd
Boral	Boral Limited
Brick	Brick and Pipe Industries Ltd
B. Tobacco	British Tobacco Company (Australia) Ltd
B.H.P.	The Broken Hill Proprietary Company Ltd
C.U.B.	Carlton & United Breweries Ltd
Coles	G. J. Coles & Company Ltd
C.S.R.	The Colonial Sugar Refining Company Ltd
C.I.G.	Commonwealth Industrial Gases Ltd
Container	Containers Ltd
Custom	Custom Credit Corporation Ltd
D.H.A.	Drug Houses of Australia Ltd
Dunlop	Dunlop Australia Ltd
Electronic	Electronic Industries Ltd
Email	Email Ltd
F. & T.	F. & T. Industries Australia Ltd
Herald	The Herald and Weekly Times Ltd
Humes	Humes Ltd

ICIANZ	Imperial Chemical Industries of Australia and New Zealand Ltd
I.A.C.	I.A.C. (Holdings) Ltd
J. & Way.	Johns & Waygood Perry Engineering Ltd
Jones	Henry Jones (I.X.L.) Ltd
McPherson	McPhersons Ltd
Myer	The Myer Emporium Ltd
Nat. Cons.	National Consolidated Ltd
Olympic	Olympic Consolidated Industries Ltd
Peters	Petersville Australia Ltd
Repco	Repco Ltd
Rothman	Rothmans of Pall Mall (Australia) Ltd
Sleigh	H. C. Sleigh Ltd
T.V.	Television Corporation Ltd
Woolworth	Woolworths Ltd

1

Introduction

Those in the community who are interested in investment in company shares and debentures, surely would believe that the millenium had arrived if it was possible to emulate the ideal of making perfectly rational decisions based on perfect knowledge. It is no more necessary to belabour the fact that such investors are known at times to act irrationally, than it is to establish the fact that many investment decisions must be based on less than perfect knowledge. The modern corporation created readily by the procedure of filing the necessary memorandum and articles of association has just completed a century of growth and development. The first statutes facilitating the incorporation of companies had little to say about the information to be made available to investors, but over the past century there has been steady progress in the information available in prospectuses to buyers of newly issued securities and in the continuing provision of information in periodic reports to existing investors.

This book outlines a century of development of the standards of disclosure applicable to the periodic financial statements of Australian companies. The compulsory requirements embodied in the provisions of companies legislation have been important in determining minimum standards with compliance demanded by legislative authority. However a study of disclosure by Australian companies is much more interesting than would be the case if it were only a study of compliance with the law. Other factors of a voluntary kind have had significant effect on commonly accepted practice. Frequently incorporation of minimum provisions in the statutes has amounted to little more than legislative recognition of the accepted norm for most publicly owned companies. (Throughout the book the term public company is used according to its Australian usage: a company the securities of which are available to the public at large and which may be bought and sold through some form of free market. This should not be confused with the usage of 'public' ownership as implying government ownership.)

In a field in which there has been continual change and evolution one can expect further change in the future. The likely direction of change and the most important forces leading to change, may be identified by reviewing what has gone before. This is an important reason for undertaking this study. However the aim of the study is not only to identify the sources of power leading to change. It is also necessary to identify the reasons which led to past changes as the same arguments may well be applicable to future situations. Understanding what has gone before may thereby help us to deal more adequately with situations in the future.

This enquiry led me to examine a wide range of official and non-official papers, journals and books. Such sources help to identify the general course of the developments discussed in following pages but frequently lack any empirically based details of practices and changes in practices over the period covered by the study. It was decided therefore to support the enquiry by a detailed study of the reporting practices of a selected list of Australian public companies. This list comprised forty-two industrial commercial companies, identified in appendix 1, and was based on the Fifty Leaders Index of the Stock Exchange of Melbourne. Two banks, one insurance company, one pastoral company and four base metal mining and investment companies were excluded on the grounds that they were special kinds of enterprises with peculiar problems of reporting not to be found among the more usual kind of industrial commercial enterprise. The forty-two companies comprised twenty-six companies registered in Victoria and fifteen registered in New South Wales. This was not considered to be an unacceptable bias because the size of the companies meant that most were businesses of a national rather than local character. In the absence of precise details it could be argued that such large companies possess the strength to ignore the voluntarily imposed norms of the business community, or alternatively that it is such large enterprises which in fact establish those norms. Neither of these extreme positions were accepted but it is trusted that the real position reflects a little of each of these extremes. In a small country such as Australia, subject to both rapid growth in recent years and increasing concentration of industry and commerce it was not possible to devise a sample of constant size over a long period. The analysis of empirical data therefore is based on an increasing size sample depending on the availability of the reports of the forty-two selected companies over a period of fifty

1 Introduction

years. The reports of a few companies were available at the earliest date surveyed, 1916, while the balance was available from later dates which coincided with either the formation of the company or the listing on the Stock Exchange of Melbourne of the securities issued by the company. The number of reports available in any one year is referred to as the 'available sample'. The importance of these forty-two companies is perhaps best illustrated by noting that, at the time they were selected, they represented 60 per cent of the aggregate market value (A.M.V.) of all companies listed on the Stock Exchange of Melbourne.[1]

Over the past forty years a number of small empirical investigations of specific features of reporting have been made and are referred to where appropriate. A list of these studies can be found in appendix 3.

During 1961–2 company legislation in all Australian States was amended on the basis of a Uniform Act. For convenience this legislation is referred to as the Uniform Acts and where relevant the section numbers cited will be those of the Victorian Act. The legislation involved is as follows:

Victoria, *Statutes,* Companies Act 1961, Act no. 6839.
New South Wales, *Statutes,* Companies Act 1961, Act no. 71, 1961.
Queensland, *Statutes,* Companies Act 1961, Act no. 55, 1961.
South Australia, *Statutes,* Companies Act 1962, Act no. 56, 1962.
Tasmania, *Statutes,* Companies Act, 1962, Act no. 66, 1962.
Western Australia, *Statutes,* Companies Act 1961, Act no. 82, 1961.

The following have been referred to as 'Public Borrowings Acts':
Victoria, *Statutes,* Act no. 7089, Companies (Public Borrowings) Act, 1963.
New South Wales, *Statutes,* Companies (Amendment) Act 1964, Act no. 20, 1964.
Queensland, *Statutes,* Companies Act Amendment Act of 1964, Act no. 10, 1964.
South Australia, *Statutes,* Companies Act Amendment Act 1964, Act no. 52, 1964.
Tasmania, *Statutes,* Companies Act, 1966, Act no. 28, 1966.
Western Australia, *Statutes,* Companies Act Amendment Act 1964, Act no. 69, 1964.

It is one of the characteristics of the developments surveyed here that, while at times great effort has been expended in securing the disclosure of specific information, there has been little attempt in Australia to define the quantitative basis of measurement underlying the published 'facts'.² This study is concerned therefore primarily with the descriptive nature of financial disclosure rather than the underlying process of accounting measurement. For all those involved in this saga to have paid so little regard to the problems of accounting measurement may be regarded as a serious matter. However it is not my task to hypothesize what might have been. On the contrary I intend to record what has been achieved and, through an evaluation of those achievements, hope to establish a clearer basis for future action.

2

Why Disclosure?

It is the nature of the modern corporation that there is a separation of the role of owner or manager as this is the only way (except for some rare instances) in which the large capital requirements of modern business can be brought together. The contributor of the financial resources (whether in the legal position of owner or not) is dependent therefore on the availability to him of information to determine whether or not the resources he has invested are being used to the best advantage. Until barely twenty years ago this investor was nearly always legally an owner, most commonly holding ordinary shares or, less frequently, preference shares. Modern developments in business finance have given an important place to investor-lenders holding unsecured notes, secured debentures or mortgage debentures. Such a change in the characteristics of the typical investor must be reflected in the demand for disclosure of information both as to the information disclosed and its availability.

Changes in society in modern times have led also to demands for information about the activities of corporations by other groups in the community who are not owners. Economists and research workers have an 'academic' interest. Statisticians seek to fulfil the needs of the research worker, aided by compulsive powers and guarantees of individual anonymity. More directed to individual companies are the interests of organized labour in gaining more adequate knowledge of the state of the company in its drive for a share of corporate productivity alongside the entitlement of the owners.

Even though our society remains firmly established on the principles of private enterprise and private ownership, the response of governments to various requests for involvement in the economic life of the nation in a variety of ways has increased the direct interest of government agencies in the ready availability of financial data of companies.

Let it not be thought that the demand for disclosure of information about the financial affairs of companies is only a modern phenomena. William Clay was a leader in a campaign in England in the middle of the nineteenth century advocating legislation to allow the routine incorporation of companies without the necessity of receiving a Royal Charter or a private Act of Parliament. Clay is said to have campaigned with the slogan 'Limited Liability: paid-up capital: perfect publicity'.[1] In England the principles of limited liability were established in the Act of 1855 and the Act passed the following year introduced the procedure of incorporation by registration of a memorandum and articles of association instead of the registration of a deed of settlement as provided for in the Act of 1844. The Act of 1844 was a remarkable document and duly recognized Clay's slogan of 'perfect publicity'. R. A. Irish expressed his opinion in the following words:

The English Act of 1844 enunciated minimum requirements for the books; it made definite rules as to audit, and provided for due publicity through publication of the balance sheet. Accent was placed on the prevention of fraud and on accounting for capital, rather than on a true determination of income. In fact, no profit and loss account was required. In this way, the accountancy profession came to regard the balance sheet as a holy document and the existing shareholders as the gods it must satisfy . . . Subsequent amendments in English Law did nothing to destroy this myth.[2]

Unfortunately the publicity practices to which Irish referred did not last. The official attitude which subsequently developed is no doubt summarized by Robert Lowe, the president of the Board of Trade, who is reported as having said that 'the only way that the Legislature should interfere [with the right of freedom of contract and the right of unlimited association] is by giving the greatest publicity to the affairs of such companies, that everyone may know on what grounds he is dealing'.[3] It remains a matter of conjecture as to just what Robert Lowe would have considered adequate publicity. What we do know is that when the comprehensive Joint Stock Companies Act was passed in England in 1856 the fulfilment of Clay's slogan of 'perfect publicity' was dependent on the adoption by individual companies of the optional articles of association set out in the schedule to the Act. Only eight years later, the same year in which the first comprehensive company law was enacted in Victoria, the editor of the *Economist* was compelled to call for more adequate disclosure by at least some companies. The editor referred to rumours of the great profits being earned by finance companies

2 Why Disclosure?

which were described as a kind of successful monstrosity which businessmen could not understand. He went on to identify the information considered desirable, holding that 'if reports are published at all, they should be so full as to enable the public really to judge of the business to which they relate'.[4]

It is theoretically correct to argue that the shareholders, as the legal owners of a company, could have secured this information by adopting appropriate articles by passing the necessary resolutions. However, the spread of ownership in the modern corporation also disperses the power of the members; so that through the use of proxies and the lack of interest of many members, it is possible for the directors effectively to control the company through control of a relatively small proportion of the shares. If directors in such a position fail to provide adequate disclosure, then it may be considered desirable for the legislature to step in and provide legislative compulsion in the interests of present and prospective shareholders. Thus there is imposed a minimum statutory standard of disclosure on all corporations. It is to be expected that, as the spread of social groups interested in companies increases, so the law will extend the disclosure requirements applicable to companies. The impact of interested parties such as political parties or organized labour may not be related directly or obviously to specific disclosure requirements such as the inclusion in the English Companies Act, 1967 of a requirement to show donations for political or charitable purposes exceeding £50. It is more likely that these demands will be reflected in the total view society has of the company at any point of time.

Professor Trevor Johnston giving one of the annual lectures endowed by the Australian Society of Accountants at the University of Melbourne argued that the traditional attitude to disclosure based on the legal status of the company needs to be replaced by attitudes which recognize the economic position of the company in the modern society. He concluded that:

In our partially controlled economies new forms of social control, particularly in the absence of effective competition, are becoming necessary if our system of free enterprise is to survive and function effectively. These new controls, including informed public opinion, with which should be associated the press and the economist, depend very largely on the availability of adequate financial reports. This means new and greater demands on financial accounting, in fact the possibility in the long run of still another branch of accounting. To the practical man there will be obvious difficulties. But the challenge is there, and the question is whether administrative difficulties are to be considered more significant than the demands of changes in social outlook which are taking place whether we favor them or not. Over a hundred years ago when the first Companies Act was passed, the failure to legislate adequately for disclosure delayed the development of standards of financial reporting to members by at least half a century; but the choice made by the legislature at that stage was consistent with the prevailing social philosophy of *laissez faire*. Today, however, the need is to match the direct action of governments, trade associations or large monopolies in creating privileges and concessions, by direct action in creating or encouraging new forms of social control including those which depend for their efficacy on full and fair financial reports.[5]

If we could assume that the standards of disclosure practised by companies were to be found in company legislation in the absence of specific shareholder resolutions, then a review of developments over the last century merely would require a recitation of the various legal provisions as they applied in the several colonies or, as they later became, the several States of the Commonwealth of Australia.

However, there have been at various times other factors at work which have had varied impacts on Australian companies. Sometimes it has been nothing more than the proselytizing fervor of an individual such as the late Sir Alexander (then Mr) Fitzgerald's efforts to define the usage of the terms 'reserve' and 'provision'. At other times it has been the leadership of one company as in 1969 when the chairman of the Colonial Mutual Life Assurance Society, W. D. Brookes, was reported by the *Herald* on 15 May as having said it had been decided to disclose the market value of the Society's share portfolio 'because other life companies were now doing so', this announcement coming on the day following a similar disclosure by the Australian Mutual Provident Society. Other influences have included the professional accounting bodies and most importantly the several Stock Exchanges. A full study of developments in disclosure must pay regard to the voluntary standards which have arisen from such sources.

3

Disclosure to Whom?

The discussion of the need for disclosure has already suggested that changes in the role of companies in our society have brought with them demands for information by an ever widening variety of interested parties.

The legal position as defined in the Companies Act still places primary emphasis on the needs of the shareholder investor. There is no evidence of recognition that even the character of shareholders themselves might change until the nineteen-fifties. In many of the industrialized nations of the world there has been a great growth in the distribution of share ownership. In a research lecture given in 1952 Sir Keith (then Mr R. K.) Yorston provided statistics that clearly demonstrated how numerous are shareholders, and how small is the average shareholding.[1] His analysis of thirty companies also showed the high proportion of women shareholders and the numerical superiority of shareholders over employees in the same companies.

Yorston made the first empirical enquiry into the information needs and attitudes of shareholders in Australia when in 1955 he circularized the members of two companies, Jantzen (Aust.) Ltd with about 200 members and Pacific Chenille-Craft Ltd with about 3,000 members, and came to the following conclusions:

(1) Shareholders desire to know more about the company and its products, for they feel they can assist in increasing the company's turnover if they have such information.

(2) Annual meetings of companies are held at a time when a large proportion of members cannot reasonably attend. Employees, self-employed persons and professional people cannot, for instance, normally attend a company meeting held during ordinary business hours.

(3) It is a general impression that a company meeting is only a brief formality and therefore it is futile to attend. Members might welcome,

for example, a tour of the factory or other operations as part of the annual meeting proceedings.

(4) Many members would like to see a greater degree of disclosure in published financial statements and to see the turnover of the company disclosed, as for instance was done by Jantzen (Aust.) Limited.

(5) I am unable to accept as valid the average member's confidence that the annual financial statements are so well understood. However, it would seem that better presentation and more liberal use of charts, diagrams, etc., are assisting in the better understanding of the figures.[2]

Yorston's conclusions that shareholders do not attend company meetings because of the inconvenient time of meeting, from the shareholder's point of view, and an impression that the meeting is only a formality must place more importance on the role of company published reports in communicating information to shareholders.

One company, not included in the 'forty-two leaders sample', recently recognized the importance of satisfying the information needs of shareholders and set out to attempt to ascertain those needs. Gibson Kelite Industries Ltd included a short questionnaire in the 1967 annual report in the form of a postcard which could be completed and returned to the company. Although only 9 per cent of the shareholders returned the questionnaire they were shown to comprise a cross-section of the company's shareholders. It appears from the published analysis of the shareholders' replies that they were generally satisfied with the company's annual report which is a comprehensive and well presented publication. Nearly half the shareholders who returned the cards did not indicate any additional information they would like included in the report. Those who did seek additional information principally sought such non-financial information as details of products, employee details and plans for the future.[3]

An American survey listed the information most sought after by the investor in company shares as 'comparative financial statements, analysis of the revenue statement by divisions or products, authoritative textual comments explaining the reasons for significant changes in operating results and financial condition, and statements explaining research and developments likely to affect the future of the company'.[4] It is interesting to compare these four items with the features sought to meet investors' needs as seen in 1955 by a Sydney stockbroker because most of these are still not generally published. J. Campbell Johnson sought a clear separation of financial data and other 'public relations' contents, the use of narrative statements,

3 Disclosure to Whom?

comparative statements over a period of years, turnover figures, and an explanation of changes in financial position.[5]

As recently as 1953 it is possible to find a spirited defence of company reports as being essentially a report of stewardship by the directors to the proprietors. Such an argument was presented by F. E. Trigg, addressing the Newcastle and Hunter Valley Conference of members of the Institute of Chartered Accountants in Australia. Trigg considered it a misconception that these reports serve multifarious purposes.

If people use them for other purposes, they may well claim that they have been misled, and it then falls to the practitioner to point out that unwarranted inferences have been drawn from them. It should be made clear that accounts laid before shareholders are primarily for their information and enlightenment...[6]

At the same time it was possible to find those who supported a wider outlook. G. L. Allard, for example, in the same issue of the *Chartered Accountant in Australia* in which Trigg's remarks appeared, was arguing that,

in order to decide how published accounts are to be prepared and what information is to be included, it is necessary to take into consideration the requirements of those who use the accounts. Although accounts are published primarily as reports to the shareholders on the progress of the company they can have a larger circulation.

Mr Allard went on to refer to the many interests in published reports and noted that in reality, 'many companies accept the presentation of annual accounts as an opportunity to acquaint the public and their employees of their activities and design their reports with care'.[7]

The Accountancy Research Foundation, established jointly by the Institute of Chartered Accountants in Australia and the Australian Society of Accountants, asked ninety respondents what should be the most important purpose of the published financial statements issued by public companies and what other purposes should be of particular significance. These respondents comprised thirty-eight auditors and accountants in public practice, seventeen chairmen, directors or managers of public companies, nineteen public company secretaries or accountants, six professors of commerce or accountancy, five officers of finance, trust and assurance companies, three chairmen of stock exchanges and two bankers. From such a diverse group one would not expect a consensus of opinion unless that opinion was widely held. Some of the respondents suggested that company annual reports do have a wider purpose than reporting to shareholders and others directly interested in the financial aspects of companies' operations, but the report of this enquiry suggests that there is 'a substantial consensus of opinion that the *prime* [emphasis mine] purpose of published statements is to report to the proprietor shareholders'.[8]

Within the last decade the difference between the needs of shareholders and debenture holders was highlighted by the circumstances revealed in the investigators' report into the Reid Murray Group. This report drew attention to matters which were reflected in the published reports to shareholders and which the auditors reported presented a true and fair view of the company. The investigators pointed out that this undoubtedly was correct from the point of view of shareholders, but they had grave doubts as to whether it presented a true and fair view to debenture holders.[9] But the investigators could not do more than make the comment because the legal position remains that company reports are issued by the directors to the members of the company.

Debenture holders are essentially creditors of the company and therefore remind us of the needs of other classes of creditors. It has been suggested that creditors particularly are interested in the realizable value of assets. This value is likely to be dependent on circumstances, and the shock effect of a receiver's statement frequently highlights the possible variations in realizable values. Apart from the values of current assets and the market values of investments, such values are largely ignored in present day reporting. It has been suggested also that the funds statement is particularly useful to creditors but, as will be shown, this statement has achieved little importance in published reports.

Sometimes it is argued that the institutional investor in shares and debentures has special needs over and above those of the individual investor. Perhaps the only ground for this assertion is the greater responsibility often brought about by the investor acting as a trustee. At the 1958 convention of the Australian Society of Accountants, F. E. Stahl suggested a number of features the institutional investor would like to see in company reports.[10] Stahl's suggestions at that time included information as to the composition of the executive, more detail in profit and loss statements, turnover figures, market valuation of stocks, fixed assets, and investments, discontinuance of grouping debtors and stocks, discontinuance of grouping creditors and taxation, consolidated statements, and a list of subsidiaries. Of all Stahl's points, increased detail of profit and loss account and the

3 Disclosure to Whom?

market value of stocks and fixed assets are the only items not realized within three years of the presentation of his paper.

The banker-creditor has also been considered to have special information needs. One prominent banker-accountant, Mr H. McE. Scambler, summarized these needs in 1958 as the quality of the management, the main products or activities, up-to-date audited position and results, earning capacity and prospects, expansion and other plans, and how they are to be financed.[11]

These special needs of bankers have been met largely in the public reports. However, it could not be expected that the demands of bankers for financial information would necessarily be met through the published financial statements and hence contribute to developing the standards required of those reports. As one banker stated: 'Close contact and the confidence enjoyed between banker and customer are probably of more value to us than anything that might be gained from general improvements that might be made in the form in which annual accounts are made public.'[12]

The use by management of the annual report as a means of communicating with employees is one of the newer uses of company reports. In 1951 R. K. Yorston conducted an enquiry among employees of certain companies. Although 89 per cent of the employees said they saw the annual report, only 78 per cent said they read it, and only 46 per cent indicated that they were able to understand it.[13] The overwhelming requirement to make the statements more useful in this context was 'simplicity'. R. K. Yorston conducted another enquiry in 1959 to determine to what extent the annual report was used to report to employees.[14] Twenty out of eighty-seven companies which replied indicated that they supplied financial information to all employees and another forty-three supplied it to a section of the employees. In thirty-seven of the companies, the annual report was the information provided. Yorston's enquiry looked at the effectiveness of this as a means of communication to employees, and he concluded that company managements were aware of problems in giving information to employees but did not have effective solutions. In the absence of a better solution, it appears from the results of Yorston's 1959 enquiry that the annual report is expected to fill an important role in reporting to employees. T. R. Johnston has pointed out that this involves a conflict of interests:

On the one hand, on the grounds of equity and stability, and in the interests of the employees, it may be socially desirable that they be regarded as members of the corporation by which they are employed and that they should be given full reports in the same way as other members. On the other hand, some degree of mobility of labour is essential in a competitive and expanding economy. The reconciliation of these interests is not easy. Unfortunately, it is organisations working under monopoly or protected conditions which are generally able to give most information to employees because they are not faced with the possible use of the information by competitors. Further, the supplying of information is often part of a plan to gain the loyalty of employees and the sympathy of unionists which may be very important when questions such as the need for tariff revision or control of monopolies are being considered by the public or by those responsible for the policies of political parties.[15]

If we accept Johnston's analysis, then we must conclude that this is a reporting problem which calls for experimentation to find a solution. Until this work is done satisfactory standards of disclosure to employees will not be established.

A. R. Hall claimed in 1958 that the relatively few people able and willing to do the required work, a lack of research funds, and the smallness and uneven distribution of the sector of economic life covered by public companies up to 1939, all contributed to Australian economists not doing detailed work on company reports until the fifties.[16] Hall suggested a considerable list of information which economists would like to see published. Among the items he then sought which are now required by statute were depreciation provision, provision for taxation, interest on fixed interest loans (this would cover most interest payments), breakdown of creditors to separate tax liability, investments divided into government securities, listed and unlisted securities, provisions for doubtful debts, and consolidated statements. Two other items which he suggested were of concern to economists have received varied treatment in published reports. They are provisions against stock fluctuations, and additional depreciation charges above the allocation of original cost. He also suggested economists would like to receive more detailed explanations of the effects of mergers and divestments. Perhaps most important of all in the information he sought was turnover. At this point we may describe the balance of Hall's requests as fantasy, extending as they did into details of the trading and profit and loss accounts and various statistical analyses of shareholdings. Not unexpectedly, Dr Hall's requests received a less than enthusiastic reception. The important feature to note is that to fulfil them places a company not only in a relationship of responsibility to its members, but also of responsibility to the community.

3 Disclosure to Whom?

Acceptance of the role of company disclosure as being the creation of informed public opinion would affect such diverse community groups as organized labour, trade unions, consumers and competitors who are affected by mergers and monopoly structures, the planners in government instrumentalities and the devisers of policies of preference or restraint through subsidies and tariffs or through political action.

The relatively short time for which these questions have been under consideration is shown by the fact that the first serious discussion in Australia of the effects of these diverse needs was in the Sixth Commonwealth Institute of Accountants Endowed Research Lecture in the University of Sydney in September 1951 given by R. K. Yorston.[17] The matter was taken further in a series of papers presented to the Australian Society of Accountants National Convention in Sydney in 1958 including those by Scambler, Stahl and Hall already referred to. Other valuable contributions to the study of this aspect of reporting include the 1960 lecture by Dr T. R. Johnston,[18] and more recently two forward looking papers presented to a one day seminar of the Victorian division of the Australian Society of Accountants, held on 30 July 1964, by a leading stockbroker and a financial editor.[19]

In Australia the pursuit of additional information has been left in large measure to the financial editors of the daily press and of certain periodicals. We have not had the kind of informed criticism of company reports represented overseas by the 'Commerce and Finance' column in the *Accountant* or 'Among the Balance Sheets' in the *Accountant's Magazine* (Scotland). Following the enactment of the English Companies Act 1929 the Finance and Commerce section of the *Accountant* changed from broad economic comment on investments in railroads and the like, to commentary on contemporary reporting. The first occasion on which this column adopted this format was on 25 February 1928, within a week of the introduction of the companies Bill into the English Parliament. In the intervening years 'the need for more informative company accounts has been fostered by the illustration in "Finance and Commerce" of existing deficiencies, and by the encouragement of improvement in examples taken from current accounts of public companies'.[20] The column in the *Accountant's Magazine* dates from the issue in July 1958 when it was titled 'Company Accounts'.

Australia has not experienced anything comparable to the crusading zeal of the Gilbert brothers in the United States of America[21] which has changed many a company meeting from a mere formality to a significant event disclosing more details about the company. The Gilberts have become an organized voice for shareholders and have contributed greatly towards obtaining more adequate recognition of the rights of shareholders to receive knowledge about the companies in which they hold shares. The Australian Shareholders' Association recently has been effective in creating a positive approach to the reports and annual meetings of some companies. This association might be able to secure widespread recognition as a mouthpiece for shareholders, represent shareholders at company meetings, and take up such causes as the association's attack on the growing practice of company chairmen insisting on answering questions 'in bulk' at the annual meeting.[22] The attendance of 500 shareholders at the annual meeting of B.H.P. on 10 September 1965 created front page headline news. This illustrated that individual shareholders could be roused to attend an annual meeting and present a united approach to the board at the meeting.[23] The *Age* commented in its columns that 'the spectacle of a majority of the meeting of the largest public company in Australia vocally opposing the board',[24] made it a meeting such as there had never been before among leading Australian companies.

Notwithstanding this particular occasion and the Shareholders' Association, the situation in Australia has not yet reached the point which caused one American writer to describe the annual meeting of the company as the 'annual headache'.[25]

The response to these demands for information has been varied and is detailed in following chapters. The most outstanding examples of an Australian company annual report addressed to an audience much wider than the shareholders must be the 1961 and 1962 reports of Ampol. These two reports were published as a supplement to the *Australian Women's Weekly,* a national magazine with an Australia-wide circulation, at the time exceeding 800,000. The directors said that they were presenting the company's report, 'not only to its Stockowners, but to Australia as a whole—to the people whose custom it strives to merit in a changing industry'. This was not just a 'newspaper' statement of the company's report. The report received by the shareholders was the *Women's Weekly* supplement printed on the same quality paper as the magazine.

We can expect that the company annual report will continue to serve a much wider audience than the shareholders, to whom it is primarily addressed and whose rights are the basis of the legal requirements defining the minimum content of the company report.

4

Attitudes to Disclosure

Just as the pressure for disclosure may come from a variety of sources, so is there a variety of attitudes to the necessity for and desirability of disclosure.

Reference already has been made to the advocacy in the nineteenth century of William Clay and Robert Lowe. It appears reasonable to support R. J. Chambers's conclusion that it is doubtful whether the publicity contemplated by these people went much further than the requirements that the annual accounts should be published.[1] The voluntary provisions of the early legislation in England proved ineffective and in 1907 the English Companies Act provided for the compulsory publication of a balance sheet. It did not prescribe any details as to the content or presentation required, apparently assuming that the publication of the company's regular financial statement would be adequate compliance with both the letter and the spirit of the law.

In Australia events had stirred the legislature to take a more serious view, at least in Victoria, for as we shall see later the Victorian Parliament had passed legislation in 1896 to compel a prescribed standard of disclosure by all companies which could not claim the anonymity of proprietary company status.

Practical businessmen did not accept readily the notion of disclosure or publicity but rather developed a clam-like attitude to the disclosure of financial information. In September 1926 the editor of the *Commonwealth Journal of Accountancy* arguing for the collection of adequate statistics of business activities was constrained to observe that: 'Australian businessmen seem to have marked objections against making trade information available to others, whether in their own line of business, or engaged in non-competitive trade.'[2]

By 1929 the Greene Committee on Company Law Amendment had reported in England and a new English Companies Act had become law. This Act was hailed widely as the epitome of company law and was adopted as the model for new legislation in three of the four most populous States of Australia. The reticence of businessmen was reflected in the limited scope of the compulsory provisions of this legislation and the opinion was expressed by a leading public accountant, Sir (then Mr) Edwin V. Nixon, that it must not be thought that this legislation had made it impossible to issue accounts which were not sufficiently informative, holding that there was always scope for intelligent discrimination.[3] Sir Edwin added a positive note to his contribution to public discussion of the issue by suggesting guiding principles. These were that the financial statements should convey, without technical reservations, the true position, show the profit fairly attributable to the period, and disclose nothing detrimental to the company and hence the shareholders.

Another accountant, L. T. Ewens, probably expressed a widespread opinion when he wrote: 'for some years past there has been a growing feeling that shareholders are badly treated in that too little information is given them'[4] and urged shareholders to assert their rights. He believed that 'much of the detail in balance sheets of the time, as presented to shareholders, conceals the true position of the company; much of the detail given is quite unnecessary, and that which is necessary is cloaked or hidden'. As T. M. Fitzgerald observed thirty years later, interpreting many items in the financial statements is like looking at the top of an iceberg for the shareholder 'must depend on the auditors, with their inside access, to assess the quality of that much larger portion of the iceberg which lies below the surface'.[5] A similar opinion was expressed by the prominent accountant and author, R. A. Irish in 1947, about normal annual reporting of companies: 'there is a common commercial tendency to limit information to the confines of legal requirements—a tendency which is indefensible and out of step with accounting evolution'.[6] Recognizing changing patterns of business finance he identified one especially significant weakness of such a practice arguing that: 'The legal obligations in respect to information are still modelled on the proprietorship theory—accounting responsibility to other parties is substantially unrecognised.'

Two American academics who surveyed a number of Australian company reports in 1960 observed these restrictive attitudes to disclosure in practice. They concluded from their analysis that 'clearly Australian management has a somewhat different concept of the responsibilities and objectives of financial reporting from that of American management'.[7] In the items these writers checked the

Australian reports clearly were deficient compared with American company reports. Many other prominent individuals have pointed out evidence of this reticence on the part of company directors. Even in 1966 at a seminar conducted by the Institute of Directors, R. L. Stock, the secretary of one of the 'forty-two leaders sample' of companies, conceded that he believed it to be 'clear that in the past the erring was on the side of too little'. 'There were some companies that grudgingly admitted they had a name, some capital and made a profit' he added.[8]

It would be a mistake to believe that this was only true in the past. In 1965 the Attorney-General for Victoria, the Hon. (now Sir Arthur) A. G. Rylah, addressing the Investment in Australia Symposium, said that the companies legislation had gone almost as far as is possible but 'this does not mean that all companies provide adequate information for the investing public'.[9]

Why do these attitudes exist among businessmen responsible for the preparation of company financial statements? F. E. Trigg, who made a significant contribution to the *Chartered Accountant in Australia* over many years, summarized the reasons for opposition to disclosure as stemming from concern for one or other of two things:

(1) whether by disclosure competitors or anybody else will gain at the expense of the company; or
(2) whether it is a good or bad thing for the shareholders to know this or that about the enterprise which they own.[10]

Writing in the fifties, Trigg observed that secrecy had 'become a bogey of fairly large proportions' and as for the second factor, he considered it 'almost borders on the preposterous'. He argued that the auditing test of truth and fairness is the essence of the matter. He advocated the auditor advancing his standards beyond legal requirements. The idea that the auditor may be used as a kind of rubber stamp he considered to be 'a position that no auditor should accept'. Trigg argued forcefully that the more proper disclosure is insisted upon, the more valuable will the auditor's contribution become.

It is not difficult to find advocates of these attitudes which Trigg described as a 'bogey' and 'preposterous'. R. K. Yorston, whose work as a textbook author is discussed later, even though maintaining the position that not enough pertinent information is being given by numerous companies in their annual reports, was able to define disclosure as being:

the clear and accurate presentation of financial information of potential importance to persons for whom the report is prepared. The doctrine of disclosure of information in annual reports of companies is *bounded* [emphasis mine] by the fact that confidential information should not be disclosed nor should information be disclosed that may be detrimental to the company or its shareholders. Sound judgment and the materiality of the item place a responsibility on the accountant as to whether or not it should be disclosed in the annual report.[11]

The Hon. A. G. Rylah was apparently in no doubt of the acceptance of this 'bogey' and 'preposterous' proposition when he said that:

Unfortunately there is a deep-seated love of secrecy in the business world. In my view the need for secrecy is vastly over-rated. Too often the failure to make adequate disclosure springs from a desire to protect the interests of directors and management rather than the interests of the company.[12]

The attitudes to disclosure advocated in the writings of some academic accountants—many of whom also have been practising accountants—stand in contrast to the attitudes described above. These writers assume that disclosure is intrinsically a good thing. This cannot be better illustrated than by referring to Stephen Gilman's *Accounting Concepts of Profit,* a pioneering attempt to survey the whole of accounting and to find a rationale for accounting practice. In this book he presented a composite list of accounting principles, from which he selected those he considered most important and codified a number of what he chose to call conventions and doctrines. Gilman assumed that there were four 'doctrines of accounting' which included the 'doctrine of disclosure'.

He wrote:

Commonly accepted by accountants as a general proposition of financial reporting is the doctrine of adequate disclosure. It is in accordance with this doctrine that the accountant prepares balance sheets, profit and loss statements, and other accounting reports with properly descriptive headings, clear explanations, and explanatory footnotes. In harmony with this doctrine the accountant indicates bases of valuation, pledged assets, contingent liabilities, arrears in preferred dividends, the effect of price declines in relation to long-term contracts, and similar matters. This doctrine is normally applicable to reporting rather than to accounting, but it should be observed that its application is required by the complexity of present-day conditions in order to supplement the limitations of the simple accounting mechanism which by its very nature can reflect only obvious relationships. When these relationships cease to be simple and obvious, application of the doctrine of disclosure is required. (p. 206)

Later on he asserts that, 'broadly speaking, the doctrine of disclosure requires the revelation of information which, if withheld, might influence a prospective creditor's decision to loan funds or a prospective investor's decision to buy securities' (p. 242), and as a final seal to the necessity for disclosure, concludes that: 'It can scarcely be doubted that the doctrine of disclosure is essential to honest, adequate reporting' (p. 244).

Gilman's contribution is peculiarly important in an examination of standards of disclosure in Australia because of the adoption of his ideas in Australian accounting literature. A. A. Fitzgerald adopted the Gilman dichotomy in the theoretical discussion in his text on analysis and interpretation. Although he does not mention explicitly the 'doctrine of disclosure', an examination of contemporary teaching aids and examination papers reveals the attention given to this 'doctrine'. Fitzgerald, it might be noted, defined a 'doctrine' as a 'belief that a given practice should be followed' and 'a dogma inculcated by teachers of accounting, text book writers or authoritative associations of accountants'.[13] The second principal stream of Australian textbooks in the post-Gilman era are those written by a group including R. K. Yorston and E. B. Smyth. These writers also adopted the Gilman approach although their particular collection of conventions and doctrines varied somewhat from the original. Over six editions of their *Advanced Accounting* they give a varied selection from eight conventions and four doctrines. Nevertheless there occurs throughout the various editions the promulgation of 'a system of beliefs' which includes in every edition a 'doctrine of disclosure' which is interpreted thus:

This doctrine suggests that all accounting statements be scrupulously honest, and full disclosure of all significant information be given. An obligation is placed on the accountancy profession that the books, records and accounting statements prepared on behalf of others are as reliable and informative as circumstances permit.[14]

In the handbook of the American Institute of Certified Public Accountants (A.I.C.P.A.) we find it argued that: 'So that the reader may reach decisions concerning financial statements in full confidence that he has all necessary information, the principle of full disclosure has long been a basic one in statement presentation.'[15] The handbook considers that in carrying this out 'the accountant has grave responsibilities with respect to the statements'. 'This responsibility relates not only to the propriety of what is set forth, but also to the inclusion of such information as is necessary to make the statements not misleading.'[16] It is not surprising to find this opinion of disclosure reflected in the results of the accounting research programme instituted by the A.I.C.P.A. which produced 'the Basic Postulates of Accounting'.[17] This attempt at formulating an accounting theory put forward three sets of propositions, the third of which were described as 'the imperatives'. As the author said: 'Because they stress what ought to be (goals, objectives, standards), they are referred to as "imperatives" '. Thus disclosure was placed in the category of what ought to be and summarized in the phrase: 'Accounting reports should disclose that which is necessary to make them not misleading'.[18] This suggests that disclosure is a little more than dogma in that it is to avoid the possibility of accounting reports being misleading. This A.I.C.P.A. study has not found a significant level of acceptance though it did have its fleeting moment of acceptance in Australia. In the third edition of *Analysis and Interpretation* Sir Alexander Fitzgerald adopted the 'imperatives' from the Basic Postulates Study.

Whether disclosure takes place because of this type of injunction will be considered in this book.

It is suggested that the opinion of the majority of Australian accountants probably lies between the extremes of the over-secretive businessman and the more zealous of the academics. Perhaps it is typified by W. R. Hartland's definition of disclosure as requiring 'the reasonable supply of information to enable shareholders to determine the results of a company's trading and its general financial stability'.[19]

Such varied attitudes to the disclosure of information by companies as we have demonstrated will lead to varying standards of practice. To the extent that the standards practised are considered to be inadequate, then the interested individuals and groups will seek to improve standards. The question arises as to how far the matter may be left to voluntary influences and how far legal powers should be invoked to compel companies to conform with what is determined to be an acceptable standard. Writing in the *Accountant's Magazine*, the journal of the Institute of Chartered Accountants of Scotland, A. F. Murray explored the pros and cons of this matter and, leaving aside the claims of certain types of company which constitute special cases, he concluded that the issues may be summarized thus:

(i) investors have a real interest in more compulsory disclosure;
(ii) companies' objections to compulsory disclosure, though sometimes justified from their own point of view, are often greatly exaggerated or even completely unfounded;
(iii) the public interest lies in the direction of fuller disclosure, since this makes for a more efficient allocation of economic resources by helping investors to channel their funds towards the better managed companies, and by helping companies to select the most rewarding lines of activity.[20]

Murray regarded the third of these conclusions as the main argument in favour of compulsory disclosure prescribed by statute. This accords with similar arguments advanced by Dr T. R. Johnston for a system which prescribed disclosure on various economic criteria instead of the traditional categories based on the legal status of the company.

This book investigates the role played by the requirements for disclosure prescribed by statute. It is particularly concerned to see how far it has been necessary to use legal powers to modify existing practice or alternatively how far the development of statutory requirements has reflected the progress of existing practice.

5

The Formative Years

None of the Australian States inherited company legislation as part of the English statutory law which followed the settlers to the colonies. The colonies inherited the existing English law as at 1828 in New South Wales, Tasmania, Victoria and Queensland, 1836 in South Australia and 1829 in Western Australia. All these predate the first English legislation facilitating the incorporation of companies by registration of a deed of settlement passed in 1844, the recognition of limited liability in 1855 or the more comprehensive Joint Stock Companies Act of 1856 later consolidated in the Companies Act 1862.

The applicability of earlier English laws in Australia involves complex issues of legal interpretation.[1] An Act of the imperial Parliament, 9 Geo. IV, c. 83, determined that New South Wales and Tasmania were to be placed on the same footing as 'settled colonies' (notwithstanding their convict settlement origins), so that they inherited English law as at 28 July 1828. This Act also determines the position for Victoria, which was separated from New South Wales in 1851, and Queensland which was separated in 1859. This legislation was considered necessary to eliminate doubts arising from the colonies starting as penal settlements. South Australia originally was regarded as part of New South Wales but subsequent enactments and decisions of the Supreme Court of South Australia and the High Court of Australia have confirmed that the application of English law to that State is to be considered as if this province never had any association with the mother colony. English law therefore applies in South Australia as at 28 December 1836 which has been defined legislatively as the State's date of settlement. It was in South Australia particularly that the question of the power of the colonial Parliament to alter this derived English law, was questioned. Notably the decisions of Boothby, J., were directed against the colonial Parliament. The position was finally resolved by the

Colonial Laws Validity Act of 1865 which established that the colonial Parliament 'could repeal or amend the British statutes and unenacted English law which had been received under the common law constitutional principles'.[2] This does not remove the application of Acts passed before or after 1865 which are held to apply to the States 'by paramount force'. Because free settlers founded the colony in Western Australia, the common law principles of the English law were applicable in the colony and the Interpretation Act of Western Australia provides that 1 June 1829 is the date on which that State 'shall be deemed to have been established' for the purpose of determining the application of English statutory law.

During this early colonial period the formation of companies was relatively difficult and involved either a special or private Act of parliament, a grant of a royal charter, or resort to the common law device of a deed of settlement company. (Such a company received its identity by virtue of a deed created under the law relating to trusts.)

One early company formed by private Act of the New South Wales Parliament and today contributing significantly to commerce and industry, is the Bank of New South Wales. This bank was formed in 1817 under a charter of doubtful validity granted by Governor Macquarie. A deed of settlement was drawn up in 1828 and in 1850 incorporation by private Act of parliament was sought and granted. An interesting case of a company operating in Australia under a royal charter is the Australian Agricultural Company incorporated in 1824.[3] In 1965 a commentator on the company's one hundred and twenty-fourth annual report described it as 'still obviously a lively and up-to-date concern' and considered the company provided a 'set of accounts which provides the investor with an adequate review of the use of his funds and the earnings arising'.[4] Perhaps one of the most interesting companies in Australian history formed as a deed of settlement company was the South Australian Company,[5] formed by a deed executed on 27 June 1836. The company registered subsequently under the English Joint Stock Companies Act on 20 November 1844 and in 1856 was granted a royal charter. This company, which contributed so much to the settlement of South Australia, was liquidated finally in 1949. Companies formed in these ways were governed by the relevant private Act, charter or deed, the conditions of which were established individually. While each company may be of interest in itself, we cannot look to these companies to find the foundations of company law generally or, the more particular concern of this study, the disclosure of financial information.

Within the colonies a number of Acts was passed governing specific aspects of the operation or management of companies before provisions were enacted facilitating the incorporation of companies.

In New South Wales in 1839 an Act was passed to make good certain contracts of banking and other copartnerships, an Act of 1842 facilitated proceedings by and against companies, another Act in 1847 facilitated the winding up of companies and one in 1848 allowed actions at law between a company and its members and vice versa. In Tasmania an Act passed in 1841 extended to all companies the legal privilege enjoyed by fourteen companies created by special Act or royal charter, but within three years this Act was restricted to the named companies. In South Australia provisions for the dissolution of companies were contained in an Act passed in 1854 while in the following year an Act modelled on the English Act of 1844 provided for the registration of deed of settlement companies. Other legislation included the extension of limited liability to banking firms in 1856 and in 1859 an Act which facilitated legal proceedings involving companies. As Victoria and Queensland were not separate colonies until 1851 and 1859 respectively, it is not surprising that these colonies were not involved in such preliminary skirmishing with company legislation.

More comprehensive steps to formulating adequate company legislation in the Australian colonies followed closely developments in England, and the date of the Joint Stock Companies Act 1856, is close to the date of legislative action in the Australian colonies. It is clear that in spite of the slow communications between England and Australia, the colonial governments were well up to date with developments in England. It is not possible to ascertain the views of the legislatures except in Victoria at this period, as the reports of parliamentary debates did not begin until 1857 in South Australia, 1864 in Queensland, 1876 in Western Australia and 1879 in New South Wales. The Parliament of Tasmania has not instituted any Hansard record.

Western Australia established its first company legislation in 1858, and this Act was copied substantially by the Tasmanian Act in 1859. These Acts relegated accounting provisions to the optional articles, reflecting the same thinking as that in the similar provisions of the English Act passed two years earlier. According to the model articles the directors were required to keep true accounts of stock, of cash receipts and payments, and of credits and liabilities of the company. The articles were unique in Australian experience, in that they specified that: 'Such account shall be kept, upon the Principle of Double Entry, in a Cash Book, Journal, and Ledger.'[6]

The articles also specified that a statement of income and expenditure and a balance sheet were to be tabled at the annual meeting. Only the balance sheet was subject to audit and to be circulated to the members. The articles also provided a model form of report which had two interesting characteristics. The first was that the statement of income and expenditure was to distinguish the several sources of income. This is a point found to recur in legislation and debate around 1938 and 1965. The second interesting feature was that where any expense was incurred which might have been spread fairly over more than one year, the whole amount was to be stated with reasons why only a portion was charged to the current period. This is a point covered by compulsory legislation around 1962 requiring the gross amount of assets at cost or valuation to be disclosed with the accumulated depreciation shown as a deduction therefrom. The specification of double entry book-keeping was dropped by Western Australia in 1893, but remained in the Tasmanian Act until 1920. This change in the accounting specifications in the Western Australian Act brought it into line with the Acts of the other colonies at that time, and the consolidating Act passed in England in 1862.

In South Australia the Act allowing registration of deed of settlement companies was considered by the government to be adequate. In 1859 the Chief Secretary remarked that the government had not seen any necessity for amendments of the legislation as the 1856 Act was 'sufficient to meet all the requirements of the colony'.[7] However, there was far from agreement on the issue for in 1859 Captain Hall gave notice of a Bill, but later withdrew it as it was impossible to proceed in that session. Again on 22 May 1862 Mr Mildred introduced an amending Bill to overcome difficulties under the present Act which he considered 'imperfect in many respects' and 'in fact was almost null and void'.[8] But this Bill was withdrawn to await the report of a 'select Committee on the mineral laws'.[9] The Act was finally passed in 1864 two years after the landmark English Act.

The Victorian legislation received a no less stormy passage. It commenced on 11 November 1862 with a notice of motion in the name of R. D. Ireland.[10] J. D. Wood claimed that legislation on the subject was required urgently. He pointed out that an important measure, in connection with it, had become law recently in Great Britain and that the Bill was based on the English Act of 1862. The origins of the Bill were identified further when in the committee debate the following June, Ireland in reply to debate on the balance sheet set out in the schedule, pleaded in justification that 'it was a transcript from the English Act'.[11] Ireland claimed the two main features of the Bill were to provide incorporation without the need for a private Act and liquidation without the necessity of resort to the Insolvent Court or Court of Chancery. At least J. McGregor was thinking on the lines of the concept of adequate disclosure as the price of limited liability for: 'He also thought that the bill did not make sufficient provision for the publication of reliable statements of the assets and liabilities of the companies formed under it. He hoped these defects would be remedied.'[12] The Bill was referred to a select committee which had been appointed to consider the Partnership Bill. Unfortunately the Bill foundered, largely because the Speaker found during the committee debate that the government printer had amended the Bill without the authority of Parliament.[13] After this incident the Bill was discharged from the notice paper. However, it was reinstated on the notice paper, passed and sent from the Assembly to the Council on 21 August 1863. In spite of these preliminaries the Bill was criticized in the Council as being a hasty measure. Mathew Hervey objected that: 'The measure was lengthy and extremely imperfect. It was supposed to be the transcript of an English act, but the fact was, that it was the transcript of a bill which never passed through committee in the British House of Commons.'[14] On 9 September the Council was presented with a petition from 'a number of the merchants, tradesmen, and citizens of Melbourne, praying the House to pass the bill during the present session',[15] but Parliament was prorogued and the Bill died. However, the promoters of the Bill returned to the effort in the following year and finally it was passed on 25 February 1864, just sixteen months after the initial notice of motion by Ireland. Similar Bills were passed by the Queensland Parliament in 1863 and the New South Wales Parliament in 1874.

The Bills passed in four of the most heavily populated colonies between 1863 and 1874 were all similar and based on the Bill which underlay the English Acts of 1856 and the consolidation of 1862. All of the Acts in the four colonies, Queensland, South Australia, Victoria and New South Wales, also relegated the accounting provisions to the optional articles in the schedule to the Act. One peculiarity of the South Australian Act was the requirement for a six-monthly return of shareholders which remained until the amending Act of 1892. The accounting provisions paralleled those in Western Australia and Tasmania except that the prescription to use double entry book-keeping was not included. Thus was established the foundation of company law in Australia, founded on the principles of English law and leaving the details of accounting and auditing to be decided by the individual company. Each company was free to adopt the standards laid down in the articles or to modify them as it saw fit. The legislature obviously concurred with the views expressed some years later by the notable jurist, Lindley, L.J., who said: 'It is not a subject for an Act of Parliament to say how accounts are to be kept; what is to be put into a capital account, what into an income account, is left to men of business.'[16]

Why was it, as this option suggests, that the legislature had moved so far away from the concept of no limited liability without disclosure and the mandatory accounting provisions of the English Act of 1844 which had even preceded the recognition of limited liability embodied in the English Act of 1855? Were the voluntary standards thus formulated observed in practice? It is not possible to answer directly either of these questions. The former, because there are no records of the arguments propounded in debate, and the latter because the company records examined did not go so far back. However it is possible to rationalize the legislatures' actions by examining more closely the concepts of the company and its finance which appear to underlie the legislation of the time.

The early companies Acts were not formulated with a view of capital as a measure of the net worth of an enterprise but as 'the minimum value of the net assets which must be raised initially and then, so far as possible, retained in the business'.[17] As Lindley, L.J., observed in the Verner case nearly thirty years later: 'the main condition of limited liability is that the capital of a limited company shall be applied for the purposes for which the company is formed'.[18] Applying the capital to the purpose of the business was seen as obtaining the necessary 'fixed' assets to operate in the chosen field of activity. When granting limited liability the legislature was concerned primarily with protecting creditors dealing with the company. This protection was based on these notions of the amount of capital agreed to be subscribed and its application to acquiring the 'fixed assets'. An assessment of the financial position of a company would therefore appear to have been regarded as establishing the amount of capital contributed and the manner in which that capital had been expended. The disclosure requirements of the 'first' companies Acts appear in accord with this. Section 24 of the Victorian Act was typical in the specification of an annual return which was to include the names, addresses and occupations of all the members and the number of shares held by each of them, and the following details:

(1) The amount of the capital of the company and the number of shares into which it is divided.
(2) The number of shares taken from the commencement of the company up to the date of the summary.
(3) The amount of calls made on each share.
(4) The total amount of calls received.
(5) The total amount of calls unpaid.
(6) The total amount of shares forfeited.
(7) The names, addresses and occupations of the persons who have ceased to be members since the last list was made and the number of shares held by each of them.

The courts in interpreting the Act emphasized this concept of the contributed capital by laying stress on a distinction between capital account and income account, which is best epitomized in the so-called double account system of accounting.[19] Under this form of accounting one part of the statement explains the sources of permanent capital and the assets on which it has been expended, while the second part outlines the current assets and current liabilities arising from routine operations. This form of accounting commonly was used by public utility companies which arose during the nineteenth century.

This emphasis on the concept of contributed capital, it might be noted, was very pervasive and early court judgments effectively extended the same thinking to the definition of divisible profits. Thus Lopes, L.J., in *Lee* v. *Neuchatel Asphalt Co.* in 1889, observed that: 'The capital and the revenue accounts appear to me to be distinct and separate accounts, and, for the purpose of determining profits, accretions to and diminution of the capital are to be disregarded,'[20] and this concept was taken the full distance in Verner's case where the court held that:

fixed capital may be sunk and lost, and yet the excess of current receipts over current expenses may be applied in payment of a dividend, though where the income of a company arises from the turning over of circulating capital no dividend can be paid unless the circulating capital is kept up to its original value, as otherwise there would be a payment of dividend out of capital.[21]

Thus the financing of a company appears to have been seen as

5 The Formative Years

the contribution of resources which may, or may not, be maintained and certainly were not repayable to the shareholders. Lindley, L.J., appears to have rejected the notion of even ultimate accountability to the shareholder for the contributed capital. In his judgment in the *Lee* v. *Neuchatel* case he observed: 'The company is not debtor to capital, the capital is not a debt of the company.'

However, the courts, when further grappling with the problem of defining profits available for payment of dividends, attempted to split the assets into two groups, 'fixed' and 'circulating', in some manner comparable with the division of capital and income. Such a division would have been a simple solution to defining capital and income if there were comparability so that fixed assets equal capital, circulating assets equal income. Such simple solutions rarely exist and the weakness in these definitions was brought out in a later case. Swinfen Eady, L.J., in his renowned discussion of this concept in the Ammonia Soda Co. case[22] in 1918, recognized that part of the 'capital'—i.e. a portion of the subscribed capital—will be applied to secure the initial circulating assets. The consequence of this is that one cannot equate subscribed capital and capital in the sense of fixed assets. Creditors therefore must be concerned not simply with knowing what assets were acquired with the subscribed capital, but will want to know 'whether the net worth of the business is maintained and whether it has assets from which they can be paid'[23] because the maintenance of the net assets of the company will indicate the maintenance of subscribed capital used to acquire both fixed assets and circulating assets. The idea of making out a balance sheet to determine profit as the surplus after recognizing liabilities to creditors and company members was suggested in *Re Ebbw Vale Steel, Iron and Coal Company* in 1877 (4 Ch.D., p. 827) but seems to have been lost in subsequent court proceedings because of the insistence on contemporary ideas of 'capital' and 'income'.

Thus the growing sophistication of business and company financing began to be recognized. It was to be expected that the simplistic attitudes and answers of the eighteen-fifties and eighteen-sixties gradually would be found to be inadequate when applied to contemporary situations. Companies today no longer rely on shareholders as the sole contributors of 'capital'. The resources of a modern company are also acquired from various classes of creditors. The security of these creditors can only be determined on the basis of the net assets of the company. Creditors do not lend so much because the shareholders have contributed a certain sum but rather because the company as a corporate unit is seen to possess assets and, where it is necessary, the ability to meet the cost of servicing an interest-bearing debt.

To know the net worth of an enterprise involves the presentation of a statement of assets and liabilities. The compilation of such a statement means that a monetary value must be given to each item. The traditional balance sheet, whatever its shortcomings may be, represents the accountants' method of compiling such a presentation. It is suggested therefore that the introduction of compulsory publication of a balance sheet was related to this developing concept of the limited liability company and what constitutes the relevant information for the protection of creditors. Such an interpretation of the information necessary for creditors' protection was recognized in the recommendation made in 1906 by the Loreburn Company Law Amendment Committee in England that:

> for the protection of persons who may deal with a company, and may become its creditors, every limited company ought to be required to file periodically a statement of its affairs in the form of a balance sheet, containing a summary of its capital, its liabilities and its assets, giving such particulars as may generally disclose the nature of such liabilities and assets, and how the values at which the fixed assets stand are arrived at.[24]

If the propositions outlined above are accepted, it may be argued that these changed circumstances would have been met adequately if companies had observed the spirit at least, if not the letter of the optional articles set out in the schedules to the first companies Acts of the colonies. These optional articles as already outlined provided for the availability of a balance sheet.

Performance in company reporting in Australia did not keep pace with these developing concepts, however. In Victoria Mr Isaac Isaacs was quite certain of the inadequacy of the existing situation when he commented that his own proposals for legislation:

> provided that the directors must keep proper books and accounts, and have their accounts audited. Various provisions are made which, to my mind, are not stringent enough for the proper keeping and purification of those accounts and the giving of guarantees to the public that the balance-sheets and accounts are fairly correct.[25]

Auditors did not escape criticism either, Isaacs saying: 'It strikes me that it is a perfect farce to direct that a company shall have balance sheets, and that those balance sheets shall be audited, unless some control is got over the auditors themselves.'[26]

5   The Formative Years

Proposals that the directors should certify the correctness of the accounting statements provoked a very hostile debate with argument on the lines that 'the fact that they had been through a panic during the last few months should not induce them to enter upon legislation of a spasmodic kind which would make it impossible for careful and prudent persons to accept any public position at all'.[27] The events of what we now know as the land boom, and the subsequent course of legislation, suggest that there could be little confidence placed in the notion that company directors would, in the interests of creditors, abide by the spirit of the optional articles contained in the schedule to the Companies Act. We can only guess how far the adoption of practices more in line with the optional articles of association would have given some protection to the shareholders in many of the ill-fated banks, building societies and other ventures.

6

Developing Concepts

The previous analysis has suggested that there was a need for, and ultimately an actual response to changing conditions which culminated in the inclusion in the companies legislation of compulsory disclosure provisions. This was not a completely spontaneous reaction, although the events of the land boom undoubtedly sparked action in the case of Victoria which was the only colony to enact compulsory disclosure requirements applicable to all public companies before the formation of the Commonwealth of Australia in 1901. There were a number of preliminary excursions into the realm of compulsory disclosure covering special types of companies which established the possible future developments on a wider basis of application.

BANKING COMPANIES

It is not unexpected that the recognition of the need for information about banks to be found in a 'balance sheet' might have come at an earlier date than the recognition of the need for trading companies to publish balance sheets. The fundamental basis of operating a bank is to secure substantial resources in the form of creditors' deposits in addition to the 'capital' or resources contributed by the shareholders.

These characteristics were recognized in provisions for disclosure enacted in Queensland in 1863, in Victoria and South Australia in 1864, in Tasmania in 1869, in New South Wales in 1874 and in Western Australia in 1893. Banks and insurance companies were required to prepare what was, in effect, a balance sheet twice each year and to keep a copy of the most recent statement *posted up* in their registered offices. The statement set out in the schedule to the Acts included details of the authorized, issued, called and paid up capital, the liabilities under five headings and the assets under four headings. Except in Western Australia, banks were therefore the first companies subject to any form of compulsory disclosure.

Legislation covering banking companies later led the way again. The first legislation for the compulsory audit of the accounts of an operating company in any of the colonies was the Queensland Act of 1889 requiring the audit of banking companies.

MINING COMPANIES

The peculiar characteristics of mining led to the enactment of separate Acts for the incorporation of mining companies. The first such Act was passed in Victoria in 1864, only two months after the Trading Companies Act. Special Acts followed in Tasmania in 1869, in Queensland in 1875, in South Australia and New South Wales in 1881 and in Western Australia in 1888. This legislation is of particular interest because of the reporting conditions imposed and the introduction of the no liability company. The mining companies legislation marked a further advance because it required these companies to *file* their financial statements with a public authority as public documents. This was the first occasion on which such a filing procedure was introduced.

The first legislation for mining companies, in Victoria in 1864, imposed obligatory accounting and reporting responsibilities. Mining companies were required to keep proper books of account, a practice which might have softened the effects of the land boom if it had been observed by some non-mining companies, and these books were to be available for inspection by creditors and shareholders. Each six months a 'full and correct account' of the company's assets and liabilities was to be published in the government *Gazette*. Similar principles were incorporated in the Tasmanian Act of 1869. In 1871 the Victorian Act was modified to delete publication in the *Gazette* and, instead, required the directors to serve the statement upon the Registrar-General 'accompanied by a statutory declaration verifying the same'. This Act also marked the first obligatory requirement to present financial statements to a meeting of the company. The directors were required to lodge at the registered office not less than one week before the meeting a statement for inspection giving 'a full and true report . . . of the state and prospects of the assets and liabilities of the company'. The substance of this Act was copied by South Australia in 1881, by Tasmania in 1884 and by Western Australia in 1888. In New South Wales the Act of 1881 did not impose any obligation for reporting on mining companies, but the 1896 amendment did require the presentation to members and filing with the Registrar of a yearly statement.

NO LIABILITY COMPANIES

It was goldmining that provided the catalyst for the tremendous growth of Victoria in the second half of the nineteenth century.

In ten years gold had transformed Victoria from a minor pastoral settlement to the most celebrated British colony. Her population of 540,000 accounted for 46 per cent of those in the Australian colonies, and was 70,000 more than the European population of Australia and New Zealand in 1851.[1]

Gold had played a most important part in developing the colony, but during this period it was alluvial gold. Deep goldmining was to follow later and would involve much larger concentrations of capital. It was to meet this that, in 1871, the Victorian government created the no liability company. Victorians seem to have been more than satisfied with their inventiveness and perhaps were even entranced by the effectiveness of this device. It will be argued later that part of the trouble over 'Mr Isaacs's Bill' arose from his enthusiasm for this type of company. The idea of no liability mining companies was received generally with enthusiasm and copied almost verbatim in Queensland in 1875, in South Australia in 1881, in New South Wales in 1881 and in Western Australia in 1888.

The importance of this development was in the way the other colonies copied the legislative ingenuity of Victoria, a practice which, as will be shown, by no means was followed on other matters of concern in this study. In fact it will be argued that Victoria remained the 'lone wolf' of innovation until the 'uniform' legislation of 1962.

LIFE ASSURANCE COMPANIES

Consideration of accounting in relation to life assurance companies would involve a complete study in its own right. At this point however, it is desirable to note a further advance which was first made with respect to these companies. Legislation was introduced for a compulsory periodical actuarial investigation coupled with a requirement to file financial statements and to circulate a statement to the members. This statement might be an abstract. It did, however, mark the first instance of compulsory requirements to *circulate to its members* the financial statements of a company. These requirements were not instituted within the companies Acts but by special Acts regulating life assurance businesses passed in Victoria in 1873, in Tasmania in 1874, in South Australia in 1882, in Western Australia in 1889, in Queensland in 1901 and in New South Wales in 1902.

FOREIGN COMPANIES

The 'first' companies Acts were enacted at a time when Australia consisted of six sovereign colonies. Companies incorporated in other colonies were just as much foreign companies as were companies registered in Great Britain or anywhere else overseas. As communications improved, undoubtedly there was an increase in trade and commerce between the colonies, and the activities of some companies extended beyond their own 'home' colony. Two events will serve to highlight this stage of development of the country. In 1883 a rail link, with a break of gauge transfer at Albury, was completed between Melbourne and Sydney, and in 1887 the two ends of the Melbourne-Adelaide railway joined to provide through services. The growing interdependence of the colonies was reflected also in the political developments of the time, for it was in 1885 that the imperial Parliament established a Federal Council which marked a significant step towards the ultimate political unification of the colonies as the Commonwealth of Australia in 1901. It is clear that the extension of the activities of such foreign companies into a colony created problems and the time came when it was necessary to register these foreign companies. South Australia acted to allow foreign companies to register in 1886 for as R. C. Baker, M.L.C. said:

the root thought . . . was that inasmuch as Corporations had no bodies to be kicked nor souls to be damned when they went into a foreign country, such as South Australia, they should have some officer appointed who could be sued if necessary, and who was the responsible person with whom they could deal, and who was really the financial representative.[2]

However, this Act provided for optional registration. The failure of the legislation provides some insight into the value of such voluntary legislation. In 1892 the registration of foreign companies was made compulsory. This lead was followed in Queensland in 1886, in Tasmania in 1895, in Victoria in 1896, in Western Australia in 1899 and in New South Wales in 1906. The Queensland Act included its own peculiarities, as Queensland legislation tended to: British companies were allowed to be registered, and could not hold freehold property unless registered or otherwise authorized to do so by Act or royal charter. Other foreign companies were permitted to register from 1895 but could only hold freehold if licensed to do so. These peculiarities continue at the present day.

This recognition of foreign companies is important because companies registered in one colony and operating in another may be required to meet obligations not imposed by the law of that other colony on the 'native' company. In subsequent years this meant that the reporting of companies operating on an Australia-wide basis could well be dependent on the State in which the company was incorporated. The spread of the activities of companies to other colonies also marks the beginnings of a movement towards uniform legislation throughout Australia, finally achieved in 1962.

7

Mr Isaacs's Bill

Never was there seen such speculation in real estate as the hysteria of enthusiasm which swept Melbourne in the eighteen-eighties. Then in 1891 the bottom dropped out of everything. 'In the year ended June 1888, no fewer than 270 new companies were registered in Melbourne, with nominal capital of £50 million and paid-up capital of about £25 million.'[1] 'Since the introduction of the Insolvency Act in 1871, there had been an average of 320 bankruptcies a year in Victoria. But in 1890 there were 445 schedules filed; in 1891 there were 420; and in 1892 no less than 509.'[2] Things were so bad that the government decided to declare a whole week a 'banking holiday' in an attempt to save the banks, only two of which remained open.[3] The poor suffered very badly. In three years, Melbourne's population fell by nearly 50,000[4] many of these people 'going bush' in an attempt to live off the land. Some said that Parliament was filled with fools and rogues who were involved with the scandals and disasters, so that the government tried to ignore what was happening. Gradually the real facts became known, largely through the work of Maurice Brodzky in his magazine *Table Talk*.[5] Then an aroused electorate expressed its revulsion of feeling in the sweeping victory of the Liberal-Protectionist Party at the elections in 1894.

Nowhere in Australia were the consequences of the 'boom and bust' of the eighties felt as acutely as in Victoria. Many saw one of the important contributing factors to have been the inadequate information available to investors who had been led to invest their savings in enterprises which could never have withstood an open investigation of their affairs. It was held by some that companies should be required to provide the correct kind of information to prevent a repetition of such disastrous events. One individual was responsible more than anyone else for achieving the passage of such legislation, Mr (later Sir) Isaac Isaacs (later Chief Justice of the High Court of Australia and first Australian-born Governor-

General of the Commonwealth). Max Gordon in his biography of Isaacs has suggested that the objective of amending the company law was the motivating factor in this gentleman's entry into politics.[6]

In 1910 when the Victorian Act was redrafted completely it was said that the legislation passed in 1896 was hasty and ill-considered. These accusations hardly fit the facts. For nearly six years under a sequence of different governments, there was a major companies Bill on the notice paper of one or other of the parliamentary chambers. The issue was so complex and raised so many fiery debates that the House was not able to make sufficient progress on the Bill to get it passed in any year.[7] It is therefore likely that Isaacs did have to adopt behind the scenes pressure tactics to get the Bill through in 1896, but it could hardly be called ill-considered.

The parliamentary tactics began when James Munro was Premier with almost the opposite objectives to those of Isaacs. When Ephraim Cox, M.L.A. asked Munro to introduce a Bill to protect the funds of depositors in the land banks, he not unexpectedly refused. Later the same year, the company directors who largely comprised the membership of the Legislative Council tried to pass the Directors Liability Bill, amending the Companies Act to enable speculators to escape the results of their actions. This Bill was introduced by W. A. Zeal who was to occupy the office of President of the Council during the subsequent wrangles of 1896. This Bill attempted to introduce 'a novel idea even for Victoria—that shareholders should not be liable to pay the uncalled capital on their shares. The Upper House passed the bill with hardly a dissenting voice' and sent it to the Assembly on 21 October 1891 'but after a shocked public outcry it was hastily buried by the Legislative Assembly'.[8]

A. Wynne, as a private member of the Council, later the same year introduced a Bill which passed the Council but did not proceed to the second reading in the Assembly. The Bill Wynne claimed was 'founded on the English acts' and 'he had endeavoured to bring the English legislation up to date'.[9] In 1892 Wynne again tried with a Bill to which he claimed he had tried to apply 'the most useful parts of the English companies law up to the present date'.[10] But this Bill was divided into two parts and only limited portions were passed ultimately. Again Wynne tried in 1893. This time he was acting as Solicitor-General in the Patterson Ministry. J. M. Davies noted that the Bill substantially had now been before the House in three consecutive sessions[11] and Wynne in the committee debate, apparently without discerning the strength of the opposition, innocently remarked that 'a large number of the clauses had been well thrashed out in committee the two [previous] sessions in succession, and he did not think there could be any objection whatever to them now'.[12] Sir Frederick Sargood on the other hand intimated that he had received a deputation from the Incorporated Institute of Accountants whose resolutions embodied no less than nine pages of proposed amendments.[13] Wynne's Bill was passed finally by the Council on 18 October 1893 but at that point the Bill 'died' as the parliamentary session came to an end.

Following elections, George Turner's government took office. Cannon has said of the electoral result:

This government had been elected with an overwhelming popular mandate to pass laws dealing with the glaring abuses of the finance and investment system, which had led to such widespread suffering . . . But at every point the Turner government was burked by a sullen and vindictive Upper House.[14]

Early in 1894 Wynne's Bill was taken up in the Assembly by Sir Bryan O'Loghlen, but the Bill failed to pass the second reading. In November 1894 Isaacs, who was now Attorney-General, commenced his 'attack' by introducing a similar Bill to the one drawn up by Wynne. Isaacs intimated that he proposed to move various amendments which 'will be all in the direction of increasing the security to the public that is intended to be given by the Bill'.[15] As the Bill had been debated over a period of four months in the Council the previous year, the leader of the Opposition, Sir James Patterson, considered: 'If the Attorney-General does not encumber the Bill with a number of fads of his own, I have no doubt it will pass very speedily.'[16] Alas, without Isaacs apparently even intimating his proposed amendments, the Bill was discharged from the notice paper on 25 January 1895. Isaacs introduced the Bill again in May 1895 but discussion of the clauses of the Bill in committee did not begin until five months later. At this stage Isaacs[17] referred to the Report of the English Company Law Committee, which he had received since the Bill was last before the House. This document was to have a most important influence as will become apparent. By the end of November the Premier advised that the government would not proceed because it was impossible to complete such a large piece of legislation in the session.[18] But this Bill was not to lapse simply because of a procedural limitation. In January Isaacs again introduced his Bill, in spite of pleas of some members not to proceed.[19] In addition, he intimated that he had incorporated into the Bill his previous amendments. He had spent the Christmas vacation virtually drafting a new Bill in the light of the English company law committee report.[20] Between the second reading of Isaacs's Bill on 21 January 1896 and its being laid aside on 5 March, the Bill was transmitted from the Assembly to the Legislative Council and back to the Assembly no less than three times.

The company directors and landowners in the Legislative Council freely amended the Bill, indicating that they did not intend to let the more revolutionary of Isaacs's ideas pass easily. Notwithstanding this continued opposition, Isaacs introduced his Bill into the Assembly again on 24 June 1896. This was the fourth attempt by Isaacs and the seventh time the proposed legislation had been before the House.

This Bill was discussed thoroughly in the Assembly, and in July was sent on to the Council. There was intense lobbying for the Bill to be referred to a select committee. Petitions were presented to the Council requesting this from the Incorporated Institute of Accountants in Victoria, the Victorian Division of the Society of Accountants and Auditors, Incorporated (England), the Melbourne Chamber of Commerce, certain banks, and Edward Knox, chairman of the Colonial Sugar Refining Company Limited, all of whom later gave evidence to the Select Committee which was appointed by the Council. Isaacs obviously considered the Select Committee to be biased in its attitude, for he described their enquiries thus:

They examined 32 witnesses who might be classified in this way:—
Directors, 6; members of companies in the position, to all intents and purposes, of managers, 4; managers of banks and companies and secretaries of institutions coming under the head of managers, 15; accountants, 5. There was also one witness whom he classed as commercial, because he did not appear in any other capacity, and one witness whose description he had been unable to find.[21]

While Isaacs's listing provides an indication of the business interests of witnesses and highlights the absence of spokesmen for shareholders and depositors, it also provides an interesting demonstration of the nature of the commercial life of the time. The witnesses represented three companies with colliery and coastal shipping interests, four wool-broking and pastoral companies, five banks, three building societies, one merchant, the Colonial Sugar Refining Company and three professional bodies and the Chamber of Commerce.[22] The Council no doubt secured the answers they wanted and subsequently returned the Bill to the Assembly with no less than 121 amendments. Notwithstanding this multitude of amendments, the accounting provisions of the Bill remained fundamentally the work of Isaacs except for the innovation of the proprietary company. Isaacs sought to hold out against some of these amendments but the Council was adamant. Isaacs finally gave in declaring that: 'The Assembly had secured, at the point of a sword, a distinct improvement on the present law, but not, in his opinion, nearly enough.'[23] At last, at a few minutes before 5 p.m. on Christmas Eve, 1896, the Governor who had come to the House formally to prorogue Parliament, gave the royal assent to the Act.

But what were the improvements that had been achieved after such a long-fought battle? Isaacs proceeded on the basic assumption that a repetition of the events of the land boom could be best prevented if investors received adequate and reliable information about the companies in which they invested. Isaacs, although a radical in his time, probably would be as astonished as his contemporaries with present day statutory obligations for disclosure. What he sought was strictly limited. He said that it would not be right for the business of a company to be disclosed in detail to all the world. He therefore distinguished between the shareholders' balance sheet and the private balance sheet on which an auditor would base his report of the state of the company.

The most important amendment introduced by the Council to the disclosure requirements proposed in Isaacs's Bill was the innovation of the proprietary company. Isaacs was not against the principle of the proprietary company but clearly had misgivings about possible abuse. It would be a matter for congratulation he said: 'If that provision could be carried out without allowing a loop-hole for evasion of the whole Act.'[24] Loop-holes did develop, but these were largely the result of further sophistication in business organization many years later and subsequently most of them have been closed. It is difficult, if not impossible, to say to whom credit for this invention of the proprietary company should be given. Sir Frederick Sargood first propounded the idea in the Council on 18 August 1896,[25] when he read an extract from the evidence of J. Herbert Tritton, vice-president of the Institute of Bankers, appearing before the select committee appointed by the House of Lords to consider the draft Bill which was the basis of Isaacs's Bill. Tritton claimed, 'it might be a hardship in the case of some private companies to enforce the filing with the registrar of a document of this character' (i.e. a balance sheet). Sir Frederick quoted extensively from the evidence presented to the House of Lords committee and discussed the difficulty of defining what constituted a private company, and called on the argument for parallel laws with England to support his stand. He argued that his quotations 'showed that this question of private companies had received very careful attention at home, [i.e. in England] and they afforded one reason why the proviso which was contained in the English Bill should be inserted in this measure instead of being omitted'. Before the Select Committee appointed by the Council, C. M. Holmes, president of the Incorporated Institute of Accountants of Victoria, was the first witness examined, and he submitted that 'the general scope of the Bill is such as almost to make it necessary that a new order of company should be instituted, in the shape of what may be called private companies'.[26] Even if Holmes was not the originator of this general proposition, it seems reasonable that he, or at least the Institute he represented, which was an antecedent of the Australian Society of Accountants, solved the dilemma of terminology by suggesting that the companies concerned be called 'limited proprietary companies'. These companies were to be exempted from the newly enacted requirements for publication of financial statements. It is clear that the Council sincerely intended this as a protection (or the more cynical observer might say a hiding place) for the company which represented a family business. These companies thus retained the privileges of incorporation with limited liability without any accompanying obligation to disclose their financial position.

Companies which were not within the definition of proprietary companies, i.e. the public companies, no longer were left wholly to determine their own accounting practices. It was now obligatory to keep proper books of account, and each year an audited balance sheet was to be sent to every member; also a copy was to be available for inspection by members and creditors at the registered office seven days before being laid before a general meeting of the company.[27] The requirement to post up a copy of the balance sheet already applicable to banks was extended to all registered public companies. Similar requirements for publication of balance sheets did not follow until 1920 in Tasmania, 1931 in Queensland, 1934 in South Australia, 1936 in New South Wales and 1943 in Western Australia.

The 1896 Victorian Act required the balance sheet to be in the form set out in the schedules. The Council insisted upon this 'straitjacket' as it did again in 1910, and it was not until 1938 that freedom of form and presentation was allowed. The form in the schedule to the 1896 Act is remarkable because instead of following the traditional tee form set out in the optional articles in the 'first acts', it represented what today would be described as a narrative format in the sequence of shareholders' called and paid capital, assets and liabilities, and then a statement of total shareholders' funds. The nominal, issued, called and paid up capital were to be shown. Debtors were to be stated after deducting bad or doubtful debts and classified into five categories. The nature of the security was to be specified for money lent on security. Separate amounts were required for real estate and shares of other companies and government securities, the last two to be specified. Stocks, plant, etc. were not required to be given in detail. The basis of valuation of all assets other than debtors was to be stated and 'whether any and if so what amount or percentage has been written off and what other provision (if any) has been made for depreciation'. These two aspects of valuation and depreciation, it will be demonstrated, were not effective, and it remained for the future to 'work them out'. Liabilities were to be classified into eight categories.

One of the more serious aspects of the land boom was the inflation, often with little real grounds, of the value of assets held. Any such increase in valuations must in future be stated. Thirty years later the folly of incorporating such ill-founded revaluations in the accounts was learned again in the Samuel Insull power company scandal in the United States of America.[28]

The shareholders' funds section of the statement provided fuel for the fire in debate. Section 24 required a statement of 'the actual amount of the reserve fund (if any) and the mode in which it is used or invested'. This was backed up by section 25 which introduced penalties for misrepresentations concerning reserve funds and their use. A member of the House, G. D. Carter, asserted those clauses showed him 'that the Attorney-General [Isaacs] did not even know what a reserve consists of',[29] and reminded Mr Isaacs that a reserve fund is 'simply an amount of undivided profits'. Isaacs clearly knew this, but was concerned at the way companies had presented their 'reserves' in publicity material. The Premier Geo. Turner declared that they wanted to get at the misrepresentation of quoting 'reserves' in the company's advertisements as a 'great draw' to people to invest in the company. Isaacs was acting in the circumstances of the day. He was not concerned necessarily with creating reserve fund investments outside the company, but was seeking to ensure that the 'reserves' presented as part of shareholders' funds were, in fact, represented by assets in the company. It also appears from his comments that it had not been uncommon in the balmy days of the boom to advertise a company as possessing large reserves which were, in fact, distributed as dividends before the issue of shares to the hapless new shareholders.[30] Isaacs's viewpoint was borne out in the schedule to the Act which included in the balance sheet format the item 'Reserved fund and accumulated profits [*specifying the actual amounts and particulars of the items of investments thereof*]'. Similar provisions were adopted by the other States when they first made publication of a balance sheet compulsory—Tasmania in 1920, South Australia in 1934, New South Wales in 1936 and Western Australia in 1943—except Queensland where it did not appear until the uniform legislation embodied in the 1962 Act.

To legislate for disclosure of financial statements was one thing, ensuring that they were reliable was another. Accordingly the balance sheet was to be accompanied by a directors' certificate that it was true and correct and a statutory declaration by the manager as to its correctness. The Act also made it mandatory for public companies to appoint an auditor, and took steps to define the necessary qualifications of an auditor. The auditor was intended to be assisted by having submitted to him the private balance sheet which was also to be filed with the Registrar-General and only to be opened by order of the Court. This was an ingenious device, if ineffective. It was anticipated that this private balance sheet would contain more details than the published documents. The filing of this document would then impose a threat against unscrupulous or dishonest practices because detailed information would be available to establish what really happened. The idea proved ineffective for two reasons: there was not, fortunately, a repeat of events such as experienced in the land boom; and the scheme was rather corrective than preventive, and in this sense was negative in its purpose. The Act also marked a breakthrough for disclosure of dealings between companies and their officers which had been such an iniquitous part of the land boom scandals. There was much debate on whether companies should be restricted in making advances to their directors. Finally, it was enacted that banking companies should file a six-monthly return of advances made to directors, managers or auditors, or to firms of which they are members or guarantees, and to companies in which they occupy similar positions. This issue was to be reconsidered by the legislature many years later when provisions were enacted to cover the reporting of loans to directors by all public companies.

One must conclude that the legislation which resulted was the outcome of the economic disaster of the land boom and the personal achievement of Isaacs. Through the newspaper stalls public awareness of the facts of the scandals as we have noted was provided by Maurice Brodzky in his magazine *Table Talk*. Brodzky dug deeply to get the facts and created an atmosphere of public hostility which undoubtedly helped to force the legislature to enact the measures which Isaacs drafted.

This 1896 Act marked the end of the era of complete freedom of action with respect to company reporting and recognition of the necessity to regulate company reporting to ensure the protection of creditors and investors through the establishment of minimum statutory requirements.

8

Mr Isaacs's Bill—Postscript

The Victorian business community settled down to working under the rules so valiantly fought for by Isaacs. No doubt there was considerable reluctance on the part of some concerned. Isaacs's Bill had not ended its ability to inspire heated debate when it became law. In a sense the ground was worked over again in 1910.

Isaacs had based his legislation largely on the Bill drafted by the company law committee of the English Parliament. This Bill was not proceeded with in England. The Victorian Act therefore had ceased to follow the form and language of the English Act. This was aggravated further when the English Act was amended in 1900 and 1907. As J. E. Mackey, who was to play an important part in redrafting the Victorian Act, pointed out, the disadvantages of this lack of similarity in the Victorian and English Acts were that decisions of the English courts were not always applicable and that English textbooks equally could not always be referred to.[1] To the still relatively small Victorian community, these were serious difficulties. No less important was the desirability of English investors being able to operate in Victoria under the same law as they were accustomed to at home. Agitation to achieve an assimilation of the law in the interests of investors was supported by the British government. W. S. Manifold when moving the second reading of the Bill prepared by Mackey expressed it thus:

> Investors at Home were shy about investing in a State whose company law they did not understand. An investor in England might write out here stating that he wanted steps to be taken in accordance with the English law, and it would be found that those steps were not legal here. That had been a great disadvantage, and the British Government had written to the various states pointing out the desirability of assimilating our law to that of the Act of 1908 passed by the Imperial Parliament.[2]

8 Mr Isaacs's Bill—Postscript

Mackey was a man of action as well as words and, assisted by a Melbourne solicitor, S. G. Pirani, prepared and submitted to the House a private member's Bill which redrafted the law for clarity on the model of the United Kingdom Act of 1908 'coupled with some of the most notable departures in our law in Victoria'.[3] The desirability of following the model of the English Act was supported verbally by Mr Justice Hodge, in writing by Mr Justice Hood and by T. a'B. Weigall, K.C., a prominent barrister and member of a legal firm which still serves many large companies. Mackey also had noted the opinions of the Registrar-General, the Law Institute and the Institute of Incorporated Accountants.[4] In fact this principle was supported by all the witnesses who appeared before the Parliamentary Select Committee on the Bill. The Select Committee[5] heard evidence from the Law Institute, the Associated Banks, the Chamber of Commerce, accountants, the Registrar-General and others before reporting to Parliament. Even Mackey found rather remarkable the unanimity of the committee on the proposition that 'it will be for the advantage of Victoria and more especially of Melbourne to make our companies law as far as possible uniform with that of England'.[6]

The evidence presented to the Select Committee by the representatives of the accounting profession deserves some detailed discussion. C. M. Holmes gave evidence on this occasion on behalf of the Australasian Corporation of Public Accountants, antecedent of the present Institute of Chartered Accountants.[7] His evidence supported proposals to require the compulsory filing as public documents of balance sheets issued by public companies, proposals recommended by the Select Committee for inclusion in the Bill. Holmes spoke in favour of the private balance sheet provisions but admitted 'my colleagues are not all with me in this matter'. His enthusiasm could probably be excused as he was the accountant concerned in the one instance where this document was used to re-establish the records of a company which had been destroyed by fire. There is no other record known of any use being made of these documents. Holmes offered an amended form of schedule and in his evidence supported a uniform form of presentation of statements. This was an attitude which the accounting profession was to repudiate in future years. C. H. Davis appeared for the Incorporated Institute of Accountants, Victoria, an antecedent of the present Australian Society of Accountants. His Institute's attitude to disclosure at the time is perhaps reflected in the comments offered on proposals to require disclosure of the amount of depreciation charged for the year, proposals which the Select Committee recommended be deleted from the Bill. This information, said Davis, 'there is no necessity to give' on the grounds that 'it is too inquisitorial and it is difficult to state'.[8] This is in sharp contrast with the lead shown by the Incorporated Institute of Accountants in shaping the 1896 Bill when it is interesting to note the Institute was represented by C. M. Holmes. This interlude is also in sharp contrast with the lead for greater disclosure given by the Commonwealth Institute at the time the 1938 Act was drafted. Thus perhaps we observe the influence that an individual may exert in the official policies of such a voluntary organization.

When the Bill was sent on from the Assembly to the Legislative Council that House maintained its tradition of the 'nineties' by fighting the Bill strenuously. The Attorney-General seized on the word 'consolidation' in the Bill and instead of arguing the contents of the Bill, argued that it was a 'consolidation' attempted without the proper procedures.[9] Stalling tactics were adopted, the Attorney-General on one occasion speaking for over an hour on the motion to report progress,[10] and on 14 December he was pulled up by the Chairman for 'repeating himself four or five times'.

There was obvious disagreement on the merits of the existing 'Isaacs Bill'. Although the Attorney-General defended the law as it stood as having been 'approved by parliament at the time' and containing provisions 'entirely in the interests of the investing community',[11] others thought 'certain stringent provisions were put in that measure which professional men, after seeing how they had worked, considered to be inadvisable and not beneficial'.[12] W. S. Manifold, who steered the Bill through the Upper House, thought it was 'useless to re-enact provisions that were of no good'.[13] The new Bill included a number of amendments of the law. For example, the Bill deleted certain procedures required on the takeover of a private business which were described thus:

This was another of Mr. Isaacs' ideas and existed here alone. Amongst other things it provided that where a company was formed to take over a particular private business there would have to be two advertisements inserted in the newspapers. All sorts of private details which were absolutely of no use to the creditors of the company had to be given.[14]

On this matter it was said that the 'Registrar-General had stated that the provision was useless, and altogether a dead letter, and that it could be avoided in more than one way'.[15] The Isaacs inspired system of no liability trading companies also was deleted. Eighteen

8 Mr Isaacs's Bill—Postscript

of these companies had been registered, fifteen were defunct, one was in liquidation and one was in fact operating.[16] Also deleted from the Bill was Isaacs's invention of the 'private balance sheet'. On this point the wishes of the Council prevailed and the requirement for the private balance sheet was re-enacted as in spite of its record of being almost no use whatever it was said to 'enable shareholders and the public to get information more readily than otherwise of the affairs of the company'.[17] The individuals who drafted the Bill did not require companies to report using a standard balance sheet but the more conservative minds of the Council added in the schedule 'a form of balance sheet which is brought up to date'.[18]

The accounting professional bodies were lobbying very actively during the passage of the Bill, not always with the aid of correct information about the Bill, as well as giving evidence before the Select Committee. This is demonstrated particularly by events relating to the introduction to the Bill of the schedule referred to above. The Incorporated Institute of Accountants sent a deputation to the Attorney-General on 13 December 1910, and in the House the Attorney-General said they were altogether against the Bill.[19] This opposition, was largely based on a press report that the form of balance sheet included in the Bill by the Council's amendment did not include a statement of profit and loss. While there was not general agreement on the imposition of the stricture of a standard form, there was agreement that if a standard form was necessary it should require an adequate presentation which presupposed a statement of profit and loss. Then on 14 December 1910 the Institute sent a letter to Manifold which, referring to a press report of the deputation said, *inter alia,* that the Institute deprecated the delay in passing the Bill and withdrew its opposition because it was said to be accidental that there was left out of a printed sheet containing Manifold's amendments, the words: 'A statement of profit and loss shall be annexed to and form part of the balance sheet'.[20] This was a hollow victory for the Institute because of the inadequacy of the profit and loss accounts published under the Act. It also perpetuated a restriction on the form of balance sheets which retarded the development of new forms of presentation.

Thus, 'Mr Isaacs' Bill' survived substantially, but it was clear that there was much disagreement about it and further changes in the legislation could be anticipated. The minimum statutory requirements for disclosure had not been significantly altered from those contained in the Victorian Companies Act of 1896.

9

Disclosure as a Safeguard

The cardinal principle of the limited liability company is that the shareholder should pay in the nominal value of the shares held by him. This principle was laid down clearly in *Ooregum Gold Mining Co. v. Roper* (1892) A.C. The background to the case was that the company's shares were discounted heavily by the market and to secure additional capital the company issued preference shares as being partly paid without receiving any considerations. Lord Macnaghten quoted the words of Mr Buckley: 'the dominant and cardinal principle of these [companies] acts is that the investor shall purchase immunity from liability beyond a certain limit, on the terms that there shall be and remain a liability up to that limit' and in his judgment, said, 'Nothing but payment, and payment in full, can put an end to the liability'; furthermore:

it is plain that the condition is one which cannot be dispensed with by anything in the articles of association, or by any resolution of the company, or by any contract between the company and outsiders who have been invited to become members of the company and who do come in on the faith of such a contract. (p. 145)

Although this dictum was defined so carefully and explicitly, the English legislature saw fit to break down the principle. The modifications to company law in turn were adopted in Australia in accord with the emphasis on assimilating the English and State laws.

Each of these modifications is of interest in this context because in each case the modification was accepted with the proviso of adequate disclosure of information concerning what it is proposed to do, to safeguard the interests of various parties. Some of these measures were introduced to Australia in the Victorian Companies Act of 1910 while others were introduced in the three similar Acts passed in Queensland in 1931, in South Australia in 1934 and in New South Wales in 1936.

9 Disclosure as a Safeguard

The first modification was to permit the payment of underwriting commissions on the issue of shares. The English Company Law Amendment Committee in 1906 (the Loreburn Committee) claimed that prior to 1900 the prohibition of part of the nominal value of a share being applied in this way was circumvented by loading the consideration paid to the vendor of the business to be acquired by the company. This vendor would then pay the underwriting commission.[1] The legislature thought it better to bring this into the open. The English Companies Act of 1900 therefore allowed the payment of such underwriting commissions on shares and debentures, or discounts on debentures. This in turn was included in the Australian States Acts in Victoria in 1910, in Tasmania in 1920, in Queensland in 1931, in South Australia in 1934, in New South Wales in 1936 and in Western Australia in 1943. Along with restrictions on the magnitude of the commission or discount allowable, all these Acts provided for disclosure in the balance sheet of any amount of such issue expenses that had not been written off.

Understandably it was an easy step for the Company Law Amendment Committee, when asked to consider the possibility of allowing the issue of shares at a discount, to see this as an extension of the payment of commissions as discussed above. As the Committee reported:

It must be apparent that what is sanctioned in Section 8 is, in its financial results, equivalent to the issue of shares at a discount, and some of us think that in these circumstances, the simpler and more straightforward course would be to authorise in express terms the issue at a discount of shares whether in the original capital or created upon an increase of capital.[2]

The matter was again considered by the Wrenbury Committee on Company Law Amendment in 1918, which recommended that the amount of discount be controlled, and that there should be ample provision for complete publicity in the balance sheet, annual summary and in every prospectus.[3] To permit the issue of shares at a discount would recognize another means of circumventing the principle of payment in full on shares issued. The acceptance, as the cash equivalent of payment, of property with a market value much less than the nominal value of the shares amounts to issuing shares at a discount. Authority to issue shares at a discount was included subsequently in the English Companies Act of 1907 and copied by the Australian States in Queensland in 1931, in South Australia in 1934, in New South Wales in 1936, in Victoria in

1938, in Western Australia in 1943 and in Tasmania in 1959. This section was coupled likewise with provisions requiring the balance sheet to show so much of any such discount as had not been written off.

The third modification of the basic principle enunciated earlier, was to allow companies to apply part of their paid up capital to the payment of interest on expenditure on capital assets which have not reached completion. The Loreburn Committee also considered this matter and reported:

We think that, subject to proper safeguards and restrictions, such as obtaining the sanction of the Board of Trade or of the Court, a Company expending paid up share capital in the construction of buildings or works of magnitude, which cannot be placed in a profit earning condition for a lengthened period, should be empowered during construction to pay interest on such expenditure out of capital, and to treat such payment as part of the cost of construction. Cases commonly arise in which the inability of companies thus to pay interest out of capital during construction discourages and impedes the construction or carrying out of works of a desirable character, and Parliament, in its Standing Orders, and in the Indian Railways Companies Act 1894, has recognised the propriety in some cases of providing for such payments. We recommend the extension of the principle.[4]

The English Companies Act of 1907 included legislative sanction of such payments out of capital and this was taken up by the Australian States Acts in Victoria in 1910, in Tasmania in 1920, in Queensland in 1931, in South Australia in 1934, in New South Wales in 1936 and in Western Australia in 1943. Again the authority was linked with the requirement of adequate disclosure of the amount on which interest is charged and the rate of interest.

The fourth aspect of company law with which this chapter is concerned, is the issue of redeemable preference shares. Serious consideration of the proposal for this type of share was given first by the Greene Company Law Committee in 1926, which thought the power to issue redeemable preference shares could prove useful and could see no reason against allowing them, provided proper safeguards were provided.[5]

The idea was not received warmly in all quarters at the time. W. O. Burt, a member of the Institute of Chartered Accountants in Australia, who for many years occupied responsible positions as a director of public companies, indicated he was 'afraid that by the redemption of certain shares, the rights of creditors and of other shareholders may be jeopardised by unscrupulous directors'. He pointed out that 'by writing up the value of assets, by inflating stocks or other similar means designed to create a profit, a reserve can be created for the purpose of redemption of redeemable shares'. He thought 'this innovation may spell uncertainty, and will shake confidence in the credit of limited liability undertakings resorting to the issue of redeemable shares'.[6] The innovation had been included in the English Companies Act of 1928 and was copied in Australia in Queensland in 1931, in South Australia in 1934, in New South Wales in 1936, in Victoria in 1938, in Western Australia in 1943 and in Tasmania in 1956. Again reliance was placed on adequate disclosure.

All these changes were permitted by the legislatures on the basis that adequate disclosure would provide the necessary protection of interested parties. This is an interesting extension of the basis on which limited liability itself was granted to companies, i.e. that adequate disclosure would provide protection for interested parties.

It is convenient to consider here also the legislative provisions relating to share premiums. Far from breaking down the concept of an inviolate company capital, the share premium amounts to the paying up of more than the nominal value of the share. Share premiums were first recognized in the Victorian Companies Act of 1896. In that Act any excess of consideration received on the issue of shares was to be credited to a 'reserve fund'. In accordance with modern terminology this term was later deleted and the present day Acts refer to the share premium account. The Act did not allow a company to issue shares at a premium until twelve months after its establishment. Share premiums were recognized by the Tasmanian Act of 1920 which followed the form of the Victorian Act in this matter. These two States were far ahead of the other States, which did not legislate on the matter until the 1961-2 Uniform Acts (England did not legislate until the 1948 Companies Act). S.60 of the Uniform Acts provides that any premium received on a share issue is to be credited to a 'share premium account'. Any balance of this account is subject to the provisions covering a return of capital just as if it were paid up capital. However, the Act does specify certain purposes to which the premium may be applied.

The importance of this section of the Act is borne out by the 'forty-two leaders sample'. In 1965 no less than thirty-four of these companies showed a balance on share premium reserve in the parent balance sheet and thirty-five showed a balance of share premium reserve in the consolidated statements.

Prior to the Uniform Act New South Wales legislation did not require the recognition of a premium not received in cash, but it could be shown if desired. Reports of the fifteen New South Wales companies in the 'forty-two leaders sample' were examined. It was found that nine companies showed a share premium reserve before the Uniform Act was in force while four companies which had not shown such a reserve previously now do so. This suggests that some companies did not recognize a premium received other than in cash until required to do so by statute.

10

'Towards Uniformity'

The adoption by all of the Australian States of a minimum level of compulsory disclosure in the form of a balance sheet is marked by the Acts passed in Tasmania in 1920, in Queensland in 1931, in South Australia in 1934 and in New South Wales in 1936. (The delay of legislation in Western Australia until 1943 is not regarded as significant because of the relative unimportance of the State to the total of company activity in Australia.) Although these Acts essentially brought the Acts of the four States concerned in line with the disclosure requirements of the 1896 Victorian Act, there is little evidence that it was simply a case of copying the Victorian example except perhaps in Tasmania. However, the Victorian legislation did have a significant effect in that the device of the proprietary company was copied by all the States when introducing compulsory disclosure.

The corporate form of organization was becoming more widely used in all the States—as it was overseas—and the abuse of the benefits of the limited liability company were not confined to the land boomers of the eighties but continued through to the thirties as unscrupulous promoters devised new ways of using the benefits of the law to their own ends. The legislation was enacted in part because of a public awareness that something should be done to curb these doubtful practices. Thus the South Australian Attorney-General, the Hon. S. W. Jeffries, observed in 1933 that there was a strong demand for new legislation from among the commercial community of Adelaide, and that the government was acceding to numerous requests to introduce the legislation.[1] The New South Wales Minister for Justice, the Hon. L. O. Martin observed in 1934 that the public demand for a better code dealing with company law had grown with increasing intensity.[2]

There is ample evidence that among the States there was a desire to enact legislation which would be uniform, an objective not achieved until twenty-five years later. The Queensland Attorney-General thought the Queensland Bill might be taken as the basis of uniform legislation[3] and the South Australian Attorney-General expressed his regret in 1931 that he was unable to introduce a Bill as one that was uniform throughout Australia.[4] But while the desire for uniformity existed, it was by no means strong enough to produce uniform legislation. Many saw the example of the English Act as the way to achieve uniformity. The Queensland Attorney-General went so far as to say that, 'if the Commonwealth goes in for a uniform measure it cannot be on any other basis but the Imperial Act which is so up to date and complete'.[5] The South Australian Attorney-General was less emphatic, merely observing that, 'when all the other Australian States have passed legislation bringing their system up to date with the English Act of 1929 there will practically be uniformity throughout the Australian States'.[6]

While public awareness of the need for more adequate disclosure by companies was a cause of legislative action, it is equally true that the catalyst was the example of the 'mother' Parliament in England culminating in the English Companies Act of 1928. The local ministers in charge of the legislation readily acknowledged this precedent. In August 1931 the South Australian Attorney-General, the Hon. W. J. Donny, said:

We are fortunate that some of the best brains in the mother country have been applied to the formulation of new rules for the protection of the public and the management of companies. These rules have been generally adopted throughout other self-governing dominions of the British Empire, and the time has now arrived when circumstances render it expedient for South Australia to fall into line.[7]

The Queensland Bill in 1931 was drafted taking the Imperial Act of 1929 as a basis with 'due regard being paid to local conditions',[8] and the Attorney-General, the Hon. N. F. Macgroarty, expressed his opinion 'that the mature consideration of English experts should weigh very seriously when people bring opposition to bear on the Bill'.[9] The influence of English experience on the New South Wales Bill was equally significant. The Minister for Justice, the Hon. L. O. Martin, described the background of the Bill thus:

In 1912 the first step appears to have been taken and the Government of the day put in hand the consolidation of our own Acts, coupled with the incorporation of the new provisions of the English Act of 1908. It was natural that my predecessor of that time should move cautiously. Our people understood and could work the code they had, and he probably hesitated to venture on amendments without further

10 'Towards Uniformity'

experience of the English system. Hence the matter proceeded somewhat slowly, but in 1914 a draft of a new measure was prepared, and printed in 1915. It was based on the English Act of 1908. It was then abandoned for a time, probably due to the war, but taken up again in the early twenties by the Commission on Law Reform which got ready a new Bill which was also printed, but dropped because of the Greene Committee's report and the introduction of the 1928 Act in England. That Act, as I have stated, was incorporated in the English Act of 1929. But action here was suspended for a time. It, however, was considered by the last Government and advanced a further stage.

The policy of the Bill, the Minister further noted was:

to make the English code the model and to follow it as far as possible, adding various provisions from the legislation of Victoria, Queensland, New Zealand, South Australia, and the Commonwealth, which have been found satisfactory, our own previous legislation being, where it has stood the test of experience, also incorporated.[10]

Before proceeding to a discussion of the particular effects of the State Acts, it is appropriate to consider briefly what were the effects on disclosure of the English developments followed so closely by the States. In 1900 the English Act had been amended to provide that every company should appoint an auditor. Then in 1907, following the enquiry by the Loreburn Committee on Company Law, the Act was further amended to require every company, other than a private company which was the English equivalent of the Victorian proprietary company, to include an audited balance sheet in the annual return filed with the Registrar. The only specifications for the balance sheet were that it contain, 'a summary of its capital, its liabilities, and its assets, giving such particulars as will disclose the general nature of such liabilities and assets, and how the values of the fixed assets have been arrived at' (s.21). A notable advance was the right given to shareholders to secure a copy of the balance sheet on payment of a fee. Other new provisions required the statement in the balance sheet of commissions paid on the issue of shares or debentures and discounts allowed on debentures, and the payment of interest out of capital linked with the disclosure of such in the balance sheet. In 1918 the Wrenbury Committee enquired into company law but nothing was done until after a further committee, the Greene Committee, conducted an enquiry in 1925 to 1926. Among the principal recommendations of the Greene Committee was one that the Act should be amended to impose a statutory obligation to keep proper accounts. The committee considered the existing requirements for filing accounts were inadequate and that to prevent companies filing the same balance sheet year after year, a company should be required to file its last audited balance sheet.[11]

The committee considered the accounts of holding companies in detail, but rejected the idea of a consolidated or combined balance sheet; but it did recommend that the holding company's accounts should include a signed statement as to how the aggregate profits and losses of subsidiary companies had been dealt with. The committee, commenting on the form of accounts, considered that shareholders and others concerned have little ground for complaint but did make recommendations which it believed would remove some of the grounds of complaint.

The Greene Committee's recommendations were reflected in the provisions of the English Act of 1928. In summary the Act required the following. Proper books of account were to be kept. Each year a profit and loss account and balance sheet were to be prepared, audited and laid before the annual meeting. The balance sheet, directors' report and auditors' report were to be circulated to members before the meeting. No details were prescribed as to the form and content of the profit and loss statement. The following details were to be shown in the balance sheet—the authorized and issued share capital; liabilities, including a statement if any are secured on any assets of the company; fixed assets, stating basis of valuation; floating assets; preliminary expenses, issue expenses of shares or debentures, goodwill, patents or trade marks if ascertainable, which have not been written off; the amount of loans made or guaranteed to directors, including amounts repaid during or outstanding at the end of the period; all fees and other emoluments paid to directors who are not full-time employees of the company. For holding companies, also the following—amount invested in shares in subsidiaries; amounts due from any subsidiaries; amounts due to any subsidiaries; a statement of how the profits of the subsidiaries had been dealt with. Disclosure within the balance sheet was continued in respect of the special provisions concerning redeemable preference shares, shares issued at a discount, payments for loss of office or on retirement of directors, and interest paid out of capital. These, then, were the English developments which we have already shown were the foundation on which the amending legislation of three States, Queensland, South Australia and New South Wales was directly based.

Hewetson Nelson, a past president of the Society of Incorporated

Accountants and Auditors, says that those who considered parliament should have insisted on companies giving certain further details, brought considerable pressure to bear in parliament, but this was resisted by the President of the Board of Trade.[12] Wide discretion remained with the directors of companies and it was left to the accounting profession and the press to exercise their influence to secure sufficient information in both balance sheets and profit and loss accounts to make them intelligible.

In Queensland a Bill was introduced in September 1931, and became law within five months. The leader of the Opposition sought unsuccessfully, on three occasions, to have the Bill referred to a Select Committee. The concern of the business community was shown by the formation of a committee which sponsored a deputation to the Attorney-General.[13] This deputation, many of whose suggestions were adopted, included the following bodies: Chamber of Commerce, Chamber of Manufactures, Brisbane Stock Exchange, Associated Banks, Fire and Accident Underwriters' Association, Bar Association, Queensland Law Society, Brisbane Merchants' Association, Institute of Chartered Accountants of Australia, Association of Accountants of Australia, Commonwealth Institute of Accountants, Federal Institute of Accountants, Secretaries' Institute, Australian Institute of Secretaries, Chartered Institute of Secretaries. The Commonwealth Institute of Accountants president considered the Act would 'make for efficiency in company management and administration, and afford greatly increased and much needed protection to shareholders and the investing public generally'.[14] The Commonwealth Institute was represented at the deputation by Mr J. S. McInnes who wrote a booklet explaining the new Act which became 'well recognised as an authority'.[15] These activities of the accounting bodies continued with the participation in the Special Company Law Committee of the Chamber of Commerce which replied to the Registrar of Companies' invitation for further submissions in 1936 directed at further improving the Act.[16]

A more tortuous path faced the New South Wales Bill which, as has already been observed, had been simmering in the administrative department since 1912. The Commonwealth Institute of Accountants had been pressing for an amended Act for some years. In the annual report of the Institute in 1926 it was reported:

It is generally recognised that the present Companies Act is out of date and does not adequately safeguard either the interests of the profession or those of the mercantile community, and therefore your Council waited upon the Attorney-General and offered the assistance of the Institute in framing any proposed amending legislation. This offer was accepted by the Attorney-General, and subsequently, representatives of this Institute met in conference delegates from the Stock Exchange, the Chamber of Commerce and other bodies, and made detailed suggestions for incorporation in the proposed New Companies Act.[17]

In December 1934 the draft Bill was presented in Parliament with the object of making 'the bill public property, so that every person interested may be enabled to get a copy from the Government Printer and study it'.[18] In the meantime the government was awaiting the report of Mr Justice Halse Rogers who was appointed Royal Commissioner to enquire into a number of investment companies which had failed. The Institute of Chartered Accountants made a submission to the Commissioner advocating strict following of the English Act with only such amendments as were necessary to meet local circumstances.[19] At the conclusion of his enquiries the Royal Commissioner included in his report the evidence of Mr Spencer Watts, who appeared as representative of the Chamber of Commerce, and who the Commissioner regarded as 'mouth-piece of the commercial community'. The only specific recommendations concerning accounts were suggestions designed to ensure that a company did have an 'annual meeting' and that 'a company with subsidiary companies be required to publish the accounts of such subsidiaries, unless such subsidiary companies publish their own accounts'.[20] The Commissioner also referred to enquiries into similar matters in New Zealand and Victoria. He demurred with the New Zealand proposal for a Corporate Investments Bureau to supervise such publications as prospectuses. He reported that he was assisted considerably by a Victorian committee. As the report of the Victorian committee was not available generally, the Commissioner included in his report a summary of the objects aimed at in the Victorian committee's findings. However, these were related generally to the issue of prospectuses and raising of debenture money, and did not include any specific mention of the provision of adequate reports of the continuing activities of a company. Meanwhile the Bill was examined and commented on by the Chamber of Commerce, Chamber of Manufactures, Institute of Chartered Accountants in Australia, Commonwealth Institute of Accountants, Sydney Stock Exchange, Bar Council and Council of the Incorporated Law Institute.[21] The revised Bill was introduced into Parliament in November 1935 and finally passed in April 1936. The effectiveness of the government's efforts in meeting the community's desires was illustrated by the remarks of the Chairman of the Institute of Chartered Accountants, Mr R. D. Bogan, who stated that many conferences had taken place between representatives of the Chamber of Commerce and his Institute and spoke of the keen appreciation of the committee with respect to the manner in which the Minister for Justice had received the representatives. 'Practically all the recommendations submitted had been adopted.'[22] Both the Institute of Chartered Accountants and the Commonwealth Institute of Accountants continued their interest by publishing explanatory booklets on the new Act, distributed gratis to members, as well as an extensive series of articles which appeared in the *Chartered Accountant in Australia*.

If the New South Wales Act had a lengthy gestation period within the administrative departments, at least it was an easier birth outwardly than that of the South Australian Act, which occupied Parliament over five years repeating some of the agonizing and time-consuming tactics of the Victorian parliamentarians of previous years which have already been discussed. While the parliamentarians dithered conditions were such that the Registrar of Companies considered it was not an exaggeration to say that half the business of successful investment was to secure what we would now call 'insider' information.[23]

As has been noted previously, there was a community demand for a new Act, but the depression had so affected the State's finances that there was no money to pay for the labour of drafting the Bill. In these circumstances a Mr Frisby Smith undertook what proved to be six and a half years' work as an honorary task. The Bill, promised in the Governor's speech on 27 May 1930, was introduced on 6 August 1931. Mr Frisby Smith had met with numerous interested parties and those who had criticized the Bill included the Law Society of South Australia, Chamber of Commerce, Stock Exchange, Chamber of Manufactures, Associated Banks of South Australia, Chartered Institute of Accountants (Australia), Federal Institute of Accountants, Australian Institute of Secretaries and Insurance Underwriters.[24] The Bill was referred to a Select Committee which reported within five weeks, but the Bill lapsed at the end of the session. It was reinstated in 1932 and again lapsed. On 27 July 1933 it was again introduced and subsequently referred to a Joint Committee of the two Houses of Parliament. The Joint Committee reported in July 1934 and in September the Bill was introduced a fourth time. It was finally passed in November 1934.

Before considering the nature of the disclosure provisions enacted in these three States, it is appropriate to comment on the position in Victoria which was far from static. The authorities in Victoria were following closely English developments. The Attorney-General was quoted by an editorial in the *Law Institute Journal* as saying, *c*.1928, that the English Parliamentary Committees had 'expressed the last modern view' on the subject and urged the desirability of incorporating in the State's legislation the committees' recommendations.[25] At the time a consolidation of Victorian Statutes was being undertaken by Sir Leo Cussen. Sir Leo proposed to the Joint Statute Law Revision Committee that it would be desirable to incorporate appropriate amendments in the consolidated Acts.[26] In a paper presented to the Committee in 1929 he indicated his reliance on the Greene Committee report and argued strongly for maintaining the Act in the same form as the English Act and for such amendments as the disclosure of directors' fees.[27] However, in order not to delay the consolidation, this approach was not persevered with, and an amended Bill was not taken further until 1936. The Victorian Act of 1896 already had established a certain minimum level of compulsory disclosure. The most important point on which the English Act differed from the Victorian position was in respect of holding companies. When the Victorian Act was amended this matter was taken much further than in the English Act. Therefore, although the Victorian Act of 1938 arose from the same events as the other State Acts discussed in this chapter, it is desirable that discussion of the Victorian Act be deferred to a later chapter as representing another stage in the development of standards of disclosure.

To return to the discussion of the three States on which this chapter is centred—what had been achieved? The compulsory standards of disclosure imposed at this time are summarized in appendix 4 and may be briefly summarized as follows: In the three States similar provisions required companies to keep proper books of account, to prepare and circulate a balance sheet and profit and loss account, and the directors' report was common to the extent of the recommended dividend and proposed transfers to reserves. The balance sheet was to show the authorized and issued capital, liabilities, noting any secured on assets, assets classified into floating and fixed, and giving bases of valuation, except that in South Australia the bases of valuation for floating assets were to be given as per details set out in the schedule to the Act. Holding companies were to show separately investments in subsidiaries, the amounts due to and from subsidiaries and a statement of how the profits of the subsidiaries had been dealt with. Various intangible assets were to be detailed, as were loans to directors and directors' remuneration. The sections of the Acts dealing with payment of interest out of capital, and the issue of redeemable preference shares required further information. South Australia and New South Wales copied the Victorian section requiring a statement on the use of reserves and reserve funds. South Australia required the balance sheet in the form set out in the schedule which went much further in specifying what was an acceptable amount of detail of the proprietorship, asset and liability items, than the broad specification, within the Act, to give such particulars as are necessary to disclose the general nature of the assets and liabilities of the company. The contents of the profit and loss account were not specified apart from the directors' remuneration and a statement of how profits of subsidiaries were treated. Queensland and New South Wales required the amount of depreciation charged and transfers from reserves to be given in the directors' report. These two important provisions are discussed in more detail later. Appendix 4 also includes for comparative purposes details of those items which were required under the existing Victorian legislation.

These Acts established statutory recognition of the balance sheet as the important document in financial reporting. The limited statement of profit and loss required under these Acts did not give any clear indication of how the profit was earned and in the case of holding companies could be credited with whatever dividend the directors chose to declare from the subsidiaries irrespective of current profitability. The recognition of the profit and loss statement by the Statutes was to follow later, and will be discussed in subsequent chapters.

While it is not intended here to discuss fully the accounting principles underlying the balance sheet, it is desirable to question whether the legislature might have misplaced its confidence in specifying the balance sheet. An appreciation of the usefulness of the balance sheet will assist in understanding later developments in standards of reporting. When discussing the Victorian Act of 1896, some reasons were put forward as to why the balance sheet was accorded the distinction of legal recognition. These included the historical concept of the company and less resistant opposition to disclosing these aspects of a company's affairs. It is unlikely that accountants did not recognize the limitations of the balance sheet —in fact in their discussion of the requirements of the 1931–6 Acts they made it abundantly clear that they did recognize at least some of these failings. It also appears that A. A. Fitzgerald was right in claiming that there was 'an urgent need for action on the part of accountants in improving the understanding by the public of the nature and functions of a balance sheet'.[28] In his editorials in the *Australian Accountant,* Fitzgerald developed the theme that the balance sheet was limited in concept and utility and that the profit and loss statement was a vital missing document. His views presaged the findings of the Cohen Committee in 1945 that the profit and loss statement is as important as, if not more important than, the balance sheet.[29] As R. G. W. Wood commented in a letter published in the *Chartered Accountant in Australia* 'the annual balance sheet of a business is a most unfortunate accounting statement, in that its purpose and construction are not properly understood by most users thereof and, consequently, too much is expected of it'.[30]

It is within the framework of this conflict of ideas, that accountants have sought to improve the form of the balance sheet. This striving for improved form is of direct concern to this book. As A. A. Fitzgerald pointed out in 1936: 'One can accept as valid the criticism of form without necessarily believing that the balance sheet is a mere anachronism which should be scrapped in favour of a financial statement which will essay to depict the market value of assets.'[31]

Thirty years later there are still advocates of such a substitution and some see legislative support for this view in the amendments of the Companies (Public Borrowings) Acts which require directors of borrowing corporations to state: 'Whether or not any circumstances have arisen which render adherence to the existing method of valuation of assets or liabilities of the company misleading or inappropriate' (s.5).

A detailed examination of how the contents of the contemporary balance sheet are derived lends support to the conclusion that it is a strictly technical document of limited meaning and utility. Nevertheless it is a useful, and necessary, financial statement. It therefore appears reasonable to conclude that the legislature did overestimate the usefulness of the balance sheet by raising it to the status achieved in the 1931–6 Acts. It did not take very long for this fact to become apparent. In fact the Acts had hardly been printed when events both in Australia and overseas emphasized that knowledge of the profit and loss account was as important as the balance sheet, and further extension of the minimum statutory requirements for disclosure were contemplated.

11

Disclosure c. 1928–1936

In a community which was as ready to follow the example of English law as shown in the previous chapter, it reasonably might be inferred that the standards of business practice similarly might be copied. If the commentary provided in the English accountancy journal the *Accountant* is any guide, then Australian practice would have gained little by such a process. The *Accountant* writer recorded the lamentable fact that a review of balance sheets of public companies issued during 1928 to 1929 would reveal quite a number which were of no practical use to the average shareholder.[1]

A. A. Fitzgerald, in a series of lectures in the infant Faculty of Commerce at the University of Melbourne published in booklet form, identified those salient features which he considered financial statements should possess. These may be summarized as:

(a) A clear separation of current liabilities, long term liabilities and proprietorship and the distinction of fixed, floating and intangible assets.
(b) The use of a settled sequence of presentation of the items.
(c) The statement of the basis of valuation of all assets.
(d) Profit and loss account in as much detail 'as is compatible with the necessity for withholding information from possible competitors' with a statement of provisions for depreciation, doubtful debts, etc. and any extraordinary profits and losses.[2]

The statutory requirements for disclosures in the Victorian Act of 1896 partly met Fitzgerald's criteria. They did not include the provision of group sub-totals in the balance sheet, the separate statement of cost price and the deduction from it of the accumulated total of depreciation written off the assets, nor any profit and loss detail beyond the net balance shown in the balance sheet. They did, however, require details of how the values of the fixed assets were arrived at. Evidence on the standard of financial reporting in Australia at the time is provided by A. A. Fitzgerald. The results of Fitzgerald's survey bear quoting in full:

I have examined the Balance Sheets of 91 companies, published in the *Melbourne Stock Exchange Record* between July and December, 1927, with the following results:—

In 17 instances there is no clear division between External and Internal liabilities.

In 15 instances the details of assets are insufficient.

In 24 instances the order of arrangement of items is faulty, and in 24 instances the basis of valuation of assets is not given.

Apart from these definitely faulty examples, many others of those examined give negative results; all that can be said in regard to them is that they appear to be satisfactory in all respects, but further investigation and fuller information might disclose grounds for criticism. It should be noted that several of the accounts examined are those of companies registered in other states, so that it is not to be assumed that there has been any general disregard of the provisions of the Act by Victorian Companies. Nevertheless there are some cases of companies registered in Victoria which have failed to comply with the Act, particularly in regard to the stating of the basis of valuation of assets.

But while 'a basis of valuation' was given by sixty-seven companies the manner of doing so was frequently such as to draw criticism. Fitzgerald said:

In many instances, apart from those classed as unsatisfactory, assets were stated as 'at valuation'. This may satisfy the letter of the requirement that the 'basis of value, whether at cost price, market price, or otherwise', is to be stated, but it conveys little information to creditors or shareholders, and is, I suggest, a breach of the spirit of that requirement. In the case of Floating Assets, the expression 'at valuation' may be assumed to indicate that correct accounting principles have been followed, and it may safely be left to the conscientious auditor to satisfy himself that such is the case. In dealing with Fixed Assets, however, it would appear to be preferable to define more clearly what is meant by the direction given in the form, and to insist upon the publication of cost price, and also of the total amount of depreciation provided up to the date of the Balance Sheet. The amount provided in the period covered by the accounts would be ascertainable from the Profit and Loss Account, if it were prepared on the lines suggested.[3]

This conclusion by Fitzgerald was borne out by an examination of the available reports of the 'forty-two leaders sample'. It is clear that at this stage financial reporting was far from satisfactory and much had to be done to bring standards up to those regarded as normal in the present day. Five years later Fitzgerald observed: 'There has so far been little, if any, attempt at improvement. With a few notable exceptions, the balance sheets offend not only in the direction of insufficient information, but in the form in which they are prepared.'[4]

This may be regarded then, as a description of the general situation when the Acts in Queensland, South Australia and New South Wales were passed between 1931 and 1936. The innovations in these Acts largely met the criteria stated by Fitzgerald, except in regard to the profit and loss account and the publication of the cost amount and accumulated depreciation to date of fixed assets. We may have expected therefore, the new enactments in Queensland, South Australia and New South Wales to have produced a significant improvement in reporting and to have been received with widespread acclaim.

However, the new requirements drew mixed reactions even from among the accounting profession. An example was the response to the requirement to classify the assets in the balance sheet. The Queensland Act required the balance sheet 'to distinguish between the amounts respectively of the fixed assets and of the floating assets and shall state how the values of the fixed and floating assets have been arrived at' (s.134). In the South Australian and New South Wales Acts it was given as, 'to distinguish between the amounts respectively of the fixed assets and of the floating assets, and shall state how the values of the fixed assets have been arrived at' (s.143 and s.104). There was an additional specification in the South Australian Act set out in the form contained in the fifth schedule to state debtors and bills receivable after providing for bad and doubtful debts and for most of the other assets a reference to a footnote 'Basis of value, whether at cost price, market price, or otherwise to be stated'. These sections gave legislative sanction to the concept of a classification grouping of assets and liabilities based on the permanence of assets in terms of intention and the urgency of liabilities assuming a continuing enterprise. But the opinion of counsel quoted by the Institute of Chartered Accountants was that it was 'not necessary to label the assets in groups as fixed or floating'.[5]

An interesting example of contrasting speed and tardiness in adopting this classified balance sheet presentation was found in the 'forty-two leaders sample'. Drug Houses of Australia Limited, a Victorian-based firm, was formed by a merger of a number of pharmaceutical manufacturing and distributing companies. One of the subsidiaries, Felton, Grimwade and Duerdins Ltd remained a listed company because of a public shareholding of preference shares. The balance sheet of the parent company was presented in a classified form in 1931 but the subsidiary company did not adopt this form of presentation until 1939, eight years later. (The parent company in like manner adopted whole pound statements in 1931, some six years before the subsidiary did so.) The classified presentation required by law in Queensland, South Australia and New South Wales, was voluntarily adopted by the parent company referred to. The subsidiary did not adopt this form until the Victorian Companies Act was amended in 1938 to require a classified balance sheet presentation. The difference between the reporting practice of the parent and subsidiary company may have reflected the degree of influence of the auditor in each case and the ideas of the particular auditor. The auditor of the parent company was E. V. Nixon who is referred to in other chapters as an advocate of up-to-date practices on more than one occasion. The auditor of the subsidiary company was the firm of Young and Outhwaite. Outhwaite is referred to later as a vigorous opponent of significant developments in reporting requirements on at least one occasion. So far as one can deduce from the available evidence this particular incident in reporting is the consequence of the auditors' influence. It appears reasonable to explain it in this way because the parent and the subsidiary companies could be regarded as being effectively controlled and managed by the same individuals.

The requirements in the 1931–6 Acts to give the basis of valuation of assets drew sharper criticism from some accountants. The extent of the criticism is surprising when it is remembered that similar provisions had been in force in Victoria since 1896. When the legal compulsion to publish a balance sheet was introduced by the Victorian Companies Act of 1896, the specifications of what was to be shown were minimal but did include the following:

The amount of debts due to the company after making a proper deduction for debts considered to be bad or doubtful. Whether the assets other than debts due to the company are taken at cost price or by valuation or on what other basis they are stated and whether any and if so what amount or percentage has been written off and what other provision (if any) has been made for depreciation. (s.24(2)(c) and (d))

When the Victorian Companies Act was 'redrafted' in 1910 this was no longer spelt out in a section of the Act in this way but the second schedule form included effectively the same note against debtors and bills and notes receivable. Against most of the other assets there was a reference to a footnote which required the 'basis of value, whether at cost price, market price, or otherwise, to be stated'. Similar provisions were included in the Tasmanian Companies Act of 1920. These requirements in Victorian and Tasmanian legislation do not appear to have raised any particular problems of interpretation and application of the Acts. Yet in 1932 one critic, W. E. Savage, wrote:

to provide for the definite basis of the values of all floating assets is merely seeking academical accuracy by trying to place under group description detailed assets, which, by their very nature, require distinct and separate valuation.

The provision gives legislative sanction to the so-called 'omnibus definition', which has been the target of professional criticism for years past.[6]

The Institute of Chartered Accountants sought counsel's opinion on how this requirement should be interpreted, and thereby helped to perpetuate some of the unsatisfactory terminology and definitions which it has taken much subsequent effort to eliminate. All of the suggestions given were supported by examples drawn from English company reports. As regards stock, counsel reported that the 'phrase generally used' was 'at or under cost'. No usual basis was indicated for shares in subsidiary companies, the examples including 'at or below cost', 'as valued by the directors' and 'at cost less realisations and amounts written off'. As regards other assets counsel's opinion supported the alternatives of:

'at cost'
'at cost, less depreciation'

and 'at cost, less amounts written off'.

These were interpreted more specifically as follows:

Freehold land and buildings:

'at cost, less amounts written off'
'at cost, less depreciation of buildings';

Leasehold properties:

'at cost, less amortisation'
'at cost, less provision for amortisation';

Depreciable assets:

'at cost, less depreciation';

Investments:

'at cost'
'at cost, less amount written off'
'at market values'
'at or under market values';

Goodwill:
   'at cost'
   'at cost, less amounts written off'.

Only in one of the eight examples cited by counsel were the assets shown at cost with the accumulated total of depreciation shown as a deduction therefrom to give the net balance remaining.[7] It will be seen that none of these recommended bases included more than one formula—although the meaning of some might be disputed. Where items within a group had different bases of valuation it was common practice at later times to state separately each item in the group along with its basis of valuation but this was not legally necessary and apparently not done by some companies at the time of the 1931-6 Acts. Nearly thirty years later good practice was recognized when the Uniform Acts required the separate total to be shown for each basis of valuation applied to a class of asset.

After the passing of the 1931-6 Acts the treatment of fixed assets followed the lines of least disclosure and rarely was Fitzgerald's ideal of showing the cost value less the total of depreciation to date, realized. In 1948 the Registrar-General in Victoria gave official acknowledgment to the presentation of fixed assets as a single figure 'at cost' or 'at cost less depreciation'. He wrote in the *Australian Accountant*:

> Another point that still appears difficult is the necessity to state in the Balance Sheet the 'basis of valuation of each class of assets'.
>
> The expressions 'at cost', or 'at cost less depreciation' cover this point adequately, but sometimes other situations make it difficult to express this 'basis of valuation'. If assets have at some time in the past been re-valued by the Directors or some other competent authority, it is sufficient to state 'at valuation of . . . at such and such a date, less depreciation'.
>
> On the assumption that the auditor has access to all these relevant matters, we have often agreed to accept the statement in the auditor's report that he 'has accepted the valuation of the manager' of the assets, or some similar wording.[8]

It is interesting to note that in 1947, some thirteen years after the South Australian Act was passed, it was necessary for the Registrar of Companies in that State to draw attention to the fact that there was a failure by companies to observe the disclosure requirements of the Act.[9] Specifically attention was drawn to the requirement to disclose directors' fees paid, the description of the *nominal* capital as such, and the statement of the basis of

11 Disclosure c. 1928–1936

valuation for all assets. (The 'forty-two leaders sample' does not include any companies incorporated in South Australia and therefore subject to this Act.)

It seems reasonable to suggest that the intervention of a world war may have explained such a tardiness in compliance with the Act on the one hand and in its enforcement on the other hand. The evidence so far presented suggests that at least until the wartime period of 1939 to 1945, there was both considerable unwillingness to meet the legal obligations for disclosure and in fact a degree of disregard of the law. Subsequently there have been significant developments in the method of giving the basis of valuation of certain assets. This is discussed in specific chapters relating to the valuation of fixed assets and depreciation of them, and the valuation of inventories.

12

The Stock Exchanges
Official List Requirements

As pointed out in the introduction, standards have not arisen only from legislative compulsion. One of the important non statutory influences has been, and remains, that of the Stock Exchanges of the principal cities in Australia. It is appropriate to review the standards sought by the Exchanges and their influence at this point because the first effective requirements of the Exchanges were introduced contemporaneously with the legislative provisions just reviewed. The Exchanges' activities will be followed through to the present time before returning to pick up the next thread in the argument.

These Exchanges are autonomous bodies but have co-operated on matters of common interest through the Australian Associated Stock Exchanges (A.A.S.E.), a national association formed in 1937. The Stock Exchanges have long shown an interest in working for adequate disclosure by companies. This objective is achieved through the imposition of listing requirements on companies seeking to have their shares listed on the Exchanges. In 1965 the A.A.S.E. Chairman summarized the purposes of these requirements as:

firstly, to ensure that a company seeking quotation of its securities in the Public Market place adheres to accepted ethical standards in matters which relate to these securities; and secondly, to ensure that a company makes available to the public—and this, of course, includes its own security holders—a specified minimum of information about its affairs so that investors and prospective investors can, at any one time, make a reasoned assessment of the value of that company's securities.

The Exchanges are not always successful in achieving these purposes, as the Chairman of the A.A.S.E. said:

it is often disappointing and disheartening to us to find a degree of lack of co-operation from companies in the matter of Listing Requirements.

We frequently find that companies which are well aware of their obligations under the listing requirements, will take no action on them until we draw their attention to their responsibilities.[1]

The Stock Exchanges first introduced listing requirements of a rudimentary nature before the turn of the century. The first printed schedule of 'Official List Requirements' was issued by the Stock Exchange of Melbourne in November 1925. It appears to have been from 1936 that the Official List Requirements of the two principal Australian Stock Exchanges in Melbourne and Sydney became identical in their specifications. It was not until 1954 that the listing requirements were issued under the imprimatur of the Australian Associated Stock Exchanges. Before this the independent exchanges had met together and decided common policies including the listing requirements. Although a considerable degree of uniformity was achieved, the listing requirements during the period before 1958, nevertheless were issued independently by each Exchange. All references are to the Official Listing Requirements of the Stock Exchange of Melbourne in the period before 1958 unless otherwise noted.

The first tentative steps taken by an Exchange towards ensuring adequate disclosure were taken at a time when financial statements of any kind were required by law only in Victoria, and it was to be another thirteen years before even Victoria required adequate statements relating to subsidiary companies, or profit and loss details. The November 1925 Official List Requirements of the Melbourne Exchange specified that the articles or rules of a company seeking listing should include provision for the appointment of the auditors (except the first auditor and the filling of casual vacancies) and the fixing of their remuneration by the company in general meeting and to require ten days' notice of candidature by anyone other than a retiring auditor. The articles should also provide that company meetings should be held on not less than seven days' notice and all notices, reports and balance sheets should be sent to every shareholder, and to the Exchange, at least seven days before the meeting to which they relate.

More specifically directed at the form of statements was the strong recommendation of the Committee that tangible assets be separated from intangible assets in balance sheets, and that separate amounts be specified for the different items. Profit and loss accounts should always accompany the balance sheets. Holding companies were covered by the requirement in clause 28: 'That any Company which has a controlling interest in another Company or Companies, shall with its own balance-sheet furnish shareholders with balance-sheets and profit and loss accounts of the subsidiary Company or Companies.' Item G of the Official List Requirements also specified that: 'Balance Sheets issued by a Company shall be accompanied by a general report of the Directors and by a statement as to the amount (if any) which they recommend to be paid out of the profits or reserve fund by way of dividend or bonus, and the amount (if any) which they propose to carry to the reserve fund.'

In December 1927 the Official List Requirements were amended in a number of respects. The recommendation concerning the separate statement of tangible and intangible assets was included as a specific item to be set out in the articles. Clause 28 of the 1925 requirements was amended to allow for the submission of an aggregate balance sheet and profit and loss account instead of individual statements of a company's subsidiary companies. Among the 'forty-two leaders sample' we did not find any instance at this time of a company having complied with the previous specification to submit the individual statements of the company's subsidiaries. Beginning from when it was first listed on the Melbourne Exchange in 1932, D.H.A. included aggregate statements of its subsidiaries thereby achieving the distinction of being the first Australian public company to issue any form of group accounts presentation. Similar aggregate statements were issued by two New South Wales companies, Email and Woolworths, in response to a Sydney Stock Exchange Listing Requirement issued in 1936. These few examples suggest a degree of success by the Exchanges in securing improved reporting by listed companies. This success was probably confined largely to newly listed companies. The three companies concerned were all admitted to the official list of the Exchanges after the requirements referred to above were introduced in 1927. Two of the companies prepared the aggregate statements as from the year in which the company was first listed but the third did not do so until nine years after being listed, which suggests the Exchanges' improved requirements had some effect.

A second amendment made in December 1927 to the previous clause 28 of the Melbourne Official List Requirements, was an extension to cover the case wherein the listed company may be one of a number of companies which possesses as its principal asset shares in an operating company, but does not own a controlling interest, i.e. more than fifty per cent of the shares. In this type of

12 The Stock Exchanges

arrangement, the operating company is therefore not a subsidiary of the listed company or companies but is what may be called an associate company. Yet the fortunes of the listed company may be wholly dependent on the success of the operating company. To cover this situation it was proposed that the balance sheet and profit and loss account of the associate company should be included with those of the listed company. In September 1936 the requirement was rephrased to cover those cases where more than one such investment existed. Two particular cases to which these listing requirements were applicable occurred in the 'forty-two leaders sample'. Australian and Kandos Cement Holdings Ltd is the present successor to Australian Cement Ltd and Kandos Cement Ltd. These two companies, one in Victoria and the other in New South Wales, merged their operations into a single operating company in 1929 so that the two listed companies each owned one half of the operating company, Australian Portland Cement Pty Ltd. The operating company, registered in Victoria as a proprietary company, was not legally required to publish financial statements until the creation of the non-exempt proprietary company under the Companies Act of 1958. (Figures for 1957, 1958 and 1959 became available retrospectively as part of the details required in the prospectus issued on formation of the new holding company.) In 1964 the two publicly listed companies were merged in the one holding company of Australian and Kandos Cement Ltd. As the holding company now controls all the shares of the operating company, the operating company is a wholly owned subsidiary. The holding company is now required to publish consolidated statements for the group. A second case centred on Australian Gypsum Products Pty Ltd. Australian Gypsum Industries Limited is the successor to Australian Gypsum Ltd. This latter company was one of three main producers which in 1931 sold their assets to a new operating company, Australian Gypsum Products Pty Ltd. As none of the three participants in the plan owned more than half the shares in the operating company, it was not a subsidiary of any of them. However, the accounts of the operating company were published as consolidated statements of Australian Gypsum Products Pty Ltd and Subsidiaries from 1957 until 1960, after which date the interests of the whole group were merged in the one public company, Australian Gypsum Ltd.

The Exchange was unable to secure the information it sought in each of these cases. Two cases does not seem an adequate basis on which to make too conclusive a statement. Without impugning the motives of individual companies or directors it does not seem unreasonable, however, to conclude that it was the advent of the nonexempt proprietary company which compelled the publication of the financial statements of the operating company and thereby rendered the particular company structure ineffective as a means of avoiding disclosure. In neither of the two cases cited were the statements of the operating company published until this was required by the Victorian Companies Act of 1958.

Among the 'forty-two leaders sample' there occurs a variation of the type of company structure discussed above with quite different reporting consequences. Carlton and United Breweries Limited is a company in which the bulk of the shares are held by a number of companies which are each in turn public companies listed on the Stock Exchange. However, the so-called 'Z' shares in Carlton and United Breweries are publicly held and the operating company is listed and reports in its own right. While the holding companies have not adopted the practice of including in their reports the statements of the operating company, the latter are readily available to the public.

The enforcement of the listing requirements at this time was dependent wholly on voluntary acceptance. There was hardly even a 'moral obligation' to comply for those companies which were listed before the Exchanges introduced any particular part of the Official Listing Requirements. At least one listed company paid so little regard to the Exchange's requirements as to publish a balance sheet showing one asset described as: 'Shares and investments in manufacturing and general merchandise companies in Australia, South Africa, New Zealand and England.' The only account given of the activities represented by these assets was the statement in the directors' report that: 'Reports and accounts from associated companies show that the volume of trade done was the largest in their history and shareholders are again assured that their financial position and soundness are undoubted.'[2] The Exchanges apparently found that some companies would present the same statements year after year. There is a report of this matter being considered at a biannual conference of the principal Exchanges,[3] held in Brisbane on 12 and 13 August 1929, where it was resolved that the Official List Requirements would in future require: 'That the accounts shall be balanced once at least in every year and at intervals of not more than 15 months; and that the Balance-Sheet shall be prepared, audited, and laid before a General Meeting.' This was included in the Official List Requirements as issued by the Melbourne Stock Exchange in May

1930. The effectiveness of the requirement was strengthened by also requiring that an ordinary general meeting of the company should be held once at least in every calendar year, and not more than fifteen months after the holding of the previous ordinary general meeting.

The Stock Exchanges became concerned at the use of share options and went so far as to withhold listing from mining companies where there was an option over unissued shares given to vendors, promoters, prospectors, or persons, other than cash subscribers, associated with the flotation of the company.[4] The Exchanges also included in the listing requirements in 1936 a clause requiring any company to show by footnote to the balance sheet: 'The number of shares under option, the price of issue, and the date of expiration of such option.' This was two years before the first legislation for similar disclosure of options was passed in Victoria.

The Acts passed in Queensland, South Australia and New South Wales between 1931 and 1936 provided for the disclosure of directors' remuneration and this also was included in the 1938 Victorian Act. The Stock Exchanges were aware of the controversy about this time which arose from the more frequent cases of company boards including executive directors. The Exchanges decided at their conference in 1936 to require all listed companies and subsidiaries to disclose the total remuneration (including fees, percentages, and other emoluments) of directors.[5] An appropriate clause was included in the Official List Requirements issued by the Melbourne Stock Exchange on 1 July 1936.

The same conference of Stock Exchanges expressed its disapproval of the unreasonable delay by some companies in the presentation of the periodical accounts. They considered three or four months was sufficient time from the close of the financial period and accordingly the Melbourne Stock Exchange Official List Requirements amendments in July 1936 imposed such a time limitation.

The listing requirements relating to holding companies were partly supplanted by legislation in Victoria in 1938. In Victoria the Companies Act of 1938 gave legislative support to the presentation by holding companies of the parent company statements together with consolidated group statements or the separate statements of each subsidiary company. The Companies Act did not favour the aggregate statement of subsidiaries as sought by the Stock Exchanges during the period following 1927. Victorian companies had to comply with this legislative requirement. This involved the adoption of consolidated statements by all Victorian companies only four years after the first example of such statements was presented by an Australian company. New South Wales companies remained subject only to voluntary compliance with the Sydney Stock Exchange Official Listing Requirements so far as any additional details of holding companies were concerned. In 1925 the Sydney Stock Exchange had adopted similar listing requirements to those adopted by the Stock Exchange of Melbourne. But in 1927 the Sydney Stock Exchange departed from the requirements as set down by the Melbourne Stock Exchange. Instead of seeking an aggregate statement of the assets and liabilities of the subsidiaries, the Sydney Stock Exchange requirements suggested that a holding company 'may' submit an 'aggregate balance sheet and profit and loss account of the company and the subsidiaries'. From 1936 the Sydney Exchange amended its requirements to seek the aggregate statement of assets and liabilities of the subsidiaries as set down in the listing requirements of the Stock Exchange of Melbourne. A further change followed shortly afterwards in the light of experience subsequent to the introduction of the Companies Act of 1938 in Victoria. The Exchanges throughout Australia agreed to include in their requirements a clause modelled on the Victorian Act seeking the presentation by holding companies of the parent company statements accompanied by either the separate statements of each subsidiary or, alternatively, consolidated statements for the group. The Sydney Stock Exchange's listing requirements therefore became an important factor in securing consolidated statements, or the separate statements of each subsidiary, from New South Wales holding companies until given statutory support in 1961. This 1941 requirement included provisions requiring disclosure of the losses of any subsidiaries and allowance in the consolidated statements for any minority outside interests in any partly owned subsidiaries. The Melbourne Stock Exchange 1946 listing requirements did not involve any alteration in the substance of the requirements except in relation to holding companies. The previously included clauses relating to the statements of subsidiary companies and of companies the shares of which constituted the principal asset of listed companies, were deleted in deference to the statutory requirements covering holding companies in Victoria.

In appendix 5 there is set out the details of when the companies included in the 'forty-two leaders sample' adopted the presentation of consolidated group statements. This shows clearly that the majority of New South Wales companies were influenced to adopt this form of presentation before being compelled to do so by the New

South Wales Companies Act of 1962. The benefits of the Melbourne Stock Exchange listing requirements on the statements of holding companies do not stand out so clearly because of the much earlier introduction of compulsory statutory requirements in Victoria. Nevertheless it is clear that the Stock Exchanges were responsible for marked improvement in the financial reporting of holding companies and to a considerable degree counteracted the deficiencies of the statutory requirements, particularly in New South Wales.

At the 1939 conference of the Exchanges the first move had been made towards more frequent reporting. The A.A.S.E. conference adopted as a requirement for new listing, the submission to the Stock Exchange for publication in the press of an interim or half-yearly report on the company's activities indicating any special matters which affected profits materially and giving a general survey of operations compared with the same period in the previous year.[6] More precise definition of the contents of these reports did not follow until two decades later.

Such new listing requirements 'are not usually made retrospective' but, in this instance, all listed companies were circularized inviting them to comply voluntarily. The Exchanges concluded from the response that most companies would accept the invitation. Seven years later the Exchanges made an important move by announcing that after 1 September 1946 companies applying for official listing would be required to enter into a form of agreement to abide by various practices set down by the Exchanges including the issue of financial statements. No longer were the Official List Requirements to be a gentlemanly guide.[7] Subsequent attempts to widen the application of this agreement reveal, on more than one occasion, a sharp clash between the Exchanges and some of the more recalcitrant companies. In 1954 the listing requirements were revised extensively and issued under the imprimatur of the Australian Associated Stock Exchanges. The agreement to be made by companies seeking listing now included the 'dragnet' clause, aimed at making all future amendments to the listing requirements retrospective. This attempt to impose the new ideas of the Exchanges upon companies already listed has led to some of the more public confrontations between the Exchanges and companies. The Exchanges have not been satisfied to confine the 'dragnet' clause to newly listed companies but have sought to make it applicable to existing listed companies. The addition to the official list of a new type of security issued by an existing listed company could provide the opportunity for the Exchange to impose the current listing requirements on companies originally listed before these two significant dates. The attempt of the Exchanges to adopt this tactic when Advertiser Newspapers Ltd issued convertible notes, led to a clash which was aired publicly in the press in the middle of 1962.

The *Advertiser* reported in its own columns on 21 June 1962 that the Board of the company 'had before it yesterday, advice from the Stock Exchange that its Unsecured Convertible Notes would no longer be quoted on the "unofficial" list after June 30, or quoted at all, unless the Company signed an agreement drawn up by the Australian Associated Stock Exchanges to cover new listings'. The company said it aired the matter, 'so that the views of directors of all public companies in Australia can be brought to bear on the Stock Exchanges to force a change in a clause in this agreement which is manifestly improper'.

The company advised that to circumvent the Exchange it would provide facilities to buy and sell the notes at its own office, including the publication of prices. It was intimated further that these facilities would also cover notes issued by two other Adelaide companies which had received a similar ultimatum, Bennett & Fisher Ltd and Adelaide Steamship Co. Ltd. The chairman of the Australian Associated Stock Exchanges, A. B. Mellor, was reported as giving a spirited defence of the clause 'pointing the bone' at these same companies for their tardiness in adopting some of the already existing disclosure requirements of the Official List Requirements. Specifically, Mr Mellor stated that Advertiser Newspapers Ltd had not disclosed its taxation provision until 1960. This item was included in the 1954 version of the Official List Requirements (O.L.R.). Adelaide Steamship Co. Ltd had not stated the taxation provision until 1960, and had not stated the amount of the charge for depreciation until 1960 (O.L.R. 1954). Bennett & Fisher Ltd still did not disclose either the taxation provision (O.L.R. 1954), or the amount of the annual depreciation charge (O.L.R. 1954). The chairman of Advertiser Newspapers, Sir Lloyd Dumas, replied that these were 'red herrings' and returned the sally with the rather embarrassing facts that the Broken Hill Proprietary Co. Ltd was in the same position because of what Mr Mellor had been only able to describe as 'an oversight by a staff member of the Stock Exchange of Melbourne'.[8] The Exchanges continued to quote the notes on the unofficial list and their conversion to shares on 1 January 1963 at least temporarily resolved the issue between the Exchanges and Advertiser Newspapers Ltd.

12 The Stock Exchanges

The ultimate weapon of the Exchanges when persuasion fails is the threat of delisting. It is to be expected that such extreme measures rarely have been resorted to. The efficacy of the threat was demonstrated in 1960 when the Queensland Lennons Hotel Group was delisted until the identity of a takeover bidder was disclosed.

The detailed financial information to be provided according to the 1954 requirements was as follows:

(i) Notification of the final dividend passed to be accompanied by a simultaneous statement of the net profit (with comparison of previous year), even if a provisional figure or subject to audit.
(ii) The final accounts to include a balance sheet showing intangible assets separately and any share options outstanding.
(iii) The profit and loss account to state the charge for depreciation renewals and diminution in value of fixed assets and the provision for and/or payment of income tax.
(iv) Holding companies to give consolidated balance sheets and profit and loss statement, or separate statements for each subsidiary. Any consolidated statement to state separately the extent of any minority interest.
(v) Where the main asset was shares in another company or companies, there was to be included the latest balance sheet and profit and loss account of such company or companies.
(vi) An interim report after the first six months of the financial year outlining any matters which had affected profits materially and giving a general survey of operations in comparison with the same period in the previous year.

An important step towards further development of a fully informed security market was the inclusion in the Listing Agreement of provisions allowing the Stock Exchange to make available immediately to its members and to the press any of the information submitted by the listed company in compliance with the Listing Agreement. This is a complementary matter to the requirement that a listed company notify the Exchange immediately of any information which will avoid a false market being established in a company's shares.

An incident in 1969 prompted a writer in the *Australian Financial Review* of 19 June 1969 to declare that 'no stock exchange in Australia has shown a readiness to examine, collate and quickly transmit to other exchanges the information contained in such . . . [reports made to the Exchanges] even if it had the personnel available'. The writer claimed that 'considerations such as this have prompted many major companies—including some of the most prestigious in the country—' to release their reports to the financial press with an embargo on publication before the date or time on which it is intended to be available to the Exchange and the public generally. He continued, 'Eastern States stock exchanges (including Melbourne . . .) have known of this practice and have accepted it.' Such a procedure was followed by Swan Brewery Ltd in 1968 but in 1969 the 'Perth Exchange . . . objected to the company sending out its annual report to all Australian Exchanges and finance editors with an embargo that the contents of the report will not be released for public information until 10.30 a.m.' on the third day after the report was sent to them. The Perth Exchange it was reported felt, 'that under the embargo, some people will obtain information on the company ahead of shareholders'.[9] The result was that for the three days the company's shares were suspended from trading on the Exchanges.

At the annual meeting of the company the chairman defended the company's position on the grounds that,

the board's primary concern was that shareholders and the general public should have information about the company's affairs at least at the same time as the stock exchange. In the promulgation of news, the relationship was between the company and its shareholders. The function of the stockbroker was to act as a link between buyer and seller.[10]

It seems extraordinary that this issue should be raised after so many years. The press comments suggest that there may have been other matters in dispute between the Exchange and the company or that some section of the press had failed to observe such an embargoed release. Neither of these assertions have been substantiated by available public evidence. The value of the incident seems to be rather in the evidence of the determination of the Exchanges to ensure that all sections of the securities market are equally aware of any relevant facts affecting the market and the assertion of the prerogatives of the Exchanges as defined in the Official List Requirements. From this viewpoint the identity of the company concerned becomes largely irrelevant.

Further action was taken by the Exchanges on the matter of interim reports in 1958, 1964 and 1967. As a later chapter shows the Exchanges proved themselves the dominant force in improving half-yearly or interim reports.

Amended Listing Requirements issued in 1961 required the disclosure of directors' fees to include the total paid or payable to both the directors of the company and the payments to the directors of any companies in which the listed company holds directly or indirectly 50 per cent or more of the issued capital.

Following the passage of the Uniform Acts, the A.A.S.E. undertook an extensive revision of the Official List Requirements in the light of that legislation. The revised requirements were issued in the form of a 'Listing Manual' in 1964. The 1964 Official List Requirements also incorporated the effect of the Public Borrowings Acts. Any public borrowing corporation is required to give to the Exchanges any reports required by Statute from such companies. Other amendments effective as from September 1967 seek an explanation of the reason for a provision for taxation differing by more than 15 per cent from the prima facie amount payable on the declared profit, and identification of subsidiaries which have incurred a loss and the amount of the loss. Without including it in the mandatory requirements, the Exchanges have recommended the publication of a schedule setting out the profit and tax and depreciation provision of each subsidiary company. A requirement which echoes problems of statutory interpretation discussed in a later chapter is one requiring the directors' preliminary profit report to the Exchanges to state whether any unusual event influenced the results for the year. These requirements will be referred to in later discussion of the relevant factors.

The Stock Exchanges have over a period of nearly forty years, sought to improve the standard of financial reporting. Their actions have been directed at some of the most controversial issues in financial reporting. The Exchanges achieved some success with improved reporting by holding companies. They have achieved more prompt reporting and exerted a continuing pressure for improvement in other less spectacular aspects of reporting. They have achieved a considerable improvement in interim or half-yearly reporting. The 'weapon' of delisting has been tested and there are indications that it may be an effective device for securing the compliance of companies with the requirements of the Exchanges. It can be concluded that the Official List Requirements of the Stock Exchanges have been a valuable source of establishing, and securing compliance with, improved standards of disclosure.

13

Reserves and Provisions

An important thread in the clarification of specific terminological issues in financial disclosure began in Australia at about the same time as the English trial of Lord Kylsant subjected to public scrutiny, among other issues, this specific problem of the lack of clarity in the definition and application of the terms 'reserve' and 'provision'. Certain problems in the clarification of these issues still persist. Just as in the previous chapter the influences of the Stock Exchanges were followed through to the present day, so this chapter will pursue the enquiry of these terminological issues before returning to consider some other aspects of the Royal Mail case in more detail.

This problem of terminology was by no means a new one, nor one that was not receiving attention. In Australia a solution to the problem was proposed by A. A. Fitzgerald. His enterprise and persistence on the topic were such that the solution of the problem may rightly be credited to him personally. It is a unique example of accounting standards resulting from an individual's personal initiative.

A clarification of the application of the term 'reserve fund' was a necessary prelude. It already has been mentioned how Isaacs included in his Bill which became the 1896 Act the requirement that the balance sheet should show 'the actual amount of the reserve fund (if any) and the mode in which it is used or invested'. It was provided further that no balance sheet, etc. should contain any representation that the company had a reserve fund unless the reserve fund actually existed and the representation was 'accompanied by a statement showing whether or not such a reserve fund is used in the business, and if any portion thereof is otherwise invested showing the manner in which and the securities upon which the same is invested' (s.24(2)(e) and s.25). It has been mentioned also that when this provision of the 1896 Act was debated,

13 Reserves and Provisions

the question was raised as to whether the Attorney-General, Isaacs, knew what was the nature of a reserve. Isaacs accepted the definition of a reserve as accumulated profits but did not consider that this technical term was understood at all clearly by the community at large. It was his object to protect investors, by attempting to ensure that when the directors of a company claimed the company possessed reserves, there would be assets in the company to support these reserves. In this context, Isaacs considered that reserves should be supported by the 'funds' invested in the enterprise or, alternatively, by 'funds' placed in some other identified or specific investment.[1] When the Victorian Companies Act was 'redrafted' in 1910 the section relating to representations of a reserve fund was re-enacted. The form of balance sheet in the schedule to the Act included the reserve fund on the liabilities side of the balance sheet and required a certificate from the manager or public officer 'that the reserve fund (if any) and accumulated profits (if any) are used in the business (or how otherwise)' (second schedule, form C). In 1934 the South Australian Companies Act took up the section as included in the 1910 Victorian Companies Act and also included in the schedule the statement to be made by the manager or public officer as included in the Victorian Companies Act of 1910. The New South Wales Companies Act of 1936 adopted a slightly different approach. It required that any representation of a reserve fund in a balance sheet should be accompanied by a statement 'showing what proportion (if any) of the reserve fund is used in the business' (s.109).

Victorian companies over the period between 1910 and 1938 dutifully fulfilled the requirements of the schedule to the 1910 Act by the secretary or manager providing a certificate as to how the reserve was employed. Among the available sample of the 'forty-two leaders' only one instance was found of a company having part of its reserve invested other than in the business. These companies therefore interpreted the law by regarding the reserve fund as equivalent to accumulated profits—which accords with the original intention of Isaacs in drafting the 1896 Act. The law read thus did not present any problems of interpretation although there lurked beneath this façade of clarity what appeared to be an absurdity. If the reserve fund was interpreted as being a separate or earmarked investment, then it was nonsensical to ask if it were invested in the business. There was little more agreement on the use of the terminology 'reserve' and 'reserve fund' in the accounting profession.

A. A. Fitzgerald recognized this difficulty in interpreting the meaning of the Act and observed that whether one considered the statutory provision as meaningless or not probably depended on which of two prominently used textbooks one had been brought up on. For as he wisely pointed out: 'There is no way in which you —or the Parliamentary draftsman—can decide which of the alternative interpretations of the meaning of reserve fund is the more "generally accepted".'[2]

On the one hand, L. R. Dicksee (quoting a Mr T. A. Welton as his authority), argued that:

the term 'Reserve Fund', properly understood, means neither more nor less than undivided profits which have been formally 'reserved' when they might have been divided; while the term 'reserve' means a provision for an *expected* loss or liability that has not as yet been definitely ascertained.[3]

Dicksee developed this theme to arrive at the use of the term 'reserve fund' to identify appropriated profits and the word 'reserve' to indicate charges made before ascertaining profits; i.e. 'reserves' was the title applied to what shall be shown later to be accepted as 'provisions' in modern terminology. Dicksee's use of 'reserve fund' was applied to what is now accepted as 'reserves' in modern terminology.

The adoption of Dicksee's view of 'reserve funds' would render redundant the question of whether the reserve funds are invested in the business. On the other hand E. E. Spicer and E. C. Pegler presented the following definitions:

A *Reserve* is an amount set aside out of profits either for some specific purpose, such as to provide for bad debts, or for the general purpose of strengthening the business by way of accumulating working capital.

A *Reserve Fund* is a reserve either general or specific, represented by investments outside the business. Sinking Funds, Insurance Funds, and Depreciation Funds are instances of specific Reserve Funds.[4]

Spicer and Pegler by including 'amounts set aside' for both specific and general purposes, effectively included amounts so dealt with before and after ascertaining profits, i.e. their term *reserve* included both of what, in modern terminology, are regarded as reserves and provisions.

If Spicer and Pegler's definition is adopted, then there is a very real question to answer as to what is the form of the investment of

13 Reserves and Provisions

the fund, though by definition, this investment is *outside* the business.

The misunderstanding of the distinction of a reserve fund as a separate fund of resources was reflected even at the highest official level, when in 1941 the Commonwealth Treasurer announced proposals to collect 20 per cent of the additions made by companies to 'Provisions for Depreciation'.[5] The fact that these are mere book-keeping entries and not represented necessarily by separate funds apparently was accepted later as the proposal was not proceeded with.

The question raised by A. A. Fitzgerald is found referred to over the following years without any very clear solution being presented. In 1946 a distinguished accountant and author of the standard Australian textbook on auditing, Mr R. A. Irish, when asked what the Act meant when it referred to a reserve fund, was able to reply only that 'possibly there is some consolation in the fact that the law is doubtful and a lenient view might be taken of an offence'.[6] On another occasion he wrote, 'No doubt you envisage, as most accountants and text books tell you, that a Reserve Fund is a reserve which is represented by specific investments. But it is by no means clear that a Reserve Fund does mean that.'[7]

Just as Victorian companies apparently obeyed the letter of the law, so too did New South Wales companies dutifully obey the Act, even if they could not agree as to what it meant.

This section of the Act was complied with by all of the New South Wales companies in the 'forty-two leaders sample', including a notation in parenthesis against the reserve item among shareholders' funds, or as a footnote, the description 'used in the business'. When the Victorian Companies Act of 1938 was passed, the relevant section was re-enacted with a slight modification. It was no longer required that the statement indicate 'whether or not such reserve is used in the business'. The requirement for a statement 'showing the manner in which and the securities upon which the same is invested' suggest more clearly a reserve fund as an earmarked fund separately invested. The 1938 Act did not specify any form of balance sheet and so the former compulsory statement by the manager or secretary as part of that form also was deleted. Among the 'forty-two leaders sample' the companies registered in Victoria all ceased to make any reference to the investment of the reserve fund from the time they issued their first financial statements subject to the Victorian Companies Act of 1938.

The Statutes in Victoria and New South Wales therefore, created two contrasting situations. In New South Wales 'reserve fund' was interpreted as referring to accumulated profits equally as to funds invested outside the business. In Victoria the Statute allowed the profession to adopt the attitude that a 'reserve fund' can only exist as a separately invested amount of resources. Thus a 'reserve fund' in Victoria was distinguished from reserves comprising accumulated profits, and the Act was interpreted as not applying other than to funds invested outside the business. This interpretation is shown in a small study of company practice in Western Australia.

As late as 1957 a survey of thirty-six Western Australian companies revealed three using the term 'used in the business' after the heading 'reserves' in the balance sheet.[8] The 1943 Western Australian Companies Act was modelled in many respects on the Victorian Companies Act of 1938. The relevant section (s.132) dealing with representations of reserve funds duplicated the provisions of the Victorian Companies Act of 1910. It therefore seems that the Western Australian companies were inclined to accept the post 1939 Victorian viewpoints as interpreting the Western Australian Act, i.e. to regard reserve funds as only applying to separately identified funds.

This difference has not been resolved necessarily by unanimity of agreement amongst accountants but by further and more recent changes in the law removing the cause of the different interpretations. All of the New South Wales companies referred to before with one exception, Bradford, have ceased to add the explanatory note to reserves shown in the balance sheet following the introduction of the Uniform Acts. These Acts have removed the doubt about the meaning of the relevant section because the section (s.162(14)) now refers only to representations about reserves made *other* than in the balance sheet. The question is irrelevant to the balance sheet where reserve is now accepted as describing accumulated profits retained in the business. In any other document it remains necessary to indicate if 'reserves' is taken to refer to this balance sheet item or whether the word is used in a common language sense of something surplus to current needs, e.g. in this sense a company may have a balance of cash held in reserve or inventories held as reserve for some future commitment or 'reserve funds' invested outside the business.

In the face of so much uncertainty in the use of terminology in the Statutes, it is right that professional accountants should have ceased looking to the Statutes to clarify the matter and to have evolved their own ideas. There are probably none who would disagree with the meaning of a reserve fund as defined in the current recommendations of the Institute of Chartered Accountants in Australia, i.e.: 'The description "reserve fund" should not be applied to a reserve unless it is represented by specifically earmarked investments (or other assets) realisable as and when required at not less than the amount of the "reserve fund".'[9]

This search for clarity may be pin-pointed as the search for agreement on the concept that a *'fund'* is in fact something that arises from the financial operation of *'funding'* resources quite apart from any other aspect of operations.

The search for clarity in meaning of the term 'reserve' was even more tortuous, however, and even if answered in practice, the search is not really completed in the pronouncement of the accounting professional bodies. Consideration of the term 'reserve' must involve consideration of the term 'provision'. Barely thirty years ago these two terms were used interchangeably with almost reckless abandon. They were used to describe a number of quite different facts or phenomena and confusion was as much a problem to trained accountants as to the layman reader. It is likely that confusion is still widely existent among lay readers of financial statements, because the two terms have been given highly technical meanings in the course of achieving consistency in their application to financial statements. We can hardly expect other than confusion when the layman is told that a provision for taxation is simply a recognition of a liability and does nothing of itself to provide for payment of the tax; or that a provision for depreciation likewise provides nothing but is a statement of the portion of original asset cost which has been allocated or matched against revenue, and finally a reserve does not mean that there is some emergency stock of financial resources but may tell us no more than the amount of accumulated profits retained in the company. The future may see both the terms 'reserve' and 'provision' discarded in favour of more descriptive titles such as implied in the above explanation.

One early writer in a prize-winning paper submitted to the Commonwealth Accountants Students Society, adopted a delightfully simple definition of a reserve as: 'the amount by which the assets of a concern exceed the sum of its paid up capital, liabilities, and unappropriated profits'.[10] The following year J. B. Tait[11] suggested that a reserve was for measuring the 'holes' in contra asset accounts, a provision was providing for some specific liability, and then ingeniously suggested a 'surplus reserve' for the true appropriation of surplus profits. The confusion of the time was illustrated by

Edwin V. Nixon 'explaining' his views in the *Commonwealth Journal of Accountancy* thus:

Reserves, etc.:—It is not unusual to find among the liabilities certain entries which represent *provisions* that have been made to meet liabilities ...
Other items of a similar nature are *reserves* which have been made to meet diminution in the value of an asset, e.g. *provision* for depreciation.[12] [Italics mine in each case]

Into this situation stepped the young A. A. Fitzgerald. Along with Edwin V. Nixon, Fitzgerald was pioneering the university teaching of accountancy at the University of Melbourne. They prepared a series of lectures as an introduction to a new university course and the series included one by Fitzgerald on reserves and reserve funds.[13] The subject was explored further by Fitzgerald taking advantage of the forum provided by the Australasian Congress on Accounting held in Melbourne during 1936.[14] In these papers, Fitzgerald argued for a new approach to what were known generally as reserves and the introduction of a classification using the terminology of reserve and provision. Fitzgerald stated that this classification was adopted at the University of Melbourne in 1925, and that it was unknown at the time that similar conclusions were being reached by independent workers in the United States of America.[15] Fitzgerald covered the familiar ground of the distinction between a 'reserve' and 'reserve fund', and came down on the side of Spicer and Pegler largely because this accords with the common usage of the word 'fund' as an identified or set apart amount of resources. Fitzgerald went on to examine the classification then advocated of grouping reserves into specific reserves and general reserves—a classification still persisted with in the official pronouncements of the Institute of Chartered Accountants in Australia and also the Institute of Chartered Accountants in England and Wales. Fitzgerald raised two objections to this classification. The term 'specific reserve' cannot be regarded as synonymous with necessary charges, since it includes some voluntary appropriations, and it is a misleading practice to group both specific and general reserves together as though they all represented undistributed profit whereas some part of them may consist of definitely necessary provisions for the replacement of assets which are being used up in the course of the business operations. He identified four classes of 'reserve', consisting of estimated liabilities, accrued liabilities, estimated amounts necessary to provide for the replacement of worn-out assets and profits withheld from distribution. Fitzgerald advocated confining the term 'reserve' to the last of these only and describing the others as 'provisions'. Fitzgerald lost no opportunity to advocate these ideas; in lectures, articles and editorials in the accounting journals he edited. Even book reviews were used by him as a medium of advocacy. Reviewing Perry Mason's monograph, *Principles of Public Utility Depreciation,* he observed that: 'The author's comment on the use of the term "depreciation reserve" reaches a sympathetic audience in the present reviewer, at least.'[16] On the other hand, a review of the Sanders, Hatfield and Moore *Statement of Accounting Principles* provided the occasion to observe that: 'The unfortunate persistence of the use of the term "Reserve" to describe a variety of things is one of the most unsatisfactory defects of accounting terminology.'[17]

An eminent accountant, A. H. Outhwaite, summarized the terminology in the following definitions published in 1936:

Any sum set aside in a company's accounts but retained in the business for some general or specific future need, which may or may not arise, is a Reserve. The common appropriation of profit to General Reserve or Reserve for Contingencies for the general purpose of strengthening financial stability is an example. If any sum so set aside is invested outside the business so as to be readily realisable in case of need, it is a Reserve Fund and the investments should appear in the balance sheet as allocated to the fund. A sum set aside in the accounts of either a company or a partnership or individual to meet an item of loss or expense which is known to have occurred but which has not accrued in any exact form should properly be described as a provision. For instance, a Provision for Taxation or Provision for Depreciation.[18]

In 1944 the Institute of Chartered Accountants in England and Wales included a pronouncement on this terminology in their Recommendations on Accounting Principles. These, in turn, were adopted with little verbal change in the Recommendations on Accounting Principles issued by the Institute of Chartered Accountants in Australia in 1946. The Institute's Recommendations VIII covered the Form of Balance Sheet and Profit and Loss Account. This recommendation included suggestions that there should be in the balance sheet a proper distinction between reserves which are, and those which are not, regarded normally as available for distribution as dividend, and that a debit balance in profit and loss account should be shown as a deduction from capital and reserves. The only significant difference in the Australian version of the recommendations was the omission of an escape clause which, in the English recommendations, allowed the sources of increases in reserves and provisions and the inclusion of provisions with other items such as creditors when 'disclosure would be detrimental to the interests of the company'.

A. A. Fitzgerald found the recommendation VI of the English Institute on Reserves and Provisions to conform closely with the suggestions he had made in 1936 at the Accountancy Congress.[19] However, he did point out the weakness in the definition of a provision as 'amounts set aside out of profits or other surpluses' which he considered to be at variance with the intention that the term should cover amounts provided to meet diminutions in values of assets.[20] In a paper delivered to the Perth Conference of the Australian and New Zealand Association for the Advancement of Science in 1947, A. A. Fitzgerald repeated his criticism of the Institute's definition but also observed the value of the recommendations. He said:

The significance of the recommendations regarding 'reserves' and 'provisions' is that it preserves this division. True reserves are part of net worth; provisions are either estimated liabilities or negative assets. Clear distinction between 'reserves' and 'provisions' and insistence on disclosure of reserves and of transfers to and from reserves or provisions, will eliminate confusion caused by mixed groups or by uncertainty whether a specific item is a true reserve. And it will no longer be possible to conceal the existence of a reserve by the simple device of calling it a provision or grouping it with provisions.[21]

What was necessary to make the definitions adopted by the Institute more precise was indicated in 1948 by L. Goldberg who suggested that the term 'provision' should be confined to a result arising from the process of matching costs and revenue, while the term 'reserve' should be applied to balances arising from the treatment of the ascertained profit or excess of revenue over costs.[22] Integrating this suggestion with Fitzgerald's earlier definition it is possible to devise a clear and unambiguous set of definitions, thus:

(1) The credit arising from a charge made in the course of matching periodical charges and revenue to be known as a Provision.

(2) An appropriation of ascertained profits to meet a specific or known liability to be called a Provision.

(3) An appropriation of ascertained profits for other general or non-specific purposes to be a Reserve.

(4) Any increase in shareholders' funds other than the paid up

value of shares, and which is not the result of ascertained profits also to be called a Reserve.

In 1964 the Institute of Chartered Accountants in Australia issued amended Recommendations on Accounting Principles which define a provision as including 'amounts set aside' for 'specific commitments and contingencies' and 'diminutions in values of assets'. These 1964 recommendations in effect suggest three categories of reserves, namely capital reserves, share premium reserve and revenue reserves. Where revenue reserves are available for distribution and not created to meet statutory obligations, the Institute is opposed to the presentation of such reserves under a variety of headings. The promulgation of the new recommendations was not unchallenged, at least by academic accountants. D. H. Briggs and R. H. Parker comment, 'the needless confusion between provisions and reserves seems to persist' for, as they point out 'the use of the phrase "set aside"—which surely suggests an appropriation —is most unfortunate.'[23] They point out that the weakness in the Institute's definition arises from the lack of consideration of the distinction between charges made in the course of ascertaining profit and charges made against the ascertained profits. Some support exists amongst the profession for minimizing the number of separately identified reserves, usually based on the argument that resources in fact may not be available for the named purposes. A clear distinction between capital and revenue reserves does enjoy substantial support. A study group of the Victorian division of the Australian Chartered Accountants' Research Society pin-pointed the basic need as to indicate the availability or otherwise of the reserves for the payment of dividends.[24]

The above account indicates the more important incidents in the development of a clear definition of the terminology. While these developments occurred at a theoretical level, were they being reflected in practice? In 1949, five years after the issue of the English recommendations and three years after the issue of the Australian recommendations, a study group of members of the South Australian Branch of the Institute of Chartered Accountants reported that a survey conducted in 1947 showed that practice fell short of the Institute's recommendations and that a number of companies did not distinguish reserves and provisions properly.[25] Isolated instances of poor terminology attracted the spotlight from time to time. The adjudicators in the Australian Institute of Management Award considered it deserving of comment in 1952 that 'one company described its Bad Debts Provision as a reserve'. In 1956

Sir Alexander Fitzgerald, who for personal reasons had missed the original incident, thought it worthwhile even after a period of twelve months to rebuke the secretary of the Myer Emporium Ltd for misusing the words 'reserve' and 'provision'.[26] In September 1957, a panel of members of the Western Australian division of the Australian Chartered Accountants Research Society reported on the financial statements of thirty-six Western Australian companies.[27] Generally the results were satisfactory, but there were a few nonconformists to be found. Two companies referred to a reserve for bad and doubtful debts. In two cases a depreciation reserve appeared as part of reserves in shareholders' funds. In one instance the word 'reserve' was used in relation to a provision for depreciation. Only one company failed to show the nature of its reserves.

With respect to the 'forty-two leaders sample', the reports were examined to determine the date at which each company adopted an acceptable usage of the terms 'reserve' and 'provision'. Table 1 sets out the results of this examination. The years shown are selected as those of significant events relating to developing standards of disclosure. At the time when A. A. Fitzgerald gave his lecture in 1928, less than one quarter of the available sample could be judged as conforming with what is now accepted as sound terminology. The table indicates that the adoption of this terminology has progressed consistently over a period of more than thirty years. This suggests that it has been the result of a

TABLE 1
Adoption of recommended terminology of reserves and provisions '42 leaders sample'

	Size of available sample[a]	No. of companies	% of available sample	Notes
1928	17	4	23	A. A. Fitzgerald's lecture
1935	24	8	33	} Australasian Congress on
1937	29	12	41	} Accounting
1940	32	18	56	
1946	33	22	67	I.C.A.A. recommendations
1950	38	28	74	
1955	41	35	85	
1962	42	41	98	Uniform Acts
1965	42	42	100	

[a] See explanatory note, p. 3.

continuing campaign of persuasion rather than of any one specific event or action. This lends further support to the view that not only was this terminology formulated by A. A. Fitzgerald, but it was also inculcated among the profession by his writing and lecturing over a period of nearly three decades and that the results are largely the consequence of his individual efforts.

The presentation of reserves within the shareholders' funds section of the balance sheet provides a detailed picture of the modern use of the terminology 'reserves'. Two American authors, in 1960, studied a sample of company reports furnished by the Sydney Stock Exchange. These companies showed a tendency to use a multiplicity of reserves in sharp contrast to the 1964 recommendation of the Institute of Chartered Accountants.

These investigators, E. DeMaris and V. Zimmerman, were shocked by the number of reserves shown, yet were aware that their judgment reflected a difference between Australian and American terminology and practice.[28] They found twenty-one different types of reserves identified in the sample with a range of one to seven for each company and an average of three or four per company.

The 1968 annual reports of the 'forty-two leaders sample' were analysed and the number of reserves used by each company are summarized in Table 2.

It should be pointed out that there is some justification for the number of reserves shown by many companies. Normally a company will create at least one reserve to indicate the amount of

TABLE 2
Presentation of reserves in consolidated statements '42 leaders sample', 1968

No. of types of reserve shown[a]	No. of companies
1	1
2	10
3	3
4	11
5	8
6	6
7	2
8	1

[a] Excludes profit and loss appropriation balance.

profits which it is intended should not be distributed at the present time as dividends. Where a premium has been received on the issue of shares, the Companies Act requires the premium to be credited to a share premium reserve and shown as such. When a company revalues some of its assets it may in some circumstances credit the amount to general reserve or profit and loss. However, it is accepted generally as good practice to create an asset revaluation reserve which keeps this credit separate from reserves made up of accumulated profits from trading. Sometimes it is suggested that credits such as those from profits on the sale of assets should be kept separate from reserves arising from accumulated trading profits. These sale of asset credits may be credited to a separate capital reserve account which may also be credited with amounts arising from asset revaluations. There are sound arguments advanced by some writers advocating the creation of specific reserves to record the financial effect of such factors as increased cost of plant replacement or the increased cost of maintaining constant physical inventories. There are other legal requirements which may give rise to the disclosure of specific reserves such as a capital redemption reserve. The reserves shown in the annual reports of the 'forty-two leaders sample' in 1968 are shown in Table 3 classified according to title. This table shows that the

TABLE 3
Descriptions of reserves in consolidated statements '42 leaders sample', 1968

Description of reserve	No. of occurrences
General reserve	35
Share premium reserve	36
Reserve on consolidation	18
Asset revaluation	22
All others	61

factors outlined above account for the majority of the companies showing the three items of general reserve, share premium reserve and an asset revaluation reserve or capital reserves. Actually seventeen companies included all three. A number of companies included two or more of these three types of reserve in a variety of combinations of types of reserve. The reserves categorized as 'all others' include a wide variety of titles and arise from a great variety of circumstances. Probably we can say only that the nine

13 Reserves and Provisions

companies which showed six or more reserves have in any way shown unnecessary detail. Even these companies can be regarded as being informative by identifying the purposes for which profits are retained or, alternatively, identifying the source of capital reserves.

The first recommendations covering Reserves and Provisions issued by the Institute of Chartered Accountants in Australia may be interpreted as requiring whatever detail of reserves that is given to be grouped under two classifications of revenue and capital reserves. The amended recommendation issued in 1964 does not suggest such a clear cut division but rather suggests that in normal circumstances three reserves should be recognized, namely capital reserves, share premium reserve (if appropriate) and revenue reserves. Among the 'forty-two leaders sample', in the 1968 reports of only nine companies were the reserves found clearly grouped under the headings of 'Capital Reserves' and 'Revenue Reserves'. Although the other thirty-three companies did not use these group headings, the titles applied to reserves did clearly distinguish those of a capital nature from revenue reserves. The Institute recommendations, it may be concluded, are being effectively followed with regard to clearly distinguishing capital and revenue reserves. However, the Institute recommendation against subdividing revenue reserves appears to be in conflict with the objective of explaining the reasons why various amounts of accumulated profits should be retained. In this respect the desire of companies to explain their policies on profit retention appears to override the Institute recommendation. Thus current practice reflects in part an Institute standard and in part the less definable standard of general practice.

14

The Royal Mail Case

In 1931 a distinguished and honourable gentleman, Lord Kylsant, chairman of the Royal Mail Steam Packet Company, and the auditor of the company, H. J. Morland, were the centre of legal action which was to have far-reaching consequences on accounting, and more specifically, the accounting requirements of company legislation, even though the company was chartered and not subject to the Companies Acts. As the case developed the precise nature of the proceedings or of the final judgment became of little relevance.

As Mr Justice Wright was at pains to point out in his summing up, the value of the prosecution of the case was in its

> revelation to the public, and the testing at law, of a state of affairs which permitted a great company, in which the money of the public had been ventured and to which new moneys had been invited, to publish over a period of seven years balance sheets and profit and loss accounts which did not show whether profit had been earned or not, and during those years to pay in dividends the sum of £5,000,000 which had not been found from current earnings, but from non-recurring items of revenue and undisclosed transfers of secret reserves.[1]

Although the summonses were issued in 1931 they related to financial statements covering the years 1926 and 1927 and a prospectus issued in June 1928. Lord Kylsant was charged under the Larceny Act of 1861 with circulating two false balance sheets and the publication of a false prospectus in that it concealed the true position of the company. Lord Kylsant was found not guilty on the charges relating to the balance sheet, as was Morland who had been similarly charged. However Lord Kylsant was found guilty on the charge concerning the prospectus, this decision being upheld on appeal.

It is the paradox of the case that, although both the defendants were acquitted of charges of issuing false balance sheets, it is in the substance of these balance sheets that the greatest importance of the case lies. Lord Kylsant was found guilty of issuing a false prospectus, not because the figures given were judged incorrect, but because it was decided as a matter of fact that they were intended to mislead in the context in which they were given. In short the company had created substantial secret reserves by using high depreciation rates and at the same time also it had built up reserves which were not disclosed in the balance sheet as part of shareholders' funds but included with sundry other items. These unpublished reserves related to taxation provisions, insurance and repair provisions and the undisclosed accumulated profits held in the accounts of subsidiary companies. A distinction may be drawn between secret reserves which are not reflected in the balance sheet figures and unpublished reserves. The latter, while included in the disclosed asset values in the balance sheet, are not revealed as part of the value of equities which represents the shareholders' rights against the assets of the company. Much of the argument in the case centred on the fact that, whereas previously the profit and loss account had contained the item 'profit for the year', in 1923 it was amended to 'balance for the year' and in 1925 the additional words 'adjustment of taxation reserves' were added at the auditor's instigation.

The case demonstrated that the profit and loss statement which complied with the law at the time gave no indication whatever of the current trading position and also failed to give any indication of how much and what reserves were being included in the 'balance'. Not only were the accounts judged as meeting the law but the most eminent of accountants gave evidence that they would have accepted them as true and correct in terms of general accounting practice at the time. As Sir Patrick Hastings submitted on behalf of Morland, the auditor: 'The evidence establishes beyond all question that the very words used in this balance sheet and profit and loss account were those which would meet with the approval of the most distinguished auditors and qualified people in the country.'[2] Lord Plender, President of the Institute of Chartered Accountants in England and Wales, said in evidence that 'it is quite usual for large commercial and industrial companies to set aside out of an unusually prosperous year sums to secret reserves'.[3] Lord Kylsant himself under cross-examination was not prepared to go beyond saying that there 'might come a time' for a company when the full facts ought to be declared to the shareholders.[4]

Although the matters concerned took place before the English Companies Act of 1929 was placed on the statute book, they were not discussed until two years afterwards. It has been demonstrated already that the overwhelming pressure in the formulation of the Queensland, South Australian and New South Wales Acts passed between 1931 and 1936, was the precedent of the 1929 English Act. Thus although the Kylsant or Royal Mail case and resulting discussion of the issues involved were contemporaneous with the consideration of these Acts, it did not lead directly to the inclusion of specific provisions in these Acts to the extent that may have been expected.

The South Australian 1934 Act followed the 1928 English Act exactly, but in Queensland and New South Wales the Act was advanced one step by requiring the directors' report to include a statement of amounts drawn from reserve and the purpose for which they were drawn. At least the profit and loss 'balance' could include only current amounts even if it could still include the result of trading, income from investments, and any other current non-recurring items. But no longer could the profit and loss account prepared under the Act in these two States show a consistent credit from year to year by the use of undisclosed transfers from reserves which were equally hidden by being included with sundry other liabilities.

The broader implications of the case were given statutory recognition in Victoria in 1938, but any further action in the other more populous States did not eventuate until the Uniform Act of 1961–2 (exceptions to this were the Western Australian Act of 1943 and the Tasmanian Act of 1958). The Victorian Act left no doubt as to its requirement of clear separation of current and non-recurring items in the profit and loss statement, specifying separate identification of the net balance of profit or loss on trading, income from general investments, income from investments in subsidiary companies, profit or loss arising from a sale or revaluation of fixed or intangible assets, and amounts transferred from reserves or provisions. If the Act had gone no further, it still would have been possible to organize the business through subsidiaries so that the only income to appear in the parent profit and loss statement would be the amount of dividends declared by the subsidiaries, as could be done under the New South Wales and Queensland Acts. Instead, the Victorian Act instituted consolidated statements which meant that each of the items listed above had to be stated for the group as well as the parent company. Effectively the group trading result

14 The Royal Mail Case

becomes known and it is no longer possible to accumulate profits in the subsidiaries to be filtered through as and when required in the parent company's accounts.

Later statutory requirements have sought to impose an obligation on directors to identify abnormal items affecting profit. These and more recent moves to identify abnormal and extraordinary items made by the accounting profession are discussed in later chapters.

The Victorian Companies Act of 1938 marked the most positive response to the Royal Mail case. In spite of the seriousness of the disclosures made in the Royal Mail case the response of others concerned with financial reporting was not very exciting. The Official List Requirements imposed on listed companies by the Australian Stock Exchanges have not at any time made a direct attack on this aspect of reporting. The Exchanges' action on some aspects of profit and loss reporting may be considered a piecemeal attack on inadequate presentation of profit and loss information, e.g. their action to secure group statements was a direct attack on the practice of reporting only so much of group profits as the directors chose to remit as dividends from the subsidiaries to the parent company. The accounting profession did not formally act until the issue of the Institute of Chartered Accountants Recommendations in 1946. The Institute's pronouncement indicated as a general principle to be followed that: 'The profit and loss account should be presented in such a form as to give a clear disclosure of the results of the period and the amount available for appropriation, for which purpose it may conveniently be divided into sections' (part I, par. (17)). This was supported by a detailed list of sixteen items which it was recommended should be stated separately. These were belated recommendations coming fifteen years after the issue was raised by the Royal Mail case and eight years after the Victorian Companies Act of 1938 compelled Victorian companies to give more informative profit and loss statements.

In conclusion it may be said that the Royal Mail case was important, not because of the particular charges that were laid, or of action directly resulting therefrom, but rather because of the publicity it gave to the uninformative nature of acceptable financial statements of the times. It identified the need for a clear statement of current operating profits and the isolation of other extraordinary items anticipating by thirty years the present day emphasis on the measure 'earnings per share'.

15

Victorian Companies Act 1938

Earlier it was mentioned how proposals to amend the Victorian Companies Act as part of a consolidation of Acts in 1928 were not proceeded with. The consequence of delay was that by the time further amending legislation was drawn up there had been significant changes in circumstances, and in the light of events of the time, radical changes were made in the accounting provisions of the Victorian Act. A. A. Fitzgerald said the Greene Committee which sat in England in 1925,

thought that the unfavourable public comments on the activities of limited companies were largely due to the abnormal conditions prevailing during and since World War I, and that, the 'return to more normal conditions' would tend to eliminate certain unsatisfactory features which had shown themselves in recent years.

But A. A. Fitzgerald had also commented in 1948, in the course of the Sixth Commonwealth Institute of Accountants Lecture at Canberra University College (now the School of General Studies of the Australian National University), 'presses on which the 1929 Companies Act was printed had scarcely ceased revolving when a series of "abnormal" storms broke over the heads of the investing public.'[1] These events included a wave of world-wide speculative investment followed by a collapse of the stock market accompanied by acute world-wide economic depression. Public discussion of provision of information to the investment market was stimulated by the legal proceedings in the United Kingdom referred to earlier as the Royal Mail case. In the United States of America action quickly followed in the formation of the Securities and Exchange Commission appointed to supervise the market in securities of nationally listed companies. In the United Kingdom legislative action was delayed until the 1948 English Act which was based on the recommendations of another company law committee, the Cohen Committee.

15 Victorian Companies Act 1938

When the Victorian government prepared to tackle company law amendment again it sought out the opinions of the accounting profession. The Attorney-General promised to allow the Council of the Commonwealth Institute of Accountants to examine the proposed legislation[2] and subsequently a joint committee of the various professional accounting bodies was formed to enable them to make a common submission on the Bill. Through this committee the accounting profession became responsible for a number of innovations in the accounting requirements of the Companies Act.[3]

The Victorian Bill as finally drafted was introduced in Parliament in 1935 but not proceeded with. Then in June 1936 the Bill was again introduced by A. L. Bussau, the Attorney-General. The reasons he gave were to bring the law more into line with United Kingdom law, to remedy defects that experience had revealed, and to provide for matters which the extended use of the company principle in trade and industry had shown to be necessary or expedient.[4] The Cussens draft Bill of 1928 had been amended according to suggestions on the files of the Law Department, by inspectors into the failure of investment trust companies and the Royal Commission by Judge Halse Rogers in New South Wales, the Joint Committee of the Australasian Institute of Secretaries, Commonwealth Institute of Accountants, Federal Institute of Accountants, Institute of Chartered Accountants in Australia and the Stock Exchange of Melbourne, and by the Melbourne Chamber of Commerce, the Law Institute of Victoria and the Registrar-General.[5] This Bill was considered by an All Party Committee but discharged from the notice paper in December. It was again introduced during the following year, 1937, in July. The debates on the Bill continued through July and August and on 26 August the committee reported progress. Further progress was not made until the Bill was again introduced in August 1938 by H. S. Bailey who was now Attorney-General. After three years of manoeuvring it was hardly surprising that the Attorney-General considered the need for the legislation to be pressing. He considered 'flaws in the existing legislation show the way to chicanery and to frauds on investors and the general public'.[6] In his explanation of the Bill he detailed the many amendments which had been introduced by the All Party Committee in 1936, by the Legislative Assembly in Committee in 1937 and by the responsible officers in his department between August 1937 and August 1938. It is worth noting that the Joint Committee of Accounting Bodies was not content with its success in gaining amendment of the Bill drafted by Judge

Cussen and debated in 1936 and 1937 but made a further report on the 1938 Bill introduced by Bailey.[7] The committee supported the principle of requiring disclosure of the annual charge for depreciation. The committee's submission appears to have been the basis of an amendment to the Bill on this matter. It was argued that to require details of depreciation charged to the profit and loss account would be circumvented by asserting that it was normally charged to the manufacturing or trading account. The Act as passed required disclosure of 'amounts charged for depreciation'. The committee re-affirmed its support for deletion of the form of balance sheet from the schedule to the Act. Perhaps the most important submission made by the committee at this stage was that relating to transfers from reserves or provisions to the profit and loss account. Clause 123(4) of the Bill required disclosure of 'amount transferred to the account from reserves or provisions shown specifically in a previous balance sheet'. The committee pointed out that such a clause would not require disclosure of transfers from secret reserves and would therefore permit the very practices which had been condemned following the disclosures of the Royal Mail case. The committee's criticism was accepted by the Legislative Assembly which deleted the offending words from the Bill. The Bill passed through the Legislative Assembly and the Legislative Council and was finally passed on 7 December 1938. The legislation had been under more or less continuous action for eight years and it was more than ten years since Sir Leo Cussen had commenced the preparation of amended legislation.

The Joint Committee of Accounting Bodies 'expressed gratification at the use that has been made of its labours'[8] but there was considerable criticism from some quarters. A. A. Fitzgerald claimed that this opposition

was aroused . . . mainly on the ground that [the contentious provisions in the Bill] represented a substantial departure from the provisions of the English Act, and that, since the English Legislature had not seen fit to amend its Act in this respect, it was unnecessary and inadvisable . . . to adopt what were regarded as repressive provisions.[9]

Among those who were critical of the recommendations of the Joint Committee was the Victorian division of the Institute of Chartered Accountants. This division of the Institute expressed itself as being, 'opposed to the provision that individual balance sheets and profit and loss accounts of subsidiary companies should be published, for the reason that it is regarded as an unnecessary

15 Victorian Companies Act 1938

disclosure of the internal working of the company'.[10] The Institute sponsored a series of lectures on the new Act, one of which by A. H. Outhwaite indicates, by its critical tone, the attitude of the Chartered Institute. By applying literal interpretations without much regard for sentence construction, this lecturer produced a series of criticisms of the requirements of the Act, as in this passage in which he commented on the provisions in the Act relating to depreciation:

I should say that the only effect of the provision is that the words 'charged for depreciation' mean actually written off or allocated to any particular asset, and that it is, consequently, necessary to show separately any such writing off or special allocation. But where depreciation of assets generally—including these investments, goodwill and fixed assets—has been covered by a general provision for depreciation, it cannot be said that any particular amount has been charged for depreciation of any particular asset, and as I have already said, I do not think the Act enjoins any such allocation of specific sums to particular assets.

Other criticisms centred on the use of the terms fixed assets, tangible assets and intangible assets. On the provision for disclosure of directors' fees, which was already enacted in Queensland, South Australia and New South Wales, he claimed it to be 'a question that cannot be answered with any degree of certainty'. The specification requiring the basis of valuation of each class of assets and the classification of the assets, gave rise to the comment that it was 'another illustration of unnecessary compulsion of a prevailing practice, and [that] the loose phrasing of the section renders this compulsion an absurdity'. It was, however, the proposal for consolidated statements which provoked the strongest objections. 'The subsection is fraught with loose expressions characteristic of this Division of the Act. I shall draw attention to them and suggest possible elucidations, but I have not the temerity to express any definite opinion of their true solution,' said Outhwaite. In reply to the suggestion that he might have prepared a sample set of consolidated accounts he stated that he had 'not felt competent to accept that responsibility, nor does your State Council, where so much is in doubt, care to sponsor anything of the kind. We hope, however, that some contributor to the Journal will, at an early date, under the shelter of anonymity, put forward something for hostile criticism by the rest of us.'[11]

This attack may be contrasted with the more mellow remarks

of Mr J. B. Tait, Q.C., who acknowledged that: 'There are, of course, certain complications and certain adjustments which may be necessary, but on the whole, the matter should present no insuperable difficulty.'[12]

What were the changes to compulsory disclosure introduced by this Victorian Act? The Act departed from the practice of specifying a particular format for the balance sheet in the schedule to the Act. This provided the freedom to experiment which is reflected in subsequent developments. The general statement as to the presentation of the balance sheet remained, but the idea of a classified presentation was introduced with the requirement to give 'such particulars as are necessary . . . to distinguish between the various classes of the assets' (s.124). Assets to be shown separately, which were not listed in the previous schedule, were preliminary expenses not written off, share and debenture issue expenses not written off, goodwill not written off if ascertainable, investments in subsidiary companies, shares in listed companies other than subsidiaries, amounts owing by subsidiary companies, and loans to directors. With respect to liabilities, new items specified were amounts owing to subsidiary companies and a statement to indicate if and when any liability is secured on any assets of the company. The balance sheet was to include details of any option existing over unissued shares, and of loans made to directors of the group and the amounts outstanding, if any, of such loans. More significant was the introduction of a detailed profit and loss statement to include the following: the net balance on the company's trading income from general investments; income from investments in subsidiary companies; amounts charged for depreciation or amortization on investments, goodwill, and fixed assets; profit or loss from revaluation of fixed or intangible assets; amounts transferred from reserves or provisions; and directors' fees paid. Finally, all of the above was extended to the affairs of subsidiary companies. This Act required a separate statement including all the prescribed detail to be presented for each subsidiary company. Alternatively, the parent company could present, together with the statements of the parent company, consolidated statements of the parent and its subsidiaries.

Through the work of the Joint Committee, the recommendations of which were incorporated in this Victorian Act, the Commonwealth Institute of Accountants could justifiably claim to have contributed to the development of accounting in the thirties and forties in a much wider sphere than Victoria alone.[13] This Victorian

15 Victorian Companies Act 1938

Act of 1938 was the first Statute among the Australian States and the United Kingdom to demand adequate profit and loss statement details and to require group consolidated statements or separate statements for each company in a group. Six years later the Institute of Chartered Accountants in England and Wales issued its Recommendations on Accounting Principles which, with respect to the reports of holding companies, adopted similar provisions to this Victorian Act.

These recommendations of the English Institute were, with minor adaptation, adopted by the Institute of Chartered Accountants in Australia in 1946. The two Institutes thus officially recognized methods evolved by members of the profession over preceding years. The English Act was not amended along the lines of the accounting provisions of the 1938 Victorian Act until after another company law committee, the Cohen Committee, submitted its recommendations in 1945. These recommendations were 'directed to a similar end in their emphasis on disclosure of operating results for the period, the segregation of abnormal or non-recurring profits or losses, and in their desire to prevent secrecy in the creation and use of reserves', and they did 'surpass the Victorian legislation . . . in their insistence on consistency, the preservation of the value of the accounts for comparative purposes and the separate statement of amounts paid or provided for taxation'.[14] The increased emphasis on reporting taxation is not unexpected in view of the much more important role of taxation with the growth of government financed activities in the modern welfare state.

It is to be expected that a change in the Statute which was so far advanced on that in other States would have a profound influence on the practice of company reporting. This has been reviewed in following chapters concerning respectively the accounts of holding companies, the presentation of profit and loss statements and the disclosure of directors' remuneration.

Legislation was also introduced aimed at preventing the situation which occurred in America when the effect of the leverage of the issuing company was multiplied by investing in companies which themselves had used leverage to the full. These provisions followed the now well established principle of relying on full and adequate disclosure to protect the investor, as well as placing certain restraints on the actions of the directors of such investment companies. The legislature found great difficulty in defining the investment company.[15] This problem was solved by the Investment Companies Act of 1938 defining them as those companies which are proclaimed by the Governor in Council. Of particular importance to our discussion are the reporting provisions imposed at the same time. The balance sheet of an investment company was to show in addition to the information required by other companies under the principal Act, any investments in securities not included in those specified to be shown by the principal Act. The manner of valuation of the investments was also to be given. A complete list was to be given of the name and quantity of all investments at the balance date together with a statement of all purchases and sales of securities during the period covered by the report. Details were also to be given of brokerage paid and of income received from underwriting. Contrary to the policy of the principal Act the Investment Companies Act set out in a schedule a prescribed form of balance sheet to be used by investment companies. When the new Companies Act was drawn up in 1958 a number of changes were made in the part dealing with investment companies. The restrictive form of balance sheet as set down in the 1938 Act was not re-enacted. Through the passage of the Uniform Acts these provisions have now been extended to all States. Not all the investment companies listed on the Stock Exchanges have been proclaimed, but the section remains available to be invoked if any company fails to provide the information which the Statute considers desirable to be given by this type of company.

16

The Profit and Loss Statement

The presentation of a statement of profit and loss together with the balance sheet had been included as part of all of the earlier statutory requirements for disclosure. In the absence of the specification of the details of the profit and loss statement, what was presented was frequently merely the balancing item in the balance sheet. The attitude to the profit and loss statement was revealed in such opinions as that, under the 1931–6 Acts passed in three States, the profit and loss statement was not one of the documents which must be annexed or attached to the balance sheet and therefore need not be circulated to the persons entitled to receive the balance sheet. It even was argued by some that the statement of profit and loss was outside the ambit of the auditor's report.[1]

Many writers and commentators regarded the advanced thinking of the Joint Committee of Accountancy Organisations as embodied in the Victorian Companies Act of 1938 as presaging a new and significant role for this financial statement. The Cohen Committee in England was satisfied that the great majority of companies were managed honestly and conscientiously, but that the fullest practicable disclosure of information would lessen the opportunities for abuse and accord with a wakening social consciousness, and considered the trend of profits as 'the best indication of the prosperity of a company'.[2] The committee recommended the inclusion in the Act of requirements to present a profit and loss statement which would separate the trading profit, income on investments in subsidiaries, income on other investments, and non-recurrent or exceptional profits and losses. It also would have to show the amount of provisions for depreciation, capital and loan redemptions, amounts set aside to reserves, and certain capital reserves, with an escape clause on the last item. In addition it was recommended that there should be shown the amount of provisions for taxation and for dividends payable. The Cohen Committee recommendations were in line with the submissions which had been made to the committee by the Institute of Chartered Accountants in England and Wales, which stated a 'general principle' that:

A profit and loss account should give a fair indication of the earnings of the year or should disclose any material respects in which it includes extraneous or non-recurrent items or items of an exceptional nature. Such a fair indication implies substantial uniformity in the accounting principles applied as between successive accounting periods; any change of a material nature, such as a radical change in the basis of stock valuation, or in the method of providing for depreciation or taxation, should be disclosed in the account if its effect distorts materially the results for the year.[3]

This memorandum to the Cohen Committee and the committee's recommendations, although English events, are important in the development of Australian practices. In the long term, this recognition of the principles adopted in the Victorian Companies Act of 1938 would assist in bringing about the adoption of these principles in all Australian States. In the short term these same principles were included in the Recommendations on Accounting Principles of the Institute of Chartered Accountants in England and Wales, issued in 1944, and the similar Recommendations on Accounting Principles of the Institute of Chartered Accountants in Australia issued in 1946. These recommendations gave the official imprimatur of the accounting profession to the recommendations of the Cohen Committee (with the exception in Australia of the escape clause referred to earlier), and, by implication, to the Victorian Act which then had stood on the statute books for eight years.

R. A. Irish observed twenty years ago that one of the curses of statutory regulation is that everybody tends to obey it so that it becomes a maximum rather than a minimum standard of disclosure.[4] Profit and loss statements issued between 1938 and 1962 provide an excellent opportunity to test this truism. Whereas the Victorian Companies Act of 1938 required substantial detail in these reports the Acts in New South Wales, Queensland and South Australia could be complied with by giving a minimum of detail. These States also provided an opportunity to test the efficacy of the Institute of Chartered Accountants' recommendations in raising the standards of reporting practice in this field. This test using the 'forty-two leaders sample' was complicated by the great variety of items which may appear in the profit and loss statement. It is

16 The Profit and Loss Statement

TABLE 4
Number of items[a] shown in profit and loss statement Victorian companies '42 leaders sample'

	Size of available sample[b]	Average no. items shown
1929	16	2·1
1939	20	3·7
1949	25	4·2

[a] As defined in body of text.
[b] See explanatory note, p. 3.

therefore not a simple process of measuring a yes/no situation. The method adopted was therefore to tabulate the number of items shown in the profit and loss statement apart from the total profits or losses, from all sources for the year, dividends paid or declared and any expenses required to be shown by statute such as directors' fees and depreciation. The reports of the Victorian companies in the 'forty-two leaders sample' were examined at three dates at ten-year intervals—in 1929 following the consolidation of the statute in 1928; in 1939 following the proclamation of Act no. 4602, the Companies Act of 1938; and in 1949 following the issue of the recommendations of the Institute of Chartered Accountants in Australia in 1946. The results of the analysis set out in Table 4 show the substantial increase in the details given following the Victorian Companies Act of 1938. The effect of the Institute recommendations issued in 1946 appears to have been only marginal in Victoria. The examination of the reports of the New South Wales companies included in the 'forty-two leaders sample' was similarly made at four dates at ten-year intervals plus the year 1965. There was an examination in 1929 prior to there being any statutory requirement for disclosure in New South Wales; in 1939 which followed the New South Wales Act of 1936, and the example of the Victorian Act of 1938; in 1949 following the issue of the Institute recommendations in 1946; in 1959 and lastly 1965 which followed the New South Wales Uniform Act. The results of the analysis of the New South Wales companies set out in Table 5 show the limited effect of the Institute recommendations issued in 1946 and the much more significant increase in the amount of detail disclosed following the passage of the Uniform Act. The tables show that there was a significant improvement in

TABLE 5
*Number of items*a *shown in profit and loss statement*
New South Wales companies
'42 leaders sample'

	Size of available sample	Average no. items shown
1929	5	1·8
1939	11	1·7
1949	12	1·8
1959	16	2·1
1965	16	5·6

a As defined in body of text.

profit and loss statement presentation in both States. This was brought about by statutory compulsion in Victoria, to a lesser extent by voluntary factors operating in New South Wales with the big change following the use of statutory compulsion in that State also.

The improvements just outlined can be described as essentially separating items which rightly represent the contents of a profit and loss appropriation statement. Neither the statutory obligations nor the voluntary factors have gone so far as to require disclosure of the detailed revenue and expenses which give rise to the operating profit. While it must be admitted that the average profit and loss statement today is a vastly improved document compared with that of thirty years ago, it does remain, however, essentially an appropriation statement. As V. L. Gole described it:

This pathetic thing masquerades under a false title. It is nothing more than a profit and loss appropriation account, which is an entirely different thing. It starts off (with a few exceptions) with a conglomerate mess graced by the vague and practically meaningless term 'Net balance of profit and loss on the company's trading'. It then proceeds to set out a few items specifically required by law to be stated separately and arrives with undignified haste at 'net profit before taxation'. The tax gatherer's share is then calculated and inserted, leaving a dangling remainder at the foot of the accounts. A study of the directors' report will probably reveal some recommendations as to what should happen to this residual item.[5]

The 'forty-two leaders sample' disclosed a few earnest attempts to do better than this. B.H.P. in its early years included a working account which gave eight expense items for its mining activities but only the net result of the steelmaking business. This detailed working account virtually ended with the cessation of the company's mining activities in 1939. A.W.A. in like manner gave details of the revenue and expenses of its wireless service until this was taken over by the government in 1946. Nat. Cons. introduced into its report in 1952 a diagrammatic representation of the company's cost structure according to wages, machines, materials and services. From 1956 this became a more formal statement until the inclusion in the consolidated profit and loss statement since 1956 of the value of sales, materials, wages and salaries, and services and other expenses. Perhaps the most notable example in the 'forty-two leaders sample' is Ansett. From 1942 the company included an itemized account setting out separately expenses of wages and salaries, materials and fuel, taxes, overhead and publicity, depreciation, and directors' fees. This continued until the period 1951–5 when economic factors appear to have limited the annual report to the minimum statutory requirement. From 1956 the report included a simplified profit and loss statement giving the expenses as described for 1942 above and this detail is now included in the statutory profit and loss statements. F. & T. in 1965 went as far as identifying separately the cost of 'wages' and the cost of 'material services and sundry expenses'. One is left, however, with the conclusion that these are only random efforts and that there is little indication of any trend towards the kind of disclosure which would answer Gole's criticism. The position concerning the disclosure of turnover or gross revenue figures represents a special aspect of this problem and is dealt with more fully later.

A clear statement of the results of the period's trading also requires identification of any abnormal or extraordinary items affecting the profit and loss account. Up to the present time the identification of such items within the profit and loss statement has not been attempted through statutory enforcement. However, the Institute of Chartered Accountants in Australia has made an attempt at defining an appropriate treatment in its recommendations on accounting principles.

The recommendations issued in 1946 provided for the disclosure of any change in accounting principles affecting the profit (par. 18), the separate statement of 'credits or charges, if material in amount, which are abnormal in nature or relate to previous periods' (par. 19 (h)) and that the profit and loss statement 'should disclose any material respects in which it includes extraneous or non-recurrent items or those of an exceptional nature, and should also refer to the omission of any item relative to, or the including of any item not relative to, the results of the period' (par. 18).

Although the tenor of the recommendations was to achieve a 'clear disclosure of the results of the period' (par. 17) the details referred to constituted an appropriation statement rather than a profit and loss operating statement.

The revised recommendations issued in 1963 recognized that within such a statement it is possible to present the profit or loss of a year as including all profits or losses arising or ascertained within the year, including those which result from transactions in the current and prior years, i.e. the all inclusive statement, or to confine the amount shown as profit or loss to the results of the operations of the year reported on (par. 40), i.e. the current operating performance statement.

The 1963 recommendations having accepted these two types of profit and loss statement, did not continue the distinction between abnormal items, those relating to prior periods and non-recurrent and exceptional items. It merely provided four alternative treatments of 'exceptional or non-recurrent' items (par. 45) which amounted to a licence to draw up the profit and loss statement in any form according to one's particular fancy. At the time of writing the Institute is involved in an attempt to establish a more precisely defined position. A statement published in the *Chartered Accountant in Australia* in October 1969 proposes that where a gain or loss results from the normal business of the firm but is unusual in magnitude, it should be included in the stated profit with some form of notation to identify the amounts involved. Items which are 'significantly different from the typical or customary business' and not recurring regularly, it is proposed should be shown as additions to or deductions from the net operating profit with a further separate adjustment to cover any items referring to prior accounting periods. This is an admirable objective although the statement as published unfortunately will add confusion because of the terminology adopted. The terms 'abnormal' and 'extraordinary' have not been used according to their dictionary definitions nor in the sense that will be shown to be relevant to the directors' duty to identify items of an abnormal nature.

As the quantity of information required to be disclosed in financial statements increases, it becomes more and more difficult for the reader to discover the most significant pieces of information. From one point of view it may be argued that the reader of financial statements is interested to discover anything which departs from

16 The Profit and Loss Statement

what may be regarded as the normal expectation, i.e. anything extraordinary, unusual or abnormal.

According to A. A. Fitzgerald it was the suggestion of the Joint Committee of the professional accounting bodies and of the Stock Exchange that the Victorian Companies Act of 1938 include a requirement for the directors to report 'as to whether or not the results of the year's operations (as disclosed in the profit and loss account or the income and expenditure account) have in the opinion of the directors been materially affected by items of an abnormal character'.[6] (There is no reference to the matter in the published notes of the Joint Committee.[7] However, A. A. Fitzgerald would have been well informed on the operation of the committee. As editor of the *Australian Accountant* he was concerned with keeping in touch with professional activities. His brother and partner, G. E. Fitzgerald, played an important part in the work of the committee.) A. A. Fitzgerald further suggests that the committee got the idea from a draft Bill included in a book by H. B. Samuel published in London in 1933 titled *Shareholders' Money—An Analysis of Certain Difficulties in Company Legislation, with Proposals for their Reform.*

The requirement as enacted appears straightforward enough yet was not without problems in its implementation because of the interpretation given to the phrase 'items of abnormal character'. As the section in the Act quite clearly refers to the results of the year as set out in the profit and loss account or statement, it would appear to infer abnormal items in the profit and loss account, e.g. windfall gains, extraordinary expenses, etc. It was A. A. Fitzgerald's interpretation that: 'The use of the term "items" clearly suggests that it is accounting adjustments about which information is required, and not the business conditions in which the company carried on during the period.'[8] A. A. Fitzgerald examined the reports of twenty companies selected at random in 1944 to determine how this section was interpreted in practice. We are fortunate that the report of this investigation includes the relevant extracts from the directors' report for each company. Only one company reported an absence of abnormal items. Three companies mentioned specific abnormal items, depreciation charged, A.R.P. (Air Raid Precaution) expenditure, and taxation rates. Seven companies specifically referred to wartime conditions. Eight other companies included varied lists of items and one company made no comment at all, thus ignoring the provision in the Act. But how relevant to the requirements of the Act was this information? We cannot do better than quote Fitzgerald's own conclusion, in which the numbers refer to the extracts set out in his summary:

(a) A surprisingly small proportion of the companies has adhered closely to the precise phraseology of the Act.
(b) Most of the companies have apparently interpreted the sub-section to mean that information is required as to whether trading results have been affected by abnormal business conditions, whereas a few only have related the requirements to the *disclosed* results. For instance of the examples given above, Nos. 1, 2, 4, 5, 6, 7, 8, 10, 11, 13, 14, 16, 17, 18 and 19 apparently relate to surrounding business conditions; Nos. 3 and 12 deal in part, at least, with adjustments in the accounts, and Nos. 9 and 15 are so phrased as to relate to either or both business conditions or account items.

Fitzgerald was correct in pointing out this difference in interpretation. However, the demarcation line between the abnormal amount in the profit and loss account and an abnormal situation leading to an abnormal overall profit result is not always defined easily. Official recognition of the difficulty was given in 1948 when an officer of the Registrar-General's office issued a statement of the attitude of that office:

The use of the words 'whether or not', in our opinion, makes it necessary for the Directors in their report to make some comment. What comment they make depends on their interpretation of 'abnormal character'. Taking the meaning of these words to be something happening during the year which is outside the normal activity of the Company, i.e. defalcation by an employee or any unusual occurrence, it is not so easy to distinguish between strikes, floods, fires, wars and so forth which, in certain circumstances, may be considered normal or abnormal.[9]

In succeeding years the situation of very few companies stating any specific items appears to have persisted, with the bulk of the companies commenting on broad conditions of business. R. A. Irish examined the reports of twenty-six companies in 1948, but found only two cases which identified abnormal items which Irish thought affected every company almost every year. 'Some of the others expressed vague generalities in the directors' report, but failed to give a remote suggestion as to their implications on the earning capacity shown in the profit and loss account.'[10] A survey of thirty-six Western Australian companies in 1957 produced even more startling results. No less than sixteen of these companies failed to make a report as required by the Statute. Of the twenty

16 The Profit and Loss Statement 119

companies that did report, '11 made the bare statutory reference without enlargement; 6 reports described circumstances and not items which could or could not affect the results and 3 only made specific reference to losses such as heavy, bad or doubtful debts, or losses on particular undertakings.'[11] (It should be noted the provision was included in the Western Australian Companies Act of 1943 in which the accounting provisions followed the example of the Victorian Companies Act of 1938.)

For about fifteen years this section of the Act was interpreted in this liberal manner and companies provided little information of a precise nature in response to the section. The Victorian Statute Law Revision Committee in its 1954 report expressed the opinion that this liberal view was not the correct interpretation and recommended that the Act be amended. The amendment should make it plain that what was required was a disclosure of abnormal items which had affected the computation of profit.[12] The subsequent amendment to the Victorian Companies Act in 1955 required a specific comment on:

Any writing off of large amounts of bad debts, any substantial increase or decrease in the value of trading stock owing to a change in the basis of valuation, any item of an unusual nature or value which appears in the accounts, and any absence from the accounts of any item usually included. (s.11(3))

The items to be commented on were made more explicit by the inclusion in 1958 of the item: 'Any change in accounting principles adopted since the last report, any transfers to or from reserves or provisions' (s.137(3)). The total of the 1955 and 1958 Victorian amendments represent the provisions which now operate in all States as part of the Uniform Acts.

The present day position appears to have moved to the opposite extreme to that described by Fitzgerald in 1944. Today we find so many items described that it is difficult to know, in the context of the report, what is abnormal. It is true that directors' reports frequently discuss general business conditions. However, to cite an example, how can one determine when a discussion of production, imports, tariff duties, overseas and local prices is only a general industry discussion or a specific discussion of the effect on the profitability of companies when engaged in industries producing products such as fine papers or chemicals? The present day position was examined on the basis of 1965 annual reports of the 'forty-two leaders sample'. Among these companies only about one-quarter stated explicitly that the result was or was not affected by abnormal items. Only one company positively identified the abnormal item referred to. This company, J. & Way., commented that profit was affected 'by a reduced provision for income tax resulting from accumulated losses in subsidiary companies recently acquired'. The other three-quarters of the companies reported the result was not affected 'except as mentioned' in the directors' report or the directors' report and the profit and loss account, etc. The reference was given in various forms, extending in one case to the whole annual report. The various categories are given in Table 6.

It is clear from Table 6 that the problem is not now the interpretation of the Act, but the interpretation of the various parts of the annual report in which we are told the details of abnormal items will be found. All of the thirty-two companies which implied the inclusion of abnormal items without specifying them, refer us to the directors' report. This in itself may involve selection from extensive details without adding the various other parts of the annual report referred to in some cases. After allowing for space occupied by illustrations and, in some cases, excluding material which, on a more generous definition, might be regarded as part of the directors' report, the average length of the directors' report in the 1965 annual reports of the 'forty-two leaders sample' was two and a half pages. The basis of this average is set out in Table 7. Although this is a sample of large and leading companies we

TABLE 6
Report as to whether results are materially affected by abnormal items
'42 leaders sample'

Detail	No. of Companies	
	1965	1968
Yes	1	3
No	9	9
Except as mentioned in:		
Directors' report	19	22
Directors' report and other parts of Annual Report	13	8
Total	42	42

16 The Profit and Loss Statement

TABLE 7
*Length of directors' report
'42 leaders sample', 1965*

No. of pages	No. of companies
½	2
1	9
2	17
3	6
4	4
5	1
6	2
9	1
Total	42

believe the pattern is followed among smaller companies. The relevant question is, how can the shareholder decide what, among the average two and a half pages of detail, is abnormal? The logical extension of this is to ascertain the effect of the item or items on the profit and loss account. A few instances were found in the 'forty-two leaders sample' where the detail given is set out with sufficient clarity to avoid these problems, e.g. Containers referred to the directors' report which indicated that the need to import tinplate led to a build up of excess stock valued at £500,000. I.A.C. referred to the directors' report which gave details of a write-down of the value of investments in listed companies. A.W.A. referred to the directors' report which indicated a change in the method of accounting for product development costs and the writing off from work in process of £126,000 development costs incurred in previous periods.

In 1968 three instances of identification of specific abnormal items were traced. A.C.I. gave the dollar value of the effect of New Zealand currency devaluation, Nat. Cons. gave a figure for the combined effect of devaluation and increased taxation. While mentioning strikes, the company did not attempt to attach any dollar value to this effect. Sleigh referred to 'the withdrawal of excess depreciation provisions' but qualified this by also referring to factors 'as indicated elsewhere in this report' whatever that may have meant.

By far the majority of reports consist of a sweeping reference to the absence of abnormal circumstances except as mentioned in the report and leave the reader to discriminate between normal and abnormal. B. Tobacco reported that the results were not materially affected 'save to the extent abovementioned'. As all that preceded this statement was a statement of the balance in the profit and loss appropriation account at the beginning of the year, the profit for the year, income tax, proposed dividends, transfer to reserve, and remaining balance, it is hard to decide just what the company considered abnormal. A.W.A. made a similar reference to what was almost an identical statement to that referred to by B. Tobacco.

Nine companies made an unqualified statement that the results were not affected by items of an abnormal nature.

The majority of the 'except as mentioned' reports clearly relate to the directors' report while a few make specific reference to other parts of the annual report. Between 1965 and 1968 there seemed to be some decline in the incidence of these references. Table 6 summarizes the situation.

The conclusion drawn is that there remains a need for the development of reporting which will highlight clearly the significant features which represent abnormal or extraordinary factors. The statutory provisions provided to date have been added to, so that there is no longer any doubt of their meaning. However, they are nullified largely by the practice of directors reporting that the results have not been affected materially by abnormal items 'except as . . .'. The statutory requirement might be more effective in solving the matter if it required directors to state 'what abnormal items have materially affected the result as shown by the profit and loss account and the balance sheet'. A possible solution to the problem of identifying the most important factors would be to require the auditor to comment on abnormal items.

The main objection to this approach might be that such comments by the auditor could be construed as a qualification to the accounts. Auditors have been reluctant to give any indication of a serious qualification of company financial statements, except in the most unusual circumstances, because of the adverse effect such a qualification may have on the company. Unfortunately empirical evidence of the auditors' attitudes is not available, although a reasonable inference can be drawn from available information about reactions to qualified auditors' reports.

In the 1969 Annual Research Lecture in the University of Melbourne endowed by the Australian Society of Accountants, Professor Goldberg identified 39 cases covering 33 companies in which a qualified auditors' report had been publicized by press comments during the period 1964 to 30 June 1969. A sample of 132 companies surveyed over a period of twelve years produced 80 qualified reports (apart from those relating to reliance on other auditors of subsidiary companies) that did not receive press publicity. Of these only 12 appear possibly to have been significant while the balance referred to the audit of branches by other auditors and acceptance of certificates relating to stock-in-trade. A more positive interpretation may be applied to the results of Professor Goldberg's research indicating a sharp increase in qualified reports commented upon in the press in 1967 and subsequently. The occasion for comment must imply the willingness of the auditor to qualify the report in the first place. Is it possible that auditors are becoming less reluctant to issue a qualified report? The fear of adverse reaction to a qualified auditors' report or to similar comments by directors may well be an inhibiting factor in developing a more informative disclosure of abnormal items affecting the results of a company's operations.

It is possible that a more specific response might follow the Australian Associated Stock Exchanges' amendment of the Official List Requirements in September 1967 to require the preliminary report of profit made to the Stock Exchange to state whether any unusual event influenced the trading results for the year.[13] The reference to 'any unusual event' would suggest the identification of specific happenings rather than the general conditions of business which we have shown to have been frequently identified as constituting 'items of an abnormal character' as called for under the statutory report in its early form or the more recent reference to 'items of an unusual nature or value'. It is to be hoped that this action by the Stock Exchanges will effectively place the responsibility on the directors to identify the 'abnormal' presently hidden among the voluminous detail of the annual reports of many large companies.

The necessity to identify abnormal and extraordinary items, particularly in the profit and loss statement, has gained increased importance in recent times with the growing emphasis on the measure of earnings per share as a basis of measuring company performance and in the determination of market prices of shares.

17

Directors' Remuneration

The Victorian Companies Act of 1938 also provides a convenient starting point to review the action taken by the legislatures with respect to the disclosure of the remuneration of directors and of loans made to directors, because this Act appears to have responded to public opinion on the matter in the light of the changed circumstances of the time. The action taken suggests that adequate disclosure may not always be a sufficient safeguard against malpractice. After outlining the facts, the question will be considered of whether the action on this particular problem has shaken the basic premise which lay behind the limited liability company, i.e. limited liability based on protection by adequate disclosure. The Greene Company Law Amendment Committee considered it was not practicable or desirable to prohibit loans being made to directors, but did consider shareholders were entitled to know what loans had been made to directors, managers, and other officers of the company, and recognized that there was a fairly widespread demand that shareholders should be entitled to receive more details than they did in some cases.[1] The recommendations of the Greene Committee were incorporated in the English Companies Act of 1928. It has been shown already that the three States of Queensland, South Australia and New South Wales modelled their amended legislation of 1931–6 on this English Act. With regard to payments and loans to directors, Victoria in 1938 followed this English Act. Later, partly by the indirect route of copying Victorian legislation, Western Australia did likewise in 1943. Tasmania also appears to have followed similar leads when drafting its 1959 Act. One of the provisions which arose in this way is the prohibition of payments to directors for loss of office unless there is full disclosure to the members of the company. Similar provisions continue in the uniform legislation now in force, except that certain bona fide payments are no longer prohibited.

17 Directors' Remuneration

At the same time the English Act enacted provisions requiring disclosure of the amount of loans made to directors during the year, the amounts repaid and the amount of any current or previous loans remaining outstanding. The proviso to the section excluded certain loans made in the normal course of business. This provision was taken up by all of the States. In South Australia and Western Australia the section was extended to cover any directors' debts due to the company for a period exceeding twelve months. (In Victoria the disclosure of outstanding amounts of loans to directors was also included in the details specified to be shown in the balance sheet.) It appears that the disclosure of these loans was designed to emphasize the fiduciary relationship between a director and the company. Disclosure does not appear to have removed the abuses at which the section was directed, because the 1961-2 Uniform Acts introduced a prohibition on loans by companies to the directors of the company. The difficulty of legislating on such matters was highlighted in the last decade by the events surrounding some company failures. While the disclosure provisions covered loans to directors, they did not cover loans to companies which may be owned wholly by the directors. If these provisions are to achieve their objectives then they must be such as to eliminate the exemption gained by a director acting under the guise of a corporate entity.

The third aspect of disclosure relating to directors covered by the English Act of 1928, was the remuneration paid to directors. The English, Queensland and New South Wales Acts followed a uniform pattern requiring disclosure of all remuneration and emoluments of directors, provided that payments to a managing director or salary paid to full-time salaried directors need not be included. The South Australian Act did not include the proviso to except these payments. The broad sweep of the South Australian Act raised questions as to how far it was meant to apply, for at least one opinion by counsel was that it applied only to directors' fees as such and not to any other perquisites.[2] Victoria also acted in 1938 to provide for the disclosure of directors' remuneration. The Victorian approach was followed subsequently in Western Australia and Tasmania. (In these three States the statement of directors' remuneration was covered also by the section of the Act detailing the contents of the profit and loss statement.) The requirements as set out in the Victorian Act, raised the question of whether it was 'necessary to include amounts paid to a director for services rendered in a capacity other than that of a director, and if so, to what extent'. The opinion of W. K. Fullager was that the prima facie meaning of the section was remuneration for services rendered as directors. He considered that the Victorian section required the inclusion of the salary paid to a managing director, but not a salary paid for any other position.[3] J. B. Tait on the other hand, attached importance to the omission of the proviso contained in the English Act. He interpreted the section as not limited to directors' fees and claimed that this was shown to be the view of the draftsman by the notes of the Attorney-General presented when he introduced the Bill to Parliament. He did not think that the section enabling shareholders to requisition for a statement of the aggregate emoluments received by directors necessarily implied that the annual statement would be more restricted in scope.[4]

The passage of this part of the Victorian legislation was not without its share of public debate. The issue was highlighted by circumstances relating to the board of directors of G. J. Coles & Co. Ltd. A meeting of the company called for 23 September 1936 was to consider three matters including: 'Whether it is in the best interests of the company that in future the Directors should publish, in the annual accounts of the company, the total remuneration of the Directors.'[5] The company was not left for more than the following two years to decide the issue for itself. However, the statement published by G. J. Coles publicizing his views among shareholders, not only provides a full documentation of the internal company position, but also reveals some of the reasons for the legislature acting to require the disclosure of directors' remuneration.

G. J. Coles & Co. Ltd had adopted the practice of distributing part of the annual profit as a bonus to directors and staff. In 1935 the then chairman, George J. Coles, considered the shareholders should be told of these payments. The board of the company would only go so far as to say, 'that the shareholders should be informed that three of the highest paid Director-executives had each received more than £10,000'.[6] George J. Coles's position was supported by the editorial policy of the *Argus* in which it was said that, 'as profits increased it might have been expected that the percentage payable to employees in addition to their salaries would have been kept within reasonable limits'. Following the annual meeting of the company the disclosure by the board of the company was interpreted by the *Argus* as indicating 'that moderate counsels have not prevailed'.[7] During the following year the board sought to displace George J. Coles from the board, together with his notions of disclosure. Without George J. Coles being involved, some shareholders briefed J. B. Tait, counsel, to ask questions on the matter at the next annual meeting on 26 August 1936. The chairman refused to disclose the information without taking a vote of shareholders. At this stage the chairman of the Stock Exchange of Melbourne entered the controversy with the issue of a public statement. This statement, in effect, said that the fact that the board of the company was almost wholly executive directors was a new feature. As such, the directors were 'in a position to fix their own emoluments' instead of being dependent on a vote of members at the annual meeting to fix 'directors' fees'.[8] As the circumstances were considered unique, the Stock Exchange did not have a rule to cover them. In March a conference of Stock Exchanges had agreed to adopt a new rule which would require disclosure of the remuneration of directors. The *Argus* considered that: 'Most of the shareholders will probably agree that a system which allows directors to occupy high executive positions in a company and thus be enabled to fix their own remuneration without consulting the people who have put up the capital is wrong in principle.'[9] (Following the settlement of the dispute with the directors of Coles, George J. Coles was reinstated as chairman of the company, a position which he continued to occupy until 1956.)

It would appear also that the public concern over directors' remuneration was not purely a domestic issue confined to G. J. Coles & Co. Ltd. At the 1935 annual meeting of Dunlop apparently strong feelings were voiced on the same issue. The directors pleaded that to disclose this information would prejudice the company. The chairman, defending the directors' point of view, quoted the case of payments in another company, adding 'and it is not the one you are thinking of'.[10] This was an obvious allusion to G. J. Coles. The chairman of Dunlop apparently anticipated the legislation by stating the remuneration of the directors at the 1936 annual meeting.

Not only were these companies, like any other public company, shortly compelled to give this information; in addition the Act was strengthened with two methods of enforcement. In all States the auditor was required to give the information both on loans to and remuneration of directors if the directors failed to do so. Various provisions were enacted to enable shareholders to move to secure a statement of the total of all remuneration and emoluments paid to directors, whether executive or salaried directors, or external directors. With certain provisos, a requisition could be served on the company by any member in South Australia or a minimum of one-quarter of the members in Queensland, New South Wales and Victoria. The proportion of members necessary to serve such a requisition was reduced to 10 per cent in the Victorian and Tasmanian Acts of 1958–9, and remains as such in the Uniform Acts.

The G. J. Coles and Dunlop incidents were echoed in England in 1944 when the Institute of Chartered Accountants in England and Wales, in a submission to the Company Law Amendment Committee, enunciated a general principle that directors should not be able to grant themselves monetary advantages without it being known to the shareholders because of the fiduciary position of directors.[11] The Institute referred to cases where directors were appointed to managerial positions so the company could avoid disclosing their remuneration. The Institute proposed therefore that the total of such 'management remuneration' should be disclosed. Alternatively, the Institute proposed that the facilities for shareholders to secure this information should be improved. The Institute's proposals were taken up by the Company Law Amendment Committee which recommended that the English Act be amended to require disclosure of the total emoluments of directors from the parent and any subsidiary companies. Emoluments excluded the reimbursement of expenses which were not taxable in the hands of the director. This committee recommended this disclosure to extend to: 'The total of all other emoluments receivable by the directors whether as directors or otherwise from such companies in connection with the management of their affairs.'[12]

The matter was considered by the Victorian Statute Law Revision Committee in 1955. The committee posed the question as to whether it was desirable to amend s.127(5) of the Victorian Companies Act of 1938 by deleting the words 'as such'. This amendment would have the effect of compelling a complete disclosure of all payments made to directors. G. E. Fitzgerald appeared on behalf of the Australian Society of Accountants and stated the Society's attitude thus:

In our opinion it is not desirable to provide for such a complete disclosure in the published financial statements; the legislation does not provide for the disclosure of remuneration paid to managers and we consider it would not be advisable to insist that such information should be presented when a manager is appointed to the Board of directors or where a director is appointed as manager.

Such a provision could be easily avoided by a managing director retiring from the Board and retaining his position as manager when his remuneration would not be disclosed.[13]

K. N. Stonier (chairman) and G. C. Tootell (vice-chairman) of the Institute of Chartered Accountants in Australia (Victorian branch) followed a similar line of reasoning in their submissions to the committee on behalf of the Institute.[14] The Uniform Acts continued to exclude the payments made to executive directors from the disclosure specified under the ninth schedule. The disclosure of this information was left subject to the requisition of members, to be given on demand of 10 per cent of members.

The passage of the 1961–2 Uniform Acts provided the occasion to question just how wide a range of forms of 'emoluments' was embraced by the clause contained in the ninth schedule of these Acts. A discussion group of the New South Wales branch of the Institute of Chartered Accountants suggested four principles as a guide to deciding what to state. These principles were: a principle of exclusiveness to test whether or not it was an asset or service enjoyed by employees not having director status, the materiality of the item, the use of an explanatory note when the value could not be ascertained, and disclosure by directors of the fact that they are partners in firms rendering professional advice whether or not the director is himself involved in the service rendered.[15]

A joint panel of members of the Victorian branch of the Institute of Chartered Accountants in Australia and the Australian Society of Accountants considered the meaning of the clause in the ninth schedule with particular attention to a director who is a member of a firm which renders management services of some kind. The committee considered that the details supplied in response to a requisition under s. 131 should be confined to payments arising from membership of the board of directors and excluding any payment for full-time employment by the company or its subsidiaries. Where a director, or a firm of which he is a member, receives fees for special services the committee suggested that the reply to the questionnaire should indicate that the director is a member of a named firm which received the specified sum for named services. In attempting to define directors' emoluments, the committee considered they should include expense allowances, contributions to a superannuation fund with undefeasible rights and free use of a motor vehicle included for part-time directors but which generally would be excluded in the case of directors in the full-time employment of the company. The committee did not consider a retiring allowance or pension paid to a director after he ceases to hold office as coming within the ambit of the clause but indicated this was not in accord with the present views of the Registrars of Companies and that further discussions were pending.[16]

It therefore appears that the advent of the 'executive director' as distinct from the 'outside director' was a significant factor in forwarding the move for legislative compulsion to disclose the remuneration of directors, and particularly affected the form of the Victorian Act which, unlike the Act in New South Wales and Queensland, did not exclude from the effect of the clause the salary of full-time executive directors.

An example of a more comprehensive disclosure of directors' remuneration is the English Companies Act of 1967 which requires a separate statement of the emoluments of the chairman and the highest paid director and the number of directors receiving each scale of emoluments in multiples of £2,500. There is an exemption where the company is not a holding company or subsidiary company and the total emoluments do not exceed £7,500. Such detailed disclosure suggests a social attitude towards business executives which might not be as acceptable in Australia. The Eggleston Committee appointed by the conference of Attorneys-General in July 1967 was directed to consider the question of disclosure of directors' remuneration. This committee recommended the disclosure of two separate amounts covering the emoluments of part-time directors and the emoluments of executive directors, but excluding the amount paid to executive directors by way of salary as an employee of the company. The Eggleston Committee however considered that disclosure of payments to directors for professional services rendered should continue to be made only on the submission of a requisition as provided by section 166 of the Uniform Acts.[17] The legislature has been able to ensure that shareholders know what has been done with respect to remuneration of and loans to directors. This form of disclosure, however, must be regarded largely as acting after the event. The prohibition of loans to directors suggests that disclosure of loans made, did not prevent the abuses attacked. At the same time, recent events have shown that prohibition has been circumvented by making loans to companies which the directors own. While it is only one aspect of company management, it is regarded here as a serious matter that disclosure has not prevented abuse. The disclosure of directors' remuneration has been successful largely. Problems have still arisen, however, where directors are receiving what are regarded as

17 Directors' Remuneration

extravagant payments under contracts entered into before the company became a public company. This moves the issue back to a stage earlier than that considered in this book, i.e. from the annual report to the prospectus.

The Stock Exchanges included provisions relating to options in their listing requirements before the recognition of the problem of disclosure of share options by the Victorian Companies Act of 1938 which required that, 'in any case where an option exists over unissued shares of the company the balance-sheet shall state the number of shares under option, the price of issue, and the date of the expiration of the option' (s.124 (1)). In recent years the option has become a more popular means of 'remuneration' of directors and other officers of companies and is likely to be used much more widely in the near future.[18] As a result of recent practices the Uniform Acts have limited options to a period of five years and require more extensive disclosure by medium of the directors' report, including the name of the person to whom the option has been granted, the number and class of shares in respect of which the option has been granted, the date of expiration of the option, the basis upon which the option may be exercised, and whether the person to whom the option has been granted has any right to participate by virtue of the option in any share issue of any other company (s.68). The Act also requires a statement of any share issues made during the period by virtue of exercising any option, and details of the options remaining outstanding at the end of the period.

18

Holding Companies

The device of the holding company can be said to have originated in the United States of America as a reaction to the outlawing of industrial 'trusts' by the Sherman Anti-Trust Laws. Originally the holding company was envisaged simply as a company holding the shares of operating companies, but has developed into a more diverse form where some small or large part of the group activity is carried out by the holding or parent company, as well as the activities conducted through the subsidiaries. It is not surprising that the 'forty-two leaders sample' representing the largest public companies in Australia are in fact all holding companies. They represent a variety of types, and originated in different ways at different points in time. Some of these companies were formed by a merger of interests to create either a company the only substantial assets of which comprised shares in subsidiary companies, or a company which holds such investments and also engages in some operating activities itself. Other of these companies were created so that two or more public companies shared the ownership of the operating companies. Some were newly created enterprises while others arose from various plans of re-arrangement of existing enterprises.

The importance of holding companies was demonstrated by the 'Directory of Top 800 Australian Companies' published by the *Australian Financial Review*. No less than 559 (70 per cent) of these companies held shares in one or more subsidiaries, thus:

    382 with one to ten subsidiaries,
    90 with eleven to twenty subsidiaries,
    69 with twenty-one to fifty subsidiaries,
    18 with over fifty subsidiaries.

The reporting problems which arise from the holding company or group form of organization, can be traced to one cause—the legal fiction of the separate legal entity of a company.

18 Holding Companies

Holding companies are diverse in nature and therefore may be expected to present diverse accounting problems. At one extreme is the company wherein all the resources are invested in subsidiaries. At the other extreme is the company which is in fact an operating company merging the interests of a number of investment-type holding companies.

It is appropriate to begin the discussion of disclosure of the affairs of holding companies at this point because legislative action was first directed to the problem, albeit unsuccessfully, in the Acts passed in Queensland in 1931, in South Australia in 1934 and in New South Wales in 1936, and with substantially more success in the Victorian Act of 1938.

While the practical problems of presenting accounting reports may have been solved, the implications of the fictional creation of the group entity still provide a difficult problem for the company auditor. E. H. Burgess, addressing the Chartered Accountants' Third Australian Congress in 1965, asserted that:

It must be obvious that if auditors are to be expected to do their work effectively, then a prerequisite is the development of a satisfactory legal concept, expressed in statutory form of the significance and limitations of the company group on the one hand, and the accounts of such groups on the other hand.[1]

Such a satisfactory concept, he then went on to demonstrate, had not yet materialized. This mirrors the editorial quoted by the *Commonwealth Journal of Accountancy* from the *Incorporated Accountants' Journal* of forty years ago which, in outlining the auditor's difficulties, also highlighted the importance of the legal concepts involved in the group organization. This editorial claimed that:

Practically every criminal case connected with company finance of the last two decades has been concerned with frauds rendered possible by the legal fiction that subsidiary companies are separate and independent constitutions from the parent company.

Although the controlling company's directors have full power to carry out their trust to both the parent company and its subsidiaries and are enabled to safeguard the assets as one whole, it frequently happens that separate auditors are appointed for the parent and some or all of the subsidiary companies.[2]

The legal distinction of the separate entity of each company means that any rights to obtain financial information which shareholders might possess are confined purely to the company in which

F

the shareholder owns shares, unless the legislatures make an extension to those legal rights. The introduction of compulsory disclosure of financial statements in Victoria in 1896 did nothing to alter this position. As all the shares in the subsidiary would be owned by the parent, the subsidiary could qualify as a proprietary company and therefore was not required to publish accounts. The balance sheet of such a holding company could convey little knowledge of the state of affairs of the subsidiaries. For example on the formation of D.H.A. in 1929, £2,416,499 of the total assets of £2,478,298 shown in the balance sheet were shares in subsidiaries. When A.C.I. transferred its operations to the subsidiaries in 1938, no less than £7,043,000 of the total assets of £7,256,000 comprised investments in the subsidiary companies. In many instances such details as were provided of profits earned, according to the first statutory attempts to tackle the problem, were completely inadequate and quite possibly grossly misleading. In the absence of any statutory or voluntarily imposed obligations to do otherwise, the directors of these companies appear to have regarded the issue of such uninformative statements as the proper thing to do and serving the interests of shareholders.

In periods of depressed trade there has been pressure to merge for economic reasons, and the failure to develop more adequate reporting accorded with the fear expressed towards disclosure, as possibly aiding competitors at a time of depressed business. Some of the companies formed by these mergers continued subsequently to establish a long record of what is considered inadequate disclosure. As late as 1964 one of these companies, H. Jones, earned the description by the *Age* newspaper of being 'renowned as the most conservative Australian company'.[3] This was a reflection of both the inadequate nature of the company's financial disclosure, and the apparently deliberate understatement of some asset values shown in the balance sheet. Or one could cite the record of Australian Glass Manufacturers Co. Ltd, as A.C.I. was then known, which was documented in the *Adelaide Advertiser* thus:

> The first three balance sheets issued by the company were very full and informative, but subsequent ones are less satisfactory. It is known that large sums have been invested in subsidiaries; but in the balance sheet the amount is coupled with loans at short call and shown as one item. In the latest publication, the figure given is £551,762 (a decrease of £43,340 for the year). The amount of the interest in Australian Window Glass Proprietary Limited has already been mentioned; but the extent of the holding in other companies is not known, so it may be that the

amount of short call money is not large. The report makes no reference to what amount, if any, the subsidiaries contributed to the parent company's earnings.[4]

Such illustrations serve to demonstrate the need for some more positive action by interested parties to ensure better reporting by holding companies.

INCLUSION OF STATEMENTS OF SUBSIDIARIES

The first attempts to deal with the problem of holding companies were aimed at obtaining the financial statements of the subsidiaries. In 1925 when the Stock Exchanges first issued codified Official List Requirements, they included a requirement for a listed company to include with its reports the balance sheet of any company in which it owned a controlling interest. This requirement effectively was directed only at newly listed companies and did not draw any response from any of the 'forty-two leaders sample'. The annual report of the Melbourne Exchange indicated its displeasure at the use of the holding company as a means of minimizing disclosure and withholding 'from those who supply the necessary capital information to which they are entitled'.[5] Where a holding company controls a number of subsidiaries, there are two objections to extending the financial reports to include the separate statement of each subsidiary. The first objection is the simple fact of the economic cost of reproducing numerous statements coupled with the diminishing likelihood that, in fact, the statements will be read. The second objection is the more theoretical question of how any individual reader can possibly obtain a significant comprehension of the affairs of a group by reading the statements of its numerous separate parts. One approach to solving this problem was that taken up by the Stock Exchanges in 1927.

AGGREGATE STATEMENTS OF SUBSIDIARIES

In 1927 the Melbourne Stock Exchange amended its Official List Requirements to allow that, where a company had more than one subsidiary company, it could issue an aggregate statement of the assets and liabilities of the subsidiary companies, instead of the separate statements of all subsidiaries. This requirement had some success, as noted in our earlier discussion of Stock Exchange Listing Requirements. The main argument in favour of this method of presentation is that it recognizes the separate legal entity of the parent and subsidiary companies. In 1928 E. V. Nixon described it in this way:

Probably the most suitable method of providing the desired information is by a method which is a compromise between the methods previously described. In this case a 'legal' balance sheet is published showing the value of the holdings in subsidiaries, and to this is appended a summary of the assets and liabilities of the Subsidiary Companies aggregated. Information is also given showing what proportion of the capital and reserves of each subsidiary are held by minority interests and by the Holding Company respectively.

A statement in this form has, however, certain disadvantages. For example, it does not disclose the position of individual Subsidiary Companies. However, the general opinion among English accountants is that this method of presentation has advantages over the other methods described.[6]

The adequacy of this type of statement is dependent in large measure on the principles upon which the preparation of it is based. Double counting will occur if the statement is not prepared so that all inter-subsidiary-company transactions are eliminated. Thus, for example, profits on sales made by one subsidiary to another would be reflected in the proprietorship accounts. If the goods concerned were still held as stock by the purchasing subsidiary, then from the group point of view, a profit has not been earned and must be eliminated. To avoid double counting it will also be necessary to eliminate any outstanding balances arising at the balance date from inter-subsidiary-company transactions. Where the group includes partly owned subsidiaries, the claims of the minority interest must be recognized and disclosed if the statement is not going to be misleading. All of these problems also exist with the preparation of group consolidated statements, but there is a further problem in the presentation which is peculiar to the use of the aggregate statement of assets and liabilities of subsidiaries. Even if a profit and loss statement is not presented, the result of profit determination is reflected in the balances shown in the proprietorship accounts in the balance sheet. The profit credited to proprietorship by a subsidiary may include profits made on transfer to the parent company. From the viewpoint of the group these are unrealized profits and their inclusion in the aggregate statement as part of proprietorship balances could give a misleading result. A further problem, and probably the most serious one, relates to the profits of the subsidiaries and the dividends paid to the parent. If the parent company is a pure holding company then the group profitability will be reflected in the aggregate statement. Where the parent company engages in operations itself, the parent company profit will include dividends from the subsidiaries as well as the parent company operating result. The increase in proprietorship (assuming profitable operations) shown in the parent statement, and that shown in the aggregate statement, may give a misleading view of the relative earning capacity of the parent and of the aggregate subsidiaries. Another distortion that could arise, would result from including dividends receivable by the parent from the subsidiaries, but not including the equivalent dividends payable in the aggregate subsidiary statement. These problems are eliminated in consolidated group statements, because the profits and dividends concerned are eliminated in the course of aggregating the parent and subsidiary company data to obtain group consolidated statements.

The alternative of consolidated statements was, even in 1928, a proven possibility. The first English book on consolidated statements, which has had a profound effect on English and Australian practice, was the publication in 1922 of the lecture of the late Sir Gilbert Garnsey. In his book Garnsey recognized the proven nature of consolidated statements, for he wrote: 'Accountants in America tell us that the case for the consolidated Balance Sheet is made out, and that there is nothing further to argue about it on the question of principle.'[7]

THE 1929 ENGLISH COMPANIES ACT REQUIREMENT

About this time the Greene Committee on Company Law was sitting in England. This committee paid considerable attention to the reporting of holding companies, and although the committee reported that it recognized 'the evidence discloses a considerable divergence of views on the subject among both commercial men and accountants', the advocates of consolidated statements were greatly disappointed when the committee reported that it did not accept the view that the issue of consolidated statements should be compulsory but on the contrary thought it should be left for shareholders to decide.[8] (This recommendation reflected a position which it was previously shown had not proved an effective means of securing adequate disclosure.) The Greene Committee recommendations were incorporated in the English Companies Act of 1928 and subsequently in the three Acts passed in 1931–6 in

Queensland, South Australia and New South Wales. The obligations imposed on a holding company by these Acts were to show in the balance sheet separately investments in subsidiaries and the amounts due to and from subsidiaries, and to provide a statement of *how* the profits in the subsidiaries were dealt with (emphasis mine).

Sir Albert Wyon, a partner of Sir Gilbert Garnsey, and recognized as his successor as an authority on consolidated statements, wrote prophetically:

I venture to think that the particulars required by the Act to be disclosed are of so general and vague a character as to be quite insufficient to supply shareholders with the information necessary for them, if they are to have a just view of the earnings of the enterprise in which they are interested and of its prospects. The provisions which I have epitomised may indeed have the unintended effect of providing justification for directors who wish so to prepare the accounts of a holding company as to conceal from those chiefly interested the actual results of its activities.[9]

STATEMENT IN PARENT BALANCE SHEET OF INVESTMENT IN SUBSIDIARIES

The balance sheet of the parent was required only to show 'a' value for the investment in the subsidiaries. Counsel's opinion secured by the English Institute and quoted in Australia, suggested the item 'shares in subsidiaries' might be quoted on any of the following bases: at or below cost, as valued by directors, or at cost less realizations and amounts written off.[10] An examination was made of those holding companies in the 'forty-two leaders sample' affected by the introduction of this legislation in New South Wales. The basis of valuation of investments in subsidiaries in 1937 was found to be 'at cost' in five out of the six cases. The results of this examination imply that there was more precision in the description used by Australian companies than suggested by the English counsel's opinion. The other company (Woolworth) described the asset as 'at cost or valuation'. Two companies whose reports are included from later dates are of interest. One (F. & T.) included from 1938, showed shares held in subsidiaries at 31 December 1936 'at independent valuation' and subsequent acquisitions 'at cost'. The other (Bradford) first acquired a subsidiary in 1939 when the shares in subsidiary were stated 'at cost' and subsequent additions 'at valuation'. Later events are not considered further because the progressive availability of consolidated statements affects the relevance of this aspect of the analysis, as outlined later. Whichever of these bases was chosen, it would not indicate whether the subsidiary had increased or decreased the net assets representing the invested resources. The absence of consolidated accounts and/or accounts of the subsidiaries thereby provided a golden opportunity to create secret reserves in the accounts of the subsidiaries, without any need to use devices which effectively exclude asset values from the books of the subsidiaries. An outstanding Australian example of this was probably a company not included in the 'forty-two leaders sample', Burns Philp Ltd: This company in 1961 showed the value of shareholders' funds in the parent balance sheet to be £17.9 million. In the following year the consolidated statements stated the shareholders' funds at £26.7 million. In other words, the increase in proprietorship which was hidden previously in the investments in subsidiaries, was no less than £6.6 million. (This ignores any effect due to adopting conservative bases of valuation in stating the balance sheet values of assets.)

The Uniform Acts now require all holding companies in Australia to publish consolidated statements or the separate statements of each subsidiary. Because of this it is no longer of great importance whether investments in subsidiaries are stated by the parent company at cost or any other basis, from the point of view of disclosing the position of the group. The figure in the parent company's statement may be high or low in relation to the value of the proprietary interest of the parent as shown by the books of the subsidiary. Whatever the position may be, the parent company's interest in the assets of the subsidiary will be included in the consolidated statement at the current book values of the subsidiary. The reconciliation of the parent company evaluation of its investment and the figures in the consolidated statement, is made by the items reserve or goodwill on consolidation and the accumulated profits (including any amounts transferred to reserves, etc.) in the books of the subsidiary.

STATEMENT OF HOW PROFITS OF SUBSIDIARIES DEALT WITH

Under the 1931–6 Acts in Queensland, South Australia and New South Wales, the second obligation imposed on a holding company was to present a statement of *how* the profits in the subsidiaries were dealt with. It should be noted that this did not require any statement of the amount of those profits. Already it has been noted that it was considered that this statement was outside the ambit of the audit.

It was suggested that there was no responsibility on the auditor for its accuracy. In discussions as to the form the report should take, a number of English company reports were quoted as precedents. Generally these English reports provided a statement saying that the profits of the subsidiaries had been taken account of to the extent of dividends received. Among the 'forty-two leaders sample' there were six New South Wales companies reporting at the time the New South Wales Companies Act of 1936 became applicable. The form of statement each of these companies gave as to how the profits of subsidiaries had been dealt with, is shown in appendix 6. Five of the six companies followed the English precedent of taking into account the profits of subsidiaries to the extent of dividends received. The statement of the sixth company was extremely vague, saying: 'Insofar as it concerns this Company, the Profit derived by the Subsidiary Company has been incorporated in the Accounts.' Subsequent to this date the New South Wales companies in the 'forty-two leaders sample' nearly all went beyond the statutory requirements applicable in that State by providing an aggregate statement of subsidiary company assets and liabilities, in two cases, or consolidated statements or separate statements for each subsidiary. This arose as discussed in chapter 12 from the effectiveness of other non-statutory factors. One partial exception was the statements of Boral in the first financial year of the subsidiary, when it made a loss. The presentation used is shown in appendix 6.

The evidence of the 'forty-two leaders sample' supports the view that the legislation adopted in Queensland, South Australia and New South Wales in 1931–6 was ineffective in providing for the disclosure of the value of shareholders' funds (at values as recorded in the books) of the group and of the profitability of the group, and improved disclosure was dependent on other measures.

CONSOLIDATED STATEMENTS

Following the publication of Garnsey's work there was an awakening among some sections of the profession to the value of consolidated statements. In England the Dunlop Rubber Company is credited with being the first public company to issue consolidated statements. The Australian company followed this lead and the consolidated statements issued by Dunlop in 1937 were the first consolidated statements to be issued by a public company in Australia. The significance of the occasion did not go un-noticed as reports of the annual meeting of the company bear ample evidence. Such a significant advance in the preparation of financial statements was sure to upset more conservatively minded investors. The directors of the company reported to the shareholders:

The Board has prepared these two additional sets of figures with the object of giving Shareholders fuller information than they have previously had of the trading results and the financial position of the company.

This form of presentation is a definite departure from custom in Australia, but it is in line with the most modern practice in Great Britain. It is unreservedly supported by the Company's Auditors, and the Board believes that it will be welcomed by Shareholders.

In recent years, the accounts of Holding Companies have been unfavourably commented upon in this country, and this new method of compiling the accounts should answer such criticism, at least as far as your company is concerned.

The thoroughness of the preparation of the company reports was indicated by the added comments of the directors:

One other innovation is incorporated in the setup of the Balance Sheet, viz. the grouping under specific headings of the various classes of Assets and Liabilities. This makes the reading of the Balance Sheet easy, and discloses the strong liquid position of the Company. The same grouping is adopted in the Consolidated Statement.

The remodelling of our Accounts has to some extent disturbed the comparisons with former years, but in all future Balance Sheets the figures for the year immediately preceding will be shown in parallel columns, for comparative purposes.

Shareholders will observe that, for the sake of simplicity, figures of shillings and pence have been omitted.

At the annual meeting, the chairman of the company defended the radical changes in the financial statements,[11] of which the presentation of consolidated statements was only one. The meeting was very well attended and the directors must have been disappointed when a shareholder, J. Jolly, who was also an influential accountant in Melbourne, opposed the motion to appoint the auditors, 'as a concrete example of dissatisfaction at the form of the balance sheet'. This motion was lost by 42 votes to 29. J. V. M. Wood was another prominent accountant who was strongly critical of the consolidated statements, claiming that 'the balance sheet as presented did not give shareholders a frank account of the financial position of the company'. One other company in the 'forty-two leaders sample', B. Tobacco, followed the lead of Dunlop before there was any legislative recognition given to consolidated statements.

It is perhaps not surprising that the first article to appear in the *Australian Accountant* dealing with the actual mechanics of preparing consolidated statements should have drawn on the English Dunlop company's statements for illustrative purposes.[12] This writer, and the first writer to deal with these matters in the *Chartered Accountant in Australia*,[13] drew on Garnsey's book as his principal source. Professional opposition was based on technical objections seen by some in the consolidated statement. The problems raised have not proved to be insuperable. At this point it is appropriate to note the problems which have been effectively summarized for us in 1948 by a South Australian member of the Institute of Chartered Accountants, G. M. Ewart, writing in the *Chartered Accountant in Australia*. He codified the following seven objections:

(i) Different balancing dates.
(ii) The consolidated statement includes assets and liabilities which are not the property or liability of the holding company.
(iii) Assets of foreign subsidiaries may not be under effective control of the holding company.
(iv) One or more subsidiaries may not, in fact, be part of the economic unit.
(v) A majority shareholding does not necessarily mean control, and vice versa.
(vi) Difficulty of ensuring assets are valued on a fairly uniform basis.
(vii) Consolidated statements do not show which subsidiaries are profitable and which are making losses.[14]

It has been mentioned already that, when the Bill for what was to be the Victorian Companies Act of 1938 was discussed, a proposal to give statutory recognition and compulsion to the issue of consolidated statements provoked some strong opposition. It appears that this opposition was expressed in the more indirect approach of arguing forcefully for Victoria to follow the 1929 English Act and thereby legislate as ineffectively in respect of holding companies as Queensland, South Australia and New South Wales had done. The official attitudes of the two principal professional accounting bodies were at variance on the question of consolidated statements. The Commonwealth Institute of Accountants, through its representatives on the Joint Committee of Professional Accounting Organisations, was the advocate for consolidated statements. On the other hand, the State Council of the Institute of Chartered Accountants made it known publicly that it did not support the proposal. This official Institute position was reflected in the hostile criticism of A. H. Outhwaite referred to earlier in discussing the Victorian Act as a whole. The Commonwealth Institute's views must have prevailed in the Joint Committee because in the Joint Committee's notes on the Companies Bill 1938, it gave unequivocal support to consolidated statements and rejected the Greene Committee requirements as reflected in the then existing Acts of Queensland, South Australia and New South Wales. 'No other provisions of the English Act have received such all-round condemnation as those relating to the published accounts of holding companies,'[15] said the Committee, and proceeded to quote from numerous authorities to support this accusation.

The Commonwealth Institute appears to have been ably represented on the Joint Committee by G. E. Fitzgerald whose brother, A. A. Fitzgerald, added his editorial support in the pages of the *Australian Accountant* rebutting the argument of those advocating adherence to the form of the existing English Act by pointing out that:

The present opportunity is too good to be lost, and if the representations of the accountancy and secretarial bodies do result in some innovations in company law in this country, it will not be the first time that Australian company law has introduced a new principle without waiting for the imprimatur of the British legislature.[16]

The advocates of consolidated statements 'won the day' and the Victorian Companies Act of 1938 became the first companies legislation to recognize the desirability of publication of consolidated statements. This Act provided that every holding company should annex to its financial statements either a separate profit and loss statement and balance sheet for each subsidiary, or a consolidated profit and loss statement and a consolidated balance sheet of the holding company and its subsidiaries. Among the 'forty-two leaders sample', the holding companies existing at the time all adopted the alternative of consolidated statements. Some ten years later, one of these companies, McPherson, chose to change to the publication of separate statements for each subsidiary. The explanation for the change given by the chairman was that: 'Directors felt that the Consolidated Accounts . . . presented in the past, were unnecessarily complicated, and that the printing of the Balance Sheet of each Company separately would enable the information to be interpreted more readily.' At this time the company had four subsidiaries, one of which was located in New Zealand. The most important of these subsidiaries was Patience & Nicholson Ltd which, as a listed public company, was required to publish its own balance sheet apart from what was done by the parent company. This situation varied little for a number of years. Following expansion in New Zealand and by takeover, the position in 1959 was that the company now had seven subsidiaries and sub-subsidiaries and the parent company's annual report was becoming an extensive booklet. In 1960 the company reverted to the presentation of consolidated statements without comment from the directors.

AUDIT REPORT ON CONSOLIDATED STATEMENTS

Differing opinions were expressed on the interpretation of some parts of the 1938 Victorian Act. Two opinions published in the *Chartered Accountant in Australia* considered the consolidated statements did not have to be audited.[17] Among the 'forty-two leaders sample' it was found that in only one case did the auditor not comment on the consolidated statements. (In three companies there was a delay of one year between the issue of consolidated statements and the inclusion of an auditor's report thereon.) This does not wholly explain the situation unless some reference is made to the form of the audit report. Until 1958–9 a large proportion of the auditors' reports on consolidated statements was merely to say that the statements were 'correctly compiled in accordance with the Act', 'in accordance with the audited balance sheets of the subsidiaries and parent company', 'correctly prepared', or that the statement 'correctly summarizes the consolidated position'. Such a report did not guarantee very much more than the correctness of the arithmetic. (These reports are tabulated in Tables 8 and 9.) This form of auditor's report was particularly prevalent in New South Wales where there was no statutory requirement relating to consolidated statements. However, in Victoria where the matter rested on an interpretation of the Companies Act there was a surprising number of reports of this type as shown in Table 8. Many auditors of Victorian companies accepted the view that the consolidated statements came within the ambit of the audit and reported as to whether the consolidated statements presented a true and correct view of the position of the group (see Tables 8 and 9). The altered phrasing of the form of auditor's report in the Victorian Companies Act of 1958 and the Uniform Acts is reflected in the adoption of the form of report which expresses an opinion whether the statements present a 'true and fair view' (see Tables 8 and 9). This legis-

18 Holding Companies

lation removed any doubt of the auditor's responsibility by requiring him to report on every balance sheet and profit and loss account laid before the company in general meeting.

Among the 'forty-two leaders sample' there were a few instances before 1959 in which the one audit report covered both statements. The uniform nature of the audit report now required facilitates the

TABLE 8
Form of audit report on consolidated statements
27 Victorian companies
'42 leaders sample'

	No Report	Separate report			Composite report		
		Other	True and correct	True and fair	Other	True and correct	True and fair
1940a	1	5	7	—	—	1	—
1946b	—	6	10	—	—	2	—
1950	—	9	10	—	1	—	—
1954	—	13	8	—	1	1	—
1958	—	9	4	3	2	3	2
1959a	—	1	—	5	1	—	16
1962a	—	—	—	2	—	—	24
1963	—	—	—	—	—	—	27

a New Companies Acts effective in Victoria.
b Institute of Chartered Accountants in Australia recommendations issued.

TABLE 9
Form of audit report on consolidated statements
15 New South Wales companies
'42 leaders sample'

	No report	Separate report			Composite report		
		Other	True and correct	True and fair	Other	True and correct	True and fair
1940	1	1	—	—	—	—	—
1946	1	2	—	—	—	—	—
1950	1	7	1	—	—	—	—
1954	1	7	1	1	—	—	—
1958	1	5	3	2	—	—	—
1959	1	5	4	2	—	—	—
1962a	—	1b	—	—	—	—	14
1963	—	—	—	—	—	—	15

a New Companies Act effective in New South Wales.
b Company balances at 31 January hence consolidated statements were not required in this report.

presentation of a report covering both the parent and consolidated statements. This development is shown in Tables 8 and 9 which summarize the auditor's reports of the 'forty-two leaders sample' according to whether there is a separate report covering the consolidated statements or one composite report covering parent and consolidated statements.

The evidence of Tables 8 and 9 supports the conclusion that even before the advent of the Uniform Acts it was a fairly general practice for the auditor of a holding company to give some form of report on the consolidated statements.

ACCEPTANCE OF CONSOLIDATED STATEMENTS

The consequence of the Victorian Companies Act of 1938 was that all of the companies in the 'forty-two leaders sample' adopted the alternative of consolidated statements. In New South Wales during the years following 1938, companies either voluntarily adopted the practice of issuing group consolidated statements (or separate statements for each subsidiary) or did so as part of their agreement to be listed on the Stock Exchanges. This development in the publication of consolidated statements is further illustrated by G. M. Ewart's reference in 1948 to a study of sixty holding companies of which forty-seven were found to 'amplify' their legal balance sheets in some way.[18] Forty-two of the companies presented consolidated statements and four presented the separate statements of the subsidiaries. (Two companies had only one subsidiary and the other two had three subsidiaries.) The remaining company gave consolidated statements of the holding company and all of its subsidiaries except one together with a consolidated statement covering that subsidiary and its wholly-owned sub-subsidiary. Among the 'forty-two leaders sample' this trend left two New South Wales companies as the only companies not publishing consolidated statements until compelled to by the Uniform Acts passed in 1962. During the intervening period between the Victorian Act of 1938 and the Uniform Acts of 1962, consolidated statements had gradually been more widely recognized and recommended as desirable practice and the remaining problems in the preparation of such statements resolved. As these developments mainly relate to a period nearly two decades ahead of the stage the main theme had reached when this chapter began, it is not intended to pursue these details further at this stage but to resume the discussion of holding companies and consolidated statements in a later chapter.

19

Verification of Stock

During the early forties a particular aspect of reporting came under close scrutiny because of the events surrounding a certain spectacular financial swindle in the United States of America. This aspect of reporting relates to the authority for ascribing the value shown in the balance sheet to the item 'stock'. The terms 'stock' and 'stock-in-trade' are here regarded as synonymous.

The verification of the value of stock is an audit problem which has been debated frequently. The problems raised range from the organization of the counting of the stock to the more technical problems of determining that the goods do in fact agree with the physical and technical description applied to them, and the appropriateness of the values adopted for each particular item. For many years auditors in England and Australia relied on the decision in the Kingston Cotton Mill case[1] as sufficient authority for accepting a certificate from the appropriate company officer as evidence to substantiate the balance sheet figures for inventories. Some auditors placed reliance on the categorical statement in the judgment of Lindley, L.J. that: 'It is no part of an auditor's duty to take stock. No one contends that it is. He must rely on other people for details of the stock-in-trade in hand.' Other auditors gave a little more weight to the opinion of Lopes, L.J. that: 'He (the auditor) is justified in believing tried servants of the company in whom confidence is placed by the company. He is entitled to assume that they are honest, and to rely upon their representations, provided he takes reasonable care.'

The lack of adequate recognition of sound audit procedures and the more cautious approach of some auditors was reflected in the correspondence between a reader and the editor, O. R. MacDonald, of the *Commonwealth Journal of Accountancy*. MacDonald considered his reader's suggestion that the auditor should check some of the stock himself by picking haphazardly, half a dozen items and checking them to see whether they had been taken at the proper costs basis would be good procedure although he considered that obtaining the manager's certificate would meet the test of 'reasonable care'.[2]

Ten years later MacDonald was inclined to the view that the auditor's responsibilities were not so easily dismissed. MacDonald pointed out that, while the audit programme may be satisfactory to the proprietors, the qualification remains that stock has been accepted as correct on the certificate of one or more of the officers of the business. He considered that: 'While this statement may relieve the auditor of all responsibility in the matter, it is apparent that a less qualified report might be more acceptable to his principals.' To this end he suggested that the auditor: 'Whilst disclaiming any additional measure of responsibility, he may yet enhance his value to his principals by incorporating into his audit investigation some methods of investigation and supervision.' MacDonald was not unmindful of the consequence of these views and noted:

It might be objected that the auditor's liability, already heavy enough, will be further augmented if he voluntarily assumes a greater part in the verification of stock. This objection cannot be lightly disregarded. No auditor should undertake duties in connection with the audit of stock-in-trade without a clear understanding between himself and his principals as to the limitation of his responsibility.[3]

Practice at the time did not reflect the procedures discussed by MacDonald because many auditors had not even progressed to the point of securing the manager's certificate far less performing verification tests.

Amongst the 'forty-two leaders sample' the auditor's report of only eleven of the 'available sample' of twenty-nine companies adopted this procedure before 1939. Another nine companies did not hold any stocks, either because of the nature of their business or because all trading was carried out by subsidiaries. (Stocks were included in the aggregate statement of assets and liabilities of subsidiaries presented by two companies. These statements were not part of the statements included in the auditor's report as required by Statute.) There were therefore nine companies with stocks where the auditor did not include any reference to a certificate as authority for the value of stocks.

Late in 1939 the whole question of the verification of stock was highlighted in an American incident referred to as 'the McKesson and Robbins incident'.[4] The significance of the incident lay in the acceptance by the auditor of certificates from the head of the company as evidence for stocks. It transpired that these were purely fictional in respect of the foreign crude drug activities of the firm. There was in fact $21,000,000 of fictitious assets on the books. Although the company suffered a cash loss of $2,869,482, it was strong and large enough to withstand the shock and continue in business. The affairs of McKesson and Robbins received worldwide publicity and were reported in Australian accountancy journals in detail.[5] The incident focused the attention of the accounting profession on the question of the verification of stock by auditors, and stimulated discussion on the matter.

On the available evidence it is difficult to draw any firm conclusion about the immediate Australian reaction to this incident as expressed in audit procedure and as indicated by auditors' reports. Among the 'forty-two leaders sample' in the 1939 reports of two companies, Peters and Herald, the auditor deleted his previous reference to the authority for the stock figure. It is difficult to know whether this was a reaction to the McKesson and Robbins incident or an interpretation of the situation arising from the new Victorian Companies Act of 1938. (At least one company, Brick, appears to have been in the reverse situation, for the auditor of this company first included mention in 1940 of a certificate covering the value of stock. This company is included in the seven mentioned next.) Among the 'forty-two leaders sample', in the reports of another seven companies, mention of such a certificate was introduced by the auditor at later dates, even as late as 1957. Each of these cases was a newly listed public company. However, this was only half the companies added to the 'available sample' after 1939, suggesting that a movement away from relying on such a certificate was beginning. In 1945 R. K. Yorston examined seventy-seven balance sheets and found:

It was interesting to note the relatively small number of accounts which indicated that the value of 'stock' was included in the balance sheet according to the certificate of an official. Only eighteen of seventy-seven companies indicated such a certification. The certification being made by: the company's officials, 6; the directors, 2; Other certifying officials were: general manager, manager, managing director, secretary, chairman of directors, the management, and in two cases it was not indicated by whom the certification was made.[6]

It would appear that the majority felt that the Kingston Cotton Mill case could not be any longer relied on and that the McKesson and Robbins affair had highlighted the need for the auditor to go beyond receiving a certificate from an official of the company. The auditor would need to verify the stock to his own satisfaction.

In 1950 the Research Co-ordination Committee of the Institute of Chartered Accountants in Australia approved the issue of a recommendation on the audit of stock prepared by the Victorian Research Society of the Institute which stated that: 'It is not sufficient merely to accept that value [of stock shown in the accounts] on the certificate of an officer of the company, relying on the fact that this is mentioned in the report.'[7] The recommendation drew one correspondent's rebuke on the grounds that auditors' responsibilities remained as they were in 1896 and that one could rely on the Kingston Cotton Mill case.[8] Other auditors joined the debate and it continued through 1951 and 1952 in the columns of the *Chartered Accountant in Australia.* The reaction to the Victorian Research Society recommendation indicated the presence of a difference in opinions borne out in the responses to a questionnaire sent to members of the Institute of Chartered Accountants by the Chartered Accountants Research and Service Foundation in 1958. The Research Society Committee concluded that there was not unanimity in the professional definition of this audit activity. It was considered by 183 of the 244 who replied that: 'The auditor was NOT justified in giving his statutory report on the balance sheet without qualification if he merely accepted the certificate of directors or responsible officers on the value of stock-in-trade.'[9] At the same time 'the committee was surprised to receive so many (113) affirmative answers' to the question of whether the auditor should state that stock valuations were on the basis of a certificate received by the auditor from the officers of the company. As the committee noted in explanation of its surprise: 'So much has been written to show that the auditor gains no protection from such a statement in his statutory report. It is not a qualification of his opinion, nor does it make clear that the auditor takes no responsibility, even if he were justified in taking that view.'[10]

Australian auditing practice is influenced strongly by developments in England. The Institute of Chartered Accountants in England and Wales issued a statement in 1962 supporting the need for appropriate tests to confirm the manager's certificate. Likewise the standard auditing reference in Australia by R. A. Irish[11] suggests physical tests although recognizing that some auditors oppose them.

By 1961 the reports of only two of the 'forty-two leaders sample' still retained in the auditor's report, or as a notation in the balance

19 Verification of Stock

sheet, a reference to a certificate covering the stock value. In the reports of all the other companies the reference had been deleted, the last references occurring as shown in Table 10. It is considered

TABLE 10
Deletion of auditor's reference to stock certificate
'42 leaders sample'

	No. of companies
1947	1
1950	1
1951	2
1953	1
1955	1
1956	1
1957	2
1958	2
1959	1
1960	1
1961	1

that the present position as revealed in the reports of the 'forty-two leaders sample' reflects the 'post McKesson and Robbins' interpretation that the auditor is not protected by a statement ascribing responsibility for the valuation of stock to an official of the company. It is interesting to note that for both of the companies in the 'forty-two leaders sample' in whose reports reference is still made to the authority for the stock valuation, there is included in the inventory a substantial portion of manufactured or partly manufactured goods. In both of these cases the reference is by notation in the balance sheet against the asset rather than a specific reference in the auditor's report. This in turn raises the further question of how far the auditor's responsibility goes and also how far his work will be permitted to go in checking the internal cost records of the company.

In conclusion it appears that the principles arising out of the McKesson and Robbins incident, given such wide publicity in the forties, has displaced in practice the dicta of the Kingston Cotton Mill case with its consequent effect on this particular aspect of financial reporting.

It is also of interest to contrast the uncertainty which may remain concerning the auditor's responsibility with the development of clearly defined responsibilities of directors concerning the value of current assets including stock. The 1961 Uniform Acts introduced a new aspect to reporting by requiring the directors' report of public companies to state: 'where the directors are of the opinion that any current assets would not at least realise the value at which they are shown in the accounts of the company their opinion as to the amount that those current assets might reasonably be expected to realise in the ordinary course of business of the company' (s.162(6)(d)). It will be shown later that these developments were a reaction to unfortunate financial events just as the development in respect of the verification of stock by auditors was a response to the McKesson and Robbins incident.

20

Format of Statements

That accountants should have bothered to argue 'why the assets appear on the right hand side of the balance sheet'[1] may appear at first to suggest a failure to realize the important issues that required attention. Alternatively, it may be regarded as the beginning of questioning by accountants as to why particular practices are followed instead of blindly obeying traditional practices. 'Tradition dies hard' may well be said when, twenty years later, a textbook author, reviewing another author's work, queries 'whether it is desirable to teach students at the elementary level'[2] to put the assets on the left of the balance sheet instead of on the right as in other textbooks. The traditional balance sheet, by its nature, was hardly designed to maximize communication of information. Not only did it largely consist of a conglomeration of items arranged without particular meaning, but its mathematical precision created a false impression of exactitude. As G. L. C. Touche writing in the *Chartered Accountant in Australia* in 1933 expressed it:

The exact balancing of the two sides of the conventional Balance-sheets is a legacy from the double-entry ledger, and adds nothing but mystery and confusion in the minds of those not acquainted with book-keeping and even, if we are to believe all we hear, in the minds of learned Judges.[3]

One approach to improve the traditional balance sheet emphasized the adoption of classified asset groups to highlight working capital or to highlight the extent to which the share capital was represented by fixed assets. Another approach, which included the concept of classified groups, proposed a departure from traditional format to adopt a narrative sequence which in many instances was given a title expressed in everyday language rather than purely technical accounting terminology.

The adoption of what were regarded as revolutionary and heretical ideas was not an easy matter, in the face of an ingrained prejudice for traditional form. As A. A. Fitzgerald expressed it: 'The grave danger which faces the accountancy profession in this respect is the danger that it may become hidebound by tradition and may cling to conventional forms long after they have outlived such usefulness as they may once have possessed.'[4]

A. Clunies Ross who was probably the first Australian accountant to put into print a proposal for a narrative balance sheet, proposed a balance sheet arranged under such generalized titles as:

>The Company Owns
>The Company Owes

which he suggested might be adopted 'if the object of the publication of the figures is to provide information "to be understood of the common people" '. But in spite of his own obvious creativity, he showed little hope for its adoption at that time and confessed, 'I have not sufficient courage to put it forward to any ordinary board of directors.'[5] Another obstacle to the adoption of the narrative form of statement, at least by Victorian companies, was the form of balance sheet that had been prescribed since the amended Act of 1910, which was set out in 'tee' form instead of the narrative form which was represented by the schedule to the 1896 Act. (The narrative form is really quite old. For example, the English shipping company, Peninsula and Orient Steam Navigation Co., used this form of presentation between 1854 and 1875.)[6] It is hardly surprising that, while some complained of this restriction in the 1910 Victorian Act, there were, at the same time, those in New South Wales who equally complained that in that State the Act did not outline a model balance sheet format. Up to this time New South Wales companies had not shown any desire to utilize this freedom by experimenting with new statement formats.

The Victorian Companies Act of 1938 did not prescribe any format of statement. The freedom of form allowed by this Act provided Victorian companies with an opportunity for experimentation and the development of new ideas. This statutory freedom has not been impeded by the activities of the accounting professional bodies. When, in 1944, the Institute of Chartered Accountants in England and Wales issued its Recommendations on Accounting Principles, the pronouncements covered a number of aspects of presentation of financial statements. But the Institute made no attempt to prescribe any particular format. This example was followed in the recommendations of the Australian Institute issued in

20 Format of Statements

1946. A. A. Fitzgerald made this question of balance sheet presentation an object of his crusading zeal. While surveying the whole problem of presentation of financial statements he pointed out that: 'The dominant considerations should be clarity of expression, the convenience of the reader and the suitability of the form to the main object of balance sheet analysis—a study of the trends in the financial structure from year to year.'[7] Fitzgerald discussed a number of proposals to improve the presentation of financial statements. Of these proposals the following are discussed separately later: classification of assets and liabilities in groups with group totals, use of tabulations in the main body of the balance sheet, inclusion of comparative figures, expression of amounts in whole pounds, and inclusion of proposed appropriations of profit. In this chapter the discussion is concerned directly with the remaining problem area which Fitzgerald identified, the use of narrative format.

An early instance of the narrative form was the annual report issued by the Adelaide firm of Crapp & Hawkes Ltd in 1941. At the time the South Australian Companies Act provided that the balance sheet should be in a traditional 'tee' format set down in the schedule to the Act. The balance sheet of Crapp & Hawkes Ltd proceeded in the sequence: fixed assets, plus current assets, deduct current liabilities and provisions, leaves total net assets representing shareholders' total investment.[8] If we, not unreasonably, attribute the format of this balance sheet to the secretary of the company, C. A. E. Sullivan, we may then conclude that he was putting into practice what he himself had advocated previously through the columns of the *Australian Accountant*.[9] The following year Manton & Sons Limited, Melbourne retailers, produced a narrative form trading and profit and loss appropriation statement which must be regarded as remarkable at that time.[10] The first company among the 'forty-two leaders sample' to adopt the narrative form of statement was Olympic. It is surely not without significance that A. A. Fitzgerald was, at the time, auditor of the company. The presentation adopted by Olympic was well received. The *Advertiser* in Adelaide commented on 13 August 1946:

This reflects a growing accounting philosophy—as yet too little in evidence—that the function of the accountant is not merely to present an arithmetically correct statement of the result of the year's operations, and the financial position of the business at a point of time, but also to do so in a manner which the average shareholder can most readily grasp.

By 1948 it was possible to list thirteen public companies as using the narrative form of balance sheet. These included two of the 'forty-two leaders sample', Olympic and Herald. What is perhaps more startling is that this form was adopted by representative companies from groups which are usually regarded as the most closely tied to traditional practices, including the City Mutual Life Assurance Society Limited which presented its reports in narrative form for the year ended 31 December 1947.[11]

The adoption of the narrative form spread slowly in the early years of its use. Table 11 shows that it took eight years after

TABLE 11
Adoption of narrative form of 'balance sheet'
'42 leaders sample'

	Size of available sample[a]	No. of companies	% of available sample	Notes
1944	32	1	3	Olympic adopts narrative form
1946	33	1	3	I.C.A.A. recommendations
1950	38	10	26	
1952	38	14	37	
1955	41	14	34	
1960	42	15	36	
1962	42	15	36	Uniform Acts
1965	42	16	38	
1968	42	17	41	

[a] See explanatory note, p. 3.

Olympic adopted the narrative form for one third of the 'forty-two leaders sample' to adopt this type of presentation. At the present time, little advance has been made on this level of penetration. This can be attributed to a more flexible interpretation of the traditional 'tee' format. The amount of detail required to be shown by many companies has reached the point where the 'tee' or double sided format requires the use of a double page layout. This improves the clarity of presentation and approaches closely a narrative form running down two pages. Table 11 shows only four-tenths of the 'forty-two leaders sample' using the narrative statement in 1968. However, only 45 per cent of the sample companies have not at any time used the narrative form of presentation. The results of the investigation of the 'forty-two leaders sample' are consistent with the results of enquiries made by other investigators using other samples at different times.

In 1948 R. A. Irish examined twenty-six 'well-known public

20 Format of Statements

companies' and found: 'Two used vertical reports for both balance sheet and profit and loss account, two others had the profit and loss statement in that form, and the remainder were in the orthodox horizontal lay-out.'[12] R. J. Chambers examined certain aspects of 250 company reports in 1956. His results of 10 per cent using narrative form in 1948 and 29 per cent using it in 1955 also fits into the pattern of the 'forty-two leaders sample'. His investigation was classified by state of incorporation and size of company as shown in the accompanying Tables 12 and 13 quoted from his report. R. J. Chambers pointed out that these results confirm the opinion that the movement towards this type of statement 'appears

TABLE 12
Form of balance sheet analysis by place of registration

Place of registration	1948 Account	1948 narrative	1955 Account	1955 narrative	Net increase in use of narrative form
New South Wales	97	2	78	21	19
Victoria	75	15	59	31	16
South Australia	20	7	17	10	3
Queensland	23	—	18	5	5
Tasmania	7	—	4	3	3
Western Australia	4	—	2	2	2
Total	226	24	178	72	48

TABLE 13
Form of balance sheet—analysis by size

Size of companies	1948 Account	1948 narrative	1955 Account	1955 narrative	Narrative form users in 1955 but not in 1948
Class 1	45	6	15	1	1
Class 2	98	8	40	18	13
Class 3	39	6	47	23	15
Class 4	19	1	36	13	10
Class 5	25	3	40	17	9
Total	226	24	178	72	48

The final column of Table 13 is not equal to the difference between the two 'narrative' columns, class by class, because of the shift in the size classification of some companies.

TABLE 14
Sequence of narrative form 'balance sheet'
'42 leaders sample'

	Beginning with	
	Assets %	Shareholders' funds %
1944	—	100
1953	—	100
1954	7	93
1957	15	85
1960	13	87
1965	19	81
1968	30	70

to have been supported initially in Victoria and South Australia'. The location of this practical support coincides with the concentration of support from Victorian authors such as Fitzgerald. He also concluded that the trend towards the narrative form was 'not confined to any class of business or to any size group'.[13] A survey of thirty-six Western Australian companies in 1957 produced a result of 'a slight majority' of companies using the narrative form. This apparent favour of the narrative form is probably the result of the composition of the particular sample of companies investigated.[14]

A great variety of format has been used in practice. The diversity of form makes it almost impossible to present a statistical summary, particularly with a sample of forty-two companies. An attempt to find any discernible trends in the sequence preferred did reveal two characteristics among the 'forty-two leaders sample'. The first is the choice of shareholders' funds or assets to begin the presentation. Table 14 shows that there is a clear preference for a sequence beginning with shareholders' funds. The alternative of beginning with the assets found limited favour among companies using the narrative form in the last decade. A similar pattern was found also by R. J. Chambers in his examination of 250 companies.[15] The second characteristic found in the 'forty-two leaders sample' was a tendency towards a narrative sequence which highlights the working capital during the first decade in which the narrative form was being developed. However Table 15 shows that since 1955, the trend has turned against emphasizing working capital and moved towards emphasizing the total assets of the company (or the group in the case of consolidated statements). These two presentations

TABLE 15
Emphasis of sequence in narrative 'balance sheets'
'42 leaders sample'

	Emphasis given to	
	Total Assets %	Working capital %
1944	—	100
1948	20	80
1954	40	60
1955	43	57
1960	60	40
1965	62	38
1968	59	41

are incompatible. This trend away from emphasizing working capital is probably related to a growing awareness that, without further information as to the nature of the items making up this item, it is a meaningless measure and a superficial reading of the balance sheet may not truly convey the position of the company. This is perhaps best illustrated among the 'forty-two leaders sample' by events relating to Ansett. In the 1962 annual report of this company the consolidated balance sheet showed 'Current Liabilities Payable within One Year' of £12,273,041 which exceeded the 'Current Assets' of £8,505,420. In the 1963 annual report 'Current Assets' of £10,049,657 exceeded the 'Current Liabilities Payable within One Year' of £6,151,050. The company now showed a separate item of 'Long Term Liabilities—Due within One Year' which had previously been included in the category of 'Current Liabilities'. Overlooking the probable schedule of payments through the year and concentrating on the static balance sheet position may well have conveyed an inaccurate view of the company's financial position.

The most recent development has been a narrative format which allows for the presentation of both parent and consolidated figures in the same statement. Six of the 'forty-two leaders sample' used such a presentation in 1968. An interesting development of this is L. A. Schumer's proposal that this objective of combining both parent and consolidated statements be combined with a traditional 'tee' form of presentation.[16]

The narrative form of statement still retains a significant part in company reporting. It is interesting that, even though there is evidence of reversion to the double sided balance sheet using a double page spread, the freedom of structure and description of the narrative form goes along with this change. The adoption by some companies of the narrative form therefore may be regarded as a most significant factor in improving the presentation of balance sheets which, on superficial inspection, appear to adhere to the traditional double sided or 'tee' format.

The balance sheet has been concentrated on because there are very few reports which include any reasonable degree of information from the operating statements (manufacturing, trading and profit and loss). The information given relating to profit and loss appropriation statements is by nature susceptible to a narrative presentation. The use of a narrative sequence for this information may not presume necessarily such adaptability in the presentation of the balance sheet. At 1968 among the 'forty-two leaders sample' only four companies used the double sided or 'tee' presentation of the profit and loss appropriation statement (A. Gypsum, B. Tobacco, Dunlop and Repco). This is clearly a more popular application of the narrative form than the balance sheet.

Without the freedom given to Victorian companies by the Companies Act of 1938 these developments could not have occurred with Victorian companies. The developments themselves must be credited to the individual initiative of the accountants and executives responsible for the company reports.

21

Classification in the Balance Sheet

A closely related matter to the format of the financial statements is the classification (if any) of the items shown in the balance sheet. A detailed examination of the development of the practice of classifying the balance sheet must go 'hand in hand' with a discussion of the relevant terminology, on the grounds that a classification scheme cannot be applied until there is knowledge of the meaning to be attributed to the terminology in which that scheme is expressed. The attempt to find a more adequate definition of terminology used has been coupled with a significant change in terminology, due to both voluntary and statutory factors examined in this chapter.

It has been indicated already how an empirical investigation by A. A. Fitzgerald found the classification of balance sheets to be inadequate in 1928.[1] There were not any statutory obligations to serve as a guide because the schedule appended to the Victorian Companies Acts of 1896 and 1910 did not require the assets or liabilities to be grouped in any particular manner.

Edwin V. Nixon, in a lecture given in 1924, suggested an appropriate method of classification and terminology from the viewpoint of either creditor, owner, or potential owner would be a classification of assets into liquid assets, circulating assets, fixed assets and intangible assets. This classification 'corresponds generally with the order in which they would be realised to satisfy liabilities', noted Nixon. He suggested the classification of liabilities into those payable on demand, that is, at the expiration of the term of credit usually allowed by the custom of the particular trade, and those payable at a fixed future date. If, however, there is any possibility of liquidation, he suggested the appropriate classification would be secured liabilities, partly-secured liabilities, and unsecured liabilities.[2]

Liquid and circulating assets were at this time regarded as making up the floating assets. This was given recognition in the Acts passed in Queensland in 1931, in South Australia in 1934 and in New South Wales in 1936, which could be complied with by using a classification such as Nixon had suggested. These Acts could be interpreted as requiring the balance sheet to contain 'such particulars as are necessary' to distinguish the amounts respectively of fixed and floating assets, or requiring the balance sheet 'to distinguish the amounts . . .' This uncertainty of interpretation is reflected in the reports of the New South Wales companies included in the 'forty-two leaders sample'. The statements of only six of the 'available sample' of ten companies affected by the New South Wales Companies Act were presented in a classified form in the first year after the Act became operative. The remaining four companies adopted a classified balance sheet in 1939, 1946, 1949 and 1959 respectively. What is perhaps even more surprising is that only three of the companies adopted the terminology of the Act, i.e. floating assets, two adopted the terminology of current assets and one did not name the groups at all until 1948. None of the Victorian companies in the 'forty-two leaders sample' have at any time used the terminology of floating assets. It therefore appears reasonable to conclude that the terminology adopted by the Statute of 'floating' assets was either considered to be synonymous with 'current' assets or else was not accepted by many persons as a satisfactory description. The problem of the literal meaning of these accounting terms was illustrated by C. Hungerford's account of the good ship *Malabar* which sailed for Australia as a fixed asset but after foundering at the port entrance, became a floating asset in the form of an insurance claim.[3] The failure of companies to follow the Queensland, South Australia and New South Wales Statutes and the continued lack of attention to classification in States where there was not any statutory obligation for classification of the balance sheet is reflected in C. B. Harvey's observation in 1936 that to secure group totals for analysing reports:

More often than not . . . necessitates the inquirer taking out paper and pencil, and engaging in an arithmetical calculation for the purpose of obtaining this information . . . In these days of rush and struggle, business men are taking a different viewpoint and are asking our profession why we make it necessary for them to do this extra work themselves . . . In other words, they enquire as to why we, as accountants, do not use our influence to see that this special work is done by our various clients before the issue of their annual published accounts.[4]

21 Classification in the Balance Sheet

Other writers at this time were seeking a better and more acceptable basis of classification than the fixed and floating subdivisions of assets implied. C. B. Harvey suggested a balance sheet classification grouping using the terminology of shareholders' funds, fixed or long-term liabilities, current liabilities, fixed assets, current assets, goodwill account and other debit balances.[5] O. R. MacDonald, former editor of the *Commonwealth Journal of Accountancy*, was another supporter of the classification of current, fixed and intangible assets with current and deferred liabilities and proprietors' funds. He recognized the difficulties of applying this classification. His test for a current asset was whether or not it is readily convertible into cash, and constantly being altered in form or value in the course of business transactions. His classification of liabilities was based on the proposition that deferred liabilities are those 'which will have to be met only in the event of the cessation of the business, or which do not become due for payment for some considerable time'. Current liabilities, on the other hand, were defined as 'those which are payable immediately or in the near future'.[6]

At this point a significant change in statutory requirements for the development of classification concepts occurred with the passing of the Victorian Companies Act in 1938. This Act did away with the restriction of a prescribed form of balance sheet in the schedule to the Act, giving a new freedom of presentation to the large number of companies incorporated in Victoria. The Act prescribed that there should be disclosed: 'Such particulars as are necessary to disclose the general nature of the liabilities and the assets of the company and to distinguish between the various classes of the assets' (s.124). The Act made no attempt to prescribe what the classes of assets should be. It was also open to an alternative reading depending on how the sentence was 'punctuated' in a similar way to the Acts of the other three States referred to previously. Victorian companies reacted little better to the statute than those in New South Wales had reacted to the 1936 New South Wales Act. In the first year after the Act was passed only twelve out of the seventeen Victorian companies in the 'available sample' had included a classification scheme in the balance sheet. All of these companies adopted the terminology of 'current' assets.

This scheme of classification incorporating categories of current assets and current liabilities subsequently has established itself as the recognized form of classification applicable to the balance sheet.

This 'modern' terminology of current assets, etc., received a degree of professional status when the Institute of Chartered

Accountants in England and Wales incorporated it in its Recommendations on Accounting Principles issued in 1944, and which were taken up in substance by the Institute of Chartered Accountants in Australia in 1946. The recommendations put forward a balance sheet classification consisting of the following groups: share capital, reserves, debentures, mortgages and long-term liabilities, amounts owing to subsidiary undertakings, current liabilities and provisions, fixed assets, shares in and amounts owing from subsidiary undertakings, current assets and preliminary and issue expenses. The Institute recommendations tackled the thorny problem of definition of terms. Current liabilities were defined by example but long-term liabilities were defined as 'not due for payment until after the lapse of one year from the date of the balance sheet'. Current liabilities are then presumably those payable within one year. Current assets were defined as assets 'held for realisation in the ordinary course of business'. The twelve month period is implied however by the recommendation that 'debts of material amount not due until after the lapse of one year from the date of the balance sheet should be separately grouped and suitably described'.

Legislative recognition of the 'current' terminology was to follow later. The provisions referred to earlier of the Queensland, South Australian and New South Wales Acts requiring the balance sheets to distinguish between fixed and floating assets, were derived directly from the English Companies Act of 1929. This Act was considered by the Committee on Company Law Amendment in 1945. This committee pointed out that the Act did not define the terms 'fixed' and 'floating' assets. Such a definition was missing also in Australian legislation. The committee considered such a definition desirable and, in its recommendations, proposed some change in terminology and the definition of 'fixed' assets as assets not held for sale or conversion into cash and 'current' assets as cash and assets held for conversion into cash.[7] The findings of this committee, though prepared for the English Board of Trade, have had a considerable effect on Australian legislation. A. A. Fitzgerald commented on the proposed definition of current assets thus:

This distinction relies on the test of intention, though it might be urged that in the long run every asset is intended to be converted into cash and that therefore a more satisfying basis for the distinction would be that of time, current assets being those which it is intended to convert, and which in the ordinary course of business can be converted into cash within a relatively short period—say one year.[8]

The Institute recommendations were not followed immediately.

21 Classification in the Balance Sheet

At the annual meeting of the South Australian division of the Institute of Chartered Accountants the chairman, A. L. Slade, while recognizing the authority of the directors of a company in such matters, upbraided the members of his Institute, claiming that: 'Unfortunately, an examination of published balance sheets discloses tendencies to adhere to the old and out-of-date system of presenting assets, liabilities and shareholders' capital notwithstanding the pronouncements of the Institute for improved presentation.'[9] The validity of Slade's comments was supported later by the publication of the results of a study conducted by a South Australian group of the Institute of Chartered Accountants in Australia in 1949, which reported that: 'The accounts examined, generally speaking, disclosed an extremely unsatisfactory classification of current liabilities and provisions. The survey disclosed (again speaking broadly), a classification of assets which did not go as far as that recommended by the Institute.'[10]

A measure of the application of the classification scheme and terminology developed and advocated by the individuals and bodies referred to may be found in the practice of the 'forty-two leaders sample'. Table 16 shows that by 1939 two-thirds of the 'available sample' were presenting a classified balance sheet, i.e. seven years before the issue of the Institute recommendations. The Institute recommendations in fact, do not appear to have had any dramatic effect on these companies at all. The increase in the proportion of

TABLE 16
*Adoption of classified balance sheet presentation
'42 leaders sample'*

	Size of available sample[a]	No. of companies	% of available sample	Notes
1934	21	1	5	S.A. Companies Act
1936	26	5	19	N.S.W. Companies Act
1938	30	13	43	Vic. Companies Act
1939	30	20	67	
1944	32	22	69	I.C.A.E.W. recommendations
1946	33	25	75	I.C.A.A. recommendations
1950	38	30	79	
1955	41	35	85	
1960	42	41	98	
1962	42	42	100	Uniform Acts

[a] See explanatory note, p. 3.

classified balance sheets appears to have been rather the result of a slow and gradual acceptance among the companies.

The results of other investigators may be compared with the results set out in Table 16. R. K. Yorston found a less satisfactory position in a sample of companies he investigated in 1945. However, he selected a larger sample than the 'forty-two leaders sample'. This wider selection may have included a greater proportion of smaller companies and companies which may tend to be 'followers' in new practices. R. K. Yorston found that only in thirty-nine of seventy-seven companies' reports examined, was the balance sheet classified. Of the thirty-nine companies, thirty-one were using the classification of current assets while eight retained the term floating assets.[11] A much more satisfactory position was revealed in an examination made by R. A. McInnes, who in 1954 found a classified presentation used by twenty of twenty-four Queensland company reports examined. Of the reports of twenty-six companies incorporated other than in Queensland examined by McInnes, twenty-five were classified.[12]

At this point it is appropriate to consider another aspect of the problem of terminology which was pursued by A. A. Fitzgerald. In an attempt to secure clarity, Fitzgerald argued against the term 'Fixed Asset' as being an inappropriate classification heading. Alternatively to the Institute's recommendations, he proposed the classification of assets into two main classes—current and non-current—which he believed would be more logical for the following reasons:

(a) Fixed and current classes are not necessarily disjunctively exhaustive, unless fixed is the antithesis of current in every respect. It has already been shown in discussions on the British Companies Act, 1948, that there are some assets which are not properly included in either class in the terms of the definitions used in accounting in United Kingdom. The true antithesis of current is non-current.

(b) The term 'fixed' is an exaggeration. No asset is permanently fixed, except possibly land, and even that, despite Ricardo's famous reference to 'original and indestructible powers', is by no means always fixed. Consider the American dust-bowl or the extent of soil erosion and depletion of soil fertility in some parts of Australia.

(c) The term 'fixed' is apt to be misinterpreted: in the accounting (or the economic) sense it does not mean immobile. Moreover, it is used in different connotations in such technical accounting terms as 'fixed costs' and 'fixed budget'.[13]

A. A. Fitzgerald no doubt has left a legacy of this thinking amongst his students and successors at the University of Melbourne.

21 Classification in the Balance Sheet

In the 'forty-two leaders sample' there is to be found one instance of the use of the term 'non-current'. Olympic adopted this classification from 1957 to 1959 inclusive. As has already been pointed out, A. A. Fitzgerald was at the time the auditor of this company. There is an echo of this logic in the specification in the English Companies Act of 1967 that headings for assets must identify separately fixed assets, current assets, and 'assets that are neither fixed nor current' (second schedule par. 4(2)).

The Uniform Acts of 1962 revised the statutory recognition of balance sheet classification. The references to floating assets in the Queensland, South Australian and New South Wales Acts were finally superseded by the term 'current assets' in the requirement to show: 'The reserves provisions liabilities fixed assets and current assets classified separately under headings appropriate to the company's business' (ninth schedule, clause 2(1)(g)). The interpretation of this requirement and the classification applied to each of the other items required to be disclosed, is left to the discretion of the individual company. Recognition is given to the desirability of stating separately the liabilities payable not later than twelve months after the date to which the accounts are made up and the amounts that are payable later than twelve months after that date.

Further recognition of the classification of liabilities followed in the Public Borrowings Acts which introduced a requirement applicable to borrowing corporations requiring a note indicating the debts receivable and liabilities payable not later than two years, later than two years but not later than five years, and later than five years from the date of the balance sheet. This provision is discussed later in the context of the Public Borrowings Acts. An example with similar intent is the provision enacted in the English Companies Act of 1967 (second schedule, par. 8(1)(d)) to show separately loans repayable more than five years after the date of the accounts together with the repayment terms and rates of interest.

In 1963 the Institute of Chartered Accountants in Australia revised its recommendations. These are now stated in more general terms than previously and recognize as 'normally appropriate headings for summaries and classifications' the terms issued share capital, reserves, liabilities, fixed assets and current assets.

The evidence of the 'forty-two leaders sample', supported by the results of other investigations, indicate that there has been a steadily growing acceptance of the practice of presenting a classified balance sheet. It seems that the important issue now is a closer examination of the specific items included under the classification headings rather than the broad categories of classification adopted in the balance sheet. In the adjudicators' report on the 1967 A.I.M. Award attention was drawn to current liabilities 'masquerading as long-term liabilities when these were borrowings falling due in the current year' and to long-term debts classified as current assets. In the 1968 report the adjudicators reiterated their opinion noting that this situation persists in 'too many reports'.

The absence of specific statutory requirements and definitions, as outlined herein, has meant that the voluntary forces have had to formulate the standards applicable to company reports in this respect. These standards established by professional practice have proved adequate to complete the appropriate classification of the assets and liabilities in terms of the broadly stated requirements of the Act.

22

Western Australia

While significant developments in the company statutes were taking place in the rest of Australia, in Western Australia the Companies Act remained substantially as it was in 1893. This State was, as the state president of the Commonwealth Institute of Accountants observed: 'Essentially a country of primary production, and its wealth or otherwise is derived chiefly from this source.'[1] With the economy of the State being predominantly agricultural, the role of companies had not developed as in the more populous and industrialized States. The main activities involving large capital aggregations were public utilities and the gold mining companies, many of the latter being based in England. It is therefore unlikely that in the early years of this century there was much need or demand for amended legislation such as arose from the land boom in Victoria for example.

However, there were stirrings in the State. R. C. Crowther tells us in 1936 that: 'For some years past Accountants and others affected by Company Legislation have realised the necessity for the drafting of a new Companies Act, or at least the amendment of or additions to the existing Act.' Crowther gives us an account of the preliminary steps that were taken in the business community. 'In 1934 Perth Chamber of Commerce initiated a movement which resulted in the passage, in that year, at the meeting of the Associated Chambers of Commerce in Melbourne, of a resolution affirming the desirability of uniform legislation in Company matters.'[2] In February 1935 the Perth Chamber of Commerce convened a meeting of the Perth and Fremantle Chambers of Commerce, the Chamber of Manufactures, the Law Society, the Junior Chamber of Commerce, the Australasian Institute of Secretaries, the Institute of Chartered Accountants, the Commonwealth Institute of Accountants, the Federal Institute of Accountants, and the Perth Stock Exchange. After much discussion, it became apparent that a number of these groups were not prepared to promote the idea of a completely new Act, although they each wanted action on particular matters. The conference sent to the Minister for Justice what were, in effect, the proposals of the New South Wales division of the Institute of Chartered Accountants in Australia. However, the Minister replied that the government was in favour of a major review rather than piecemeal amendment, and the end of the Parliamentary session made this impracticable.[3] On 13 November 1940 the Minister introduced into Parliament a Bill to amend the Companies Act, and later a Joint Select Committee was appointed to consider the Bill. In his second reading speech on 26 November 1940, the Minister expressed the view that: 'Happenings in this State during recent years, particularly in connection with the operation of so-called investment companies and the flotation of mining ventures, have definitely indicated that the present State laws are inadequate to deal with the new conditions.'[4] The Minister also supported the principle of uniform company law throughout Australia, and indicated that the Bill sought to conform with legislation in the other States as far as possible. He also acknowledged at this juncture that the reporting provisions of the Bill were modelled on those of the Victorian Companies Act of 1938. The Select Committee later was turned into a Royal Commission, thereby increasing its powers and, at the same time, facilitating the parliamentary process of the Bill. The Bill as amended by the Royal Commission was restored to the notice paper on 20 August 1941. It was debated through the following months but was not taken up in the new year. Then in May 1942 Parliament was prorogued. The Seventeenth Parliament opened on 5 August 1943 and the Bill, after being debated by the Legislative Council, was finally passed on 8 October 1943. Although the Act was passed in 1943 it was not to be proclaimed to operate sooner than six months after the cessation of hostilities of the war. It was later intended to be proclaimed to operate from October 1947. Administrative difficulties delayed the operation of the Act a further three months.

Before the Act became effective an attempt was made to have it redrafted and brought in as an even more up-to-date measure. This move was initiated by A. A. Fitzgerald and was given serious consideration. The Deputy Registrar of Companies has recounted the story:

Some of you will remember that Mr. A. A. Fitzgerald, who is well known in the accountancy world, last September suggested through the press that our new Act be brought up-to-date—that is, in line with the recommendation of the Cohen Committee and the Institute of Chartered Accountants in England—before its proclamation. The suggestion was referred to the Registrar by the Attorney-General. The Registrar expressed the view that the new Act represented a great improvement on the Act of 1893, and it brought our company legislation substantially into uniformity with the Acts of the Eastern States. Further, any attempt at that stage to adopt Mr. Fitzgerald's suggestion would have had the effect of delaying indefinitely the supersession of the archaic Act of 1893. The new English Act of 1947 embodying the recommendations of the Cohen Committee was introduced in the House of Lords and more than 300 amendments to the bill were moved. It could not be hoped that a Bill to radically amend our 1943 Act would have a smooth passage through Parliament. In other words, it was better to have half a loaf of bread presently than no bread for a long time.[5]

Thus Western Australian companies were, for the first time, made subject to statutory requirements to disclose their financial position. The legislation followed the 1938 Victorian Companies Act requiring the publication of sufficient profit and loss detail to indicate the operating result of the company, as well as the publication of a balance sheet. Holding companies were required to publish consolidated statements or separate statements for each subsidiary. Provision was made for proprietary companies and companies meeting the relevant tests were exempted from the requirement to publish financial statements.

23

I.C.A.A. Recommendations

The development of standards of disclosure in the period preceding World War II may be said to be the development of the statutory obligations for disclosure coupled with the efforts of the Stock Exchanges. It has been shown that it was not until 1936 that the second major State had any compulsory requirement for companies to publish financial statements. The only State not to impose this obligation until after the war, Western Australia, represented a very small segment of the Australian economy. The existence of a measure of compulsion provided a framework within which other voluntary agencies could exercise their influence to improve what was done in compliance with the law.

The most formalized voluntary factor has been the Recommendations on Accounting Principles issued by the Institute of Chartered Accountants. These were first issued by the Institute in England and Wales in 1944, notwithstanding the wartime conditions. The recommendations were taken up, after some time lag, with little modification, by the Australian Institute. As recently as 1963 the Australian Institute reported that the 'policy of the Council is to keep the Institute's recommendations as close as practicable to the recommendations of the Institute of Chartered Accountants in England and Wales, having regard to Australian conditions and legal requirements'.[1]

When the recommendations were first issued they were received generally with acclamation as a positive step by the Institutes to improve accounting. Although the Institute in England and Wales had received its Charter in 1880, and the Australian Institute its Charter in 1928, neither had attempted to lay down criteria for good accounting before this. A. A. Fitzgerald was among those who welcomed the Institutes' action and expressed the opinion in his address to the A.N.Z.A.A.S. Congress in Perth that: 'It may confidently be expected that the recommendations of the institutes will result in a substantial and rapid improvement in the general standard of company financial statements in England and Australia.'[2] G. E. Fitzgerald and A. E. Speck welcomed the recommendations on holding companies as 'the most important statement made in the British Empire in regard to the best methods of presenting the accounts of holding companies'.[3]

The matters on which recommendations were made by the Australian Institute were, form of balance sheet and profit and loss account, the treatment of taxation in accounts, the inclusion in accounts of proposed profit appropriations, reserves and provisions, disclosure of the financial position and results of subsidary companies in the accounts of holding companies, and depreciation of fixed assets. These covered the same ground as those of the English Institute except for stock-in-trade which was covered by a recommendation issued in 1949.

The way in which the Institute tackled the task has been described by A. A. Fitzgerald as an approach through three distinct but closely related channels:

(a) Specification of certain items which should be separately stated in balance sheets or in profit and loss statements.
(b) Removal of ambiguities and other causes of obscurity by classification of balance sheet or profit and loss statement items into logical groups, and
(c) Standardisation of the meaning of accounting terms hitherto commonly used in accounting statements, almost indiscriminately, to describe essentially different kinds of items.[4]

The success of the recommendations has been of a threefold kind. As will be shown later, some of them have made a significant impact on published reports. These are the recommendations which do not require any fundamental difference in the details of the financial position portrayed in the financial statements, but rather are concerned with the arrangement and presentation of what is given already. This is directed at what may be described as a 'pretty balance sheet'. Much less success has been achieved with those recommendations which require the presentation of financial facts which are not required to be given to comply with the Companies Act. Later chapters will demonstrate the complete failure of recommendations relating to stock, the tardy response to recommendations concerning depreciation and the presentation of fixed assets in the balance sheet, and the confused position concerning adjustments made to take account of changing price levels. (The last is a matter where the Australian Institute has not followed the action of the English Institute.) A third group of recommendations merely gave official Institute blessing to developments that were established already as accepted practices or as legal requirements. Two examples which have been discussed before are the definitions of the terms 'reserve' and 'provision', and the presentation of appropriate classifications within the balance sheet.

It is true that in some matters the recommendations have been in advance of the statutes, but it frequently required the force of statutory obligation to give the accountant support to enable him to secure compliance. The Institute recommendations on the profit and loss statement closely followed those of the Victorian Act of 1938 with an additional obligation to state the amount provided for taxation on the result of the year's trading. These recommendations were incorporated substantially in the English Companies Act in 1947. These important recommendations did not receive the support of legislative compulsion in Tasmania until 1959 and in New South Wales, Queensland and South Australia, not until 1961 when the Uniform Acts were passed.

The recommendations both as originally stated and in subsequent amended versions sought to improve on the statutory position covering the treatment of abnormal or extraordinary items as outlined in the discussion of the profit and loss statement earlier.

Earlier reference was made to the complaint in 1948 of Slade, the chairman of the South Australian division of the Institute of Chartered Accountants in Australia, that many company reports did not comply with the Institute recommendations. This was an assertion borne out by the study conducted about the time by M. S. Esau and others,[5] while the survey of the reports of Western Australian companies conducted by E. M. Jones and others in 1957 was also critical of the failure of many Western Australian companies to adopt the Institute recommendations.[6]

In 1963 the Australian Institute revised its recommendations, publication having been delayed until the passing of the Uniform Acts. The 1963 recommendations included a new section on accountants' reports for prospectuses, and a revised recommendation on valuation of stock which is discussed fully later. The 1946 recommendations on the treatment of taxation in accounts, disclosure of the financial position and results of subsidiary companies in the accounts of holding companies, and depreciation of fixed assets, remained unaltered. The general objective of the recommendations on presentation of balance sheet and profit and loss account remained unaltered. Changes in detail occurred relating to classification in the balance sheet and the definition of reserves and provisions.

It was indicated before that some of the more important of the Institute recommendations were not put into practice as widely as might have been hoped, except in so far as the recommendations involved the better presentation of a given body of information. Nevertheless they have provided an official expression by the accounting profession of desirable practices. To this extent they have been valuable support for the development of statutory provisions on those matters on which the law has been trailing the Institute's recommendations.

It remains for the future to test the ability of the accounting profession to promulgate standards in advance of current practice. The Institute's recommendations up till the present have tended to be well and truly tried and accepted accounting principles. These recommendations have been successful in developing standards in practice in so far as they were directed at the presentation of a 'pretty' balance sheet as the following comments indicate.

WHOLE POUND STATEMENTS

The mesmerism sometimes engendered by the seeming mathematical precision of the balance sheet may well have been accentuated by the persistence of accountants in adding the odd shillings and pence to figures amounting to even millions of pounds. The suggestion that such details were redundant, however, could on occasion provide the excuse for lengthy discourse.[7] The argument for deletion usually is stated as the lack of materiality of the information in relation to the total values stated. The results of an examination of the reports of the 'forty-two leaders sample' set out in Table 17 definitely suggest that the practice of presenting statements expressed in whole pounds was given impetus in Australia by the desire to conserve paper during wartime shortages and that, after the cessation of hostilities, there was little point in reverting to the inclusion of data which nobody had missed. R. J. Chambers examined the reports of 250 companies in 1948 and again in 1955 and found the proportion of whole pound statements to be 63 per cent and 89 per cent respectively,[8] which agrees with the pattern shown by the 'forty-two leaders sample'. Chambers classified the results he obtained according to the size of the company. His analysis suggests that the medium sized company was more reluc-

TABLE 17
Adoption of whole pound statements
'42 leaders sample'

	Size of available sample[a]	No. of companies	% of available sample	Notes
1934	21	nil	0	
1935	24	1	4	
1938	30	6	20	
1939	30	12	40	World War II
1942	32	18	56	
1945	33	23	70	Cessation of hostilities
1950	38	33	87	
1962	42	42	100	Uniform Acts

[a] See explanatory note, p. 3.

tant than the very large or very small to delete the shillings and pence from the statements. R. A. McInnes records that only sixteen of twenty-four Queensland companies had eliminated the shillings and pence from the reports he examined in 1954.[9] It does not seem possible to draw any conclusion from these findings that 'whole pound statements' were less acceptable in the smaller States because E. M. Jones's survey of Western Australian companies only three years later showed 'nearly all the companies' using whole pound presentations.[10]

The presentation of shillings and pence appears to have suffered its final defeat with the necessity to include comparative figures in statements as enacted in the Uniform Acts. The continued inclusion of shillings and pence would have robbed space which might better be employed to set out the comparative figures. One company in the 'forty-two leaders sample', Jones, presented its 1965 statements stated as to the nearest one hundred dollars. This would seem to be an extension of a logical measure of materiality to a very large enterprise.

BALANCE SHEET HEADINGS

An aspect of presentation which the Institute recommendations condemned and have been singularly successful in ending was the practice of heading the two sides of a conventional balance sheet 'assets' and 'liabilities'. With this practice may be considered the practice occasionally found of including as headings the titles 'Dr' and 'Cr', which might be argued for as serving to underline the true nature of a balance sheet as a classified schedule of ledger account balances. The balance sheet includes amongst the credit items proprietorship accounts, and to label them as liabilities is inaccurate. Apparently this was sufficiently clear to the legislatures, for modern company statutes have seen no necessity to prohibit this misuse of titles, any more than to prescribe such unnecessary detail.

TABLE 18
*Deletion of general headings from balance sheet
'42 leaders sample'*

	Size of available sample	No. of companies	% of available sample	Notes
1928	17	2	12	
1935	24	5	21	
1940	32	9	28	
1944	32	12	38	I.C.A.E.W. recommendations
1946	33	15	45	I.C.A.A. recommendations
1950	38	29	76	
1955	41	36	88	
1960	42	37	88	
1965	42	39	93	
1968	42	38	90	

Table 18 sets out the relevant data of the practices of the 'forty-two leaders sample' in this respect. This shows a very marked increase in the number of companies deleting these headings following the issue of the Institute recommendations. It was disappointing to find four companies continuing to include these headings in 1968 (B.H.P., Boral, I.A.C. and Woolworth), grouping shareholders' funds under the title of 'liabilities'. R. A. Irish found 60 per cent of twenty-four reports he surveyed in 1948 had deleted the headings.[11] R. J. Chambers found two-thirds of the 250 companies he surveyed in 1955 had dropped these headings.[12] These results of other researchers accord with the results of the investigation of the reports of the 'forty-two leaders sample'. It is concluded from the sharp rise in the proportion of companies deleting these titles after the issue of the Institute recommendations, that this action was predominantly a direct result of the Institute pronouncement.

INCLUSION OF PROPOSED APPROPRIATIONS

The inclusion of proposed appropriations, including proposed dividends, in the financial statements may mean that a substantially different financial position will be portrayed. Recommendations that provisions for intended dividends and other appropriations should be included in the published statements gained widespread recognition. The Uniform Acts now require the directors' recommendations to be included in the financial statements (ninth schedule, clause 1(k)). The adoption of this practice among the 'forty-two leaders sample' is summarized in Table 19 which shows that the

TABLE 19
Inclusion in statements of proposed appropriations
'42 leaders sample'

	Size of available sample	No. of companies	% of available sample	Notes
1935	24	4	17	1938 Victorian Companies Act
1940	32	13	41	1944 I.C.A.E.W. recommendations
1945	33	18	55	1946 I.C.A.A. recommendations
1950	33	25	76	
1960	33	32	97	
1962	33	33	100	1962 Uniform Acts

practice was followed by half the companies before the issue of the Institute recommendation. Most of the remaining companies adopted the recommendation within the following four years. All of the companies which are included in the 'forty-two leaders sample' after 1946 adopted this recommendation at least from when their reports were available. For this reason Table 19 has been restricted to companies included in the 'available sample' before 1946. In this way the response of the existing sample is highlighted without the bias of subsequent additions to the sample which all followed the recommendations. R. A. Irish, in his survey of twenty-six companies in 1948, found that fourteen (54 per cent) had included the proposed dividend in the appropriation statement.[13] R. A. McInnes in 1954 found ten out of twenty-four (42 per cent) Queensland companies and twenty out of twenty-six companies incorporated in other States reporting statements prepared as after giving effect to the directors' recommendations.[14] It is possible that the Queensland companies were 'trailing the field'. The judges for the A.I.M. Award reported in 1953 that: 'Only 6% of the companies did not give effect to the directors' recommendations in the profit and loss account and balance sheet.'[15] It therefore would appear that this Institute recommendation was adopted readily and was followed effectively by all except a very few companies within a period of five or six years.

23 I.C.A.A. Recommendations

COMPARATIVE FIGURES

The final aspect of the recommendations aimed at securing a 'pretty' balance sheet refers to the inclusion in published statements of comparative figures for the previous accounting period. The earliest instance of a company including such comparative figures in its financial statements for which documentary evidence was found was an English company, S. Instone & Co. Ltd which drew praise for doing so in 1928 although its statements were deficient in other respects.[16] Legislative support was not given until the Uniform Acts were passed when, as Table 20 indicates, the inclusion

TABLE 20
Inclusion of comparative figures in statements '42 leaders sample'

	Size of available sample	No. of companies	% of available sample	Notes
1934	21	nil	0	
1935	24	2	8	
1939	30	6	20	Vic. Companies Act, 1938
1944	32	13	41	I.C.A.E.W. recommendations
1946	33	17	52	I.C.A.A. recommendations
1950	38	25	66	
1955	41	34	83	
1960	42	39	93	
1962	42	42	100	Uniform Acts

of comparative figures in financial statements had become standard practice. At the time the Australian Institute's recommendation was issued one half of the available sample of the 'forty-two leaders sample' had already included comparative figures in their reports. The Institute's recommendation appears to have been successful in securing the compliance of nearly all the remaining companies. In the 'forty-two leaders sample' only two remained to be compelled to do so by the provisions of the Uniform Acts (ninth schedule, clause 5(2)). R. A. Irish similarly found twelve of twenty-six companies (46 per cent) he surveyed in 1948 giving comparative figures.[17] R. J. Chambers survey of 250 companies showed 43 per cent including comparative figures in 1948 and 72 per cent doing so in 1955. His analysis suggests leadership in this item by Victorian companies. He reported: 'Of companies registered in New South Wales, only 21 [of those included in his sample] gave comparative figures in 1948. The improvement in the figures over the period is thus largely due to belated recognition in New South Wales of a practice which was already in 1948 much more generally adopted in Victoria.'[18] R. A. McInnes found in 1954 only thirteen of twenty-four (52 per cent) Queensland companies including comparative figures.[19] In Western Australia E. M. Jones's examination of thirty-six reports of Western Australian companies in 1957 showed only twenty-three (64 per cent) to have included comparative figures.[20] Both of these results show a substantially lower proportion of companies including comparative figures than found in the 'forty-two leaders sample' or in the overall results of Irish and Chambers. This, it is suggested, supports Chambers's conclusion of 'Victorian' leadership.

There are, however, four problems which have arisen from the adoption of the principle of including comparative data in reports: maintaining clear presentation in spite of an increasing mass of detail, the adequacy or otherwise of only including comparative figures for the previous accounting period, adjustments that become necessary to previously published figures, and in some circumstances the usefulness or otherwise of what are regarded as comparative statements. Some writers have gone so far as to argue that comparative figures ought not to be included within the statements for the current period, but stated quite separately.[21]

The adequacy of a one-year comparison is another matter altogether. Support for the necessity to present tabulations extending over longer periods, of at least certain details, has come from no less a body than the Jenkins Company Law Committee and the recommendations of this committee are almost certain to be noted in future Australian legislation. This committee proposed that the annual accounts should include a five-year summary of issued share capital and reserves, including the balance on profit and loss account, the annual profits before and after tax, the annual dividend, and the turnover.[22] The inclusion of tables of comparative data for more than two accounting periods is now common in the better published reports.

This analysis shows that the recommendations of the Institute of Chartered Accountants were effective in achieving the presentation of whole pound statements, the omission of general headings from the balance sheet, and the inclusion of the directors' proposals for appropriations (with the exception of the appropriation for taxation discussed later), while that covering the inclusion of comparative figures appears to have been less successful in the other States than in Victoria. In this way the Institute contributed toward the presentation of 'prettier balance sheets'.

24

The Valuation of Stock

There is little doubt that for most trading companies the two most important figures in the determination of the profit or loss on trading are the valuation placed on stock and the amount charged as depreciation. Of the Recommendations on Accounting Principles issued by the Institute of Chartered Accountants in Australia in the forties, those dealing with stock and depreciation were the only ones capable of having any effect on the process of accounting measurement as distinct from the form of presentation of reports.

The importance of the item stock is shown by the Tables 21, 22, 23. In Table 21 the proportion of total assets represented by stock and the ratio of profit to stock is shown for each of the 'forty-two leaders sample'. As Table 22 shows, in almost half of the companies included in the sample, stock represents more than 25 per cent of the asset values as disclosed in the balance sheet. It is not difficult to see that any error in the valuation of stock or different definition of the basis of valuation adopted can have a marked effect on the valuation of total assets shown in the balance sheet. The summary shown in Table 21 of the profit as a percentage of stock highlights the position even more clearly. In view of the importance of this item it could be argued that there should be clear agreement on how to deal with it. It will be shown that there has been little agreement and, furthermore, that actual practice has been far different from that advocated in the literature and by the professional bodies as correct and desirable practice.

All of the Australian State Acts have required the basis of valuation of stock to be given since the first compulsory publication of balance sheets. We do not have any adequate evidence of recommended or actual practice at the time of the Victorian 1896 Act, but we do know that at the time of the passage of the 1931–6 Acts the Commonwealth Institute of Accountants sought and published opinion of counsel which reported that English companies used a

TABLE 21
Importance of stock and basis of valuation stated
'42 leaders sample'[a]

Company	Stocks Total assets %	Profit Stocks %	Basis of valuation given
A.W.A.	43	22	lower of cost and market value [b]
Ampol	5	173	lower of cost or replacement
Ansett	13	32	lower of cost or market value [c]
APPM	23	53	lower of cost or selling price [d]
A. & K.	10	66	lower of cost, realizable value and replacement price [e]
A.C.I.	18	56	lower of cost, market or replacement value [f]
A. Gypsum	11	109	lower of cost or market value
A.P.M.	11	55	lower of cost or valuation [f]
B.M.I.	8	108	lower of cost or net realizable value [g]
Bradford	29	30	cost or market value, whichever is the lesser
Boral	8	66	lower of cost or net realizable value
Brick	5	300	lower of cost or market value
B. Tobacco	35	26	lower of cost or market value [h]
B.H.P.	14	45	lowest of cost, market selling value or replacement [i]
C.U.B.	4	249	not exceeding cost
Coles	18	57	lower of cost and net realizable value
C.S.R.	9	55	normal and customary methods of valuation [j]
C.I.G.	17	63	lower of cost or realizable value [k]
Container	32	27	lower of cost or market value
D.H.A.	29	21	lower of cost or market selling value
Dunlop	26	33	lower of cost or replacement value [l]
Electronic	31	15	lower of cost and market value [m]
Email	37	17	lower of cost or market value [f]
F. & T.	32	20	lowest of cost net realizable and replacement price
Herald	15	120	at cost or under [n]
Humes	29	25	lowest of cost, net realizable value and replacement price
ICIANZ	22	29	lowest of cost, net realizable value and replacement price [o]
J. & Way.	25	47	at valuation
Jones	32	17	lowest of cost, current market and estimated realizable value
McPherson	34	18	lower of cost or net realizable value
Myer	21	67	cost or values permitting disposal at normal margins
Nat. Cons.	40	42	lowest of cost price market selling price or replacement value [p]
Olympic	26	34	lowest of cost, net realizable value and replacement price
Peters	30	21	lowest of cost market or replacement value

24 The Valuation of Stock

TABLE 21 (continued)

Company	Stocks / Total assets %	Profit / Stocks %	Basis of valuation given
Repco	34	28	lower of cost or market value
Rothman	63	15	lower of cost or net realizable value
Sleigh	7	102	lower of cost and net realizable value
T.V.	14	85	cost less amortisation q
Woolworth	23	34	lowest of cost net realizable value or replacement price

a   Excludes Australian Guarantee, Custom Credit and I.A.C., which as finance companies, do not hold stocks. All figures taken from consolidated statements where appropriate.
b   Less provision for future adjustments.
c   Less provision for stock obsolescence of aircraft stores, etc.
d   Stores and raw materials at cost.
e   Less a small provision shown.
f   Less provision for fluctuations in stock values.
g   Livestock at average cost and at market value.
h   A small proportion at market value.
i   Stocks other than 'trading' at cost.
j   Described also as taking into account the nature of the product, cost, market or selling value and requirements of the respective industries and less a provision for diminution of value.
k   Cost for manufactured goods identified as on an absorption costing basis.
l   'As certified by the companies' officials'.
m   Excluding stocks on floor plan valued at market value not exceeding cost.
n   Less provision for stock price fluctuations.
o   Less provision for possible measuring inaccuracies and other losses.
p   'As certified by the management'.
q   Other stocks at cost or at lower of cost or realizable value.

variety of bases for valuation of stock, of which it was said that the most usual was 'at or under cost'.[1] This gave an aura of authority to an unsatisfactory practice. This basis of valuation was among those to be soundly condemned within ten years as the following narrative will show.

The outstanding feature of stock valuation in Australian reports in past years has been the diversity of definitions used. R. J. Chambers surveyed the reports of fifty companies published in 1938 and found no less than twenty-two different bases of stock valuation. The same companies, ten years later, produced twenty-three different bases. While seven of the bases used previously had been dropped, another eight new bases had been adopted.[2] In 1944 A. A. Fitzgerald found fourteen bases shared among the forty companies which he surveyed.[3]

It was this diversity of description which led some writers to advocate the use of cost as the only appropriate basis of valuation. Such a definition at least had the characteristic of clarity of expression. As A. C. Littleton expressed it, the rule that inventories should

TABLE 22
Importance of stock to total assets ratio
'42 leaders sample'

Stock as % of total assets	No. of companies
0	3
1–4	1
5–9	6
10–14	6
15–19	4
20–24	4
25–29	6
30–34	7
35–39	2
40–44	2
45 and over	1
Total	42

TABLE 23
Relationship of profit and stock valuation
'42 leaders sample'

Profit as % of stocks	No. of companies
0–19	5
20–29	9
30–39	5
40–49	3
50–59	5
60–69	4
70–99	1
100 and over	7
No stocks held	3
Total	42

be valued at cost on a first-in first-out basis, 'has no mingled bloodlines to weaken its character'.[4] At least 'cost' would avoid the ambiguities of definitions such as 'cost or market' which were advocated frequently.

It appears that, in spite of the evidence to the contrary there was a body of opinion in the accounting profession which held that there was a commonly held or 'usual' basis of valuation. The editor of the *Commonwealth Journal of Accountancy* in an editorial in October 1935, was rash enough to suggest that: 'The principle that stock-in-trade at balancing date must be brought into the accounts at cost or market, whichever is the lower, is universally accepted.'[5]

A. A. Fitzgerald wrote in 1944 that:

It is sometimes assumed that there is a tacit acceptance by business men in Australia of what has come to be known as the 'golden rule' of stock valuation, viz., that stock should be valued for balance sheet or profit and loss purposes at cost or market replacement price, whichever is the lower.[6]

He demonstrated that few companies in fact used the so-called 'golden rule' but that 'the guiding rule was caution' and 'that in the great majority of cases "cost" determines the ceiling value'. Only two out of the forty companies surveyed by Fitzgerald used the 'golden rule', although thirty-three indicated a basis of valuation which effectively meant 'cost or less'. Similarly, R. J. Chambers found only nine out of fifty companies using terms equivalent to the 'golden rule' in 1938 and ten of the same fifty using it in 1948.[7]

This 'golden rule' has a long history. A. C. Littleton quotes from a German scholar writing of the manuscript records of an Italian businessman as evidence that this rule was practised as early as A.D. 1393, or nearly a century before the first book on double entry book-keeping was written by Lucas Pacioli.[8] The application of this rule has been tied in closely with the desire to avoid any possible taking into account of unrealized profits and the desire to recognize all possible and probable losses whether they have yet eventuated or not. This has been lauded frequently as 'sound' or 'prudent' business sense. The rule was therefore in accord with the views of those who felt that financial statements should be prepared on a 'conservative' basis.

A. A. Fitzgerald himself examined the justification for the assumption that the 'golden rule' was accepted. The summary given by him in the First Commonwealth Institute of Accountants Research Lecture in the University of Sydney based on an earlier lecture in Adelaide was:

(i) Neither in England nor in U.S.A. is there any longer dogmatic assertion that the 'lower of cost or market' rule must always be followed;
(ii) The extent to which reliance is placed on the rule as a guide to practice depends in particular on the relative importance attached to conservatism on the one hand, and disclosure and consistency on the other;
(iii) Whatever may be thought of the suitability of the rule for balance sheet purposes, its use for profit and loss statement purposes is not satisfactory.[9]

It would appear from the surveys conducted by Fitzgerald and Chambers, as well as those by R. K. Yorston[10] in 1945 and K. C. Keown[11] in 1951, that businessmen were inclined to insist on a more conservative basis of valuation of stock than the 'golden rule' permitted. It could well have been that the failure to follow the 'golden rule' was in part due to the inconclusive nature of the rule itself.

There was not any authoritative pronouncement which could be relied on by anyone seeking a guide to action on the matter, until in 1945 the Institute of Chartered Accountants in England and Wales issued its Recommendations on Accounting Principles covering the valuation of stock-in-trade. This recommendation was made available to Australian accountants through the medium of the local professional journals, and could be said to have regularized in the profession, the dictum of the lower of cost or market rule. The recommendation amounted to a disclaimer of the view that market value should be calculated with reference to replacement price so that the rule was interpreted effectively as the lower of cost or realizable value. A similar recommendation was not pronounced officially by the Institute of Chartered Accountants in Australia until 1949. A. A. Fitzgerald told the Congress of the Australian and New Zealand Association for the Advancement of Science in Perth in 1947 that he thought there was little chance of theoretical arguments shaking the faith of practical accountants in the lower of cost or market rule, but he did think that, 'the recommendations of the English Institute will be most useful in checking excessive conservatism and in removing both the temptation and the opportunity for manipulation of secret reserves.'[12] In 1960, an amended recommendation, issued by the English Institute, spelt out the 'golden rule' more fully, and recognized the acceptable basis of valuing stocks as the lowest of cost, market selling value or replacement price. These recommendations also were adopted by the Australian Institute, with appropriate changes of words, in 1963.

Table 21 shows that among the 'forty-two leaders sample' in 1968 only seven companies used the basis set out in the current Institute recommendations and another three used a description which could be regarded as an equivalent. Nine companies used the lower of cost or realizable value while the eleven companies which used the 'lower of cost or market' constituted the largest single group. Thus, these twenty companies, or approximately half the 'forty-two leaders sample', are still following the superseded Institute recommendations issued in 1949. The lower of cost or replacement value

24 The Valuation of Stock

was used by two companies, and another five indicated a basis of cost or lower defined other than in the terms already referred to, including one defined as cost or 'values permitting disposal at normal margins'. The remaining two cases could not be regarded as giving any precise basis of valuation. One described stocks as 'at valuation' while the other proclaimed the use of 'normal and customary methods of valuation'. The conclusion that is drawn from this examination is that there has been a very slow response to the Institute recommendations. The Institute recommendations appear to have contributed towards a reduction in the number of different bases of valuation currently used or at least a standardization of terminology sufficient to allow closer classification of the bases used. It is also noticeable that many of the vague terms found by Chambers in 1938 and 1948 and by Fitzgerald in 1944, are not now found, e.g. terms such as 'valuation', 'as certified', 'cost or under'.

Whereas the lower of cost or market, even if defined as lower of cost or realizable value, may be regarded as vague, it does indicate the principles followed. It certainly does not indicate the extent of the reduction below cost. Such bases of valuation represent long standing means of creating provisions against loss of value without indicating the magnitude of such provisions. The guidance to practice given in the Institute of Chartered Accountants in Australia recommendations is that the amount of any provisions necessary to meet the recommended basis of the lowest of cost, net realizable value, or replacement price need not be stated, but only that 'provision should be made to the full extent of expected losses'. However, in referring to any statement of stock at a value lower than the recommended value, i.e. lowest of cost, net realizable value, or replacement price, it says this would, 'create a reserve which should be so described and disclosed and should not be treated as a charge against revenue'.

Action taken by a company to recognize possible losses of value of stocks could be any of the following:

(a) Creation of a provision which may be considered to be the amount necessary to reduce the inventory value from cost to the basis recommended by the Institute.

(b) Creation of a provision by a charge made before ascertaining profit which may be considered as reducing the value of inventory from cost to a value less than that recommended by the Institute.

(c) An appropriation of ascertained profits to create a reserve against possible loss of value of inventory (including any such appropriations incorrectly described as a provision).

Those instances of the creation of stock provisions or reserves found among the 'forty-two leaders sample' were examined with this classification in mind.

Among the 'forty-two leaders sample' there were five instances where it was considered that the adjustment to the value of stock was correctly described as a provision because it related to likely events 'in the ordinary course of business'. These provisions were considered to refer to events in the normal course of business because three of these examples related to the rapid rise in prices of some world trade commodities at the time of the Korean war, while the other two related to industries where technological change could cause quite sudden loss of value of stocks, e.g. the effect on the value of aircraft spares of a decision to re-equip with a new aircraft type. In another ten instances a provision was made which it was considered would reduce the value of the inventory below the Institute's recommended basis. These adjustments are correctly described as provisions inasmuch as they relate to charges made in the course of ascertaining profits. The assessment on the limited information given was that these adjustments did not refer to losses expected 'in the ordinary course of business' and ought therefore to have been made as appropriations to reserves to comply with the Institute recommendations. There were six cases which fitted the third category of reserves created by an appropriation of ascertained profits. One of these cases actually arose from a revaluation of inventories which had been stated consistently and deliberately at standard values determined some decades previously with consequent reduction in stated profits over the years concerned. In four of the cases the reserve concerned has been merged subsequently with general reserve or used for other purposes. It is of interest that two of these cases arose from wartime circumstances, three arose during the worst of the post-war inflationary period and one, as noted before, from the necessity to adopt more up-to-date and realistic stock values. The individual reporting incidents referred to, involve no less than eighteen of the 'forty-two leaders sample'.

On this evidence relating to the 'forty-two leaders sample' it appears reasonable to conclude that there has been developing in recent years an increased willingness to go beyond the mere statement of a stock valuation and to give some further explanatory information. No less than nine of fourteen cases of adjustments described as provisions it is considered ought to have been described as reserves to accord with the Institute recommendations. This high proportion of treatments assessed as failing to meet the Institute recommendations parallels the previous conclusion that there has been little acceptance in practice of the Institute's recommendation on the appropriate basis of valuation of stocks. Finally it may be questioned whether it is indicative of dissension within the Institute of Chartered Accountants of Australia that the other Recommendations on Accounting Principles which were made by the Institute followed the issue of the English recommendations within two years, but that five years elapsed before the Australian Institute followed the English lead with respect to stock-in-trade.

25

Depreciation

The introductory remarks to the previous chapter pointed out the importance in accounting measurement of the valuation placed on stock and the amount charged as depreciation. Having discussed the first of these it is logical now to review the second. There is, however, a significant difference in the developments concerning disclosure of these two items for while the accounting profession has given reasonably clear guidance on the principles of valuation to be applied to stock, it has given little guidance on the matter of depreciation, except to support the traditional accounting concept of depreciation as a process of cost allocation. The Institute of Chartered Accountants recommendations recognize this concept but do not provide any guidance as to how the allocation should be made. The Institute in its advocacy of the disclosure of depreciation expense was in essence doing little more than affirming an existing statutory requirement.

The discussion of the reporting of depreciation involves two aspects which may be considered conveniently as chronologically following each other, but which nevertheless are related fundamentally in accounting theory. The first is the statement of the depreciation expense for the accounting period reported on, the second the reporting of the accumulated total of depreciation taken into account with respect to each item of fixed assets shown in the balance sheet.

The question of depreciation has received little attention in Australian literature apart from the work of Professor L. Goldberg and G. T. Webb,[1] notwithstanding the importance of the item in the accounts of most commercial and industrial enterprises. A. A. Fitzgerald attributed this lack of attention, compared with the overseas situation, to the public ownership of most public utilities creating a lack of awareness of depreciation problems in these areas,

25 Depreciation

TABLE 24
Importance of depreciation expense '42 leaders sample, 1968'

Company[a]	Depreciation expense as % of profit	Depreciation as % of asset value[b]	
		Cost or valuation per balance sheet	Book value per balance sheet
A.W.A.	32	8·1	26·1
Ampol	55	3·0	4·2
Ansett	170	8·3	14·2
APPM	45	5·0	12·3
A. & K.	76	5·3	7·7
A.C.I.	45	9·9	14·2
A.G.C.[c]	60	17·3	22·0
A. Gypsum	34	9·0	23·3
A.P.M.	80	6·0	12·0
B.M.I.	37	8·2	15·4
Bradford	53	6·3	9·7
Boral	98	7·7	11·9
Brick	29	6·8	9·7
B. Tobacco	31	9·0	16·3
B.H.P.	109	8·2	9·0
C.U.B.	22	6·6	3·9
Coles	19	6·9	10·2
C.S.R.	56	5·2	8·1
C.I.G.	58	6·9	13·3
Container	37	6·7	16·1
Custom[c]	6	12·1	17·0
D.H.A.	19	9·7	14·3
Dunlop	38	10·1	17·4
Electronic	26	7·9	15·0
Email	29	7·5	28·3
F. & T.	48	8·9	18·0
Herald	19	10·7	68·6
Humes	82	15·1	24·8
ICIANZ	81	9·3	15·0
I.A.C.[c]	32	15·4	19·2
J. & Way.	22	8·6	15·6
Jones	34	8·2	14·8
McPherson	31	6·3	11·5
Myer	16	12·1	14·7
Nat. Cons.	11	7·7	15·3
Olympic	43	8·7	24·3
Peters	67	8·3	17·3
Repco	34	11·9	24·3
Rothman	34	13·7	30·2
Sleigh	21	5·7	9·7
T.V.	20	8·4	18·6
Woolworth	32	6·0	8·3

[a] All calculations based on consolidated statements.
[b] Real estate excluded when separately stated.
[c] Based on values for plant and equipment leased to clients.

the fact that Australians had been less critical of financial statements than their contemporaries overseas, and:

the relatively slow development of cost accounting in Australia. This slow development is a natural reflex of the fact that Australia has not hitherto been a highly industrialised country, and the need for cost accounting as a method of control has not been universally felt as a matter of urgency. Consequently, depreciation has been regarded rather as a problem in balance sheet valuation than as a problem in the accurate ascertainment of current operating expense.[2]

The importance of depreciation in the measurement and reporting of profitability is shown in Table 24 in which the depreciation expense of each of the 'forty-two leaders sample' is expressed as a percentage of the profit for the 1968 year. The results of this analysis demonstrate the extent to which profitability may be affected by the depreciation expense. In the majority of cases the depreciation expense is between 20 and 50 per cent of the stated profit. In two instances (Ansett and B.H.P.) this ratio exceeds 100 per cent. To demonstrate this more clearly Table 25 gives a

TABLE 25
Depreciation as percentage of profit '42 leaders sample', 1968

Range %	No. of Companies
0–9	1
10–19	5
20–29	7
30–39	12
40–49	4
50–59	4
60–69	2
70–79	1
80–89	3
90–99	1
Over 100	2
Total	42

frequency distribution for this ratio. The importance of this item stands in contrast to the tardy development of reporting practice.

When the Bill which became the Companies Act of 1910 was considered by the Select Committee of the Victorian Legislative Assembly, C. M. Holmes appeared for the Australasian Corporation of Public Accountants (now the Institute of Chartered Accountants in Australia), and argued for showing the balance of the value of assets at the beginning of the year less the amount written off during the year (i.e. the annual depreciation), to arrive at the net balance sheet figure.[3] On the other hand, C. H. Davis for the Incorporated Institute of Accountants, Victoria, an antecedent of the Australian Society of Accountants, argued against requiring banks to disclose depreciation allowed on their premises as 'too inquisitorial' and as 'difficult to state'.[4] The Act as finally passed did not bring in any compulsory disclosure of depreciation either by banks or trading companies. The disclosure of the annual depreciation expense was first given legislative support in Queensland in 1931 and New South Wales in 1936, when new Acts required directors to report the amount written off as depreciation. (In this respect these Acts went beyond the requirements of the English Companies Act of 1929 on which these Acts were modelled.) Details of depreciation expense were required as part of the profit and loss statement under Acts passed in Victoria in 1938, in Western Australia in 1943, in Tasmania in 1959 and in South Australia in 1962.

This item of expense has been required by Statute for a large part of the period during which the reports of the 'forty-two leaders sample' are available. An examination of this aspect of reporting was confined therefore to those New South Wales companies in the 'available sample' at 1936 and those Victorian companies in the sample at 1938. This examination showed that very few companies disclosed depreciation expense voluntarily. In fact, three of the four companies which disclosed this information as early as 1919 subsequently ceased to do so by 1930. In 1936 not one of the available sample of nine New South Wales companies was giving this information voluntarily. In Victoria the information was given voluntarily by three companies of the available sample of nineteen companies before the passage of the Victorian Companies Act 1938. This can only be regarded as a most unsatisfactory record.

Although depreciation expense was thus singled out in the thirties as a necessary item of disclosure, the New South Wales and Queensland legislation was ineffective in one particular respect—holding companies. The directors' report of the holding company was only required to give the depreciation provided by the parent company. Therefore there was not any disclosure of depreciation where the physical assets were held by subsidiary companies, a situation found with three out of the available sample of nine New

South Wales companies. In Victoria the consolidated statements of a group, or separate statements of each subsidiary, published in compliance with the 1938 Act, were required in the same detail as the statements of the parent company. Where the physical assets of a group were held by subsidiary companies the consolidated profit and loss statement would give the amount of depreciation provided by the group. There were thus few circumstances where disclosure would depend on the effect of voluntarily imposed standards such as the Institute of Chartered Accountants recommendations.

The Institute recommendation to show the depreciation expense in the profit and loss statement as well as the directors' report had little influence on practice according to the evidence of L. Goldberg's examination of seventy-eight companies between 1945 and 1953.[5] However my examination suggests more success in later years because among the New South Wales companies included in the 'forty-two leaders sample' at 1961 (immediately before the Uniform Act came into force requiring the profit and loss statement to include depreciation expense), there was only one company which did not include the depreciation amount in the profit and loss statement presentation.

As depreciation in its accounting connotation is the allocation of original cost over a number of accounting periods, it follows that the most obvious way to check the adequacy of the annual depreciation is by comparing it with the original cost of the assets concerned. Likewise, the knowledge as to what extent this cost has been taken account of in depreciation, indicated by the accumulated depreciation, may assist one to form an opinion as to whether the depreciation allowed to the present time has been calculated at an appropriate rate. If the only information available concerning fixed assets is the written down or book value, considerable distortion may result in any financial analysis that may be attempted. This can be demonstrated in respect of the 'forty-two leaders sample'. The capitalization basis given by the net book value of the assets for two-thirds of the sample summarized in Table 26 is between 41 and 70 per cent of the capitalization base using the gross balance sheet amount before deducting accumulated depreciation.

The almost universal Australian practice in the past of stating fixed assets at only the net amount, after deducting the accumulated depreciation, can in no small measure be attributed to the opinion of counsel obtained by the Institute of Chartered Accountants in England and Wales on the 1929 English Companies Act, which was accepted as an interpretation of the local laws. This opinion suggested that appropriate expressions covering assets generally were:

'at cost'
'at cost, less depreciation'
'at cost, less amounts written off'.[6]

The desirability of showing separately the assets at cost and the deducted amount of accumulated depreciation, was supported in the 1946 recommendations of the Institute of Chartered Accountants in Australia and in the 1945 report of the Cohen Company Law Committee.

TABLE 26
Ratio of net fixed asset value to gross value as stated in balance sheet
'42 leaders sample', 1968

Range %	No. of companies
0–10	—
11–20	1
21–30	1
31–40	3
41–50	9
51–60	10
61–70	10
71–80	5
81–90	3
91–100	—
Total	42

L. Goldberg conducted an extensive enquiry over the period 1945–53 and concluded there had not been a very strong tendency towards using this form of presentation. In some cases the reverse had occurred. These conclusions were supported by his finding that:

Of the seventy-eight companies in the sample, fifty-one, or over 65 per cent have not at any time during the post-war period shown the amount of the accumulated charge for depreciation, whether in total or for each group of fixed assets. The proportion, based upon the number of reports available, has fallen from 77.6 per cent in 1945 to 66.6 per cent in 1953, but this latter figure still appears to be a high proportion of companies which have not found it practicable (to use the term in the Institute's recommendations) to show the accumulated depreciation charge separately from the fixed assets.[7]

Goldberg's conclusion echoes the sentiment in the report of the adjudicator for the A.I.M. Annual Report Award in 1953 that 'it is a pity that Companies do not show the accumulated provisions for depreciation in the balance sheet'.[8] It was much more encouraging than R. A. Irish's finding in 1948 that only five companies out of the twenty-six he surveyed, showed the accumulated depreciation separately.[9] As recently as 1960 two American authors surveyed a selection of twenty-five annual reports selected for them by the Sydney Stock Exchange and contrasted the failure of these companies to identify the accumulated depreciation with generally accepted practice in the U.S.A.[10] It is clear that legislative support was needed to secure compliance with this recommendation of the Institute of Chartered Accountants, and this was provided by the Uniform Acts. Only half of the 'forty-two leaders sample' included the information before the Uniform Act. The figures quoted in Table 27 include both the case where an aggregate depreciation 'reserve' is shown among the liabilities as well as the inclusion of the depreciation as a deduction from the assets.

The grouping of the accumulated depreciation with the assets concerned is another aspect of this presentation. If the accumulated depreciation is shown in close proximity to the asset it is more likely to be allocated against each particular class of asset. It will also

TABLE 27
Statement of accumulated depreciation in balance sheet '42 leaders sample'

	Size of available sample[a]	No. of companies	% of available sample	Notes
1917	5	1	20	
1921	10	3	30	
1930	19	4	21	N.S.W. Companies Act, 1936
1937	29	8	28	Vic. Companies Act, 1938
1940	32	10	31	
1946	33	9	27	I.C.A.A. recommendations
1950	38	15	47	
1960	42	19	45	Uniform Acts
1963	42	40	95[b]	

[a] See explanatory note, p. 3.
[b] The table does not show 100 per cent acceptance of the practice of showing the accumulated depreciation because one company does not provide for depreciation but instead provides for replacement of assets and at the date for which the table is compiled one company held shares in the operating company as its only asset and therefore did not have any depreciable assets.

25 Depreciation

TABLE 28
Presentation of accumulated depreciation
'42 leaders sample'

	Associated with assets % of cases	Separate item under liabilities or proprietorship % of cases	Notes
1926	0	100	
1933	17	83	
1937	25	75	N.S.W. Companies Act, 1936
1939	44	56	Vic. Companies Act, 1938
1943	33	67	I.C.A.A. recommendations, 1946
1949	47	53	
1952	57	43	
1957	72	28	
1961	75	25	
1962	100	0	Uniform Acts

mean that the assets are shown at 'unallocated cost' giving smaller balance sheet totals than if the accumulated depreciation is shown as a provision or reserve among the liabilities or proprietorship. The reports of the 'forty-two leaders sample' showed that there was a significant proportion of cases where only an aggregate reserve or provision was shown among the first companies to disclose the accumulated depreciation. There has been, however, a distinct movement away from this presentation in more recent years. By 1961 immediately before the Uniform Acts only one-fifth of the companies which disclosed the accumulated depreciation used this form of presentation. These observations are set out in Table 28.

As the above analysis shows, the disclosure and the manner of presentation in company reports, of depreciation expense have been primarily the result of statutory requirements.

One of the interesting side effects of this statutory requirement has been the clarification of the basis of valuation of the asset amount from which the accumulated depreciation is deducted. At the time of the Uniform Acts nearly all companies brought forward existing assets at the written down values and showed new additions at cost. So far as operating plant and equipment is concerned by 1968 the whole amount was stated on the basis of cost by nineteen of the companies in the 'forty-two leaders sample' and in another nine cases the proportion stated at other than cost was less than 5 per cent of the total asset group amount. In only six cases was more than 20 per cent of the asset amount stated on a basis other than cost. This clarification of asset costs does not remove the element of opinion embodied in the accumulated provision for depreciation and the net amount resulting from the deduction of the provision.

The Institute of Chartered Accountants unequivocally excludes from its concept of depreciation any amount intended as a charge exceeding the allocation of original cost. The Institute recommendation on this matter, first issued in 1946, still reads that:

> Amounts set aside out of profits for obsolescence which cannot be foreseen, or for a possible increase in the cost of replacement are matters of financial prudence. Neither can be estimated with any degree of accuracy. They are in the nature of reserves and should be treated as such in the accounts.[11]

An examination was made of the reports of the 'forty-two leaders sample' to ascertain what these companies had done to recognize any expense of 'depreciation' exceeding the allocation of original asset cost and how it had been dealt with in the financial statements. It should be made clear that such an analysis cannot possibly identify those companies which simply adopt a shorter life span over which to allocate the cost of an asset than may be normally appropriate, if this action is not revealed by some comment in the annual report. Among the 'forty-two leaders sample' a number of instances were found in which such additional depreciation charges had been made and identified in the financial statements. There has been little uniformity of treatment: six companies have followed the Institute recommendation by treating these charges as appropriations; two other companies made appropriations following periods when other treatments were adopted; nine companies however, treated the charges as provisions made in the course of profit determination. In summary then, it can be said that, when increased depreciation charges relating to increased costs of plant replacement have been made, only half the companies have followed the Institute recommendations and treated the charges as appropriations of profits.

Those companies which made charges before determining profits may be classified further into three categories: three companies simply increased the credit to provision for depreciation (one of these used different treatments in later years); three companies credited the amount to an appropriately titled provision, e.g. provision for increased cost of plant replacement; another three companies credited an appropriately titled provision after using different methods previously. Of the six companies having credited a provision for increased cost of plant replacement at some time, three have transferred the credit subsequently to a reserve account. Two of these companies have merged the balance with general reserve, and only one retains the balance as a specific reserve titled 'reserve for increased cost of plant replacement'.

The remaining treatment to note is that where a charge in addition to normal depreciation has been included before determining profit, and the credit raised as a reserve instead of as a provision. Five companies followed this practice for varying lengths of time. Two of them subsequently amended their terminology to that of a provision.

Some aspects of this recognition of costs over and above original asset cost is illustrated by what B.H.P., Australia's largest company, has done (Table 29). Between 1954 and 1961 this company made charges to the profit and loss statement and credited a provision for increased cost of plant replacement. When the company first made

TABLE 29
Depreciation expense and profitability of B.H.P.[a]

	Provision for increased cost of plant replacement £'000	Depreciation expense £'000	Net profit per cent of shareholders' funds[b]
1954	852	4367	8·2
1955	838	5038	8·3
1956	2995	6719	10·9
1957	4145	7864	10·1
1958	6120	10125	11·1
1959	6200	11260	10·7
1960	7025	11655	12·2
1961		22001	7·1
1962		24378	6·1
1963		26951	6·6

[a] Based on group consolidated figures.
[b] Net profit is stated after the provision for increased cost of plant replacement.

these additional provisions they were of relatively insignificant amounts. By 1956 the amount provided was nearly one-half of the annual depreciation, and in 1960 had reached 60 per cent of the annual depreciation. At the end of this period the company altered its practice. The assets of the company were revalued and henceforth depreciation was charged on the basis of replacement cost. The annual depreciation expense in 1961 increased to £22 million, an increase of £3.3 million on the combined total of depreciation and provision for increased cost of plant replacement for the preceding year. The revaluation of assets makes it difficult to assess the increase in the physical resources of the company during the year. The ratio of profit to shareholders' funds would have been substantially affected by the revaluation of assets which led to shareholders' funds being stated in 1961 at approximately twice the figure stated in 1960. This ratio of profitability would also have been reduced by the increase in depreciation resulting from the adoption of the different concept of depreciation as an allocation based on replacement cost. The presentation adopted from 1954 to 1960 revealed the extent of the charges made above an allocation of original cost of fixed assets to create the provision for increased cost of plant replacement. The presentation, subsequent to 1960, does not indicate the extent to which depreciation exceeds what it would be based on an allocation of the historical cost of fixed assets, and it is therefore considered to be a less informative and desirable form of disclosure.[12] Another problem is that the provision for depreciation based on replacement costs soon may exceed the stated asset values unless they are revised regularly in an upward direction. B.H.P. has recognized this by announcing in the 1969 annual report that henceforth the fixed asset values will be 'reduced by only that portion of the "Fixed Asset Utilisation" charge which relates to the gross asset values carried in the accounts. The remainder of the charge appears in the balance sheet as "Fixed Asset Value Adjustment"' within the shareholders' funds. In 1969 the latter sum amounted to 16 per cent of the 'Fixed Asset Utilisation' charge. The extent to which opinion may determine the result was shown clearly by the review (undertaken by the company) of the basis of calculating the total charge which resulted in an expense 9 per cent less than would have resulted from the procedures followed in the previous year and a 20 per cent increase in profit after taxes.

Among the business community there has not been a lack of advocacy for what the Institute describes as 'financial prudence', i.e. providing for possible unforeseen obsolescence and increased costs of plant replacement. The evidence from the 'forty-two leaders sample' shows that the directors of many companies are aware of these factors, but the action taken has however, been spasmodic and lacking in uniformity of approach. How many other companies may be making increased depreciation charges without disclosing the fact, we cannot tell. Even among the companies which have revealed a measure of their actions, it cannot be said that they have accepted the Institute recommendations for among the 'forty-two leaders sample' half of the companies revealing such charges reject the Institute view that it is an appropriation and not an expense.

It appears that while there is definite evidence of a recognition of the need for additional charges beyond those arising from an allocation of the historical costs of assets, the treatment of such charges is lacking in any uniformity and not by any means in accord with the official view of the Institute of Chartered Accountants in Australia.

26

A.I.M. Award and Report Production

In 1950 another factor which would contribute to the development of disclosure came into being, with the decision of the Australian Institute of Management to make an award for company annual reports. The A.I.M. Award (as it will be referred to herein) was instituted: 'To make known the important place of private enterprise in the community and to raise the standards of company reporting'.[1] The objects of the Award were amended in 1957 to include business enterprises outside of private enterprise, but otherwise remain as originally stated. These objects are:

To encourage the presentation and distribution of adequate financial and other information regarding business enterprise to proprietors, employees, and to the public generally in a form which those without business training can readily understand.

To establish better employee-employer relations by making known facts about business enterprises, and the financial results of their activities, and to create employee pride in organisations and in the products and services which they provide.[2]

The reports of all companies now are included automatically in the competition for the Award. An initial selection is made by the Stock Exchanges. Therefore companies do not have the choice of entry. Such a choice might reflect something of the company's attitude to disclosure. The A.I.M. Award each year has attracted considerable notice from the press and undoubtedly has done much towards developing a wider community awareness of good reporting practices.

The A.I.M. Award was instituted before the period in which company annual reports developed into extensive booklets making free use of colour printing and illustrative material. The period after the A.I.M. Award was instituted was also marked by a growing awareness of a wider readership of reports than the company's

26 A.I.M. Award and Report Production

shareholders. It is not unexpected, therefore, to find that the most effective work done by the A.I.M. Award is to be found in the development of better presentation and style and in those aspects of reporting which concern a wider reading audience. The A.I.M. Award has been less successful in respect of purely accounting issues. It is not meant to suggest that all improvements in the quality of the production of company reports can be attributed to the A.I.M. Award, but because of the emphasis given to these matters by the A.I.M. Award it is proposed to review these developments in the context of the impact of the A.I.M. Award.

In the early years covered by this study the typical company annual report consisted of a single quarto or foolscap pamphlet. Nearly always there are exceptions to a rule and B.H.P. and Jones were exceptions to this rule as early as 1917. There were those companies which realized the utility of a more substantial report and which progressed to producing a booklet often having a light pasteboard type of cover. This movement was accelerated when consolidated statements began to be published in the late thirties.

TABLE 30
Quality of production—booklet
'42 leaders sample'

	Size of available sample[a]	No. of companies	% of available sample	Notes
1930	19	5	26	
1935	24	9	38	Consolidated statements under
1939	30	15	50	Vic. Companies Act, 1938
1945	33	18	55	End of hostilities
1950	38	30	79	
1955	41	34	83	

[a] See explanatory note, p. 3.

Table 30 shows that a substantial proportion of reports from the 'forty-two leaders sample' became booklets and by 1950 the 'pamphlet' quality report very nearly had disappeared. The development of a more than two colour report on calendar paper and the introduction of illustrations, etc., took place approximately a decade later. Among the 'forty-two leaders sample' Dunlop and F. & T. showed leadership in issuing this quality of report in 1940. Such experiments were set back by paper and manpower shortages during World War II. Wartime conditions and their aftermath no doubt

TABLE 31
Quality of production—full colour booklet
'42 leaders sample'

	Size of available sample	No. of companies	% of available sample
1946	33	3	9
1950	38	7	18
1955	41	16	39
1960	42	34	81

acted as a restraint during the immediate post-war years. However, Table 31 shows how from 1948 onwards there was an increasing proportion of these reports, and by 1960 practically all reports of the 'forty-two leaders sample' were judged to be 'full colour booklets'. Any assessment of the quality of production of reports involves subjective analysis. Even an assessment based on the size and number of pages cannot avoid an element of subjectivity because the quality of the report will depend on how the available page space is utilized.

In 1948 R. J. Chambers made an analysis of the size of 250 company reports. He drew attention to the large number of companies still issuing a purely formal report, although the proportion displaying such economy was declining. He also drew attention to the cost factor and its possible relation to the tendency for larger reports to be issued by the larger companies. Distinctive covers he noted were added to otherwise formal reports whilst some larger reports did not appear to consider the cost of such a cover necessary or justified.[3] It would be easy to argue that good reporting depended on the amount of expenditure if size of report were the only criterion. The Institute of Management, however, through its A.I.M. Award, has been at pains to stress that, 'cost alone was no criterion of a good report and, in fact, that the Institute had penalized companies which otherwise may have won an award because of obviously excessive cost of production'. One company, we are told, wrote to the Institute giving 'its opinion that the award could not be won unless a company was prepared to spend a great deal of money on the presentation of its report'.[4] This company, Larke Consolidated Industries Ltd, appeared in the Merit Award List the following year, in the Special Award List in the next year and in 1964 and 1965 won the award for the best annual report.

If it did cost a great deal of money we can only assume that the company considered it justified. Further evidence that size and large expenditure were not necessary factors was given in 1963 when an award was made to J. Conkey & Sons Ltd, a company whose principal place of business is in the country town of Cootamundra in New South Wales. There is always the danger that excessive cost may not lead to improved reports, a condition noted in the 1965 report of the adjudicators. In their 1966 report the adjudicators noted that the 'tendency to increase cost has been reversed and the reports are better for it', and perhaps more importantly 'several awards this year are to relatively small Companies or organisations which have produced attractive, informative and yet inexpensive reports' (p. 3). However, the cost bogey does not seem to have been so easily put down because in 1967 the adjudicators reported that some reports had been marked down 'where cost appeared excessive in relation to the organisation' (p. 3).

What the A.I.M. Award has achieved towards the better use of this additional space in and expenditure on, company annual reports has been commented on by adjudicators in a statement prepared each year by E. S. Owens. Some of the matters on which the adjudicators have found it necessary to comment appear to be trivial, yet in practice are real problems.

In 1961, 1962 and 1963 the adjudicators criticized companies for failing to display the company's name clearly on the report. The adjudicators' report has consistently advocated the inclusion on the front cover of an indication that the report also includes the notice of annual meeting lest a member 'complain that he received no Notice if he consigned the Report to the wastepaper basket in the belief that it was one of the many brochures he did not have to read'.[5] The inclusion of this information was reported as being 'often shown' in 1964 but in 1965 drew the rebuke that 'too many companies made no reference' to the notice of meeting on the front cover. Among the 'forty-two leaders sample' in 1968 only thirteen companies included information on the cover of the report indicating that the report included the notice of meeting. Although practice might not have progressed so far as the adjudicators would like, it seems that they have achieved something worthwhile. As they pointed out in their 1962 report, there was a time when the notice of meeting was not even placed prominently in the report, far less referred to on the cover.

The title indicated on the front cover of the annual report varies widely. Among the 'forty-two leaders sample' in 1968 it was

TABLE 32
Title on front cover of Annual Report
'42 leaders sample', 1968

A (Including notice of meeting)		
Annual Report	10	
Annual Report and Financial Accounts	3	
	—	13
B (Not including notice of meeting)		
Annual Report	20	
Annual Accounts and Report	4	
Directors' Report and Accounts	1	
Directors' Report	1	
Annual Report and Balance Sheet	1	
Report and Chairman's Review	1	
Company Name	1	
	—	29
Total		42

possible to classify the titles used as shown in Table 32. The adjudicators have also pointed out that even where the name of the company is given: 'When the report was first instituted it was possible to examine a report from cover to cover and not know whether the organisation made jam or ran an airline. This is not the case today.'[6] The adjudicators have consistently drawn attention to this and pointed out its importance in circumstances such as takeovers. The 1965 A.I.M. Award report goes so far as to suggest that there should be some symbol on each page of the report which indicates the nature of the business (p. 7).

This is clearly not a problem confined to Australian companies because it was apparently considered necessary to rectify a lack of disclosure when the English Companies Act of 1967 introduced a requirement for the directors' report to include details of the principal activities of the company or group (s.16(1)). The adjudicators have continually advocated a more positive use of the reverse cover of the report. Among the 'forty-two leaders sample' the 1968 reports showed little evidence of any imaginative use of the back cover of the report. As Table 33 indicates nearly half the reports were completely blank on the back. Twenty-one of the forty-two reports gave an indication on the back cover as to who the booklet came from which is an increase of four on the number doing so in 1965. Only ten reports included any information on the back cover which would indicate to the reader that it was the annual report of the company. This compares with only six doing

TABLE 33
*Content of back cover of Annual Report
'42 leaders sample', 1968*

Blank page	17
Continuation of overall design pattern of front cover	3
Monogram or symbol	6
Pictorial material	4
Company name only	2
Other information	10
Total	42

so in 1965. One company very effectively used the back cover to detail the divisional structure of the group and the products of each division.

The adjudicators have commented regularly on 'layout, type suitability, etc.' and 'use of colour and illustrations'. These comments have been too wide in scope and too generalized to have been of very much help. Improvement in this respect is probably the product of the skill of compositors and commercial artists. However, the adjudicators were specific in their condemnation of too many personal photographs of directors and managers in 1961. Although this was not supported unanimously by the adjudicators it apparently had some impact because they reported in 1963 that, 'it was interesting to note that the number of personal photographs were fewer than in the previous year' (p. 3). In 1965 the comments on typography were made more specific by commending the type used by a nominated company.

The adjudicators have not advocated any particular sequence for the contents of the annual report. In a recent report of the adjudicators it was pointed out that the adjudicators were not in agreement amongst themselves on this although they did agree that the consolidated profit and loss statement should be associated with the consolidated statement of assets and liabilities rather than the parent company profit and loss statement. They have been successful in their advocacy of a 'highlights' page, placed in a prominent position. Such a page details selected key facts and interpretative ratios. More recently they have advocated this to be a perforated page that may be torn out for convenient filing for future reference. Table 34 shows the pattern of adoption of this aspect of presentation among the 'forty-two leaders sample' nearly half of which now include a highlights page in the annual report. It is only fifteen years since the first occasion when a highlights page was presented by one of the 'forty-two leaders sample'.

TABLE 34
Inclusion of highlights page
'42 leaders sample'

	Size of available sample[a]	No. of companies	% of available sample
1952	38	1	3
1955	41	6	15
1960	42	14	33
1965	42	20	48
1968	42	18	43

[a] See explanatory note, p. 3.

It is surprising to find that as far back as 1928 a writer in the *Commonwealth Journal of Accountancy* was advocating that many of the details of financial statements should be set out in supporting schedules so that the statements are not cluttered up.[7] Equally surprising is the advocacy by C. B. Harvey in 1936 of the use of notes to the financial statements:

As a result of the modern trend to give more information in published accounts, it is noticeable that in many balance sheets appearing at the present time (I am referring more particularly to those in England) explanatory notes are given against individual items in the balance sheet. Not only is this information of real value to shareholders and other parties interested, but it also has the twofold effect of modifying the responsibility of the auditor, by disclosing much important information which would influence shareholders in forming their opinions as to the financial position and possibilities of the company.[8]

These comments are surprising because they anticipate the general use of the technique of notes in Australian company financial statements by between fifteen and thirty years. The A.I.M. Award would appear to have been a great encouragement to the technique of using notes to set out a great deal of the detail required or desired to be included in the financial statements. The first instance of the use of this technique identified among the 'forty-two leaders sample' was in 1948, only two years before the commencement of the A.I.M. Award. The use of notes increased slowly until about 1959–60 when there was a rapid increase in the use of notes as indicated by the 'forty-two leaders sample' and set out in Table 35. As the A.I.M. Award adjudicators noted in 1961, there were excellent examples of notes among the award winning reports. This undoubtedly brought to the attention of

TABLE 35
Adoption of the technique of notes to the accounts '42 leaders sample'

	Size of available sample	No. of companies	% of available sample	Notes
1947	34	—	—	
1948	36	1	3	
1952	38	3	8	
1954	40	4	10	Vic. Companies Act, 1958
1959	42	10	24	
1962	42	22	52	Uniform Acts
1965	42	32	76	
1968	42	39	93	

companies what might be done. In the following year the use of notes was encouraged to meet the needs of the Uniform Acts. Information had to be given in many instances for the first time, and in considerably greater detail. Not only has the number of notes increased considerably but the extent of the notes has likewise increased. An attempt was made to measure this twofold effect among the 'forty-two leaders sample'. A points system of rating incorporating an arbitrary weighting was devised as follows: Each note scored one point. To this number of points was added 50 per cent if the notes occupied two pages, 75 per cent if they occupied three pages and 100 per cent if they occupied four or more pages. The points scored were grouped in intervals of five represented by the ratings A to H in Table 36. The arbitrary nature of the analysis is recognized. However, the results, set out in Table 36, in some measure indicate the trend towards more notes and more detail in each note.

The adjudicators of the A.I.M. Award have consistently advocated the wider use of 'graphs, charts and diagrams' (though a statistician may well take them to task for their apparent liking for pie charts). This is an aspect of reporting on which it is difficult to establish any general rules. While such devices may be useful, they do not always add to the information conveyed, nor are they always necessary. Even the adjudicators were forced in 1963 to

TABLE 36
The extent of notes to the accounts
'42 leaders sample'

No. of cases	1959	1962	1965	1968
	10	22	32	39
Rating[a]	% of cases			
A	30	23	13	13
B	20	23	19	23
C	20	18	22	18
D	10	18	6	10
E	—	9	25	3
F	20	4	—	15
G	—	5	3	13
H	—	—	12	5

[a] As defined in text.

mellow their advocacy by noting that: 'The award-winning report is notably lacking in use of these devices' (p. 7).

In addition to the above aspects of presentation, the A.I.M. Award appears to have been a significant factor in broadening the appeal of company annual reports. As the adjudicators noted in 1964:

There has been a marked trend this year towards the type of annual report which presents the company to the public instead of merely recording statistics. This is something which the Australian Institute of Management has encouraged since the beginning of the Award and it is rewarding to see so many companies taking this approach. (p. 2)

The A.I.M. Award appears not to have added very much to the treatment of such purely accounting issues as the classification of assets, the statement of taxation provisions, the inclusion of accumulated depreciation in the presentation of fixed assets in the balance sheet or the basis of valuation of stock. The A.I.M. Award however, does appear to have contributed to the extension of profit and loss and trading details. The adjudicators for the A.I.M. Award have adopted a firm attitude towards the necessity to disclose turnover. This has been taken so far as to attach a sufficient points penalty for non-disclosure, and in 1964 one company missed securing a Merit Award because of its failure to disclose this one item of information (p. 6).

In 1967 the A.I.M. Award introduced into the adjudicators' assessment a new factor which gives some more positive recognition of the quantitative basis of the report. This is the inclusion

26 A.I.M. Award and Report Production

in the report of information showing how the company's performance measures up to its past performance, the conditions in the business sector in which it operates and the future prospects of the company.

The adjudicators' Steering Committee in addition to their written reports have offered to discuss the reports submitted with the companies and organizations concerned. In 1966 twenty-three interviews resulted from this action.

During the period that the A.I.M. Award competition has operated there has been a significant improvement in the standard of company reporting and the Award may fairly claim credit for at least part of this improvement.

27

Operating Account Details

As the size and quality of company reports have grown in the period following World War II, so attention to more detailed aspects of the financial affairs of companies has grown. A number of these developments relate to the operating accounts of companies and it is these matters with which this chapter is concerned. Previous chapters have detailed earlier moves directed at such matters as the separation of extraordinary gains or losses from the operating results of the company, the disclosure of various forms of directors' remuneration and the depreciation expense.

It remains true, however, that companies have been, and remain, reluctant to concede very much detail of operations other than the final ascertained profit. Some chinks have been forced in the protective screen thus erected by companies. One small chink is the progress made in securing details of sales or turnover. As recently as 1964 K. W. Halkerston, a partner in a leading firm of sharebrokers, described the failure of companies to disclose their turnover as being, 'perhaps the biggest deficiency'[1] in company reporting in Australia. The absence of this information was described by two American investigators in 1960 as: 'one of the striking features of Australian financial reports'.[2] The case cannot be better stated than by R. A. Irish who, in 1948 questioned the persistence of the prejudice against the disclosure of turnover and declared:

Surely there is every reason why the shareholders should be informed as to the success of the company's sales policy. Competitors are not deluded for they can generally arrive at a ready approximation; in fact, in certain cases, there is no prospect of effective competition anyhow. Non-disclosure prevents the shareholder from effectively comparing the control of expenditure; it creates misconceptions in many quarters when a large sum of net profit is shown, although in reality it is a minute fraction of sales; it plays up to the technique of secret reserves in stock valuation; it prevents the assembly of statistics of value to the industry and to society.[3]

It is true that, for some companies, there are problems in correctly reporting this item including discounts and intercompany sales, extraordinary items, treatment of by-products, the relationship to minority interests of a group, a diverse product or service mix, that value added may better reflect productivity, taxes included in sales, and the overseas trading content in the total.

The disclosure of turnover was supported by the Jenkins Company Law Committee in England[4] and was made a statutory requirement under the English Companies Act of 1967 (second schedule, par. 13A) except for companies with a turnover less than £50,000 per annum. This Act has not attempted to define turnover but calls for a statement of the method by which the figure is arrived at. This may be the better alternative even if some companies try to maximize their turnover figures by use of debatable formulae, explained in an obscure note at the end of the report.

In Australia the Eggleston Committee established in 1967 to advise the Attorneys-General of the States and Commonwealth recommended that companies should be required to disclose turnover figures but at a conference in Hobart in March 1969 the committee of Attorneys-General rejected this recommendation.[5] Progress in this respect does not look promising at present. In the absence of statutory enforcement there has been consistent progress in disclosure of turnover details. There have even been instances of companies going further and giving divisional turnovers separately. Ansett, as the private enterprise section of the two airline policy of the government, may be regarded as in a special position which not only justifies, but requires, more disclosure than usual. Whether this is accepted or not, the company has issued some tables which are of special note here and which present a commendable standard of performance in financial reporting. Since 1958 the company has given the proportionate division of the company's financial resources among six divisions with the addition of a seventh division in 1964 after the company entered the television industry. (Originally expressed as a fraction of shareholders' funds, the statement has been expressed as gross assets since 1959.) The company also gives its gross revenue according to five divisions similar to the division of assets. Airline revenue has been published since 1954, road passenger revenue since 1954, road freight revenue since 1957 and the remaining revenue divided between 'Hotel and tourist resort operations' and 'Manufacturing and trading operations' since 1960.

The results of an examination of the practice of the 'forty-two

TABLE 37
Statement of turnover
'42 leaders sample'

	Size of available sample[a]	No. of companies	% of available sample
1939	29	—	—
1940	31	1	3
1950	36	7	19
1955	38	11	29
1960	39	16	41
1965	39	17	44
1968	39	16	41

[a] Three finance companies are excluded from this table on the grounds that the information is not relevant to this type of business.

leaders sample', presented in Table 37, indicate that there has been a steady growth in the proportion of companies giving actual turnover figures throughout the post-war period, until at present nearly half of the companies disclose this information. Many of the 'forty-two leaders sample' are companies occupying such a dominant position in their respective industry that there can hardly be an argument that disclosure of turnover would benefit their competitors. We must conclude that the move to secure turnover cannot be said to have progressed nearly so far as to only leave a 'hard core' of companies failing to disclose this information. There remains considerable scope for the exercise of the persuasive power of voluntary factors towards disclosure of turnover.

A very small number of instances were found among the 'forty-two leaders sample' of companies giving the quantitative amounts of production. This may hardly be regarded as significant disclosure because in the industries concerned the argument may be readily sustained that this information should be available as basic statistics of the economic life of the community. The companies moreover, occupy monopoly or duopoly positions, whereby the industry and the company or pair of enterprises are equivalent to each other. Two cases, B.H.P. and C.S.R., are companies which are the sole producers in Australia of steel and refined sugar respectively. Two paper manufacturers, A.P.M. and A.P.P.M., who give production tonnages, operate in different segments of the industry to a large extent.

Changing circumstances may be expected to lead to pressure

for disclosure of information not available previously. This is illustrated by the new emphasis on debenture finance in the post World War II period, leading to the introduction in the Victorian Companies Act of 1958 of a requirement to state the amount of interest paid on debentures and other fixed loans (ninth schedule, clause 1(e)). This measure was extended to all States by the Uniform Acts.

A later corollary to this development was the requirement introduced in the Uniform Act for companies to state separately the income from investments in shares and debentures, income from other investments and income from subsidiary companies (ninth schedule, clause 1(c)).

In a similar way, the modern development of directors determining the auditor's remuneration has led to a statutory requirement to disclose that remuneration. The principle underlying the appointment of auditors is that the auditor is appointed by, and responsible to the members of the company. When the appointment of auditors was made compulsory it was logical therefore that it should be the shareholders who fixed the auditor's remuneration. However it became practice for the annual meeting of members to delegate this power to the directors. This is frequently more convenient because, if the auditor is paid on a time basis, the charge would not be known until after the work was done. However, lest the directors 'avoid' an adequate audit by underpaying, or conversely attempt to 'bribe' the auditor, the shareholders should know what remuneration the auditor appointed by them receives.

It is perhaps not surprising that some auditors have objected to the distinction thereby imposed on their profession. The Victorian Act of 1958 (ninth schedule, clause 1(1)) required such disclosure and when it was proposed to carry this into the Uniform Act the general council of the Institute of Chartered Accountants in Australia did not think the auditor's fee should be singled out but should be available on request at an annual general meeting. The council recognized that its motives might be misconstrued and therefore suggested that alternatively the Institute's policy should be to seek for a limitation on the disclosure to cover fees received only in respect of the actual audit function.[6] Subsequently the Uniform Act did require disclosure of the auditor's remuneration 'for their services as auditors' (ninth schedule, clause 1(m)). This amounted to something of a compromise compared with the Victorian Act of 1958. That Act required disclosure of payments for all services rendered by the auditor. With the development of the field of management services, many auditors now provide much wider services than those of the audit. The principle of the shareholders knowing the financial relationship of the auditor to the company, however, has been preserved. This has been done by providing that 10 per cent of the members (or holders of 10 per cent of the issued shares) may petition to receive a statement of all emoluments paid to or receivable by the auditor.

A development affecting only a relatively small number of companies, but frequently of substantial significance to those few companies, concerns the treatment of unearned income on terms contracts. This was brought to notice as a direct consequence of enquiries into the affairs of certain companies in the sixties by government-appointed inspectors.

It is not part of the purpose of this book to argue the question of whether, on some types of terms contracts, the profit on the trading transaction should not be taken until payment is completed. The matter specifically dealt with here is the treatment in the published statements of the unearned terms charges and the information given about how that unearned income figure is determined. The argument proceeds on the basis of general acceptance of the assumption that the revenue on a terms contract can be regarded as being earned over the period of the contract.

During the post World War II period there had been a rapid expansion in the field of consumer finance which gave these aspects of accounting and reporting a new importance. The first evidence of any formal action by professional accountants was the establishment in 1959 by the general council of the Institute of Chartered Accountants in Australia, of a special committee to study the topic. The committee's findings were adopted by the council of the Institute and published in January 1960. The Institute pronouncement at this stage was that income yet to mature should be shown as a deduction from the relevant asset and not among the liabilities in either a balance sheet or prospectus.[7] It did not concern itself with the effects of this item on the operating accounts.

Among the 'forty-two leaders sample' there are six companies for which 'unearned income' is a significant item. Three are hire purchase and finance companies, one a retailer, one a manufacturer and retailer of electrical appliances, and one a manufacturer of electrical consumer durables. Each of these companies stated its debtors at the full amount including the income yet to mature which was shown amongst the liabilities in the balance sheet. Four of these companies adopted the Institute recommendation issued in January 1960 and treated income yet to mature as a deduction from the gross debtors. The other two companies were later compelled to adopt this presentation by the Uniform Acts. At the time in 1961 the directors of A.G.C. reported:

You will note the deferred income is deducted from gross receivables in conformity with good accounting practice, and not shown as a detached liability on the opposite side of the balance sheet. This practice conforms with a suggestion made by the Institute of Chartered Accountants in Australia, in which this Company fully concurs.

The directors of I.A.C. reported in 1962 that, 'this year in accordance with a change in the Companies Act, it is shown as a deduction from the assets'.

A second and perhaps more important aspect of unearned income on terms contracts is the calculation of the sum to be accounted for and the disclosure of the method followed in making the calculation. In some circumstances an awareness of the problem of calculating the amount of unearned income stems directly from altered business circumstances. Thus in 1958 Myers attributed to the growth in sales of television sets, the necessity to 'alter the accounting treatment to properly apportion the hiring charges and profits on these transactions as between one year and another over the full duration of the hiring agreements'. In some finance companies the matter was brought to attention when they entered into contracts which tended to be for longer time intervals, e.g. Custom reported in 1961 that the proportion of motor vehicle finance had fallen from a one time level of 70 per cent to somewhere nearer 25 per cent.[8] It appears that the unearned income formulae used by the company failed to meet this altered position and led to the adjustments made to the company's accounts for 1962 when, as a Sydney paper reported: 'Custom Credit Corporation's heavy addition of £1,145,770 to its unearned income provision represents an over-statement of previous years' declared profits by this amount. . . . This would represent about a 25 per cent over-statement of the taxable profits published in the three years.'[9] Such events drew attention to the adequacy or otherwise of currently accepted methods of calculating 'unearned income'.

The Institute of Chartered Accountants did not say anything on how income yet to mature should be calculated until June 1961. A pronouncement made in that month supported the 'rule of 78' as the only acceptable basis of apportionment of the income on a terms finance transaction but did not require any publication of the method used.[10] Writing in the *Chartered Accountant in Australia* B. J. Hill and M. F. Desmarchelier pointed out that the error in the rule becomes substantial when the interest rate chargeable exceeds 5 per cent or the contract extends beyond twelve months.[11] The argument that the rule was that used in the hire purchase Statute was dismissed by these writers as a preoccupation with rebating and an illogical justification of its use.[12] Their comments may be contrasted with the increase in the provision for income yet to mature made by Custom in the 1962 accounts so that, 'the provision at 30 June . . . represents the sum of the rebates or charges on Hire Purchase, Mortgages and other Charges which the Company would have made if all contracts, both short and long term, had been paid out in advance on 30 June, 1962.' The general council of the Institute of Chartered Accountants reported in June 1962 that its special committee was evolving a formula in consultation with the Australian Hire Purchase Conference, to cover the treatment of longer term contracts.[13] There was little need to argue the necessity for the council's action because as N. Runcie pointed out four months later in the *Chartered Accountant in Australia*, 'at least three important Australian finance companies have disclosed deficiencies in their unearned income provision in recent years'.[14] Runcie argued that any formula should take account of the whole cost structure of the finance industry and not only the funds invested. In November the council of the Institute reported progress and announced that: 'Authority was given for this work to continue to the point where any agreed-upon formula may be endorsed by the Executive of the Council for promulgation to the hire purchase industry through the Australian Hire Purchase Conference.'[15]

A pronouncement was made in the following April by the Australian Hire Purchase Conference, which proposed:

(a) That the 'Rule of 78', modified to meet individual companies' particular types of business, should be retained in assessing unearned income on short-term contracts—up to five years.

(b) That a specially devised set of actuarial factors, known as 'Collins' factors should be used in assessing deferred income on long-term contracts—beyond five years.[16]

The response of the six companies in the 'forty-two leaders sample' for which unearned income on terms contracts is a significant item, have varied greatly. The appliance manufacturers and retailers have not indicated how they calculate the provision shown in their reports. The intimation by Custom in 1962 of how

27 Operating Account Details

they calculate the amount rebatable has already been referred to. This effectively means the 'rule of 78' on hire purchase contracts because this is the basis of calculating rebates under the hire purchase Acts of the States. The statement by the directors of the company does not tell us the formulae used on other types of contract, but only that electronic equipment is used to make the calculation. I.A.C. reported in 1962 that the methods of calculation it used were:

In respect of hire purchase transactions—by the rule of 78, [and] in respect of mortgages and other loan transactions where the principal and interest are merged and repayable by equal monthly instalments—by means of an electronic computer using the true rate of interest for each transaction on a formula approved by the Company's Consulting Actuary.

In 1962 A.G.C. had included an actuary's certificate that the 'deferment of income' was more than that required to meet actuarial methods of calculation. The company has continued to include an actuary's certificate in the annual report. The chairman claimed in 1964 that he was, 'proud to say that we are, as far as I know, the only company which does produce such an assurance to its shareholders'. In 1965 the company intimated that it had adopted a method of calculation described as the 'Collins Factor $- T + 1$', i.e. in accordance with the recommendations of the Australian Hire Purchase Conference.

Although neither voluntary nor statutory forces have yet led to, or required, the statement of the direct adjustments in the operating accounts for unearned income, we have moved to a situation where the basis of calculating the balance of unearned income stated in the balance sheet has been clarified and made known to readers of the financial reports of most companies with large amounts of instalment debtors. While the Institute of Chartered Accountants played some role in this development it is clear that the primary contribution came from the Australian Hire Purchase Conference.

The discussion of the treatment of unearned income provides an appropriate point to review the development of disclosure procedures applicable generally to transfers to and from reserves and/or provisions. Earlier discussion showed how the modern terminology of provisions and reserves developed. At this point amounts arising from adjustments before the ascertainment of profit are described as provisions and those arising afterwards as reserves except where the appropriation is made to meet a specific liability of known amount.

The first statutory requirements for disclosure in all the States, except Western Australia, required no more information on operations than a statement of the balance remaining in the profit and loss appropriation account and, in some cases, the disclosure of the amount charged for depreciation. The Acts passed in Queensland in 1931 and New South Wales in 1936 required disclosure of any transfers from reserves, but did nothing towards uncovering any transfers from balances rightly or wrongly regarded as provisions. The Acts passed in Victoria in 1938, in Western Australia in 1943 and in Tasmania in 1959, required disclosure of transfers made *from* either reserves or provisions and transfers made *to* reserves. This meant that any drawing on such reserves or provisions had to be disclosed but a company could 'salt away' unlimited resources by transfers to provisions without having to disclose any details, so long as it was earning profits to cover the charges to the profit and loss account. This situation continued until the Uniform Acts were passed including requirements to state the amounts of transfers to and from reserves and, more importantly, for the operating accounts to state the amounts of transfers *to* and *from* provisions subject only to the qualification of materiality. Whether the information is disclosed is therefore dependent on the interpretation of what is 'material'.

An examination was made of the practices of the 'forty-two leaders sample' and this indicated an increasing level of disclosure of provisions other than those for depreciation, taxation and proposed dividends (the latter two arising from appropriations to meet specific claims of known amount). The number of these 'other' provisions shown was:

	1965	1968
One item	9 cases	15 cases
Two items	6 cases	3 cases
Three items	Nil	2 cases
Four items	1 case	1 case
Total	16 cases	21 cases

The description of the provisions comprised:

	1965	1968
'Other' provisions	6	5
Doubtful debts	3	3
Various	16	15
Long service leave	4	8

In each case where an amount was described as 'other' provisions in terms of the Act, the amount exceeded $200,000. This suggests that for these companies this sum may represent what is regarded as a 'material' amount. The disclosure in the profit and loss statement only represents the amounts added to a little more than one fifth of the number of the provisions disclosed in the balance sheet. For the purposes of balance sheet analysis provisions were confined to those arising from charges made before ascertaining profit except for depreciation provisions. Provisions arising from appropriations of ascertained profits were excluded so far as this fact could be identified. Only one of the consolidated statements presented by the 'forty-two leaders sample' failed to disclose any such provisions. The provisions disclosed in the consolidated statements were classified as in Table 38, indicating that provisions

TABLE 38
Provisions shown in consolidated statements '42 leaders sample', 1965–8

Title of provision	No. of cases		% of total	
	1965	1968	1965	1968
Doubtful debts	28	34	27	29
Long service leave	27	30	26	26
Unearned income, etc.	8	11	8	9
Stock	9	8	8	7
Unexpired risks, etc.	—	11	—	9
Other	32	24	29	20
Total	104	118	100	100

disclosed related primarily to doubtful debts and long service leave with a smaller number relating to unearned income and stock.

The discretion of showing 'material' provisions has clearly led to very limited disclosure of provisions made in the course of determining profit, other than the provision for depreciation.

The treatment afforded provisions for taxation are discussed separately in the next chapter.

So far as items in the operating accounts other than those already referred to are concerned, there is little to be said of developments or even pressures for disclosure. Development of this aspect of disclosure remains largely for the future. The few cases found in the 'forty-two leaders sample' may be individually mentioned. In the days when B.H.P. was engaged in mining, the Mine Working

Account gave some twelve expense items comprising eight functional activities and four other items. With the closure of the mine and the entry into steelmaking, the company moved to give only the net result of all operations. C.U.B. from 1914 included ten expense items in the profit and loss statement. This was reduced to five in 1922 and became only one aggregate item in 1924. Ansett has included in its report since 1942 (except for the years 1951–5 inclusive), either as part of the consolidated profit and loss statement or a 'simplified' statement, details of expenses divided into wages and salaries, fuels, and materials (more recently including tourist accommodation in this item instead of as a separate item), taxes of all kinds, and overhead expenses. With the technological change of some of its re-equipment programme, this information provided an insight into the changing cost structure of the air transport industry. Perhaps the best example of what might be achieved in this aspect of reporting is provided by Nat. Cons. This company in 1952 introduced into the annual report a diagram which gave the company's cost structure according to wages, machines, materials and services. From 1956 this became a more formal statement. Later this information was incorporated in the 'legal' consolidated profit and loss statement.

28

Taxation

It was a common practice in years past to include the company's liability for taxation in the balance sheet although this was combined frequently with other liabilities and likely as not, grossly overstated. As E. S. Wolfenden pointed out in 1928, the tax liability frequently was overestimated to the extent that it ought to have been regarded as a reserve to be added to shareholders' funds.[1]

The Institute of Chartered Accountants recommendations issued in 1946 sought the separate statement of the liability. This had little effect on practice. For example although a little more than half of the 'forty-two leaders sample' were disclosing an estimated tax liability at the time, Table 39 shows there was a slow response from the other companies. Similar evidence was provided in the report of the judges for the 1953 A.I.M. Award. It remained for the Uniform Acts to give statutory support to the disclosure of the estimated tax liability in the balance sheet.

TABLE 39
Disclosure of tax liability in the balance sheet
'42 leaders sample'

	Size of available sample[a]	No. of companies	% of available sample	Notes
1920	9	nil	—	
1930	19	3	16	
1935	24	8	33	
1940	32	18	56	
1946	33	19	58	
1950	38	24	63	
1956	42	31	74	
1960	42	36	86	
1962	42	42	100	Uniform Acts

[a] See explanatory note, p. 3.

Even if the tax liability was stated correctly in the balance sheet, we still could not be sure of the amounts provided for and/or paid during the year unless we were to assume actual payments were made equal to the reported liability. Moves for disclosure in respect of taxation therefore have been directed primarily at the reporting of the provision necessary to cover the estimated liability on the current year's taxable income.

The disclosure of the provision made during the financial period for estimated taxation was covered by the 1946 recommendation of the Institute of Chartered Accountants in Australia. The inclusion of this item in the profit and loss statement was recommended by the Cohen Committee[2] and included in the 1947 English Companies Act (first schedule, clause 8(1)(c)). Table 40 shows that the

TABLE 40
Disclosure of taxation appropriation
'42 leaders sample'

	Size of available sample	No. of companies	% of available sample	Notes
1917	5	2	40	
1920	9	2	29	
1930	19	11	58	
1935	24	8	33	
1940	32	14	44	
1946	33	16	48	I.C.A.A. recommendations
1950	38	21	55	
1956	42	33	79	Vic. Companies Act amendment
1960	42	37	88	
1962	42	42	100	Uniform Acts

Institute recommendations could at best be regarded as being followed reluctantly and that progress in disclosing the annual taxation provision remained dependent on legislative action. The first statutory recognition in Australia of the practice of disclosing the taxation provision came in the amending Victorian Act of 1955 which added to the items to be shown in the profit and loss statement, the 'provision made for payment of income tax in respect of the year ending on the date to which the account is made up' (s.11 (2)). This requirement was included in the Uniform Acts by all States in 1961 (ninth schedule, clause 2(1)(g)).

The reporting of actual taxes paid rather than the provision made has rarely occurred. During the period from 1941, Woolworth adopted this course although they had disclosed a provision for estimated taxation since 1929. The directors in this case explained their action on the grounds that: 'Owing to the increasing rates of taxation on account of war costs and the retrospective incidence of some of the recent taxation enactments, it is not possible to estimate with any degree of certainty the Company's taxation liability in respect of a year when the accounts are being closed.' The inability to calculate accurately the provision required is a rather dubious reason for non-disclosure. Aspects of taxation law may cause substantial variations in the estimate. Some of these are such that disclosure of the provision amount may suggest disclosure of additional information as to the cause of the variation in the amount of the provision if the statements are not to be misleading.

The low proportion of the 'forty-two leaders sample' disclosing the tax provision (see Table 40) appears to be at variance with the Report of the Adjudicators of the A.I.M. Award in 1953 that: 'In most cases the tax provision was indicated in the profit and loss account.'[3] This was before the A.I.M. Award competition automatically included all listed companies, and it is highly probable that the adjudicators could be regarded as therefore commenting on a better-than-average sample of company reports.

The results of the examination of the reports of the 'forty-two leaders sample' suggest that the Institute recommendations had little effect and the significant change in the proportion of companies disclosing this information was related closely to the amendments made to the companies Acts.

It has been recognized over a considerable period that the calculation of taxable income on which the tax liability is based, and accounting profit need not necessarily agree, and therefore, that the amount of taxation payable may not always bear the same ratio to the disclosed accounting profit.[4] The fact that the disclosed taxation liability bears a ratio to the disclosed accounting profit different from the ruling rate of tax payable on taxable income of companies, serves to highlight a difference between taxable income and accounting profit. It is helpful to the reader of the report to know why this situation exists. It may arise from: (a) the inclusion of expense items, such as depreciation calculated at different rates; (b) a different distinction between capital and revenue outlays; (c) the dis-allowance for tax calculation purposes of what are regarded as legitimate expenses; or (d) the allowance for tax calculation purposes of deductions which are not represented by current expenses, such as past losses, or special allowances for such items as plant investment and export incentives.

One of the first occasions on which this difference of taxable income determination and profit measurement drew any widespread attention, arose from the introduction of initial depreciation allowances. As an incentive to investment to aid in the development of export markets and to assist in offsetting inflated cost of machinery, the government introduced a 40 per cent initial depreciation allowance for the determination of taxable income. This was introduced in 1946 for a period of five years, and operated on taxable income up to the year ended 30 June 1951, with a twelve months' period to cover plant in the course of delivery.[5] There is no fundamental reason why the depreciation rates used for taxation purposes, and those used for profit determination and reporting, must be the same. However, a difference between the rates can contribute towards a variation in the relationship of taxation and profit. Such a variation ought to be explained. If, in calculating taxable income, depreciation rates are increased arbitrarily, this does not mean that the depreciation expense in the profit statement ought to be increased similarly. Such action would be tantamount to creating hidden reserves. An indication of the incidence of these initial depreciation allowances among Australian companies is given by the study undertaken by J. McB. Grant and R. L. Mathews in South Australia. Of twenty replies received, fourteen companies had claimed the initial depreciation allowance, and of these, nine had included the additional depreciation, 'with ordinary depreciation in their books of account and published reports'.[6] The magnitude of the amount involved compared with normal depreciation expense is indicated by Table 41 taken from another report of Grant and Mathews' study and reproduced here. Grant and Mathews obtained this information by questionnaire. How many companies had claimed the initial depreciation allowance and what was the magnitude of amounts included in the financial statements would have been impossible to determine from an examination of published reports.

Seven of the companies in the 'forty-two leaders sample' made some form of report to indicate that the company had taken advantage of the initial depreciation allowances. The simplest treatment would be to give a note setting out the amount of the tax benefits gained in this way. The advocates of 'tax allocation' would consider that this high initial deduction for tax purposes represents the bringing forward of a tax deduction which should be regarded as part of the profit determined later in the lifetime of the asset. The acceptance of this view would require the creation of a provision for deferred taxes which would give relief to those later periods when the assets were still in use but no further tax deduction of the asset cost would be available. In four cases it was possible to identify the amount involved and to trace the subsequent running down of the 'provision for deferred' taxes. In one other case information in a report of a much later year suggested the continuation of a balance sheet item arising from these allowances.

TABLE 41
Initial depreciation allowances in relation to total depreciation
(£'000s)

	Initial allowances claimed	Initial allowances recorded	Total depreciation recorded
1945–6	28	16	128
1946–7	47	27	163
1947–8	40	14	113
1948–9	94	69	221
1949–50	120	69	258
1950–1	369	93	364
1951–2	207	77	478
1952–3	2	2	389
1953–4	1	1	532

SOURCE: J. McB. Grant and R. L. Mathews, 'The Response of South Australian Companies to the Post-War Inflation', *Australian Accountant*, 27 (March 1957), p. 151.

The Grant and Mathews figures suggest that quite a large number of companies recorded the allowance as an effective depreciation of assets. The 'forty-two leaders sample' evidence is that few companies were ready to disclose the effect of the allowance, but that when they did, it could be expected that they would make provision for the 'deferred tax'. At least twenty-nine companies in the 'forty-two leaders sample' were in the available sample at the relevant period, and would be expected to have been entitled to the benefit of these allowances. The eight instances of positive action being taken in reporting the effect of the allowances therefore, suggests little acceptance at the time of this as a desirable standard of disclosure.

Initial depreciation allowances continued to be used as a taxation device in later years for agriculture. In more recent times the government has made investment allowances, i.e. the deduction from assessable income of an amount apart from the allocation of the cost of the asset. That such an allowance is calculated as a proportion of the asset cost may be regarded as simply an arithmetical device. These investment allowances were introduced through s.62AA of the Income Tax and Social Services Contribution Assessment Act of 1962, 'as part of the Commonwealth Government's proposals designed to stimulate the economy', and were to apply to plant 'delivered on and after 7 Feb 1962 and will be allowed in the year in which such plant is first used, or installed ready for use, in manufacturing processes'.[7] Writing in the *Australian Accountant* three members of the Victorian State Research Committee of the Australian Society of Accountants identified four possible methods of accounting treatment of these allowances: the taxation saving taken in full in the first year as a reduction in the provision for income tax for that year, either with or without disclosure of the amount involved; the saving spread over the estimated useful life of the related plant, as a reduction of the provision for income tax; the saving used to reduce the cost of the assets which gave rise to the saving, thus leading to lower charges for depreciation over the estimated useful life of the assets; the saving excluded from the determination of profit in any period and transferred to a reserve account.[8] Whichever of these methods is adopted, it is clear that the provision for taxation account will be affected, and possibly other accounts.

Among the 'forty-two leaders sample' only sixteen companies made any mention of the matter in their 1965 reports. This represents half of the companies likely to be entitled to claim the investment allowance. Probably ten of the 'forty-two leaders sample' would not be entitled to these allowances because they are financial companies, retailers, television and newspaper companies and manufacturers in industries unlikely to qualify under the conditions which apply. Of the sixteen companies, thirteen reported that the allowance had been taken into account in determining the provision for income tax, and nine of these companies gave the monetary value of the tax saving involved. Two companies created a 'secret reserve' by not taking the allowance into account in calculating the provision for income tax. The other company had not taken the allowance into the current year's accounts but showed the item in the previous year's comparative figures. The place of presentation of the relevant information in the annual report was equally varied. Of the sixteen companies which made some mention of the investment allowance, nine gave the details in the notes to the statements, five included the detail in the directors' report, one in the general manager's report and one in a separate pamphlet of the chairman's address to the annual meeting of the company.

Up to this point the treatment of the tax consequences of these matters was largely a matter of individual company *ad hoc* adjustments as and when it was considered necessary. Similar treatment was given to the consequences of such measures as the double deduction of export promotion expenses and the effects of past tax losses. For example, three of the nine cases in which monetary values were given in 1965 for the tax consequences of the investment allowances also included the consequences of export marketing allowances, losses of subsidiaries or calls paid to a forestry company.

Some statutory recognition of these problems was incorporated in the English Companies Act of 1967 which calls for advice by way of note of any deferred taxation (second schedule, par. 14 (3A)), but up to the present there has not been any attempt to legislate on the matter in Australia.

The Australian Associated Stock Exchanges approached this problem by amending the Official List Requirements in 1967 to require a company to give an explanation of and the major items responsible for any difference of more than 15 per cent between the stated amount provided for taxation and the prima facie tax payable if normal tax rates were applied to the disclosed profit.[9]

The response to the move by the A.A.S.E. as evidenced by the 'forty-two leaders sample' suggests some improvement in the standard of reporting. Whereas in 1965 dollar amounts of the tax effect were given by nine of the sixteen companies acknowledging the effect of the investment allowance, in 1968 the dollar tax savings were given by ten out of thirteen companies identifying themselves as benefiting from the investment allowance. Another two companies recognized the investment allowance but only gave the total tax effect of these allowances together with other deductions including past losses and export deductions. All of these companies took account of the allowance to reduce the taxation provision for the year although this effect was more than offset by other factors in two cases.

The existence of tax savings in addition to those arising from the investment allowance were identified and given dollar values by four of the above companies while one company mentioned the existence of other deductions without giving a dollar value. Another three companies identified similar items and gave either the tax saving or the deduction involved.

Thus in 1968 among the 'forty-two leaders sample' no less than fifteen companies gave a dollar amount of the reduction in tax provided due to these deductions.

The approach adopted by the Stock Exchanges is in line with the widely held view that the amount reported as provision for income tax should represent the tax assessment for that year. This view demands the disclosure of the main components making up the tax assessment to explain the variations from year to year. R. A. McInnes prepared a survey of current practice in 1968 for the Australian Society of Accountants and concluded that 'present practices . . . do not follow any cohesive pattern and few (companies) provide a reconciliation with the single amount shown in the published statement'.[10] The procedure of tax allocation[11] as practised in the U.S.A. does not appear to have gained general acceptance in Australia but there are signs that there is some trend towards adopting the procedure. McInnes found that ten of the ninety-four companies he examined in 1968 had disclosed some provision for future taxes[12] which arose in a number of cases from circumstances such as give rise to the tax allocation procedure followed in the U.S.A. A wider acceptance of these concepts will place new demands on company reporting.

Among the 'forty-two leaders sample' in 1968 seven companies were identified which had introduced some element of tax allocation. Three of these companies have shown a separate provision for future tax in the balance sheet, while the remainder have simply adjusted the usual taxation provision shown. One company has made this adjustment to offset tax deductions of past losses, and depreciation, but noted that the adjustment did not represent the current tax savings. Another company simply explained that the matter arose from the timing of deductions while the remaining five all explain their actions as arising from differences in depreciation for tax purposes and the depreciation included in the financial statements. Five of these companies gave the dollar amount of this adjustment or included it in a dollar amount for the net effect of all tax adjustments.

It is clear that the new requirements of the A.A.S.E. have already produced a substantial improvement in the disclosure of the circumstances affecting the reported tax liability on the disclosed profit.

A general presumption that the reported tax liability on the disclosed profit should be as nearly as possible the tax assessed for the year[13] reflects the legal nature of the liability, and recognizes the function of tax planning by management. This approach to reporting taxes however, does require the additional disclosure along the lines of the A.A.S.E. requirements of those factors which have caused the actual tax to vary from the prima facie tax payable on the disclosed profit. The alternative approach is the procedure of 'interperiod allocation of income taxes'. This concept implies that assets and expenses have an inherent tax deduction which 'attaches' to the asset or expense until it is matched against revenue. The application of the procedure to the allocation of fixed asset costs in a firm continually acquiring new assets may lead to recording a deferred liability which is unlikely to ever be payable.[14] It reaches its ultimate extreme when a loss is reported reduced by the amount of the future tax saving which may result from the deduction of the loss if profits are earned in the future.[15] The procedure appears more plausible where accrual accounting requires recognition of an expense such as doubtful debts while tax law may recognize only the actual event of finally writing off the bad debt. Interperiod tax allocation is at least as misleading as the non-disclosure of the relevant factors affecting the tax liability.

29

Group Accounts

In previous discussion of the problems relating to disclosure of the affairs of holding companies and their subsidiaries, the broad scope of developments was indicated but discussion was deferred of some of the more detailed problems which have been given attention as the scope of disclosure practised by holding company groups has grown. In this chapter these problems of disclosure by such groups are examined.

The statutory recognition of consolidated statements in the Victorian Companies Act of 1938 made the solution of the supposed problems in the preparation of such statements more urgent. Fortunately there were leaders in the accounting profession ready to make a contribution to this task. The most notable efforts were the two series of articles, one by R. K. Yorston[1] and the other by G. E. Fitzgerald and A. E. Speck,[2] the latter of which formed the basis of what was to become, for nearly twenty years, the only Australian specialist textbook on the subject.[3] It also seems that examples of consolidated statements published and commented on in the 'Commerce and Finance' section of the *Accountant* proved valuable in assisting the development of Australian practice. Readers of the *Australian Accountant* were given in 1939 a guide to the relevant materials in the *Accountant*.[4] Official support of consolidated statements was given by the Institute of Chartered Accountants in England and Wales Recommendations on Accounting Principles no. 7, which were in turn adopted in substance as Recommendations on Accounting Principles V of the Institute of Chartered Accountants in Australia in 1946. In addition to recommending consolidated statements, these recommendations represented an advance on the legislation in England and in Queensland, South Australia and New South Wales by recognizing that the group accounts should also include sub-subsidiary and further derivatives if they exist.

The resolution of problems in the preparation of consolidated statements and the acceptance of such statements has been sufficiently successful to cause some writers to question whether there is any useful information in the statements covering only the group parent company.

In company reports where separate parent and consolidated statements are given, there is a noticeable trend to give priority of position to the consolidated statements. In 1968 among the 'forty-two leaders sample' the consolidated statements were given more prominence than the parent company statements in the reports of twenty-four companies. Two companies have gone so far as to draw attention to the importance the company gives the consolidated statements. In 1950 the report of Ansett carried the note to the parent statements: 'The Victorian Companies Act, 1938 requires the publication of the Balance sheet of a Holding Company. As the major assets of this organisation are held by subsidiary Companies, the position of the entire group of Companies is only seen in the Consolidated Balance-sheet attached.' Similar notes are made in all subsequent reports. Nat. Cons. included a similar comment in its report from 1955 until 1961 inclusive. In twelve companies the parent company statements retained their position as the primary statements. There has also been a noticeable trend, illustrated in Table 42, to the use of a composite statement which

TABLE 42
Presentation of parent and consolidated figures in composite statement '42 leaders sample'

	No. of reports
1957	1
1960[a]	2
1961	3
1962	7
1963[b]	7
1964[b]	9
1965[bc]	9
1968	6

[a] One company, composite balance sheet only.
[b] One company, composite profit and loss statement only.
[c] In addition, one company included statements combining pounds and dollar figures.

includes the parent and consolidated details in one statement, this being used by six companies in 1968. The first reference to this type of presentation appears to be the reference to the statements of Borax Consolidated in the *Accountant* of 12 March 1949 reported by F. E. Trigg writing in the *Chartered Accountant in Australia* in May 1949 (p. 714). The rapid growth in this type of statement appears to have been accelerated by the requirements of the 1961–2 Uniform Acts to include comparative figures in all statements. This form of presentation is suited particularly to include comparative data. The presentation generally is arranged with the descriptive titles in the centre. On either side of these titles are the parent and consolidated figures respectively, while outside of these are placed the comparative figures for the previous accounting period.

The first problem in the preparation of consolidated statements is the definition of what constitutes the group entity. Under Australian companies legislation the definition of a subsidiary company has been accepted as being ownership of more than half of the voting rights attached to the shares, or having the power to appoint a majority of the directors of the company. Therefore, consolidated statements generally have included at least those companies in which the parent owns more than 50 per cent of the shares. This may extend to more than one level of the company structure. Among the 'forty-two leaders sample' there occurred an instance, namely Bradford in 1954–7, of a company only including wholly owned subsidiaries. It should be noted that at the time the company was not subject to any statutory obligations to publish consolidated statements. The Victorian Companies Act of 1938 however, adopted a definition which was sufficiently wider in scope to include sub-subsidiary companies and further 'generations' of companies if need be (s.126). The acceptance of more than 50 per cent ownership or voting control is based on the operation of the legal powers of members of the company. It may be argued that for accounting purposes other definitions may be more appropriate. Thus G. Garnsey suggested consolidation based on a criterion of 75 per cent ownership.[5]

A company may be effectively part of a group even when no more than 50 per cent of the shares are owned by the group parent company. Manufacturing agreements between Australian and overseas companies often lead to the formation of joint enterprises in which the Australian company may own only 50 per cent of the shares. While this does not legally constitute a subsidiary relationship, the operating company is controlled effectively by the Australian shareholder company, and logically may be regarded as part of the group. This situation was illustrated in the 1963 annual report of Industrial Engineering Ltd which included an additional financial statement incorporating the two 50 per cent owned associate companies. If the company had not done this, it would not have shown the extent to which the value of its investments in these companies, even on the basis of the associated companies' book values, had appreciated from the value shown in the group parent company's statements. This remains a singular example of this approach and one which is to be commended as improving the standards of disclosure by such company groups. It is known that there are a considerable number of listed companies with substantial holdings of not more than 50 per cent in other companies. The inclusion of these investments in the consolidated statement at the book value recorded by the parent company may involve a substantial understatement of the group interests.

A Tentative Statement on Accounting Practice published by the Australian Society of Accountants in the *Australian Accountant* in November 1969 supports the inclusion in the consolidation of companies where one effectively controls the operations of another although this is not required under the present Statute. At the time of writing further action by the Society suggests that this position may be abandoned in favour of the alternative equity method.

Opponents of group statements including associate companies argue that although they may represent the extent of effective control exercised by the parent company realistically, they include too large a proportion of net assets over which the parent and its subsidiaries do not have legal control. This strict legal viewpoint is met by the equity method. Under this method investments in associate companies are stated at cost plus a share of profits since acquisition, according to the proportion of shares held, less dividends received out of these profits. This method has been used to a limited extent in the U.S.A. but is an innovation in Australian practice where disclosure of these investments is usually confined to the cost of the investment.

Where the investment is in a listed company the Statute now requires publication of the market value of the securities even if the identity of the investments is not disclosed. Any attempt to assess the value of investments in non-listed companies must begin with identification of the company so that if necessary the filed financial statements may be examined at the office of the Registrar of Companies. In 1968, of the thirty-eight companies of the 'forty-two leaders sample' disclosing such investments only eleven indicated any details of name of the company in which the investment was held, the percentage ownership or the cost of the investment. In another four cases some details could be obtained by an examination of the directors' report. These investments which are described so inadequately represent activities which, in many instances, constitute an important segment of the business of a group, when regarded as extending beyond the confines of the more than 50 per cent owned or controlled subsidiary.

Knowledge of the composition of a group depended on the personal enquiries of the reader even of a report prepared under the Victorian Companies Act of 1938, unless the company voluntarily provided these details. The Uniform Acts ensured that the composition of a group was known to a reader of the financial statements by requiring group consolidated statements to be accompanied by a schedule of the subsidiary companies included in the consolidation (ninth schedule, clause 4(2)).

An interesting extension of this form of disclosure was included in the English Companies Act of 1967 which requires the annual report to identify in addition to investments in subsidiary companies any investment which constitutes more than 10 per cent of the shareholders' funds of the company in which the investment is held, or where the investments constitute more than 10 per cent of the book value of the investing company's assets. These requirements recall those instituted in Victoria in 1938 and applicable to proclaimed investment companies. Similar rules based on 25 per cent ownership have been applied by the London Stock Exchange. The London Stock Exchange requirements include loan capital as well as share capital. These requirements point the way for further developments in Australia towards the disclosure of group investments in associate companies. The Eggleston Committee appointed in 1967 has been giving consideration to requirements that would lead to the disclosure of the identities of significant shareholders in companies. The committee's deliberations have been principally concerned with takeover strategies but any such action would have to apply to all companies. Whether the findings of the Eggleston Committee will lead to a more positive identification of holdings in associate companies will depend on whether any subsequent enactments are phrased in terms of public companies and/or non-exempt companies, which now includes any company in which one or more shares is held by a listed company.

A partial consolidation might be more appropriate where one or more subsidiary companies had such unusual characteristics that their inclusion could distort the financial statements so that they would not represent a true and fair view of the group. This would be true particularly where a subsidiary was established for a highly speculative venture and the group intended to take advantage of its limited liability to the subsidiary and not to make good any losses sustained.

The Tentative Statement on Accounting Practice published by the Australian Society of Accountants, referred to earlier, rejects partial consolidations, among other possibilities, as inadequate financial reporting. This is clearly too narrow a view although the condemnation of the practice of adopting various devices to include or exclude particular subsidiaries according to their financial position must be supported. Such variations in consolidation practice would not lead to the presentation of a true and fair view of the group. The only circumstances in which a partial consolidation was allowed by the Victorian Companies Act of 1938 was where a subsidiary was incorporated outside of the State. In such a case it would be sufficient to present the separate statement of that subsidiary and not to include it in the consolidation. The separate statement is only required in the detail stipulated by the law applicable in the place of incorporation (s.125(1)). This provision now applies in all States under the Uniform Acts (ninth schedule, clause 4(5)). An example from the 'forty-two leaders sample' in 1968 was the exclusion from the consolidated statements of McPherson of the New Zealand subsidiary. The Uniform Acts also allow the exclusion from the consolidation of companies which are subsidiaries only because of control of the voting power or of the composition of the board (i.e. without the ownership of more than 50 per cent of the shares).

Apart from these matters the Uniform Acts do not allow for a part consolidation although one can resort to the separate publication of the financial statements of the parent company and each of the subsidiaries. However there is evidence to demonstrate what could be done if partial consolidation was allowable.

Before 1962 in New South Wales, consolidated statements were not prepared in order to comply with statutory requirements, and there was therefore more freedom for the presentation of partial consolidations and some experimentation took place. One example from the 'forty-two leaders sample' was the exclusion of the accounts of Ampol Exploration Ltd from the consolidated statements of Ampol from 1953 until the introduction of the Uniform Acts. Two other interesting experiments within the framework of a statutory obligation to publish consolidated statements, indicated what might be done by adopting different group definitions. Humes's treatment arose from the need to recognize a complex group structure, while Electronic sought to give its shareholders more up-to-date information by recognizing a significant transaction which occurred after the end of the financial year. Humes acquired the balance of the shares in its partly owned subsidiary, Hume Steel, and subsequently liquidated the subsidiary. For the two years 1950 and 1951 the report included statements for Humes Ltd, Humes Ltd and Subsidiaries, Hume Steel Ltd and Subsidiary, Hume Industries (Far East) Ltd. Electronic included a supplementary statement in its 1960 report consisting of a consolidated balance sheet prepared as if the sale (at a subsequent date) of the company's shares in General Television Corporation Pty Ltd had taken place on 30 June 1960.

The limited recognition of partial consolidation given by Australian company legislation is in contrast with the English Companies Act of 1948 which provided that where the directors' opinion is that a better presentation will be achieved and will be understood readily by the members of the company, the company may present separate statements for any company or any *part* of the group. In Australia a unique situation led to a demonstration of what might be achieved in the application of this principle. An unusual corporate structure required the publication in 1968 of a composite report which presented separate financial statements for each unit in the four-tiered grouping of Consolidated Press Holdings Ltd, Television Corporation Ltd, Australian Consolidated Press Ltd and Conpress Printing Ltd. Each of the latter companies is a subsidiary of the previously named. The ordinary shares of the first two named companies are listed in Melbourne at time of writing, while the unsecured notes and preference shares of the latter are listed.

While the Uniform Acts do not allow specifically for any of these variations in the definition of the group for consolidation purposes it is surprising that there has not been a more positive move to publish such statements relying on the overriding statutory requirement that the financial statements should present a true and fair view of the group.

The Victorian Companies Act of 1938 did recognize the possibility of distortion of consolidated statements by including unprofitable subsidiaries and therefore provided that the total of any losses incurred by subsidiaries should be disclosed in a note to the consolidated profit and loss statement (s.125(1)(a)(ii)). The intention of the section was sound, i.e. to prevent an apparent air of overall prosperity by combining profits in some subsidiaries with losses in others. The effectiveness of the section is, however, doubtful, for it could be avoided by simply merging the unprofitable subsidiary to become a division of a profitable subsidiary. The Victorian Statute Law Revision Committee enquired whether the section could be amended to 'ensure that the profit or loss of each subsidiary company is shown in the consolidated profit and loss account of the holding company'.[6] The committee considered that this could be done to prevent 'losses in one subsidiary being hidden by setting them off against profits in other subsidiary companies'.[7] The Australian Society of Accountants, through its representative, G. E. Fitzgerald, submitted that nothing was gained by a statement, according to the existing section of the Act, showing the total losses, if any, of the subsidiary company or companies, basing its objection on the organizational similarity of divisions of a company and subsidiaries of a holding company.[8] The Institute of Chartered Accountants in Australia, represented by K. N. Stonier, was more inclined to support the proposal as a safeguard to inform shareholders of the existence of an unprofitable subsidiary (or subsidiaries). The Institute suggested the relevant section might be clarified by adding the words 'without offsetting any profits of a subsidiary company or companies'.[9] The difficulty of the problem was reflected by the government's not proceeding with the committee's recommendation, the provision not being carried into the amended Victorian Companies Act in 1958, nor appearing in the Uniform Acts. In view of the recognition of the difficulties of isolating loss activities among a group, it is surprising to find that in 1967 the Australian Associated Stock Exchanges amended the Official List Requirements to require a company to include with consolidated statements a notation of the names of any subsidiaries which made a loss for the period reported on and the extent of such loss. Such a statement was included in the notes in the report of Jones in 1968.

At the same time the Exchanges recommended that published statements be accompanied by a schedule setting out the trading results, the provisions for depreciation and taxation, and the final net profit of each subsidiary.[10] Such a statement may still be open to manipulation by appropriate adjustments between the subsidiaries. In 1963 Coles included such a schedule of profits earned by subsidiaries in the annual report, and has continued to do so up until the present time.

The opportunity for the result of one subsidiary to differ markedly from the general trend disclosed by a consolidated statement is likely to increase with a widely diversified group.

The creation of a company group suggests policies of vertical or horizontal integration or, alternatively, the creation of what is known today as a conglomerate. When a company expands by vertical integration, it is probable that the fortunes of the industry at each level of operations will move along the same path. There is more possibility of an uneven pattern of success or failure of individual parts of the enterprise if a company enters into a scheme of horizontal integration. The individual units may meet substantially different conditions in their respective types of business and produce quite different financial results. When a company expands by diversification, then the various activities of the company may bear no relation whatever to each other. In fact it may be quite inappropriate to regard the diverse activities as one integrated unit. R. K. Mautz who conducted the project on 'Financial Reporting by Diversified Companies' for the Financial Executives Research Foundation gives in the research report a definition which identifies these characteristics and the resulting problems. He defines a diversified company as one

which either is so managerially decentralized, so lacks operational integration, or has such diversified markets that it may experience rates of profitability, degrees of risk, and opportunities for growth which vary within the company to such an extent that an investor requires information about these variations in order to make informed decisions. (p. 9)

The creation of such a diversified group or conglomerate suggests a need for partial consolidation statements. However, where the diversification is made within the one company even this solution would not apply. Whether we consider a group structure or a diversified company there is a need for disclosure of the results of the different classes of business conducted which is not bound to the definition of corporate limits.

Changes in company law discussed later in this chapter mean that where an organization structure based on subsidiary companies is retained, the financial statements of subsidiaries must be filed with the Company's Registrar. These statements are available as public documents but cannot be considered as readily accessible to the readers of company reports. An examination of these filed documents may not give adequate information because of the effect of inter-company transactions in the group. Assuming that such technical problems were to be solved, this still does not meet the need for adequate standards of reporting in the circulated company report.

This question received some public attention and newspaper coverage because of the takeover of Ready Mixed Concrete Ltd by Blue Metal Industries Ltd and Colonial Sugar Refining Co. Ltd. The Chairman of C.S.R. was not amenable to suggestions to give a breakdown of the investment of assets and profits earned in the units of such a diverse company as it now is, and said he was, 'sure that the shareholder [who requested the information] is convinced of the right as I am convinced of the wrong'.[11]

Such instances of disclosure as were found among the 'forty-two leaders sample' may be regarded as the pioneers or leaders in a new aspect of reporting. The few instances found of disclosure of divisional financial information tend to concentrate on a breakdown of only one aspect of the group, e.g. the asset values, the shareholders' funds or the revenue. Such presentations do not enable the reader of the report to assess the divisional profitability. A fully detailed statement of assets and liabilities according to divisions has been included in the report of Boral since 1962. At first this statement had four divisions, increased to seven from 1964 to 1967 and reverted to five divisions in 1968. No analysis of group profits is provided.

In 1965 Sleigh included in the annual report a simplified balance sheet for its major subsidiary, Hardie Rubber Company Pty Ltd, but did not indicate anything of profitability.

Ansett has included in its report a table of 'Distribution of shareholders' funds' which indicates the proportion of group resources used in each of seven operating divisions without identifying specific assets. However, this company does go some way towards allowing an analysis of divisional performance because the gross revenue has been reported on a divisional basis and the company also gives extensive statistics of passenger and freight activities.

The disclosure of information on the divisional activities of diversified groups or companies being the most recently raised issue concerning the published reports of Australian public companies may be regarded as a problem to be solved in the future.

Action is being taken overseas on this matter at the time of writing. The Companies Act passed in England in 1967 requires an analysis of turnover (unless under £50,000) and profit into the differing classes of business engaged in by a company or group without defining how this is to be done. The matter is also receiving much attention in the U.S.A. and revised rules issued by the Securities and Exchange Commission in September 1968 called for the disclosure of the sales and contribution to profit attributable to each class of products representing 10 per cent or more of the company's activities.

Possibly the most significant accounting procedural problem in the presentation of consolidated statements is the treatment of the goodwill or reserve on consolidation, i.e. the difference between the value at which the acquisition of shares in a subsidiary are recorded in the parent company accounts, and the book value of the portion of the subsidiary company acquired according to the books of the subsidiary company.

Where an investment is acquired with settlement made in cash there is usually little difficulty in identifying the value to be ascribed to the investment. Where settlement is made by the issue of securities, either notes, debentures or shares, it is necessary to determine the value to be ascribed to these securities. Whatever value is adopted will affect the statement of the shareholders' funds and/or liabilities of the group. While the adoption of the book value of the net assets in the subsidiary acquired may eliminate any reserve or goodwill on consolidation it may not lead to a correct statement of the financial resources that the issue of the securities might be expected to produce. The determination of the value to be ascribed to such issues of securities remains one of the significant unresolved issues in accounting with consequences for the published financial statements. A committee of the Australian Society of Accountants considered this matter and could not do better than to conclude that

> while it is not possible to lay down a precise procedure which can be applied in all cases for establishing a basis of accountability, it is reasonable to say that the basis adopted should be a fair value of the property acquired arrived at from a consideration of the objective evidence available and subjected to such adjustments as the directors deem applicable in the circumstances.[12]

The committee was not able to offer any more conclusive statement even though it considered the use of such measures as the alternative cash offer, if any, the market value of the securities issued and the earning capacity of the assets acquired.

The problem of dealing with this difference between recorded cost of the investment and the book value of the net assets acquired is not difficult to solve in terms of the mechanics of preparing consolidated statements, but there has been little consistency in the treatment of the resulting reserve or goodwill in the financial statements. Divers descriptions have been applied to the item as presented in the consolidated statement of assets and liabilities. They have tended to be descriptive of the calculation giving rise to the item. A selection of these descriptions is given in appendix 7. Such expansive descriptions can be useful because of the variety of factors which may give rise to the item. They also cover the situation where the item represents an 'adjustment' to the asset values as recorded by the subsidiary rather than an 'adjustment' to the price paid by the holding company. Some writers have advocated the use of the short terminology 'reserve on consolidation' or 'goodwill on consolidation'. Among the 'forty-two leaders sample', even including such variations as 'surplus on consolidation' and 'capital surplus' as reasonably synonymous terms to 'reserve on consolidation', there has been little use in the past of this short terminology. An examination of the reports of the 'forty-two leaders

TABLE 43
Use of terms 'reserve on consolidation' and 'goodwill on consolidation' '42 leaders sample'

	Reserve on consolidation[a]	Goodwill on consolidation	Total Number of companies reporting an equivalent item[b]
1953	—	—	24
1954	—	1	28
1955	2	1	29
1958	3	1	29
1960	5	1	29
1961	6	4	34
1962	7	3	34
1963	5	4	33
1964	3	5	32
1968	4	5	29

[a] Includes capital surplus on consolidation and surplus on consolidation.
[b] Excludes companies presenting consolidated statements where reserve or goodwill on consolidation appears to be non-existent or to have been eliminated.

TABLE 44

Classification of reserve or goodwill on consolidation in the consolidated statement of assets and liabilities

	Reserve				Goodwill					No. of cases[a]	Notes
	Shareholders' funds	Separate asset	Separate liab.	Total	Shareholders' funds	G'will and intangibles	Separate asset	Total	None		
	% of total cases for year										
1935						100		100		1	Dunlop issues consolidated statements
1939	14	—	7	21	—	14	36	50	29	14	Vic. Companies Act 1938
1946	14	5	9	28	10	5	38	53	19	21	I.C.A.A. recommendations
1950	17	7	3	27	7	22	24	53	20	29	
1955	15	9	3	27	12	37	12	61	12	33	
1960	22	3	3	28	17	28	8	53	19	36	
1962	29	2	2	33	20	22	7	49	18	41	Uniform Acts
1965	19	—	2	21	21	30	7	58	21	42	
1968	17	—	5	22	24	19	4	47	31	42	

[a] This is effectively the number of companies in the 'forty-two leaders sample' issuing consolidated statements at this time.

sample' suggests that adoption of the short terminology has gained a little in momentum in recent years, as demonstrated in Table 43. Even so, the number of companies using this terminology is only a small proportion of those companies presenting consolidated statements in which an amount representing a reserve or goodwill on consolidation appears.

An examination of the classification in the consolidated statement of assets and liabilities of the item representing the reserve or goodwill on consolidation, adopted by the 'forty-two leaders sample' shows that these classifications may be categorized as shareholders' funds, goodwill and intangibles, a separate asset category, and a separate liability category. Tables 44 and 45 have been compiled using these categories. The former table shows the cases of reserve and goodwill separately while the latter gives the total proportion irrespective of whether it was a reserve or goodwill.

TABLE 45
Classification of reserve/goodwill on consolidation in the consolidated statement of assets and liabilities

	Shareholders' funds	Intangibles	Separate asset	Separate liability	None	No. of cases[a]	Notes
	% of total cases for year						
1935		100				1	Dunlop issues consolidated statements
1939	14	14	36	7	29	14	Vic. Companies Act
1946	24	5	43	9	19	21	I.C.A.A. recommendations
1950	24	22	31	3	20	29	
1955	27	37	21	3	12	33	
1960	39	28	11	3	19	36	
1962	49	22	9	2	18	41	Uniform Acts
1965	40	30	7	2	21	42	
1968	41	19	4	5	31	42	

[a] This is effectively the number of companies in the 'forty-two leaders sample' which issued consolidated statements in the particular year.

From Table 45 it can be seen that there has been a very marked fall in the proportion of cases where the item is classified as a separate asset, and as a separate liability. On the other hand there has been an increase in the proportion of cases describing the item as an intangible asset or as part of shareholders' funds. The inclusion of a reserve as part of shareholders' funds and the description of goodwill as either an intangible asset or a deduction from shareholders' funds may be regarded as better descriptions than separate liabilities and assets. Table 44 indicates that there is now as large a proportion of cases involving a deduction of goodwill from shareholders' funds, as there is of cases involving the addition of a reserve amount. The deduction of goodwill in this way means that a smaller figure is quoted for shareholders' funds and a smaller figure for total assets, in the consolidated statements, than would be the case if the goodwill on consolidation were presented as an asset. This can be regarded only as a desirable trend because the item concerned is not an asset in any real sense, but is the consequence of recording the assets at the date of acquisition in the subsidiary records, at a value greater than what is regarded in the parent company records as the cost of those assets. It may also be said that this is a conservative approach which facilitates the creation of secret reserves, if the purchase price recorded by the parent company is unrealistic in terms of what is actually acquired.

Whatever may be the correct theoretical answer to this accounting problem, it may still be true that the reporting practice revealed in this examination is a manifestation of attitudes favouring the adoption of conservative (i.e. less than might otherwise be) values in the accounting records of the parent company's investments in subsidiary companies.

Where companies have paid for what amounts to goodwill on consolidation, there has been a tendency in recent years to eliminate this item from the consolidated statements by a revaluation of the investment in the parent records, or a revaluation upwards of the net asset values recorded in the records of the subsidiary company. Table 44 shows that the proportion of consolidated statements published by the 'forty-two leaders sample' which do not indicate any reserve or goodwill on consolidation had been fairly constant but has significantly increased in the last three years. There has been a marked change in the reasons for this non-statement. Where a company forms a subsidiary by investing in a newly formed company, there will not be any reserve or goodwill to account for if the company contributes to the subsidiary capital equal to the nominal value of the shares held in the subsidiary company. Where a company acquires control of an existing company by buying the shares, there is almost certain to be some amount of reserve or goodwill. The decrease in the proportion of cases where such a reserve or goodwill appears to be non-existent could be attributed to the formation of subsidiary structures being related more frequently to the acquisition of shares in an existing company than the formation of new companies. The elimination of a previously reported amount of reserve or goodwill can be attributed to two possible causes. Firstly, it appears reasonable for a group to revalue the assets of a subsidiary and give them the value regarded as the value of those assets by the group. From an accounting point of view, this seems reasonable where it involves a downward valuation of the subsidiary assets, i.e. an elimination of a reserve. An upward valuation in some circumstances may be considered an undesirable inflation of values. The second reason reflects the explanation offered previously for classifying the reserve or goodwill as part of shareholders' funds, i.e. to avoid an overstatement of both assets and shareholders' funds.

The acceleration after 1960 of the move to eliminate reserves or goodwill on consolidation reflects tougher bargaining in more difficult and more competitive business conditions, suggesting the desirability of eliminating the premium paid on the acquisition of subsidiaries so that the basis of calculating the earning rate of the group is not inflated by high premiums which may have been paid in a period of unbridled optimism.

The accounting treatment of the minority shareholders' interests in subsidiaries has been normally the inclusion in the consolidated statements of all the assets and liabilities of the subsidiaries. When preparing a consolidated group statement the inclusion or exclusion of the proportion of the assets and liabilities representing the minority interest in a subsidiary may lead to differences in the total group assets reported. If the minority interest is included there is a further choice of whether the claim of the minority interest is disclosed or merged with some other liability.

The application of the possible alternatives was illustrated by the reports of the 'forty-two leaders sample' for 1968. Twenty-nine of the 'forty-two leaders sample' disclosed a minority interest in the consolidated statement of assets and liabilities. Thirteen of these showed the minority interest as a separate item of 'equities' (i.e. used in the sense of assets = equities). In seven of these cases the minority interest was insignificant and only in one case did the minority interest represent more than 10 per cent of the total group assets. Three companies included the minority interest as a liability and in each instance this interest was not of significant magnitude. The remaining thirteen companies all presented the minority interest as closely allied to shareholders' funds. Seven of these companies showed the minority interest as a separate amount added to shareholders' funds to give 'total funds used'. None of these minority interests exceeded 4 per cent of the total group assets. The remaining group of six companies included the minority interest as part of the shareholders' funds. This would appear to be a direct contradiction of terms, because by definition a minority interest in a subsidiary is represented by an ownership exercised outside the structure of the parent company. Of this group of six companies, the minority interest was less than 4 per cent of the total group assets in five cases, and in the other case the minority interest was about 10 per cent of total group assets. A similar analysis of these companies made in 1965 showed a number of instances of minority interests representing a larger proportion of group assets which now appear to have been eliminated. At that time the analysis showed a sharp contrast between the incidence of large minority interests included under shareholders' funds and the small minority interests shown as a separate equity. This analysis led to the conclusion that those responsible for the financial statements are unwilling to recognize in the statements the distinction between group ownership and minority interest ownership if this is likely to portray the group as having smaller shareholders' resources.

Purely on logical grounds it would appear inconsistent to prepare a consolidation of financial statements prepared on different balance dates. There are circumstances which may make this a practical necessity, however. The natural business years of the different members of a group may not coincide, it may not be possible to avoid delays by waiting for some subsidiary company details (a most unlikely event with modern communications), or it may be desired to declare and pay dividends from the subsidiaries to the parent company before closing the books of the parent company.

In England the 1947 Companies Act (s.16(2)) made uniform balance dates compulsory unless approval was obtained from the Board of Trade. In the first year only twenty-nine companies applied for a subsidiary company to use a different balancing date than the parent. Of these applications, twenty were granted and one was refused. (Three applications were not proceeded with and five were outstanding at the end of the year.) In Australia, the idea of a uniform balance date within a group did not become an issue until the publication of the report of the investigators into certain company failures in the sixties. These reports highlighted blatant examples of 'juggling' the books of a group using different balance dates. The State governments acted quickly on many of the matters raised by the investigators, including these variations in the balancing date within a group. All States enacted legislation requiring a common balance date in the Public Borrowings Act, although Queensland deferred the operation of the relevant section until 1 July 1965 because although the Minister for Industrial Development, the Hon. A. W. Munro, thought it desirable he claimed there were unresolved questions concerning taxation.[13] Provision was made in the Public Borrowings Acts for granting special permission to continue using non-uniform balance dates (s.4). A number of companies since have been given this special permission. Statutory compulsion for a uniform balance date for a group of companies led to nine of the 'forty-two leaders sample' altering their procedures. In two instances the next accounting period of the parent company was reduced to nine months so that the balance date coincided with that of the subsidiaries. In both these cases the consolidated reports still included twelve months of the subsidiaries' activities. Formerly these companies presented consolidated statements which were prepared three months later than the balance date of the subsidiaries so that the consolidated statements did not reflect the activities of the subsidiaries for a period of three months before the date of the consolidated statements. The other seven companies all indicated that the adoption of uniform balance dates had led to including more than twelve months' results for some subsidiaries in the changeover period. The monetary value of the additional profits included in the consolidated statements was given by only two of the seven companies.

It appears improbable that these changes would have occurred without legislative support. The legislation probably would not have been enacted except for the disastrous events surrounding a small group of companies which directed attention at some of the grosser abuses that the non-uniformity of balance dates in a group could permit.

30

Subsidiaries and Divisions

In the administration of a large and complex business enterprise it is necessary to create an organizational structure to facilitate management planning and control. Whether this organization is based on a divisional structure or separate corporate entities will not affect greatly the management function. The use of separate corporate entities however, will be important where there is a desire to isolate specific legal responsibilities whether known or merely contingent.

Changes in statutory requirements have increased the opportunity to obtain information about activities conducted by separate subsidiary company units. Some company groups have reacted to these changes by reverting to a divisional structure, thereby frustrating the disclosure objectives of modern Statutes.

The privilege of confidentiality of the financial affairs of proprietary companies established in the Victorian Companies Act of 1896 was used as a device to avoid the disclosure of the financial position of companies by transferring the operations and assets of public companies to subsidiaries which enjoyed the privileges of proprietary companies. While there was questioning of whether this privilege should continue to be used in this way, there was no clear force of opinion against it. The Greene Company Law Committee did not think that the evils justified a change in a similar situation existing in England in 1925.[1] The Cohen Committee in 1945 thought that consolidated statements as required in Victoria since 1938 provided adequate disclosure of the affairs of groups, but just the same the committee sought to confine the privilege of non-disclosure to the 'small family business'. It sought to do this through the creation of the non-exempt private company.[2] Attitudes in England have 'hardened' further and the Jenkins Committee in 1962 recommended that exemption from publication of financial statements should be a privilege only available to unlimited companies.[3] Accordingly the English Companies Act of 1967 (s.2) abolished the exempt private company and it is believed that many companies which are of the nature of family trusts or investment companies will retain the privilege of non-disclosure by embracing the status of unlimited liability. It is too early yet to make any precise judgment so far as companies which may be thought to have some chance, albeit slight, of falling on bad times. The exemption from disclosure granted to proprietary companies became a political issue in Victoria when the American company, General Motors Corporation, acquired the preference shares in General Motors-Holden's Ltd, thereby converting the Australian company into a wholly owned subsidiary. This would have avoided the necessity to publish the Australian company's financial statements. The company's activities were a sensitive public issue because, as the *Age* finance editor noted: 'With the tremendous success of the Holden car, profits and dividends have risen to controversially high level in recent years and have brought criticism from many quarters.'[4] The report of the proposed takeover of the preference shares brought forth comment from both the government party and opposition members of Parliament. The Deputy Leader of the federal Opposition, A. A. Calwell, called for an amendment of the Constitution to allow the Federal Parliament to compel publication of the company's financial statements, if necessary.[5] The importance of the issue was brought out by the Victorian Premier, the Hon. H. E. Bolte, who on the same day, issued a statement saying that: 'if the purpose of the General Motors' proposal to acquire the whole of the preference shares capital was to avoid publication of accounts relating to General Motors operations the move would be to no avail.'[6] The Premier pointed out that the conference of State Ministers which had met in Perth the previous week to consider uniform company law had agreed unanimously that the model companies Bill should provide for the disclosure of the accounts of proprietary companies when any interest in a proprietary company was held by another company. In answer to a question in the House as to when the legislation would be introduced, the Premier replied on 10 May 1960 that he:

was quite prepared to introduce legislation if there was any suggestion that General Motors-Holden's Limited did not intend to publish their balance-sheet.

However, I have been assured that the accounts of General Motors-Holden's Limited will be published as usual this year. In these circumstances, it is considered that there is no need for urgent legislation, and the question will be covered in the uniform company law Bill which it is hoped will be introduced in March, 1961.[7]

The matter remained an issue over the following two years. Support for extension of disclosure provisions to cover this particular case was given on a national level. The Prime Minister, the Right Hon. R. G. Menzies, on 12 September 1961, in reply to a question, said that so far as he was concerned, 'if I had power to enforce the disclosure of the profits I certainly would do so'.[8] The outcome of the issue was that ultimately the net had to be more widely cast and thereby include a considerable number of other companies operating in Australia as wholly owned subsidiaries of overseas companies.

This development in the legislation took place in two stages in Victoria. The concept of the non-exempt proprietary company entered Australian legislation first in the Victorian Companies Act of 1958, which declared a company to be a public company if, 'more than fifty per cent of the paid up value of its issued share capital is beneficially held directly or indirectly by two or more public companies (whether incorporated under this Act or not)' (s.135). This section was directed at the 'associate company'. Exemption from publishing financial statements was narrowed down further in the Uniform Acts which excluded from the definition of an exempt proprietary company any company in which a share was held by a public company and any proprietary company included in a pyramid or chain of more than four levels of proprietary companies. The case of proprietary companies owned by overseas companies was dealt with by implying that foreign companies were included in the reference to public companies in the definition of an exempt proprietary company with certain specified provisos. This effectively means that the exemption from filing financial statements is lost by any company in which a share is held by a foreign company unless the foreign company meets the prescribed tests. The types of foreign company ownership which retain the character of an exempt proprietary company include exempt proprietary companies under the English Companies Act (this would now imply the unlimited company under the English Companies Act of 1967), exempt proprietary companies or their equivalent under the laws of any other State, Territory or country as declared by order, proprietary companies under the laws of any other State, Territory or country as declared by order and in which shares are held only by natural persons, and certain non-profit sporting, educational, charitable and similar corporations or associations.

This has not solved the problem of securing information on the activities represented by these companies. If the company does publish its statements, the statements may be highly suspect. As John Elsworth remarked on the subject of wholly owned subsidiaries:

With the compulsory filing of non-exempt proprietary company accounts, it has become newsworthy to report the annual results of subsidiaries of public companies, as they become available. If there is some scope for the over- or under-statement of a consolidated profit, there is much more scope in the case of the results of wholly owned subsidiary companies.[9]

What has happened however, with many public companies, is that the activities of the subsidiaries have been merged into the business of one company, frequently the parent, as divisional activities.

Among the 'forty-two leaders sample' there is evidence of this trend towards divisional structures resulting from this change in statutory reporting requirements. In 1939 A.C.I. sold its assets to its subsidiaries as part of a plan to sectionalize the company's major activities. In 1965 we find Peters noting the effects on the accounts of the transfer of marketing operations from the holding company to subsidiary companies. An opposite change of organizational plan was undertaken by F. & T. in 1954 when it was decided to amalgamate the wholly owned subsidiaries with the parent company. This process the chairman thought might take two or three years, but would 'make a significant contribution to the simplification of the financial and administrative structure of the Company and its overall taxation position'. Some other companies gave similar reasons for their reaction to the inclusion of the concept of the non-exempt proprietary company in the Uniform Act. Email transferred all trading to the parent company and the subsidiaries ceased to trade as from 30 June 1962. The subsidiaries thereby only remained as holders of real estate on the first day that they were subject to the requirement to file their financial statements as non-exempt proprietary companies. Similar action was taken by D.H.A., the general manager reporting in 1965 that 'the voluntary liquidation of the majority of the subsidiary companies which ceased trading in 1962 was concluded during the year and it is anticipated that the remainder will be liquidated during the current year'. A more gradual elimination of subsidiaries has been undertaken by some other groups. In the 1964 report of Ansett there was an announcement of an intention to eliminate most of the subsidiaries: 'Due to the increased accounting and secretarial requirements of the Uniform Companies Acts including that of audited half-yearly accounts for the entire organisation and *the publication of each subsidiary's accounts*' (emphasis mine). B. Tobacco in 1965 reported of some of the company's numerous subsidiaries: 'To achieve greater administrative efficiencies, the Leigh-Mardon group of companies has, during the year, undergone a major change in organisational structure, whereby the major operating units will in future function as divisions of Leigh-Mardon instead of as separate subsidiary companies.' Bradford was less specific in reporting in 1965 that: 'In conformity with the policy initiated by the Board to reorganise the structure and operations of the Companies of the Bradford Group, the Assets of several Subsidiary Companies were sold to the Parent Company during the year.' Even more generalized was the comment in 1965 by the directors of B.M.I. that: 'Steps are being taken to consolidate the activities of the Group and to liquidate a number of the subsidiary companies which are no longer required.'

Yet while there is this evidence of moves towards a divisional structure, there remain particular enterprises which appear to find the multiple subsidiary structure of particular advantage to them. The most numerous subsidiary structures among the 'forty-two leaders sample' are associated with the rubber industry and its attendant motor vehicle tyre service businesses. Thus it was found in 1968 that Dunlop had 262 subsidiaries and Olympic had 170 subsidiaries, while in 1965 before a rearrangement of group activities, Sleigh had 102 subsidiaries. In another field B. Tobacco in 1968 had 117 subsidiaries.

31

Value in the Balance Sheet

The dominant role of the balance sheet in early developments in company financial disclosure was discussed in an earlier chapter. There it was suggested that this may have been a misplaced reliance. Subsequently the ascendancy of the profit and loss statement was commented upon. In more recent years there has been some resurgence of the role of the balance sheet and of attempts to portray the 'value' of the enterprise.

One small step towards improved balance sheets was the provision in the ninth schedule of the Uniform Acts for the statement of separate monetary amounts according to each method of valuation applied to an asset. Furthermore a company is permitted to change the basis of valuation of any item without indicating the financial effect of that change. All that is required is that the directors' report should identify the fact that there has been a change.

The English Companies Act of 1967 has gone one step further by requiring the year in which each valuation of fixed assets was made to be shown against the value and the names and qualifications of the valuers for any valuations made in the current year to be stated. While such moves improve the presentation in the balance sheet, they do nothing toward resolving the basic issues as to what kind of a statement the balance sheet should be. The alternatives available range from conventional accounting procedures, whereby the balance sheet is essentially a statement of costs carried forward, to proposals to state all assets at current market or realizable values or an attempt to apply concepts of value based on the discounting of expected future cash flows. It is not intended to explore the mechanics of the techniques suggested in the literature nor to argue the merits of the alternatives but rather to note the changes to published balance sheets which have occurred and which have given some recognition to values other than those which represent costs carried forward. This examination takes into account the distinction now generally recognized in accounting literature that values of commodities may change due to either general price level influences or specific price level changes relating to specific commodities.

Conventional accounting practice has afforded recognition to realization values of current assets such as debtors and stocks. Statutory recognition of the importance of these values was given in the Uniform Acts which instituted a requirement for the directors of the company to report

where the directors are of the opinion that any current assets would not at least realize the value at which they are shown in the accounts of the company their opinion as to the amount that those current assets might reasonably be expected to realize in the ordinary course of business of the company. (s.162(6)(d))

The reporting of the valuation of stocks has been dealt with before. There has been little discussion in the literature of the valuation of debtors although the magnitude of bad debt losses incurred by a number of retailers and land developers in the sixties directed some attention to the matter. As a result the general council of the Australian Society of Accountants issued a pronouncement in the *Australian Accountant,* December 1967 (p. 672). This pronouncement declared that 'the only acceptable basis for valuing book debts is expected realisable value in the ordinary course of business'. It should be recalled that the recommendation of the Institute of Chartered Accountants in Australia covering the valuation of stocks is the lowest of cost, realizable value or replacement price. We thus have professional and statutory support for recognition of realization values in the balance sheet for these two important current assets.

A rather different situation exists in respect of the recognition of 'current' values of assets other than stocks and debtors. No evidence has been found of any attempts by Australian companies to publish financial statements incorporating adjustments recognizing general price level changes. In this matter Australian companies are not necessarily lagging behind practice in other developed countries. The first instance recorded of any published company financial statements adjusted for general price level changes and carrying an unqualified audit report, was the statements of Champion Celulose S.A., a Brazilian company, issued in 1964.[1]

It is quite certain that an awareness of the effect of both general

31 Value in the Balance Sheet

and specific price level changes has led in many cases to the adoption of appropriate financial policies, but a failure to spell out the effects of these policies in the financial statements. Rather they have been hidden by adopting over-conservative asset values thereby creating secret reserves and a tendency to state lower dollar profits. There has been, however, a number of instances of Australian companies incorporating charges in the financial statements recognizing specific price changes of some assets belonging to the company. These adjustments may be incorporated as expenses by making charges before determining profit or by appropriations of ascertained profits. J. McB. Grant and R. L. Mathews in their 1956 study of South Australian companies, found out of twenty companies, three instances of transfers to asset replacement reserves and three instances of transfers to stock revaluation reserves.[2] In the earlier discussion of stock valuation it was pointed out that, among the 'forty-two leaders sample', three companies had made appropriations to special stock reserves to take account of changes in the price levels of commodities. Apart from these three cases it is not possible to identify positively any of the other 'reserves' or 'provisions' in respect of stock as being created specifically in recognition of inflation.

In earlier discussion of the use of special 'reserves' or 'provisions' for increased cost of plant replacement it was noted that no less than eighteen of the 'forty-two leaders sample' had made some additional charge or appropriations. It appears unlikely that many of these companies applied any systematic method to calculating the amounts involved and in many cases it seems that it was a convenient description to reduce stated profits. On this evidence it can be concluded that there is very little acceptance by Australian companies of any formalized approach to the disclosure of the profit effects of specific price level changes.

A greater degree of recognition has been afforded appreciation in asset values resulting from price level changes. The principal argument for the revaluation of assets is that it presents 'more closely the current position of the company' while the main objection would appear to be that 'additional profits will need to be earned to enable a company to pay the same dividend rate on the increased capital'.[3] However, there is evidence that there has been a considerable number of companies which have revalued at least some assets.

Grant and Mathews found that more than one-third of the South Australian companies they examined in 1956 had made a revaluation, 'usually confined to freehold land and buildings and were carried out on a once-for-all basis'.[4] Among the 'forty-two leaders sample' the examination of reserves revealed that in 1968 the statements of twenty-one companies included an asset revaluation reserve. This does not necessarily mean that more companies did not undertake revaluation. Many companies may well have eliminated a previous asset revaluation reserve by an issue of bonus shares or similar action. It is clear, however, that there has been a fairly widespread recognition of the usefulness of more up-to-date values in the balance sheet for at least some assets.

Legislative action to secure current appraisal values of assets has been confined, at this time, to the requirement introduced in the Uniform Acts to state by note the aggregate quoted market value of any investment in government, municipal and other public debentures and in companies where a market value may be ascertained (ninth schedule, clause 5(3)(b)). As with any attempt at appraisal, these market values are only estimates based on the opinion of the 'market', but they frequently represent more realistic values than the conservative balance sheet figures presented by the owning company. Previous comments have noted the importance of investments in non-listed companies for which such market values are not available. At this time no statutory measure has been enacted in Australia to secure disclosure of any adequate details concerning these investments.

This recognition of current values has been extended to investments in shares not listed on a Stock Exchange by the English Companies Act of 1967 which requires either the directors' valuation or prescribed details concerning the profitability of such an investment to be shown (second schedule, par. 5A and 8(I)(a)). Attempts to place a value on such non-listed investments are fraught with many difficulties and recognition of this emphasizes the extent to which this recent enactment provides a lead towards the incorporation of more current value information in the balance sheet at least by way of supplementary notes. The new English Act also requires the directors' report to identify the difference between the market value and the book value of land and interests in land held as fixed assets, information which may perhaps be more readily compiled than that in regard to non-quoted investments.

Changing practice and legislative requirements applicable to the balance sheet have not been confined to the statement of assets but have recognized some necessary developments in the treatment of liabilities. Where a company is engaged in a large scale expansion, the financial position of the company may be portrayed far from completely if the cost of completing that expansion is not taken into account. The Institute of Chartered Accountants in Australia recognized this in its Recommendations on Accounting Principles issued in 1946 and statutory support for disclosure of capital expenditure commitments was given in England by the 1947 Companies Act (first schedule, clause 7(b)). The importance of future capital expenditure necessary to complete a project was highlighted by the Chevron Hotel project in Sydney. The results of subsequent investigations have shown the desperate measures which were adopted to keep up the necessary flow of money to support the project.[5] This was only one of a number of companies which faced the problem of inability to meet the capital expenditure necessary to complete projects in the period following the supplementary budgetary measures introduced on 15 November 1960 by the Commonwealth government. These events highlighted this particular aspect of reporting, and it is not surprising that the Uniform Acts required the disclosure of obligations on contracts for capital expenditure not otherwise accounted for (ninth schedule, clause 2 (1)(r)(iii)). There is, however, an inadequacy in this statutory requirement because a much more important item may be the expenditure planned by the directors rather than that to which they are committed formally by contract. This was recognized by the Jenkins Committee[6] and the English Companies Act of 1967 (second schedule, pt I, cl. (6)) calls for the particulars of capital expenditure authorized by the directors but not yet contracted for. However, as a legal requirement this may well be regarded as worthless as there may be cases where board approval long precedes any actual expenditure while in other cases events may have made heavy expenditure inevitable long ahead of any board approval. An attempt to define the requirement in terms of expenditure necessary to complete projects already begun might be more workable. Professional action in Australia has recognized the necessity for such an approach. The Institute of Chartered Accountants in Australia, in contrast to its habit of only taking up established practices, already has issued a new recommendation in 1965 suggesting that: 'Where a company has entered into contracts for only part of the work on a project of capital expenditure . . . further information should be given indicating the total expenditure expected to be incurred in the project.'[7]

Among the 'forty-two leaders sample' in 1965 only three companies specifically indicated the total expenditure on capital projects in hand. In the case of another company the directors' report indicated a plan for capital expenditure on new premises. In this respect the year 1968 showed little progress for only two companies gave this type of information. One company included approved expenditure in the statement of liabilities for capital expenditure not included in the accounts while another company indicated planned expenditure by a note in the 1968 directors' report. Apart from this many companies give some general description of expansion and development plans. Nevertheless this is a very small response to the Institute recommendations.

Closely related to disclosure of future capital expenditure and attempts to make balance sheet values more current is the disclosure of actual current outlays as capital expenditures. In this respect there has been a much more significant change in reporting as shown by reports covering the most recent financial year. This information is not always easily found. In 1968 the details were given in the funds statement in ten reports, in the directors' report in five instances, in both the funds statement and directors' report in one case, while one company included the figure in the highlights page.

The requirement of the Uniform Acts to show the cost of fixed assets less the accumulated depreciation as a separate deduction has enabled the reader of the statements to discover the change in assets excluding the depreciation factor. However, this can only reveal the net change due to additions and disposals. In the absence of the supporting detail as given in 1968 by seventeen of the 'forty-two leaders sample' the reader cannot validly determine the amount expended on new assets during the year. This deficiency in disclosed information has been dealt with in the English Companies Act of 1967 which calls for the directors to report significant changes in fixed assets during the year giving the amounts of additions and disposal of fixed assets under each fixed asset heading in the balance sheet (second schedule, pt I, cl. (6B)). Although this may lead to the presentation of some complex notes it would appear to have a simple objective, i.e. to identify changes which may occur in the nature of the assets owned and the activities carried on by the company.

Much less progress has been made in the treatment of lease obligations which have become more important with a more diverse and widespread use of lease financing as one of the modern weapons in the armoury of business financiers. Even in the traditional area of leasing land and buildings, practices have developed of companies selling and leasing back property on a more wide-

31 Value in the Balance Sheet

spread scale than was formerly the case. One of the 'forty-two leaders sample', Woolworth, has for many years had a partly-owned subsidiary which has raised much of the finance to acquire properties which it leases to the principal trading company. Very little discussion of the problems of these new financing methods has taken place in Australia. A report of the Victorian State Research Committee of the Australian Society of Accountants was published in November 1965. The committee surveyed the treatment of leases in the reports of 100 companies. The conclusion stated was that:

Present Australian methods of accounting for and reporting lease transactions appear to the committee to be inadequate . . . financial statements are presented for companies which have similar lease rights and obligations showing in each case a quite different statement of financial position. Similarly, present reporting practices do not facilitate comparability between the published financial statements of companies which finance asset acquisition by means of equity capital or borrowings and the financial statements of companies which acquire property rights through leasing.[8]

The English Companies Act of 1967 was the first step in the direction of codifying disclosure of leases by requiring a statement of amounts paid for hire of plant and equipment but did not attempt any move towards a statement of the capitalized value of such obligations or of the value of the assets rented. Under the Uniform Acts there is no question of the disclosure of sums expended on improvements to leasehold property or even leases where the whole lease payment is made as one initial sum. In both these cases the outlays appear in the balance sheet to be amortized over the life of the lease. However where the form of lease is such that only an annual payment is required there is no statutory requirement to disclose any details of the lease. In 1968 only six of the 'forty-two leaders sample' gave any information of this kind. Nevertheless these few cases illustrated the problems involved and the possible treatments. Both Ansett and ICIANZ indicated the annual rental amount and the total future liability in respect of leases of operating equipment. (Apparently no attempt was made to discount these obligations to determine a 'present value'.) Ansett also stated in a note the amount of hire purchase obligations. Two companies, ICIANZ and Myer, indicated the amount of annual commitments on property leases. Olympic simply noted that there were liabilities for the unexpired values of agreements for leasing of premises, signs and other equipment. Two companies, Sleigh and Humes, indicated the conditions pertaining to options on leased properties occupied by the company.

Currency conversion provisions were enacted in the Victorian Companies Act of 1958 and carried into the Uniform Act requiring disclosure of the basis of conversion to Australian currency of the assets and liabilities of foreign subsidiaries when incorporated in consolidated statements.

Among the 'forty-two leaders sample' in 1965 there were no less than twenty-six companies whose financial statements included some items which were subject to conversion from some foreign currency. The materiality of the items concerned varied greatly as some cases covered the incorporation of the accounts of foreign subsidiaries comprising substantial business units, while others may only have involved the inclusion of the accounts of an overseas buying or marketing branch office.

The traditional balance sheet also is deficient in that it does not include necessarily all of the assets of a company. It is not uncommon to find a company chairman recognizing an important asset not shown in the balance sheet in the contribution to the success of the company made by the staff. There are, however, other tangible assets of a material kind which equally may fail to appear. Two examples are those of discovered deposits of minerals, oil and gas and created assets such as growing timber owned by afforestation companies. Moves towards making the balance sheet a more informative statement of values must include developments in the reporting of this type of asset.

Each of the measures outlined in this chapter has led to the development of a more informative balance sheet. What has been achieved has in part relied on professional action and in part on legislative compulsion.

32

Victoria and Tasmania 1958

A number of the developments discussed in the last seven chapters in particular carried through to the time when the Uniform Acts came into being and, as has been noted, many of these developments were carried into this legislation or depended on these Acts for their culmination. This chapter now proceeds to a discussion of the Uniform Acts including some prior discussion of the Acts passed in 1958 in Victoria and in 1959 in Tasmania, which were substantially the basis on which the Uniform Acts were modelled. The purpose of this chapter is to outline the differences in the accounting and reporting requirements these Acts imposed, compared with the previously existing legislation, the Victorian Companies Act of 1938 and the Tasmanian Companies Act of 1920.

In Tasmania, two significant differences were the introduction of requirements for consolidated statements for a group or separate statements for each company in the group, and for reasonably detailed profit and loss statements. These were essentially aspects in which the Tasmanian legislation was brought up-to-date with the Victorian Act of 1938. Similarly, the Tasmanian Act took up the amendments made in Victoria in 1955.

The 1958 and 1959 Acts in Victoria and Tasmania introduced a number of innovations in the reporting provisions including the distinction between exempt and non-exempt proprietary companies, disclosure of interest paid on debentures and other fixed loans, inclusion in the profit and loss statement of dividend appropriations, amended details concerning the statement of directors' remuneration, and of the auditor's remuneration, and a statement of the currency used where the financial statements are not in Australian currency and the basis of any conversion made into Australian currency. Another new requirement was for a statement of the amount provided for redemption of share capital and for redemption of loans.

The requirement for a public company to keep posted up at the registered office a copy of the last audited balance sheet was 'omitted as being archaic and useless'[1] according to the Attorney-General.

These Acts introduced an aspect of draftsmanship worthy of comment. They were the first Australian Acts to relegate the whole of the specification of the financial statements into a separate schedule to the Act. However, they did not go so far as to give the executive power to modify the schedule from time to time.

Evidence of the effect of the reports of English company law committees on Australian legislation was demonstrated by the redrafting of the requirement that the balance sheet state the 'basis of valuation of each class of assets' (s.124(1)) to require the balance sheet to show 'the method used to arrive at the amount or value of assets under each heading' (ninth schedule, cl. 2(h)). The Cohen Company Law Amendment Committee in 1945 had commented on the reference to 'values of fixed assets' in the existing English Act as being 'inappropriate since the balance sheet does not purport to give their realisable value as at the date at which it is drawn up', and therefore recommended that the balance sheet should 'state how the amounts at which the fixed assets are stated have been arrived at'.[2] A comparison of the Victorian and Tasmanian Acts with the English Act of 1948 shows how far English law still guided the local legislators, although the Australian legislation retained its individuality and forward thinking on disclosure requirements.[3]

The private balance sheet, Isaacs's invention of 1896, which had caused such bitter argument in the past, was dropped from the 1958 Victorian Act. The private balance sheet procedure had been retained in the Victorian 1938 Act and even extended in its operation. That Act required subsidiaries of public companies to lodge the private balance sheet, thus indicating the likely pattern of steps towards disclosure by a wider range of companies. Even in 1943 the section did not appear to be subject to effective policing. It was understood 'that the private balance sheets of all subsidiary companies are not being filed'.[4] As E. T. Spackman pointed out in 1953: 'Of what use is the lodgment of the private balance sheet in a sealed envelope in the Registrar-General's office?'[5] This question was answered by A. Clunies Ross fourteen years earlier. In his imaginary conversation between a 'foreigner' and a 'Victorian' the following exchange takes place:

F.: By the way, have you perpetuated Victoria's speciality—the private balance sheet?
V.: Yes, indeed—and you are not to jeer at the mass of dusty envelopes —already weighing somewhere between ten and a hundred tons— resting till the crack of doom in the R.G.'s vaults. They *have* been of use—after fires and other disasters.[6]

In 1954 Spackman had appeared before the Victorian Statute Law Revision Committee in his capacity of Chairman of the Companies Auditors Board and an office-bearer in two professional bodies, to advocate the deletion of the private balance sheet procedure from the Act as he contended it was a useless provision.[7] The comment of the Attorney-General, the Hon. A. G. Rylah, in 1958 that the sections had been omitted as of no value[8] does not appear to have caused so much as a 'raised eyebrow'.

Queensland was the only other State to have even a brief flirtation with anything akin to the 'private balance sheet'. In Queensland in 1954 an amendment to the Act required private companies to file audited balance sheets. However, to ensure the privacy of the affairs of these companies, the Registrar was required to seal the papers in an envelope which could only be opened by order of a Supreme Court Judge or the President of the Industrial Court. Under the Queensland Companies Act Amendment Act (s.53) of 1942 private companies incorporated anywhere within the British Commonwealth of Nations had been given an automatic exemption from the sections of the Companies Act requiring companies to post up and file their financial statements. This exemption was henceforth only available at the discretion of the Crown Law Officer under the amendments made by the Companies Act Amendment Act of 1953 (s.8). The position of private companies incorporated elsewhere within the British Commonwealth was later eased by restoring the automatic exemption from posting up the financial statements. The necessity to file the financial statements with an envelope in which they would be sealed, remained subject to the discretion of the Crown Law Officer.[9] This filing procedure as applied to private companies in Queensland was to die with the advent of the Uniform Acts.

This legislation is also important because it strengthened the Victorian provisions relating to unit trusts and as a derivative of this, led to changes in this aspect of the legislation in all States.

The first unit trust in Australia was First Australian Unit Trust launched in Sydney by Australian Fixed Trusts Pty Limited. The development of unit trusts in Australia was very slow compared with the United Kingdom where, between 1931 and 1937, over £71,000,000 was invested in unit trusts. It is possible that the controls imposed in Victoria in 1938 on investment companies indirectly contributed to the growth of the unit trust movement which did occur. The attention of the legislature was drawn to the sale of units and like interests, not by the legitimate unit trust but more particularly by the sale of interests in olive and timber plantations and the resultant enquiry.[10]

Following the Statute Law Committee enquiry in Victoria action was taken to legislate for a trustee to be appointed and for the trustee to forward an audited statement covering the interests to each of the holders.[11]

It was this legislation which was found to need strengthening to ensure that unit holders should receive with the annual report of the company a summary of all purchases and sales of securities, the amount of brokerage paid or charged and the proportion paid to any broker related to the company and a full list of investments held at the balance date.[12]

The conduct of the affairs of the promoters of vending machines led to the appointment of inspectors into the affairs of the company concerned in Victoria and to a further enquiry by the Statute Law Revision Committee[13] which found that the 1958 Act did not cover vending machines, as the definition to be found in the 1958 Act only covered rights or interests to participate 'in any profits assets or realization of any financial or business undertaking or scheme' (s.63(1)). This deficiency was covered in the drafting of the legislation in New South Wales, Queensland, South Australia and Western Australia. It was necessary to amend the definition as originally enacted in Victoria and Tasmania. This common definition to be found in the uniform legislation includes, in addition, any rights or interests in 'any common enterprise whether in the State or elsewhere in which the holder of the right or interest is led to expect profits rent or interest from the efforts of the promoter of the enterprise or a third party', and 'any investment contract'. This legislation is now incorporated in the Uniform Acts operating in all States (s.76–89). More recently some promoters have sought to avoid this widened definition of interests by forming syndicates of not more than twenty members and thereby operating under partnership law. Some syndicates it is believed have voluntarily appointed a trustee company or placed themselves under the Companies Act. As the *Australian Financial Review* pointed out on 27 August 1968, 'one very obvious advantage in not coming under the Companies Act lies in the scope given for claims in advertising and brochures', but as it also noted, 'most syndicates have been going less than four years (and) their claims have yet to be tested by time'.

These then were some of the significant matters dealt with in the review and revision of the Victorian Act. As the Attorney-General, A. G. Rylah, observed in his second reading speech on the Victorian Bill, company law and practice 'are far from static' and the Bill was intended to redraft and streamline the existing legislation.[14]

Drafting of the Bill had begun in 1956 in the light of the recommendations of the Cohen Committee and the English Companies Act of 1947. In May 1957 the Bill had been submitted for comment to Amalgamated Institute of Secretaries, Chartered Institute of Secretaries, Australian Society of Accountants, Institute of Chartered Accountants in Australia, Stock Exchange of Melbourne, Law Institute of Victoria and Bar Council of Victoria, which all provided useful comments, and also to Australian Bankers' Association, Life Officers' Association for Australasia, Chamber of Mines, Australasian Institute of Cost Accountants and a few individual experts.

Practically identical legislation was passed in Tasmania. The Victorian legislation had not come into actual operation when a project aimed at uniform legislation throughout Australia began in 1959. Nevertheless the Ministers representing all States and the Commonwealth agreed to take the Victorian legislation as the basis of their discussions and thus it became the model on which the Uniform Acts were based.

33

The Uniform Acts

The President of the New South Wales division of the Commonwealth Institute of Accountants, addressing the Institute 1927 annual meeting, observed that:

When the business history of Australia is written, future generations will marvel at the unique and somewhat ridiculous spectacle of a comparatively small business community allowing itself to be shackled and confused with some thirty-odd Companies Acts—some of them being mutually antagonistic, and others obsolete—where the community might all along have been working comfortably and harmoniously under one Commonwealth Act.[1]

Proposals for uniform law had been considered by the Premiers' Conferences almost since federation.[2] The President of the Commonwealth Institute of Accountants, L. A. Cleveland, referred to the matter in his annual report in 1924 and again in 1926 when he urged the members to press members of parliament to allow a referendum on the proposal to give the Commonwealth a clear power to legislate.[3] The Commonwealth Institute of Accountants strongly advocated a uniform law and the council of the Institute urged its members to vote 'Yes' when the matter was included in a referendum to amend the Constitution. The referendum proposal was linked with other more contentious issues and the referendum failed to secure the required vote when put to the people in August 1926. The biennial conference of the principal Stock Exchanges held in Brisbane on 12 August 1929 agreed to press for a uniform law.[4] The result of these pressures was that the Commonwealth draftsmen prepared a model Bill following the 1934 Premiers' Conference. The fate of this Bill was outlined earlier in the more detailed discussion of the 1931–6 Queensland, South Australian and New South Wales Acts. The prospect of uniform legislation receded further when in 1938 Victoria again moved ahead in its legislation.

Following World War II, there was a move for more modern companies legislation in all States.[5] This movement was promoted by the issue in 1945 of the report of the Cohen Company Law Committee and subsequently the passage of the 1947 Companies Act in England. A committee of the Commonwealth Institute of Accountants general council had decided by June 1948 that uniform legislation could be achieved by using this English Act of 1947 as a model.[6] The Commonwealth Institute acquainted other accounting professional bodies with its activities and was prepared to offer its advice to the State governments when the time was right. At the 1957 annual meeting of the general council of the Institute of Chartered Accountants in Australia the proposal for a conference sponsored by the Commonwealth to formulate a uniform law was put forward.[7] This proposal was re-affirmed at the 1959 meeting[8] following the passage of the Victorian Companies Act of 1958.

In July 1952 it was reported in the Sydney press that the Prime Minister 'contemplated the formation of an expert committee to examine the existing statutes with a view to bringing about a greater degree of uniformity'.[9] According to the Hon. A. G. Rylah: 'By approximately 1956 exactly nothing at all had been achieved.'[10]

Uniform Bills were ultimately presented to each of the State parliaments. The preceding steps are outlined in a foreword to the model Bill issued over the signatures of the Attorneys-General of the Commonwealth and all the States dated 16 June 1961:

The preparation of a draft uniform companies Bill began almost exactly two years ago to-day when Commonwealth and State Ministers met in Melbourne on the 18th June, 1959. Since then the Ministers have met to consider the problems on seven occasions. The first draft prepared under the direction of the Ministers was circulated widely in October, 1960, and the Ministers are deeply appreciative of the valuable comments that were made on that draft by persons and professional organisations in the legal, accountancy, secretarial and commercial fields.

After a close study of these comments the Bill was re-examined and substantially amended at a meeting of the Ministers in Hobart in February of this year. The Bill in its present form is the result of that consideration and also of careful revision of the drafting. It is believed that the Bill is now in as good a form as can be expected in complex legislation covering such a wide field.

The general approach of the Ministers to this matter has been firstly to simplify the requirements of the legislation with the object of facilitating operations of legitimate business and secondly to strengthen the provisions aimed at fraudulent and undesirable practices and those designed to safe-guard the investing public.

These two objectives are to a degree irreconcilable but it is believed that the streamlined procedure of the legislation will be of great benefit to the community and that the strengthening of the provisions relating to disclosure and prevention of fraud will not interfere unduly with the operations of legitimate business.

Indeed it is probably true that legislation designed to curb fraudulent activity must assist legitimate business. It is impossible in any field to prepare legislation that pleases everyone and this draft will no doubt have its critics; but the Ministers believe that, when considered as a whole, the draft is a measure which fairly balances the interests of the business community against that of the public generally and the investing public in particular.

Being conscious of the constant developments in the field of commercial law and of the probability of further reforms being recommended by the report of the committee at present considering company law in England under the chairmanship of Lord Jenkins, the Ministers fully realize that this measure, even if adopted by all States and Territories in the near future will soon require further consideration. So that company law can be kept abreast of these developments, it is proposed to review the position periodically and to maintain close contact between all administrators working in this field. This draft is offered as a proposal for a Bill for adoption throughout the States and Territories of Australia. If the draft is acceptable to the Legislatures of the various States and Territories concerned, Australia will have a law regulating corporations equal to any in the Commonwealth of Nations and well suited to its needs in these times of vast manufacturing and commercial growth.[11]

At the Hobart conference, decisions were made on 600 separate items drawn from the 1,000 separate representations that were made concerning the draft Bill.[12] At a national level the Institute of Chartered Accountants and the Australian Society of Accountants formed a joint committee which prepared a submission to the conference of Attorneys-General.[13] This co-operation of the accounting profession was evidenced at the State level.

QUEENSLAND

In Queensland for some years there had functioned a group calling itself the Queensland Company Legislation Standing Committee consisting of representatives of Australian Society of Accountants, Brisbane Stock Exchange, Queensland Law Society Incorporated, the Bar Association of Queensland, Brisbane Chamber of Commerce Incorporated, Chartered Institute of Secretaries,

Institute of Chartered Accountants in Australia and Queensland Chamber of Manufactures. A report was submitted by this committee to the Queensland Minister on 18 February 1959.[14] This report appears to have initiated the preparation of a Bill to amend the companies legislation in Queensland, only a few months before the first meeting of Attorneys-General agreed to endeavour to secure uniform legislation. A Bill was introduced subsequently into the Queensland Parliament on 7 December 1960 so that it could be printed to allow it to be debated early in 1961. The model Bill prepared by the Standing Committee of Attorneys-General was sent to the Queensland Company Legislation Standing Committee on 7 November 1960 with an invitation for comments.[15] On 23 February, the week after the Hobart meeting of Attorneys-General, the Queensland Minister made a statement pointing out that the Bill introduced the previous December would need to be redrafted in the light of the Hobart conference.[16] On 23 August 1961, Queensland became the first State to submit a Bill in 'general conformity with the decisions of the conferences of Ministers held in February and June 1961'.[17] The Bill was passed on 30 November 1961.

WESTERN AUSTRALIA

In Western Australia a Bill was introduced into Parliament on 25 October 1960, based on the first draft prepared under the Attorneys-General, but this Bill was not proceeded with as, following the further conferences of Attorneys-General, it was considered expedient to present a new print of the Bill. It was reintroduced as the Uniform Bill on 31 August 1961, and finally was passed by the Assembly on 24 October 1961. The Council's amendments were received and accepted by the Assembly on 15 November 1961.

VICTORIA

The third parliament in which the Uniform Bill was introduced was Victoria, where it was introduced on 4 October 1961. It was passed by the Assembly on 23 November 1961 and the Council's amendments were dealt with on 12 December 1961.

NEW SOUTH WALES

The New South Wales division of the Institute of Chartered Accountants was active in seeking amended legislation. In 1957 the State council had set up a committee and proposed to offer its services to the Minister for Justice.[18] In New South Wales the first draft of the Uniform Bill was introduced into Parliament on 9 November 1960. The Bill was passed through both Houses by 29 November 1961.

TASMANIA

In Tasmania the Uniform Bill was introduced on 21 August 1962 and passed little more than a week later on 29 August 1962.

SOUTH AUSTRALIA

Last of the States to act on the matter was South Australia. The South Australian division of the Institute of Chartered Accountants in Australia was concerned that the South Australian Act should be brought up-to-date. As far back as the 1948 annual meeting of the South Australian division it had been reported that copies of a report on the form and content of published accounts of companies, at that time in preparation, would be sent to the relevant government departments, when the South Australian Act was to be amended.[19] The report referred to was published the following May.[20] At the following annual meeting it was notified that the government reaction to the proferred assistance was qualified. The chairman thought it unfortunate that the Institute had been excluded from the early discussions.[21] The delay in acting meant that the Uniform Act was already in force in three States, and a similar Ordinance in the Australian Capital Territory, when the Uniform Bill was introduced into the South Australian Parliament on 4 September 1962. However, the Parliament was not as slow as the executive had been and the Bill passed all stages by 9 October 1962.

THE TERRITORIES OF THE COMMONWEALTH OF AUSTRALIA

It is convenient at this point to note the progress made in the company ordinances of the Territories of the Commonwealth of Australia. These have not been referred to previously because of the relative unimportance of private economic activity in the Territories. In recent years, public companies had adopted the practice of registering in Canberra to avoid State stamp duty on share transfers, a tax advantage which lasted until 1969. Among the 'forty-two leaders sample' one company newly incorporated to carry out a scheme of rearrangement of a group, A. & K. Cement, is in fact a company registered in the Australian Capital Territory (A.C.T.).

33 The Uniform Acts

Companies in the A.C.T. were governed by the New South Wales Act of 1899 until 1954 when the Companies Ordinance adopted the form of the 1936 New South Wales Companies Act. As from 1 July 1962 the Companies Ordinance of the A.C.T. has been similar to the Uniform Acts. Although in the past the A.C.T. Ordinance has not played an important role in the development of company law, and more particularly the development of disclosure by Australian companies, it does not follow that this will remain true in the future. The growing importance of the A.C.T. as a place of incorporation of national companies, provides an avenue through which the Commonwealth government may affect the development of company law just as much as it is possible for some of the State governments to speed up or retard developments in company law and the reporting requirements embodied in the Acts.

Ordinance no. 1 of 1964 of the Territory of Papua and New Guinea is also modelled on the form of the Uniform Acts. In this instance the Ordinance replaced legislation still modelled on the English Act of 1862.[22]

REQUIREMENTS OF THE ACTS

The changes in accounting requirements may be considered to fall into three broad categories:

(a) The inclusion in the legislation of Queensland, South Australia and New South Wales, of provisions first introduced into Victoria in 1938, requiring consolidated statements or the separate statements of each company in a group, and a reasonably adequate profit and loss statement which would identify the result from current operations and the disclosure of share option details.

(b) The inclusion in the legislation of all the other States except Tasmania, of specific items introduced by Victorian legislation in 1955 and 1958 and the Tasmanian legislation of 1958 including dividend appropriations, provisions for taxation, directors' and auditors' remuneration, interest on debentures and the concept of the exempt and non-exempt proprietary company.

(c) The introduction of provisions which were entirely new requirements in all States. These included the form of presentation of data on fixed assets, inclusion of comparative figures in statements, the names and places of incorporation of subsidiaries and the directors' declaration on the realizable value of current assets. Details of each of these matters have been given in the relevant chapters.

Thus was Australia brought to the point of having uniform company legislation throughout the Commonwealth sixty years after federation and three decades after the previous serious though abortive efforts towards this goal.

Following chapters include a review of some of the subsequent changes in the Uniform Acts. The course of events very quickly raised questions as to whether the uniformity could be maintained. Regular meetings of the Commonwealth and State Attorneys-General have continued towards this end. An important step was taken in July 1967 when Mr Justice Eggleston was appointed chairman of a three-member committee to advise the Standing Committee of Attorneys-General. The terms of reference of this committee were 'to enquire into and report on the extent of the protection afforded to the investing public by the existing provisions of the Uniform Companies Acts and to recommend what additional provisions (if any) are reasonably necessary to increase that protection'. The committee made its first report in 1968 and this was reviewed by the Attorneys-General in Hobart in March 1969. The course of these events gives confidence to the belief that the uniformity achieved in the 1961–2 Uniform Acts will be continued in the future.

34

Public Borrowings Acts

One of the traditional ways for a company to secure additional finance was by the issue of preference shares. In 1933 debentures still were regarded as sufficiently unusual for a writer to claim that companies 'are forced to resort to borrowing by debentures, specific mortgage or bank overdraft',[1] because of difficulty of raising capital due to the abnormal economic conditions. This situation changed dramatically in the post-war period and, aided by the effect of the taxation policies of the Commonwealth government, debenture borrowing became the accepted form of financing and preference shares became virtually a 'museum piece'.[2] This change in methods of financing went even further with the use of unsecured notes as a common type of debt finance. Not all was plain sailing and it came to be seen that some action was needed to prevent the worst of abuses which became apparent.

The practice of some companies of accepting money on deposit without issuing a debenture and hence avoiding the necessity to issue a prospectus, was prohibited in the Victorian Companies Act of 1958 (s.36) on the recommendation of the Victorian Statute Law Revision Committee.[3] The necessity of issuing a debenture also meant that the investor, whether receiving a secured or unsecured debenture, was now entitled to secure the annual financial statements of the company as a debenture holder. This move created a new problem because both the secured and unsecured investor had to receive a 'debenture'. While many companies followed the Stock Exchange practice of referring to such unsecured investments as unsecured notes, this was by no means a universal practice. The documents issued as 'debentures' were often given names which indicated a 'security' which was spurious. The Uniform Acts tackled this in part by requiring that, where a deposit or loan was not to be secured by a charge over assets, the document recognizing the deposit or loan must be described as an unsecured note or unsecured deposit note (s.38). The Act thereby imposed a specific terminology on accounting in this respect. More significant issues were to be raised as a result of the shock of the disclosure of the full details surrounding a series of spectacular company failures revealed in the reports of the investigators appointed to probe the companies concerned.[4] The Victorian government acted quickly, some would say hastily, and enacted the first of the Public Borrowings Acts.

The Attorneys-General of all the States met in December 1963 and confirmed their support for the Victorian legislation which they felt would deal with many of the weaknesses revealed by the investigations into the recent financial events.[5] In due course the other States preserved the uniformity of company legislation by enacting similar legislation. Among the business community some joined P. C. E. Cox in wondering what was the logical end to the attempt to legislate for every possibility devised by human ingenuity,[6] though others joined E. St John and P. Grogan in declaring that the amendments were the minimum demanded by the recently disclosed abuses.[7]

To preserve the uniform character of the legislation, the Victorian government had to pass a further Act modifying some of the more stringent provisions of Act no. 7089. These modifications related to half-yearly reports which are discussed later. The amendments made to legislation have preserved uniformity except in Queensland, where provisions for the issue by borrowing corporations of half-yearly financial statements have not been enacted.

The Acts created new categories of companies—the borrowing corporation which is:

A corporation that is or will be under a liability (whether or not such liability is present or future) to repay any money received or to be received by it in response to an invitation to the public to subscribe or purchase debentures of the corporation. (s.2(a))

and guarantor corporation defined in relation to a borrowing corporation as one:

that has guaranteed or has agreed to guarantee the repayment of any money received or to be received by the borrowing corporation in response to an invitation to the public to subscribe for or purchase debentures of the borrowing corporation. (s.2(a))

In both these definitions debentures are mentioned, and this term in this context includes both debentures and unsecured notes.

The Public Borrowings Acts went further than the Uniform Acts in prescribing terminology which must not be departed from by declaring that, according to the terms of issue, a debenture henceforth could only be called an unsecured note or an unsecured deposit note, a mortgage debenture or certificate of mortgage debenture stock, and a debenture or certificate of debenture stock (s.2(c)).

In the application of this terminology some companies found a problem in endeavouring to identify securities ranking in priority between debentures and unsecured notes. According to Bryan Frith writing in the *Australian* on 7 March 1968 this was resolved by an agreement between the Australian Finance Conference and the State Companies Registrars to call such securities 'debentures (second ranking)' and anything ranking ahead 'debenture stock'. This informal agreement was not recognized by F.N.C.B.-Waltons who, Frith says, issued a prospectus for debenture stock (two classes), designated initially inside the prospectus and later on the cover, as 'first ranking' and 'second ranking'. It has now become common for companies to distinguish different rankings of securities with such descriptions as 'first charge' debentures and 'debentures (second ranking)' used by I.A.C. While this situation has initially arisen in respect of prospectuses it will no doubt be reflected in the periodic financial statements included in annual reports.

The Acts more importantly introduced two new compulsory reports to be issued by any borrowing corporations. Firstly, there is a requirement to issue to the trustee for the debenture holders a three-monthly report from the directors identifying anything affecting the security and interests of debenture holders including any exceeding of borrowing limitations, any events which might cause debentures to become enforceable, any change in the nature of the company's business since the issue of the debentures not previously reported, and whether or not all the covenants and provisions of the debentures or trust deed have been performed (s.3).

This report is also to give details of any amounts lent to, or deposited with, a related company, or of any liability assumed on behalf of a related company except where the related company has 'guaranteed the repayment of the debentures of the borrowing corporation and has secured the guarantee by a charge over its assets in favour of the trustee for the holders of the debentures of the borrowing corporation'. This is supported further by the requirement to provide details of any charge given over the assets of the borrowing corporation or a guarantor corporation. Where such a charge is indeterminate, such as to secure a bank overdraft, the quarterly balance is to be reported to the trustee.

The second new report is a half-yearly report to be issued to the trustee and lodged with the Registrar by every borrowing corporation and every guarantor corporation. This report consists of a balance sheet and profit and loss statement.

The Public Borrowings Acts also added to the ninth schedule (clause 2(4)) of the principal Act the requirement for borrowing corporations and guarantor corporations to include as a note to the balance sheet, a statement of the amounts of liabilities payable by and the debts payable to the company not later than two years, later than two years but not later than five years, later than five years, calculated from the date to which the balance sheet of the company was made up. This marks a significant development of the classification of the balance sheet on the traditional lines of permanency and urgency, and the more recent statutory obligation to distinguish liabilities payable not later than twelve months, and those payable beyond twelve months from the balance date. This form of statement has been received most favourably by users of company reports and some have advocated the extension of this part of the ninth schedule to all companies.

Of more general impact was the requirement commented on earlier for all holding companies, unless specially exempted, to adopt a common balance date for the preparation of group consolidated statements.

These Acts had very direct impact on certain aspects of terminology and presentation and most importantly gave the first legislative support to the publication of audited interim financial statements.

In 1966 a questionnaire was circulated to all companies, other than speculative mining companies, listed on the Melbourne Stock Exchange. This survey indicated that the Public Borrowings Acts extended to one in eight of the listed companies at that time. Although affecting a relatively small proportion of listed companies, the half-yearly and quarterly reporting and the schedule of amounts due and payable required by the Public Borrowings Acts have provided a significant forward step in the development of the reporting standards applicable to these 'public borrowing' companies. However the legislation has so far paid little attention to any problems that might arise particularly from the issue of any of these debt securities with rights to convert to ordinary shares. This reflects the fact that the revocation of the tax deductibility of interest paid on convertible debentures or notes in 1960 virtually has eliminated this form of security from the new issue market. Proposed changes in taxation law are expected to restore the convertible to the market although on terms somewhat different from those which applied to some issues before 1960.

The most important reporting issue arising from the existence of convertible securities is the possibility of dilution of the reported earnings per share if the conversion rights are exercised. If this effect of conversion is not reported by the inclusion of a *pro forma* calculation in the annual report, then the report is misleading. Therefore any moves encouraging the issue of convertible debt securities should be accompanied by moves to ensure that the issuing companies subsequently report the profit or earnings per share, both on the basis of the number of shares currently issued and the total number of potential shares if the conversion rights on debt securities are exercised.

35

Interim Reports

Although instances can be found of companies regularly issuing half-yearly reports about fifty years ago (e.g. Herald until 1920, B.H.P. until 1917, Brick until 1925, C.S.R. until 1938 when the company obtained the approval of the Supreme Court to new articles in place of those in the original deed of settlement of the company), the practice, which might be considered to be universal in the 'modern' period of company reporting, has been to issue an annual report on the company's affairs. Details were given in an earlier chapter of the recognition of half-yearly reporting in some legislation governing mining companies.

It is the length of the reporting interval which is the foundation for all demands for interim reports. This becomes even more important when the delay between the date of preparation of financial statements and their issue is considered. If the issue of the financial statements takes four months, then an annual report covers a period extending from four to sixteen months earlier. At least a half-year report would confine the reporting to events within ten months, assuming the same four-month interval between balance date and issue of the report.

The Stock Exchanges consistently over many years have maintained the attitude that twelve months is too long a period between reports and that the shareholder is entitled at least to be told there has not been any change in the trend of the company's affairs. The first move for half-yearly reports was made by the Stock Exchanges in 1939, when it was resolved to include in the Official List Requirements for new issues a requirement for the directors of the company to supply a general report on the company's operations after the first six months of each financial year. Companies already on the Official List were invited to adopt this practice and by 1955 this form of report was being provided by 70 per cent of listed

35 Interim Reports

companies.[1] In 1957 the Stock Exchanges decided to make the form of half-year report more explicit and to require a:

report by the directors concerning the company's activities for that period, stating *inter alia* the relationship of volume of sales (or revenue) compared with the volume of sales (or revenue) in the corresponding period in the previous year, and any unusual factors affecting the earning capacity of the company.[2]

Then in 1964 the Exchanges moved another step forward, deciding that the specification in the Official List Requirements covering the half-year report should state for the company and, where appropriate, the corporate group, the relationship compared with the corresponding period of the last preceding year of profitability and volume of sales (or revenue), and any material factors affecting the earning capacity of the company.[3] This requirement applied to new listings and to any existing listings covered by the 'dragnet clause'. Nevertheless the Exchanges achieved a high degree of acceptance for, as my 1965 analysis shows, only 8 per cent of the 547 companies issuing an interim report in the six months period failed to extend the report to cover the trend of profitability (see Table 46).

It was during this period that the facts relating to two of the company crashes which occurred drew the attention of the authorities to the need for adequate interim reporting leading to the inclusion in the Public Borrowings Acts of provisions designed to ensure more adequate interim reporting (s.3).

The interim reporting provisions contained in the Public Borrowings Act as passed in Victoria, and the action of the Stock Exchanges, provided the cue for one section of the press to release a fusillade against the concept of half-yearly reports. Space does not allow the inclusion here of all that was written in the resulting debate which continued during the following three months. Barrie Dunstan said in the *Age* 1964–65 Business Review (21 December 1964): 'Cries that "interim reports can be misleading", have been given widespread publicity by sources with a domestic interest in the matter.' This appeared to be an allusion to the sentiments expressed in the columns of the *Herald* by John Eddy, *Herald* economist, who referred to the danger of 'part-year, off-the-cuff reports' (1 September), and wrote that some interim reports 'could be most misleading' (5 September). The opposite role in this debate was taken by the *Age* finance editor who considered that if one company chairman's remarks were to be construed as direct opposition to the Stock Exchanges seeking interim reports, then it was 'to be deplored' (17 September), and that the case for these reports generally was not weakened because some 'have not in the past been fully revealing' (11 September). A columnist in the Sydney-based *Australian Financial Review* went so far as to argue in effect that the worse the news the more frequent the need for reporting becomes. 'Taking the view that shareholders should be protected from the truth about their companies', he wrote, 'strikes right at the heart of public investment, decisions on which should be made in possession of as many of the facts as possible' (3 November). During the period occupied by these press exchanges two companies added fuel to the debate by producing end-of-year results opposite to the earlier indications given in the interim reports.[4] Perhaps the attitudes were best typified in the headlines following the annual meeting of Stramit Boards Ltd at which the chairman, J. B. Hobart, had discussed the special accounting problems of the building industry. The *Herald* (8 October) interpreted this with a headline 'Stramit Chief Warns on Interims', but on the following morning the *Age* headline was 'Helpful Hints from Stramit'. A similar interpretation was given to the remarks of A. B. Mellor, the chairman of the Melbourne Stock Exchange, at a press conference on 26 October. The *Herald* noted his remarks that 'you cannot generalise and say it should be mandatory on all companies to issue interim balance sheets'. The *Age* (27 October), however, made no mention of this remark and emphasized Mellor's remarks concerning the standard of enforcement of interim reporting in London and New York. The *Herald*'s attack may well have been the most vigorous and concentrated ever waged by the press against a move to extend the information required to be disclosed by Australian companies to comply with the Statute. It is therefore worth noting that its efforts do not appear to have retarded progress effectively but perhaps have served only to justify the position of the *Herald* company as the only large company, other than some of the financial institutions, which steadfastly refuses to issue a half-yearly report of any kind.

In Queensland the Public Borrowings Act did not introduce the requirement for half-yearly financial statements from borrowing corporations which the Minister claimed 'is not a desirable provision' although the requirement for the more generalized quarterly report to the trustee for debenture holders by the directors of such borrowing corporations was enacted. The Minister argued that Queensland companies were either engaged in seasonal primary industries or heavily dependent on the seasonal trade of primary producers with the consequent accounting problems. Half-yearly stocktaking, he suggested, could be 'inconvenient' and the results of profit measurement 'may be misleading in a very material extent'.[5] In Victoria the requirement for half-yearly reports was amended shortly after the Public Borrowings Act was passed and to this extent the opponents were successful. The special seasonal nature of the pastoral industry was recognized and provision was made to exempt pastoral companies even though they might be borrowing corporations.[6]

The auditing profession unexpectedly included some aggressive critics of the half-yearly reporting requirements, this criticism being based largely on the difficulties of completing more than an annual audit.[7] In answer to these criticisms, the Victorian Act was further amended to allow the trustee for debenture holders to dispense with so much of the audit as the trustee considered unnecessary. The amendment also specifically allowed the acceptance by an auditor of an estimated stock figure for the purpose of preparing half-year financial statements.[8] The interim reporting requirements of the Victorian Act as thus amended became the model for the legislation passed in all the other States except Queensland.

A further advance was made when, in September 1967, the A.A.S.E. recommended that the half-yearly report include a statement of the percentage relationship of profitability and sales volume with the corresponding period. The A.A.S.E. did not go so far as to include this in the Official Listing Requirements and thereby invoke the 'dragnet clause' but relied instead on its powers of persuasion. At the same time the A.A.S.E. did amend its requirements by calling for the half-yearly report not later than three months after the end of the first six months of each financial year in an attempt to eliminate tardy reporting by some companies.[9]

The Exchanges have not stopped at framing requirements or recommending desirable procedures. There is evidence of the Stock Exchanges acting where a half-yearly report fails to meet the letter of the listing requirements. The *Australian Financial Review* of 18 April 1969 reported that the Stock Exchange of Melbourne had queried one company because it had not reported on the trend of profitability, the directors claiming that 'owing to the seasonal nature of the fruit-processing industry, it is not practicable'. The company subsequently reported the percentage change in sales for the period but still declined to report the trend of profits.

The legislation and the A.A.S.E. Official Listing Requirements thus established four standards of interim reporting as follows: (i) full financial reports subject to audit (except to the extent that this is not required by the trustee) by public borrowing companies, (ii) a statement of the trend of profitability and volume of sales (or revenue) by those companies which have made listing agreements with the A.A.S.E. since the inclusion of the 'dragnet clause' and therefore are bound to comply with the September 1964 listing requirement and later amendments, (iii) a statement of the trend of volume of sales (or revenue) by those companies which elect to comply with the A.A.S.E. listing requirement before September 1964, and (iv) no information from those companies which are not affected by any of the former and do not voluntarily adopt one of these standards.

A trend of sales or profitability can be described in precise figures or by a generalized descriptive comment. It has been found possible to classify the form of interim reports into six categories: the actual monetary values of profit or sales, a percentage or proportionate change, a statement which applies a qualitative adjective to the increase or decrease without including any quantitative values, a statement that the item has increased or decreased without any further qualification or details, the omission of any comment on the item, and other forms of report which either explicitly or by implication indicate a continuation of a similar position to that in the previous period.

This classification was used in a survey of interim reports issued by companies with ordinary shares listed on the Stock Exchange of Melbourne directed at assessing the impact of the legislative and A.A.S.E. requirements. The periods surveyed reflected the progressive changes in these requirements between 1964 and 1969.

The period January to June 1964 covered the 1957 A.A.S.E. requirement for a report on trend of sales only, the period January to June 1965 followed the extension of the A.A.S.E. requirement to cover the trend of sales and profitability. The additional factor of the Public Borrowings Acts applied in the period July 1965 to June 1966. The most recent move by the A.A.S.E. to secure a quantitative statement of the trend of sales and profits applies in the last period of the survey, July 1968 to June 1969.

The results of the survey are set out in Table 46. The survey was based primarily on the summarized interim reports as appearing in the *Official Record of the Stock Exchange of Melbourne*. In order to gain a measure of the economic importance of each company, the analysis also included tabulations weighting each com-

35 Interim Reports

TABLE 46
Form of half-yearly report

Contents of reports	% of companies						Shareholders' funds repr.						Total assets represented					
	1964	1965	1965–6	1968–9			1964	1965	1965–6	1968–9			1964	1965	1965–6	1968–9		
Report on trend of sales (or revenue)																		
No. of companies	444	470	599	565			444	470	599	565			444	470	599	565		
	%	%	%	%			%	%	%	%			%	%	%	%		
Actual value of sales	4·5	4·7	5·0	4·8			6·6	8·5	11·2	8·6			7·9	9·7	12·6	9·3		
Proportionate change	12·4	20·7	12·2	24·1			8·7	21·0	7·3	12·7			9·1	20·5	7·8	13·0		
Qualified change	22·1	23·4	18·5	9·0			24·1	19·6	13·8	11·3			23·0	18·8	14·2	11·6		
Change not qualified	28·5	30·3	30·7	31·5			24·9	27·0	21·9	19·5			24·0	25·0	22·7	18·9		
No comment	16·7	13·4	19·7	22·8			19·1	13·6	22·9	25·4			19·9	15·9	23·8	26·9		
Other	15·8	7·5	13·9	7·8			16·6	10·3	22·9	22·5			16·1	10·1	18·9	20·3		
Report on trend of profitability																		
No. of companies	511	547	704	673			511	547	704	673			511	547	704	673		
	%	%	%	%			%	%	%	%			%	%	%	%		
Actual profit amount	4·5	24·9	26·0	29·7			6·3	38·6	33·7	36·5			5·7	47·9	42·7	43·9		
Proportionate change	11·4	4·8	3·7	8·8			7·9	4·1	2·0	6·7			7·8	3·3	1·8	6·0		
Qualified change	20·2	25·6	18·6	12·6			22·2	21·9	14·4	23·6			21·3	17·6	12·6	19·5		
Change not qualified	26·2	20·8	24·7	32·7			24·8	17·3	20·3	19·9			22·9	14·3	17·9	18·1		
No comment	20·9	8·0	8·8	5·4			22·2	6·2	18·9	6·6			25·7	4·9	15·0	6·6		
Other	16·8	15·9	18·2	10·8			16·6	11·9	10·7	6·7			16·6	12·0	10·0	5·9		

pany according to the value of each of shareholders' funds and total assets. These values were obtained from the published figures in the annual reports as summarized in the 'Stock Exchange of Melbourne Investment Service'.

It was necessary to limit the first two intervals in the analysis to periods of six months in order to isolate the factors of concern to us. This, however, means that these periods do not include Australia's largest company, the presence of which may affect significantly the analysis including financial weightings. The two latter periods each cover a full annual cycle and survey all companies with ordinary shares listed in the January of the period surveyed. These periods therefore include in the 'no comment' category those companies which failed to issue any interim report during the year. Three companies were excluded on the grounds that they were essentially overseas companies with an Australian division representing only a small part of the activities reported upon. Seven trading banks and one life insurance company were excluded as special institutions covered by special legislation. Companies involved in such finance activities as hire purchase, investment, underwriting, insurance, trustee, pastoral and property investment were excluded from the analysis of reporting related to turnover.

There now remains a very small proportion of companies which have failed to respond to the call for interim reports. In January 1969 there were 673 companies with ordinary shares listed on the Stock Exchange of Melbourne. The exclusion of banks and a life insurance company, of companies not trading because of the appointment of receivers and liquidators, and of those for which interim reports would not be expected as new listings or delistings within the survey period, left 596 companies from which interim reports could be expected. After including reports traced in other sources and information given at annual meetings of eight companies interpreted as valid interim reports, there remained only fourteen companies which do not appear to have issued an interim or half-yearly report. These include eight insurance trustee and investment companies, two public utilities and only two large commercial undertakings. These few companies we may regard as clearly failing to meet widely practised standards of disclosure by failing to issue a half-yearly report.

As noted earlier a survey disclosed that one in eight listed companies was subject to the statutory obligations imposed on borrowing corporations. It is clear, therefore, that while the legislation has been important in advancing the standards of disclosure, it was not responsible for the increase to nearly 30 per cent of companies giving actual profit figures in the interim report. However the incidence of borrowing corporations would be above average among finance companies. 28 per cent of companies included in this category disclosed actual profits in the interim report in 1964 but since the Public Borrowings Acts were passed this has approached 50 per cent. Among this group of companies it appears that this statutory requirement has had a significant impact on reporting. What is perhaps more important is that the companies reporting actual profits represent nearly 44 per cent of all assets of the companies surveyed and 72 per cent of the assets of the finance companies in particular.

The A.A.S.E.'s actions have encouraged the publication of actual profit figures and the latest recommendation clearly has led to the reporting of the proportionate change of profit, where actual profit is not given, by a higher proportion of companies. The 'other' category reflects periods in which profits remain relatively stable. The A.A.S.E.'s actions would appear also to have contributed to the continued decline in the number of companies not giving any comment on profitability and the use of meaningless adjectives to describe the magnitude of the change in profits instead of giving a quantitative measure.

The reporting of turnover is not affected by any statutory requirements and we therefore may regard improvements in this respect as more directly attributable to the A.A.S.E. requirements and recommendations.

The reporting of actual sales figures remains a practice of barely 5 per cent of listed companies, comprising about 10 per cent of total assets of the surveyed companies. Against this must be matched the one-fifth of these companies which do not give any report on the trend of sales or revenue in the interim report. On these results we may well consider the efforts of the A.A.S.E. as not having been as successful as might have been hoped. However, the strength of the A.A.S.E. is more revealed in the last period of the survey. In this period the recommendation to give the percentage change in sales was responded to by nearly one-quarter of the companies. It appears that this may rather reflect smaller and more recently listed companies in view of the fact that these companies comprise only one-eighth of the total shareholders' funds or assets of all the companies (excluding the finance group of companies). The apparently higher result in 1965 reflects in part the difference between a six-month and full-year survey. It may indicate also a responsiveness in the form of reporting to current business conditions. As the call for a proportionate or percentage change in turnover only requires a voluntary compliance, not being included in the Official List Requirements, these results may suggest a greater willingness to give a more informative report among smaller and 'younger' companies and a greater responsiveness by these companies to Stock Exchange moves.

The Public Borrowings Acts have been the dominant force in securing the inclusion of actual profit figures in half-yearly reports. At the same time it is clear that the Stock Exchanges have been a dominant force in the establishment of the general standards applicable to the reporting of both sales or revenue and profitability in half-yearly reports.

The survey questionnaire conducted among companies listed on the Melbourne Stock Exchange invited comments from companies on half-yearly reporting. The question asked was designed deliberately as an 'open-ended' question. Nearly a quarter of the respondents availed themselves of this invitation. The results may contain an element of bias arising from the conduct of the survey. The design of the questionnaire encouraged the respondents to comment on the question of seasonality, and may have drawn replies from those with 'hostile' feelings. Of the questionnaires returned with comments about 45 per cent revealed themselves strongly against the issue of half-yearly reports, 30 per cent were judged to favour them and the remaining 25 per cent expressed caution based on the point that six months' trading may not necessarily equal one-half of the year's result. About half of those opposed to the issue of half-yearly reports relied on the assertion, without much substantiation, that such reports may be misleading. The claims of one small group of companies involved in heavy construction and engineering are based on significant problems peculiar to those companies. The claim by these companies that interim statements of dollar profits 'can be grossly misleading' probably is not unreasonable. It is a gross over-statement to assert (as one company's reply did) that: 'All half-yearly reports can be misleading.' Perhaps this would be the case if there were general truth in the reply which noted that it is likely that errors occur because the half-yearly accounts are not given close scrutiny. A number of companies objected to half-yearly reporting on the grounds of cost. In some cases there seems little justification for this although one company pointed out that it had arranged to repay its publicly-raised debentures to avoid the public borrowings provisions 'in view of the excessive cost of preparing

35 Interim Reports

half-yearly accounts in such a large and diverse manufacturing company'. The third main opposing group included those companies which only issued a half-yearly report to satisfy the Stock Exchange requirements. As one company put it, half-yearly reports are 'to be avoided if at all possible', or to quote another: 'The annual report is the one of real importance.' There was also the company which commented that 'for a company such as . . . it appears unnecessary to prepare a half-yearly balance sheet.' In spite of the publicly-voiced objections to half-yearly reports as simply a device to activate sluggish stock markets,[10] only one company objected to half-yearly reporting 'because of the risk of inflating share values' on the basis of what may prove to be only short-term factors. Among the replies favourably disposed to half-yearly reports the reasons given generally followed the idea that they are 'a worthwhile means of communication' and something which the shareholder is entitled to receive. One company went so far as to say that the half-yearly report is 'essential as a guide to shareholders'. Some companies even offered support for the general requirement for half-yearly reports to be given statutory recognition.

The objection to half-yearly reporting on the grounds of seasonal trading is voiced so often that information was sought to determine the importance of this factor. One-third of the companies which replied considered that this was a factor with them (we may assume it was not a factor in two-thirds of the companies). The proportion was higher among textile and garment makers, some chemicals, food, retail trading and service industries. The comments made by companies on this particular point were summarized by the company which stated it was reluctant to give more precise half-yearly figures 'because of a fear of misrepresentation' of the information disclosed. The danger that many companies see is in attempting to forecast the year's profit by simply doubling the half-year result.

The conclusion to be drawn from the comments proffered would appear to be that there is more widespread positive thinking about the merits of half-yearly reporting than outright opposition. Any attempts to extend existing legislation or other requirements to ensure more adequate half-yearly reporting will require the position of particular classes of companies to be defined. These classes of companies include those involved in long-term contracts where half-yearly reporting increases the technical accounting problems of revenue and cost allocation, and those companies involved in activities having a distinctively annual cycle such as agricultural producers and processors of annual agricultural crops.

The important role of the Stock Exchange in securing improved standards of disclosure was brought out in an analysis of the distribution of copies of the half-yearly reports. All of the borrowing corporations sent the reports to the Stock Exchange, and about three-quarters of them sent details direct to the newspapers. The content of the reports issued to the Stock Exchanges included balance sheet and profit figures in about 40 per cent of cases, actual profit figures without a balance sheet in 40 per cent and no dollar value information in the remaining 20 per cent. Less than one in five of the borrowing corporations issued the half-yearly report to shareholders. Of those reports sent to shareholders about one-quarter included a balance sheet although practically all included the actual dollar profit result. Less than one in ten issued this report to debenture holders. Apart from a few exceptions, all of the companies which were not borrowing corporations reported to the Stock Exchanges, and more than 80 per cent sent the details to the newspapers direct. However, only about 10 per cent of these companies issued the half-yearly report to shareholders. Although nearly one-sixth of these companies reported to a trustee for debenture or note holders, the number of reports issued to debenture holders is negligible. These results were typical of all industrial and commercial groups. While it is recognized that the costs of issuing half-yearly reports to shareholders can be substantial, it is clear that this information would not be available if it were not for the facilities provided by the Stock Exchanges to disseminate the contents of reports sent to them. But, while many issued reports may remain unread, this failure of some to use the available information is not a valid argument against issuing a report. One company secretary ruefully remarked: 'I am sure that the majority of annual reports remain unread and that the dividend cheque is regarded as the vital statistic.'

36

Additional Information

The discussion up to now has paid little attention to questions other than the form and content of the traditional financial statements of the balance sheet and variations of operating statements and profit and loss appropriation statements including the more modern concept of group consolidated statements. The more diverse audience for company reporting which has been referred to earlier has called for an ever-widening range of information. Within the last two decades these new demands for information have been able to be taken into account as the size of company reports increased. Some of this disclosure may be regarded at this time as being experimental in nature.

One such type of experiment has been the inclusion in the annual report of a funds statement. This statement has been advocated and written about by teachers of accounting for nearly thirty years, with apparently little practical consequence so far as published company reports are concerned. The first recorded contribution to Australian literature was an article in the Students' section of the *Commonwealth Journal of Accountancy* by A. A. Fitzgerald in 1935. Fitzgerald saw the purpose of the statement as: 'to emphasise the relationship between the sources of new funds and the investment or use of those funds' (p. 500), and suggested that this would be achieved if the statement were prepared as if in answer to two questions: what new funds came into the business during the period under review, and in what ways were those funds applied? Fitzgerald's article was followed within twelve months by a contribution by O. R. MacDonald, who presented the funds statement as the means of answering the question: 'You show that I have made a profit of so much. Where is it?'[1] It is probably significant that the numerous articles on this type of statement which have appeared in Australia are almost wholly directed at students and student problems. Little attention has been paid to it by writers more concerned with the problems of business. It seems that the teachers have not been able to establish the importance of this statement with sufficient strength to gain widespread acceptance by those responsible for company financial statements.

Although the A.I.M. Award adjudicators have mentioned the funds statement each year, their support does not seem to be based on a precise concept of this statement. The adjudicators' reports have complimented companies on the use of diagrammatic representations of the contents of the funds statement. The danger with diagrams is that precise figures may not be given and the presentation therefore becomes vague and generalized. It is likely also that the failure to gain widespread adoption of this statement may reflect the extent of dispute over what should be the scope and concept of the statement. Various concepts advocated by different writers include a statement including all changes in economic power including unrealized gains; a statement based on a concept of economic resources which only recognizes realized gains although being a broader concept than a statement expressing changes in working capital items, or even a statement only dealing with cash transactions.[2] If the advocates of this type of report cannot show more agreement as to what they are advocating, then there is little chance of widespread practical acceptance.

In 1953 the adjudicators of the A.I.M. Award reported that: '21% of the Companies were making use of the "Statement of Funds" compared with 13% in the previous Award'.[3] This was before the decision to include the reports of all listed companies in the award and therefore represents the results of a 'selected' sample of reports which aspired to gain the A.I.M. Award. A survey of Western Australian companies in 1957 produced two funds statements from thirty-six companies.[4] R. J. Chambers likewise found little acceptance of the statement. Among 250 reports he examined in 1955 only seven companies included a funds statement.[5] An analysis in 1965 showed that of those among the 'forty-two leaders sample' to have at some time included a funds statement in the annual report half had discontinued the practice. In 1968 eleven of these companies included a funds statement (see Table 47). This very significant increase suggests that perhaps this statement is at last about to be given its proper place in financial reporting. The statement presented by Ansett is of some note because of the long-term comparison given beginning with a seven-year statement in 1963 and having covered ten years' figures in the reports since 1965. Nat. Cons. has presented a five-year comparative statement.

TABLE 47
*Inclusion of funds statement
'42 leaders sample'*

	Size of available sample[a]	No. of companies	% of available sample
1953	38	Nil	
1954	40	1	2·5
1956	42	2	5·0
1957	42	5	12
1958	42	8	19
1960	42	6	14
1963	42	8	19
1968	42	11	26

[a] See explanatory note, p. 3.

There has been an advocacy for longer-term comparative statements to be included in annual reports for purposes of financial analysis.

The first year after the Act required companies to include the previous year's figures the A.I.M. Award adjudicators in their report on the 1963 Award said that: 'All companies in the award-winning list give comparisons ranging up to ten-year periods' (p. 5). Thus the award-winning companies have, in recent years, established an example. This is more encouraging that the earlier situation revealed in the examination of the reports of 250 companies by R. J. Chambers. He found only 4 per cent giving such comparisons in 1948 and by 1955 this had increased to 13 per cent.[6] The results of the analysis of the reports of the 'forty-two leaders sample' indicate a significant increase in the inclusion of this type of statement between 1952 and 1957 with little change in the last decade of the survey which follows the institution of the A.I.M. Award (see Table 48.) It appears reasonable to conclude that the desire to meet the standards set by the A.I.M. Award competition was the significant factor in this particular development of reporting. The adjudicators of the Award competition have consistently advocated the inclusion of long-term comparison tables. These comparisons have been described by the adjudicators of the A.I.M. Award in the report of the 1963 Award as, 'most valuable to the analyst and layman alike' (p. 5).

The enthusiasm of some companies to extend the time period covered by these statements drew the comment of the adjudicators in their report on the 1964 Award that: 'Five years' figures would

TABLE 48
Inclusion of long-term comparison tables
'42 leaders sample'

	Size of available sample	No. of companies	% of available sample
1947	34	2	6
1950	38	2a	5
1952	38	6	16
1955	41	12	29
1960	42	17	40
1965	42	19	45
1968	42	22	52

a Excludes one company which included more than two years' figures in statutory profit and loss statement.

TABLE 49
Long term comparison tables
Percentage of tables according to number of years' detail shown
'42 leaders sample'

	5 years or less	6 years	7 years	8 years	9 years	10 years	more than 10 years
1947	—	—	—	—	—	100	—
1950	—	—	—	—	—	100	—
1952	33	—	—	—	—	67	—
1955a	16	—	17	17	—	50	—
1960	23	6	—	—	12	47	12
1965b	21	—	16	—	5	58	—
1968	40	5	5	—	—	45	5

a One company included as giving eight or nine year table also gave some information as a five year or less table.
b One company included as giving a ten year table also gave some information as a five year or less table.

in most cases be quite adequate' (p. 5). An analysis of the time period covered by the tables given by companies in the 'forty-two leaders sample' indicates some preference for tables containing ten years' information (see Table 49). Although tables including ten years' data have been the most common, there has been considerable variety in the choice of the number of years' data to be shown.

There is much more variety in the items included in the long-term comparisons than in the choice of the number of years of data to be included in the comparison. Because of the great variety of content in the examples included in the reports of the 'forty-two leaders sample' it was only possible to make a general survey of this aspect of the comparisons. This analysis indicated that nearly all the comparisons included both balance sheet items and profit and dividend information. Less than half the comparisons included a variety of other statistical facts or financial ratios (see Table 50).

TABLE 50
*Long term comparison tables
Analysis of content of published tables
'42 leaders sample'*

	'Balance sheet' items %[a]	Profit, dividend details, etc. %	Other statistical measures %
1947	50	50	—
1950	50	50	—
1955	83	75	33
1960	76	88	41
1965	95	89	42
1968	95	95	36

[a] These percentages should not be added together. Some tables include more than one type of information.

In 1927 the Melbourne Stock Exchange added a note in its Official List Requirements recommending 'that Companies follow the practice set by the leading banking and industrial companies of issuing to their Shareholders full reports of proceedings at their General Meetings'. This practice is still followed by some companies, but there has been a distinct move towards issuing any comments to be made by the chairman as part of the annual report. This may be done by including a separate chairman's statement in the annual report or extending the directors' report over the chairman's signature. In a few cases the chairman's speech is issued with the annual report, but as a separate document. Among the 'forty-two leaders sample' thirty-nine companies included a review of the company's activities in the annual report, and only in three cases was no review of activities traced (see Table 51).

The 'annual review', however it is presented, may disclose information on a great variety of aspects of the activities of a company. This, in turn, may be supported by other specific details on aspects such as the products produced and the factories, warehouses, retail stores or offices owned by the company. Among the 'forty-two leaders sample' twenty-one have given some directly descriptive details of the products manufactured or traded by the company, and twenty-three have included descriptions of their factories, stores, etc. This information has only been given spasmodically by many of these companies. In some cases the presentation is exceedingly informative. We would mention as examples the schedule of the number of different types of stores trading in each State given by Coles or the analysis of sales by using industries given by ICIANZ.

TABLE 51
Form of review of company activities '42 leaders sample', 1968

Expanded directors' report	24
Expanded directors' report with chairman's review[a] in separate booklet	3
Expanded directors' report and chairman's review in annual report	6
Chairman's review in annual report	4
Chairman's review in separate booklet	2
No review	3
Total	42

[a] Includes report of general manager, managing director or chairman.

The success of the operations of a company will depend on the skill and dedication of the executives and the efficiency of the organization structure. Therefore it may be of interest to shareholders to know something of who are the executives of the company and how the company is organized. Twenty-three of the 'forty-two leaders sample' were found to have given information of this kind at some time. At 1965, sixteen of these companies included some detail of these matters, but by 1968 only twelve were doing so.

The published results of an investigation of shareholder attitudes sponsored by Gibson Kelite Industries Ltd in 1968, suggested that more information on senior executives would be welcomed by shareholders although some shareholders were emphatically against such a move.[7]

Statistical information on the senior executive personnel of a company appears to be less frequently disclosed than information about the employees. Of the 'forty-two leaders sample' only fourteen companies were found to have given details such as the number of employees, and related personnel statistics. Only six companies included any details in 1965 but this had increased to nine by 1968. Only five of the fourteen companies could be regarded as having followed any consistent policy of including this type of information in the annual report.

An interesting comment on the social position of company senior employees is provided in the requirement introduced in the English Companies Act of 1967 for disclosure of the numbers according to salary multiples of those employees receiving more than £10,000 per annum individual emoluments. However the 'lesser' employees have not been overlooked in the English Act which also requires a statement of the average number of employees (unless under 100) and the aggregate remuneration of all employees for the year. At present there is no evidence of serious moves in Australia to secure this type of information. As the adjudicators' report on the 1967 A.I.M. Award noted, 'without people the assets of a Company become almost junk, and in most reports far too little mention is made of this valuable asset which is not reflected directly in the balance sheet' (p. 8).

It appears that even less recognition has been afforded the shareholder than the employee as regards the details disclosed in the annual report. Up until 1965 twelve of the 'forty-two leaders sample' have at some time disclosed details of the number of shareholders. In 1968 there were twelve cases of disclosure of this type of information. When this information is given it is sometimes accompanied by an analysis of such aspects as the size of holdings, residence of the shareholders, etc. Only four of these companies have for any length of time followed a consistent pattern of disclosure of details relating to shareholders.

Rather more serious in intent and implications was the consideration given by the Eggleston Committee in 1967 to proposals to require that the actual ownership of all holdings of 10 per cent or more of the voting power in a company should be revealed. The committee recognized the need for this information but considered there should be some flexibility in its imposition.[8] The 10 per cent figure reflects an ownership level accepted in Australian legislation where the rights of minority and majority shareholder groups are concerned.

The Attorneys-General according to the *Australian Financial Review*, 25 March 1969, held that disclosure of substantial shareholdings was

justified by the consideration that in the case of companies whose shares are traded on stock exchanges shareholders are entitled to know whether there are in existence substantial holdings of shares which might enable a single individual or corporation or a small group, to control the destinies of the company, and if such a situation does exist, to know who are the persons on whose exercise of voting power the future may depend.

This has become a more important matter as a number of companies have made issues of shares to each other, apparently as a defensive strategy against takeover bids. By the existence of a large block shareholding the directors are ensured substantial proxy support which would be difficult to secure from a widespread shareholding and it may be possible to deny an intending takeover bidder the opportunity to use the statutory provisions to secure the compulsory acquisition of a minority of shares whose owners are reluctant to accept the takeover terms. The financial implications of such 'share exchanges' are less serious where the two companies have similar earning and dividend rates, similar market prices apply to the shares and the two companies have similar opportunities of growth. Where the market price of the shares is markedly different the number of shares issued will differ and may lead to quite different degrees of dilution of earnings per share in the two companies. The short-term position may be offset if the dividends of the two companies are in the opposite proportion although it would be unusual to find the dividends paid by both companies on the shares involved in the share exchange to balance exactly the dilution of earnings per share in both companies simultaneously. Where there is the added complexity of different growth potentials and risk it may become extremely difficult to judge the fairness of such share exchanges.

The development of a more widespread pattern of share ownership may be regarded as having created a new audience of shareholders less 'sophisticated' in reading financial statements. This would appear to be the logic underlying a number of shortlived experiments in presenting simplified financial statements in the annual report. Among the 'forty-two leaders sample' only seven companies were found to have experimented with this type of presentation. No less than five of the seven persevered over a period of some years. By 1968 only one example was to be found of the presentation of a simplified balance sheet or profit and loss statement. It may be that the development of the use of notes and the increasing flexibility of format of the statutory financial statements have tended to reduce the need for further simplification of

36 Additional Information

these statements. Alternatively, it may be that there is not an audience among shareholders for the simplified statement.

This examination of the presentation of various types of additional information by Australian companies, as evidenced by the 'forty-two leaders sample', leads to two inescapable conclusions. Firstly, there has been a great deal of experimentation in the inclusion in company reports of many kinds of financial information beyond the statutory reports, and of other non-financial data. Secondly, there has been little consistent adoption of specific practices. There has rather been a great deal of spasmodic inclusion of this type of information.

It does not matter however extensive the information disclosed by a company might be, it will be of little value if it is not made available promptly. At least among some companies there has developed a new awareness of the need for prompt reporting. Custom Credit Corporation Ltd is a notable example of the prompt issue of the annual profit figure. This company has consistently issued the year's profit result not later than 8 July each year since 1959. The columnist Keith Dunstan in the *Sun* has suggested there is a race to publish among some companies, or what he called the 'statement stakes'. On 22 July 1966 he reported that Robert Hutchinson's issued their profit figures on 1 July and quoted the secretary of the company as saying: 'We could do it any time. We get a profit statement every day. Seeing that we have a quick turnover we work it out on manufacture, not sales.' Even though upstaged by Indoor Bowling which announced its 1968 result a day before the year ended, Robert Hutchinson 'still took first prize for trading companies' in 1968 and was predicted by the *Australian Financial Review* on 30 June 1969 as 'likely to once again take the honours'. But, as Dunstan observed: 'Oddly, those who don't make any profits don't seem to try for a victory in the statement stakes.'

37

Conclusion

There is absolutely no doubt that the most important source of applicable standards of disclosure for Australian companies has been the companies Statutes. This analysis has demonstrated this and also shows how the statutory developments broadly may be summarized into four important stages. The first stage was the introduction of the first compulsory standards of disclosure generally applicable to companies under the Victorian Companies Act of 1896. The emphasis on the balance sheet in this Act continued in the second stage in which the first statutory requirements were enacted in 1931–6 in Queensland, South Australia and New South Wales. The third stage is marked by the Victorian Companies Act of 1938 which introduced adequate profit and loss reporting and group consolidated statements. These innovations were extended subsequently to the other States in the fourth stage which is marked by the culmination of the efforts towards achieving uniform company legislation throughout Australia in 1961–3.

While the Statutes may be regarded as a primary standard, there is also the secondary question of how the Statutes came to be enacted. This analysis has shown two very effective influences. The accounting professional bodies in Australia at all times have been given an opportunity of expressing their minds on proposed company legislation. They have had varying levels of success, probably having gained the most in the suggested innovations which were incorporated in the Victorian Companies Act of 1938. The second continuing influence on Australian company law which has been examined in detail here is the example of English law and a series of Company Law Committees which have operated in England. In recent decades some Australian States have shown themselves ready to accept the English Committee recommendations ahead of the United Kingdom Parliament. At the other extreme have been the

37 Conclusion

instances where Australian legislation has been rewritten deliberately in order to assimilate it to English law.

One could be forgiven for looking for the accounting profession to have had the greatest non-statutory influence on what has been essentially a matter of financial reporting. This analysis has shown on the contrary that recommendations made by the accounting profession have done little to gain additional disclosure, although they have been very successful in achieving a 'prettier' presentation of the available information. On the other hand the Stock Exchanges have had substantial success in obtaining information above and beyond the statutory requirements. Particular success was achieved in respect of the statements of groups and, more recently, in respect of more frequent reporting.

In modern times there has been an ever-widening range of interested readers of company reports and the needs of these readers have called forth a response in the disclosure of a widening range of information. This movement is perhaps best illustrated by the activities relating to the A.I.M. Annual Report Award which has emphasized the development of the company report as an informational document directed at a diverse audience.

Particular innovations have been attributable directly to large scale financial disasters such as the land boom of the nineteenth century or such specific incidents as the Royal Mail case in England in the thirties. Similarly some developments have been supported by widespread advocacy while others have been the result of individual crusades such as Sir Alexander Fitzgerald's to clarify the use of the terms 'reserve' and 'provision'.

Such diverse sources of change in the past mean that we do not find any easy or ready-made solutions to the question of how we should expect future change to take place. We may expect that the readers of company reports will comprise an ever-widening audience of increasing diversity and therefore we may expect the demands for disclosure of information to continue to cover a widening range of information. The question remains as to how far we can go on relying on statutory requirements to enforce rules which must be of universal application when the need may well be rather for specific information for particular kinds of enterprise. The Stock Exchanges show little sign of easing up in their endeavours and the accounting profession may be expected to have a more specific influence through their own activities if the recently launched Australian Accountancy Research Foundation is successful in better formulating Australian accounting principles.

An important unknown quantity in the future success of the Stock Exchanges and, more particularly, the accounting profession acting through company auditors, is the resistance which may exist in the 'boardrooms' of companies. It is an unfortunate situation that there is not available any adequate information on which to assess the extent to which differences exist between the directors and auditors of a company. Already the community's attitudes to qualified auditors' reports have been referred to. On one hand there are to be found auditors who will assert that the threat of a qualified audit report has led to changes in the financial statements of many companies, while on the other hand there are those who declare that the directors determine the profit required and expect the accountants and auditors to conform to that requirement. Whatever the real position may be, at this stage we can only resort to the judgment of 'Not proven'. Resistance to further disclosure is justified where it would favour one interest at the expense of another. Therefore future developments must allow more opportunity to ensure that the demands made and the new disclosures achieved are a reasonable reflection of the existing equitable arrangements among the various parties concerned.[1]

A superficial analysis would suggest that the most controversial issue raised by the Eggleston Committee was the formation of an Australian Companies Commission which, among other duties, would include the altering of statutory requirements for company accounts, group accounts and directors' reports, the granting of exemption from or approving alternatives to prescribed disclosure requirements, and determining materiality of information in certain circumstances.

Proposals for a body of this kind were put to the Eggleston Committee in a number of the submissions made to it, including the submission of this writer, and there is reason to believe that at least one member of the Committee strongly advocates such a move. The basis of such a proposal is the difficulty of continually expanding the statutory obligations for disclosure to close off every conceivable avenue of deceit which the more innovative and less honest company directors may devise. The continued expansion of statutory requirements to catch the few cases of deficient disclosure causes unnecessary complexity and commonly difficulties. There is a real need for some form of administrative tribunal with the power to deal with individual cases within the broad principles of the Statute and to act as a moderator between directors and auditor should they face an unresolved dispute. The standing committee of

Attorneys-General was reported as having agreed at Hobart in March 1969 that there was a need for this power of dispensation, but that at present this should be exercised by the Registrars of Companies. It is clear that the matter is not a dead issue and that the comment in the *Australian Financial Review*, 10 March 1969, that the Attorneys-General 'gave short shrift to the suggested companies commission', and that 'strong opposition by powerful sectors of Australian business was apparently a major factor underlying the rejection' is probably too strong a statement. There is little doubt that much of the vocal opposition was based on the false assumption that the Eggleston Committee proposal was for a body on the lines of the United States Securities and Exchange Commission, but as the New South Wales Attorney-General, the Hon. K. M. McCaw, was reported in the *Australian Financial Review*, 11 March 1969 as saying: 'The Standing Committee of Attorneys-General have not entertained any proposal of this kind.'

It is appropriate to conclude this study with wholehearted support for this Eggleston Committee proposal for a Companies Commission, because the statutory requirements for disclosure have now become so all-embracing in scope that the problem is now only rarely one of the lack of disclosure of facts. The important area of development which remains barely touched is that of the quality of the specific items of data given in compliance with the statutory standards of disclosure. A Companies Commission could provide the necessary flexibility of administration of the law to allow for progress in this important area of improving the quality of the information rather than the number of facts available to the readers of the reports of Australian public companies.

The alternative is for the accounting profession to attach a greater importance to the overriding statutory requirement that the financial statements are such as to present a true and fair view of the state of affairs of the company. As was pointed out earlier the profession has been found wanting in so far as its treatment of group or consolidated statements is concerned. It is to be hoped that there may be developing a new awareness of this responsibility and that it will be regarded as sufficiently important to allow a conflict with the secondary duty of presenting the financial statements in accordance with the details specified to be shown according to the schedule to the Act.

William Clay's slogan from last century calling for limited liability and perfect publicity progressively becomes more of a reality as time passes and we move closer to perfection in disclosure of the affairs of Australian public companies.

APPENDIX 1

Details of Forty-two Companies comprising 'Forty-two Leaders Samples'

Company	Predecessor[a]	Place of incorp. and date Vic.	Place of incorp. and date N.S.W.	Rank market value[b]	Rank value of share t'over[c]	Earliest accounts avail-able[d]
A.W.A.			1913			1919
Ampol	(Aust. Motorists Petrol)		1936	18	14	1936
Ansett	(Ansett Airways)	1937				1940
APPM		1936				1937
A. & K.		1962 A.C.T.[e]				1965
	Australian Cement Ltd	1924				1925
A.C.I.	(Aust. Glass Mfg Ltd)	1922		11	9	
	Aust. Glass Mfg Co. Ltd					1920
A.G.C.			1925			1928
A. Gypsum		1961				
	Australian Gypsum Ltd					1925
A.P.M.	(Pty Coy till 1937)		1926	15	17	1937
B.M.I.			1953			1954
Bradford	(Bradford Cotton Mills Ltd)		1927			1935
Boral	(Bitumen & Oil Refineries Ltd)		1946		16	1947
Brick	(New Northcote Brick Co. Ltd)	1886				1918
B. Tobacco	(reorganized in 1927)	1927				1920
B.H.P.		1885		2	1	1917
C.U.B.		1907		16		1914
Coles		1927		8	8	1928
C.S.R.			1887	6	7	1921
C.I.G.			1935			1935
Container		1949				1950
Custom			1953			1954
D.H.A.		1929				1932

304

Company	Predecessor[a]	Place of incorp. and date Vic.	Place of incorp. and date N.S.W.	Rank market value[b]	Rank value of share t'over[c]	Earliest accounts available[d]
Dunlop	(Dunlop Perdriau Rubber) Dunlop Rubber Australasia Dunlop Rubber Australia Ltd	1929		20	13	1917
Electronic Email		1939				1940
F. & T.	(Electric Meter & Allied Ind.) (Felt & Textiles of Australia Ltd)		1934			1936
Herald		1902	1921	13	3	1937
Humes	(Hume Pipe Co. (Aust.) Ltd)	1920				1916
ICIANZ		1928		5	12	1922
I.A.C.	(Industrial Acceptance Corp.)	1929				1933
J. & Way.	Johns & Waygood Ltd (Johns & Waygood (Holdings) Ltd)	1957				1948
Jones	(Henry Jones Co-operative Ltd)	1909				1925
McPherson	(Pty Coy till 1945)	1913				1914
Myer	Myers (Aust.) Ltd	1925		7	6	1945
Nat. Cons.	(National Radiators)	1948				1922
Olympic	Olympic Tyre & Rubber Co. Ltd	1954				1949
		1933				1935
Peters	(Peters Ice Cream (Vic.)) (Peters American Delicacy)	1929				1930
Repco		1937			10	1938
Rothman			1955			1956
Sleigh		1947				1948
T.V.			1955			1955
Woolworth			1924	9		1929

[a] This column indicates antecedent companies for which data was available and which logically could be included in the analysis. Names in brackets indicate where the only change has been of name without any break in continuity of the company.
[b] Per Annual Report by the Committee of the Stock Exchange of Melbourne, 1965, p. 12.
[c] Per ibid. p. 22.
[d] This column indicates the commencement date of available files. Most of the earlier material was available from the library of J. B. Were and Son, members of the Stock Exchange of Melbourne.
[e] Incorporated in Australian Capital Territory.

APPENDIX 2

Companies included in Stock Exchange Fifty Leaders excluded from 'Forty-two Leaders Sample'

Name of company	Type of business
Bank of New South Wales	banking
Commercial Union Assurance Co. of Aust. Ltd	insurance
Conzinc Riotinto of Australia Ltd	base metals
Elder Smith Goldsbrough Mort Ltd	pastoral
E. Z. Industries Ltd	base metals
Mount Isa Mines Ltd	base metals
The National Bank of Australasia Ltd	banking
North Broken Hill Ltd	base metals

APPENDIX 3

Empirical Surveys of Company Reporting

ARTICLES

A. A. Fitzgerald, 'The Published Accounts of Companies', in E. V. Nixon and A. A. Fitzgerald, *Some Problems of Modern Accountancy*, Melbourne, 1928.
Survey of balance sheets issued by 91 Australian companies between July and December 1927.
(Also reported in A. A. Fitzgerald, 'The Reports and Accounts of Limited Companies', *The Stock Exchange Official Record*, 26 (May 1933), p. 151.)

―――, 'Items of an Abnormal Character', *Australian Accountant*, 14 (March 1944), p. 80.
Surveys contents of directors' report per section 123(5) of the Victorian Companies Act 1938.

―――, 'A Further Note on the Valuation of Trading Stocks', *Australian Accountant*, 14 (December 1944), p. 424.
Surveys basis of valuation of stocks and relates its significance to disclosed profits.

R. K. Yorston, 'Stock in Trade', *Chartered Accountant in Australia*, 16 (November 1945), p. 199.
Surveys basis of valuation of stocks, certificate of stock value, and classification in the balance sheet.

(Contributed), 'Life Assurance Company Adopts Vertical Form', *Australian Accountant*, 18 (July 1948), p. 227.
Lists companies using the narrative form of presentation of balance sheet.

R. A. Irish, 'Current Developments in Corporate Accounting', *Australian Accountant*, 18 (December 1948), p. 427.
Surveys 14 aspects of reporting by 26 selected companies.

[Study Group, South Australian Branch of the Institute of Chartered Accountants in Australia], 'The Form and Content of Published Accounts of Public Companies', *Chartered Accountant in Australia*, 19 (May 1949), p. 755.

Compares reporting of selected companies with the Institute Recommendations but does not give any precise statistical results.

R. J. Chambers, 'The Spice of Accounting', *Australian Accountant,* 19 (November 1949), p. 398.
Surveys the basis of valuation of stocks in 50 companies.

K. C. Keown, 'Stock on Hand in the Balance Sheets of Victorian Companies', *Australian Accountant,* 21 (July 1951), p. 265.
Surveys basis of valuation of stock in 181 Victorian companies.

R. K. Yorston, 'Some Accounting Implications Arising from the Corporation Viewed as a Social Unit', *Australian Accountant,* 22 (February 1952), p. 41.
A survey of the employees of Jantzen (Aust.) Ltd covering knowledge of and attitudes to company reports.

R. A. McInnes, 'Better Financial Statements, The Accountant Must Help', *Australian Accountant,* 24 (March 1954), p. 111.
Surveys the reports of 50 companies listed on Brisbane Stock Exchange and compares them with the Institute Recommendations.

R. K. Yorston, 'Control in the Corporation', part 2, *Australian Accountant,* 25 (July 1955), p. 293.
Surveys the opinions towards reports of shareholders of two public companies.

L. Goldberg, 'Depreciation in Published Company Reports', *Accounting Research,* 6 (1955), p. 155.
Detailed examination of reporting of depreciation and fixed assets by 78 companies.

J. McB. Grant, & R. L. Mathews, 'Inflation and Company Accounts', *Australian Accountant,* 26 (February 1956), p. 61.
Surveys various consequences of inflationary pressures as affecting South Australian Companies, and the reporting or otherwise of action taken.

R. J. Chambers, 'Trends in Corporate Reporting', *Australian Accountant,* 26 (December 1956), p. 493.
Surveys details of eight different aspects of the reports of a sample of 250 companies.

J. McB. Grant & R. L. Mathews, 'The Response of South Australian Companies to the Post War Inflation', *Australian Accountant,* 27 (March 1957), p. 143.
A more extensive treatment of the material contained in the previous article by these authors.

E. M. Jones and seven others, 'A Review of Published Accounts of 36 Selected Western Australian Public Companies', *Chartered Accountant in Australia,* 28 (September 1957), p. 101.
A detailed survey of a limited sample of reports.

E. Joe DeMaris and Vernon K. Zimmerman, 'An American View of Australian Financial Reports', *Chartered Accountant in Australia,* 30 (January 1960), p. 343.

Survey of 25 Australian reports with special reference to turnover, fixed asset presentation, and reserves.

R. K. Yorston, 'Reporting Financial Information to Employees', *Australian Accountant,* 30 (February 1960), p. 80.
Further treatment of results of questionnaire to employees of a public company covered by article in 1955.

R. W. Gibson, 'Survey of Company Interim Reports—Are They Substantially Satisfactory?', *Australian Accountant,* 36 (March 1966), pp. 133-6.

——, 'Survey of Company Interim Reports', ibid. (December 1966), pp. 667-72.

——, 'Improvements in Company Interim Reports', ibid., 39 (December 1969), pp. 557-60.

BOOKS

R. J. Chambers, *The Function and Design of Company Annual Reports.* Sydney, 1955.

R. K. Yorston & S. Owens, *Annual Reports of Companies.* Sydney, 1958.
Both these books have a great many illustrations drawn from actual company reports, but do not contain statistical analysis of contents, etc., except that Chambers lists the reports indicating size, number of pages and quality of production.

A. A. Fitzgerald and G. E. Fitzgerald, *Form and Contents of Published Financial Statements.* Sydney, 1948, 1960.

A. A. Fitzgerald, G. E. Fitzgerald, L. C. Voumard and M. O. Jager, *Form and Contents of Financial Statements,* 3rd ed., Sydney, 1964.
These volumes include reproductions of a number of examples of actual reports which are taken as representing good practice at the time.

APPENDIX 4

Comparative Table of Disclosure Required by Companies Acts, 1931-1936

Item	Victoria 1910	Queensland 1931	South Australia 1934	New South Wales 1936
Company to keep proper book of account of all receipts and payments of cash, and sales and purchases of goods, assets and liabilities.	s115	s132	s141	s102
Profit and loss account to be presented to annual meeting.		s132	s142	s103
Balance Sheet to be presented at annual meeting.	s115	s132	s142	s103
Directors' report to be attached to balance sheet showing:				
Report of state of company's affairs.		s133	s142	s103
Recommended dividend.		s133	s142	s103
Amount to be taken to reserves.		s133	s142	s103
Amount of depreciation charged.		s133		s103
Basis of valuation of stock.		s133		
Whether all contingencies provided for.		s133		
Amounts drawn from reserve and the purpose for which drawn.		s133		s103
Balance sheet to be:				
Signed by two directors.		s139	s149	s110
Circulated to members of public companies, with attachments.	s115	s140	s150	s111
Copy to be furnished on demand, to every shareholder and debenture holder of a public company.		s140	s150	s111

310

Appendixes

Item	Victoria 1910	Queensland 1931	South Australia 1934	New South Wales 1936
Balance Sheet to contain:				
Authorized Capital.	s115	s134	s142	s104
Issued Capital.		s134	s142	s104
distinguishing classes of shares	sched.		sched.	
amounts paid in money and	sched.		sched.	
amounts paid up otherwise	sched.		sched.	
arrears of calls.	sched.		sched.	
Liabilities.	s115	s134	s142	s104
Statement if any secured on assets of a public company.		s140	s150	s111
Eight categories.	sched.		sched.	
Assets.	s115			
Thirteen categories.	sched.		sched.	
Floating assets.		s134	s142	s104
Bases of valuation.	sched.	s134	sched.	s104
Debtors after provisions for bad and doubtful debts	sched.		sched.	
Fixed Assets		s134	s142	s104
Bases of valuation.	sched.	s134	s142	s104
Provision for amortization of leaseholds.	sched.		sched.	
Preliminary expenses ⎫ not		s134	s143	s104
Issue expenses ⎬ written	s98	s134	s143	s104
Purchased goodwill ⎪ off		s134	s143	s104
Patents and trade marks ⎭		s134	s143	s104
Shares in subsidiaries		s135	s144	s104
Debts due from subsidiaries		s135	s144	s104
Debts due to subsidiaries		s135	s144	s104
Loans to directors made and amount outstanding.		s138	s147	s108
A statement of how reserve fund used or invested.	s115		s148	s108
Discount on shares issued.				s147
In form of schedule	s115		s143	
Capital on which interest paid out of capital, and rate.	s99			s157
Profit and loss statement to contain:				
Statement of profit or loss.	sched.			
Directors' remuneration.		s138	s147	s108
A statement of how profits of subsidiaries dealt with.		s136	s145	s106

APPENDIX 5

Presentation of Group Accounts by 'Forty-two Leaders Sample'

VICTORIAN COMPANIES

WITHOUT LEGAL COMPULSION

Publication of aggregate statement of assets and liabilities of subsidiaries

D.H.A.   1932–8   (consolidated statements adopted in 1939)

Publication of consolidated statements before legislative compulsion

B. Tobacco   1937–
Dunlop   1935–

WITH LEGAL COMPULSION

Publication of consolidated statements in first year following the Victorian Companies Act 1938 and since

A.C.I.   Humes
Brick (except 1952–60 inclusive   ICIANZ
    when company had no subsidiaries)   J. & Way.
B.H.P.   Jones
C.U.B.   Myer
D.H.A.   Repco

Companies with subsidiaries only after 1939

Publication of separate statements for each subsidiary

Ansett   1944–5
I.A.C.   1948–53   (newly listed in 1948)
McPherson   1949–59   (following four years of consolidated statements)

312

Publication of consolidated statements

Ansett	1946–	(following publication of separate
I.A.C.	1954–	statements of subsidiaries—
McPherson	1945–8 and	McPherson's first four years following
	1960–	Listing in 1945)

APPM	1946–	
Coles	1949–	
Herald	1954–	(first year with subsidiary companies)
Olympic	1952–	
Peters	1944–	
Sleigh	1953–	

Container	1950–	
Electronic	1940–	(newly listed companies)
Nat. Cons.	1949–	

A. & K.	1965–	(follows change in group structure)
A. Gypsum	1961–	

NEW SOUTH WALES COMPANIES
WITHOUT LEGAL COMPULSION

Aggregate statement of assets and liabilities of subsidiaries

Email	1934–45	(newly listed in 1934)
Woolworth	1938–49	

Separate statement of each subsidiary

Custom	1955–8	(consolidated statements later)

Consolidated statements

Email	1946–	(following aggregate statements)
Woolworth	1950–	
Custom	1959–	(following separate statements)
Ampol	1948–	
A.G.C.	1949–	
A.P.M.	1948–	
C.I.G.	1948–	
F. & T.	1937–	(first available statements)
Bradford	1939–	(first year subsidiary operating)
Boral	1950–	(first year subsidiary profitable)
T.V.	1961–	(first year with subsidiary)
B.M.I.	1954–	(newly listed)
Rothman	1956–	

WITH LEGAL COMPULSION
Consolidated statements

A.W.A.	1962–	
C.S.R.	1961–	(actually year ended three months before new legislation effective)

APPENDIX 6

Report on Treatment of Profits and/or Losses of Subsidiaries per s.106 New South Wales Companies Act 1936[a] by 'Forty-two Leaders Sample'

A.W.A. (1937)

The profits of subsidiary companies have been brought into the accounts of A.W.A. to the extent of dividends received from those companies during the year ended 30th June, 1937. Small losses made by two Subsidiary Broadcasting companies . . ., have been covered in the accounts of A.W.A. by provision made in this company's reserves.

A.G.C. (1937)

The profits of the Subsidiary Company so far as they concern the Company, have been dealt with in the accounts of this Company by the inclusion of the dividends received.

A.P.M. (1937)

Insofar as it concerns this Company, the Profit derived by the Subsidiary Company has been incorporated in the Accounts.

C.S.R. (1937)

Profits of subsidiary companies have been included in the attached accounts to the extent to which they have declared dividends during the period covered by these accounts. No subsidiary company has made a loss during the period covered by the last accounts of the respective companies.

[a] This Appendix covers those companies in the sample incorporated in New South Wales, which were affected by the 1936 New South Wales Companies Act and which did not publish aggregate statements of assets and liabilities of subsidiaries or consolidated statements for the group, or separate statements for the parent company and each subsidiary.

C.I.G. (1937)

The Company's proportion of the profits of Subsidiary Companies has been included in the Profit and Loss Account to the extent to which dividends have been declared by those Companies. All Subsidiary Companies have made profits.

WOOLWORTH (1937)

The Dividends received from the company's investments in Subsidiary Companies have been included in the accounts under review.

BORAL (1949)

The first financial year of the Subsidiary Company ended on 30th September, 1949. The loss incurred by the Subsidiary Company for the period to 30th June 1949, has not been dealt with in the attached accounts of the holding company. [Consolidated statement given in the following year.]

APPENDIX 7

Description of Reserve or Goodwill on Consolidation, Selected Cases from 'Forty-two Leaders Sample'

Capital surplus arising on acquisition of subsidiary companies.

Difference between par value and book value of subsidiary companies shares less amounts below par paid in acquiring interests in certain subsidiary companies.

... includes profits of subsidiaries at time of merging adjusted by the difference between book values and par values of inter-company holdings.

... excess of cost of shares in subsidiary over book value of net assets acquired.

Premium arising on the incorporation in the Consolidated Balance Sheet of the tangible assets and liabilities of Subsidiary Companies at Book Value less Reserves in these Companies when the shares were acquired.

Difference between the values at which inter-company holdings of shares are entered as Assets in the Balance Sheets and their par values.

Goodwill on Consolidation shows the net difference between the book value in the accounts of the parent company of shares in subsidiary companies and the amount of shareholders funds in those subsidiary companies accounts at the date of acquisition, less amounts subsequently written off.

Amount by which Cost of Shares and Stock in Subsidiary Companies exceeded their Net Assets.

Adjustment arising on Consolidation;

This item represents the net excess of the book amounts of net tangible assets of subsidiary companies at the dates of acquisition of the shares of those companies over the total cost of the shares of those companies.

Difference between consideration paid for the Shares of the Subsidiary Companies, based on independent valuations of Assets, and the nominal value of such shares.

Excess of cost over par value of Shares held in Subsidiary and Affiliated Companies.

REFERENCES

1 INTRODUCTION

1 Stock Exchange of Melbourne, *Annual Report by the Committee* (Melbourne, 1965).
2 For a brief outline of these problems see R. W. Gibson, *An Introduction to the Theory of Financial Statements*.

2 WHY DISCLOSURE?

1 Quoted by B. C. Hunt, *The Development of the Business Corporation in England 1800-1867* (Cambridge, Mass., 1936), p. 69.
2 'The Evolution of Corporate Accounting', *Australian Accountant*, vol. 17 (November 1947), p. 489.
3 *Parl. Deb.* (U.K.), 1856, vol. 140, pp. 110-38.
4 *Economist*, 23 July 1864.
5 'The Role of Financial Reporting in a Partially Controlled Economy', *Australian Accountant*, vol. 31 (January 1961), p. 34.

3 DISCLOSURE TO WHOM?

1 'Some Accounting Implications Arising from the Corporation viewed as a Social Unit', *Australian Accountant*, vol. 22 (February 1952), pp. 41-54.
2 'Control in the Corporation', ibid., vol. 25 (July 1955), p. 295.
3 L. Goldberg and R. C. Clift, 'An Investigation into Shareholder Attitudes', ibid., vol. 38 (June 1968), pp. 297-305.
4 'Some Accounting Implications Arising from the Corporation viewed as a Social Unit', ibid., vol. 22 (March 1952), p. 77.
5 'The Stock Exchange Viewpoint on Company Annual Reports', ibid., vol. 25 (January 1955), p. 555.
6 'Principles or Profits', *Chartered Accountant in Australia*, vol. 23 (May 1953), p. 645.
7 'Presentation of Accounts for Publication', ibid., p. 654.
8 'What's Wrong with Financial Statements', *Australian Accountant*, vol. 38 (July 1968), pp. 385-96.
9 *V. & P.* (L.A. Vic.), 1963-4, 1(C3), pp. 828-9.
10 'The Annual Report and Accounts as a Source of Information to Investing Institutions' in *Proceedings of Convention*, May 1958, Australian Society of Accountants, pp. 191-7.
11 'The Annual Report and Accounts as a Source of Information to Bankers', ibid., pp. 183-90.
12 R. K. Yorston, 'Some Accounting Implications Arising from the Corporation viewed as a Social Unit', *Australian Accountant*, vol. 22 (March 1952), p. 78.

13 Ibid., (February 1952), p. 51.
14 'Reporting Financial Information to Employees', *Australian Accountant*, vol. 30 (February 1960), pp. 80-8.
15 'The Role of Financial Reporting in a Partially Controlled Economy', ibid., vol. 31 (January 1961), p. 28.
16 'The Annual Report and Accounts as a Source of Information to Economists' in *Proceedings of Convention*, May 1958, Australian Society of Accountants, pp. 173-80.
17 'Some Accounting Implications Arising from the Corporation viewed as a Social Unit', *Australian Accountant*, vol. 22 (March 1952), p. 78.
18 Op. cit.
19 K. W. Halkerston, 'Financial Statement Presentation, What the Investing Public Needs (no. 1)', ibid., vol. 34 (November 1964), pp. 625-31. John Elsworth, 'Financial Statement Presentation, What the Investing Public Needs (no. 2)', ibid., vol. 34 (December 1964), pp. 663-71.
20 'Reports of Public Companies', *Accountant*, vol. 129 (October 1953), p. 489.
21 Lewis D. Gilbert and John T. Gilbert, *Annual Report of Stockholder Activities at Corporation Meetings During* . . .
22 'Bulk Questions Under Fire', *Age*, 16 November 1966.
23 'The Essington Lewis House Curtain Raiser', *Age*, 10 September 1965 and 'Hundreds at B.H.P. Meeting, Bigger Hall for "Battle"', *Herald*, 10 September 1965.
24 'A Memorable Meeting', *Age*, 11 September 1965.
25 O. Glenn Saxon, 'Annual Headache; The Stockholders' Meeting', *Harvard Business Review*, vol. 44 (January-February 1966), p. 132.

4 ATTITUDES TO DISCLOSURE

1 'Accounting and Business Finance', *Australian Accountant*, vol. 22 (July 1952), p. 220.
2 [O. R. MacDonald], vol. 6, p. 1.
3 'The Shareholder's Right to Information', *Accountant in Australia*, vol. 2 (June 1932), p. 265.
4 'The Modern Balance Sheet', *Chartered Accountant in Australia*, vol. 5 (November 1934), p. 180.
5 'Comments on "Should We Blame the Auditing Profession" by R. A. Irish', ibid., vol. 34 (August 1963), p. 91.
6 'The Evolution of Corporate Accounting', *Australian Accountant*, vol. 17 (November 1947), p. 491.
7 E. DeMaris and V. Zimmerman, 'An American View of Australian Financial Reports', *Chartered Accountant in Australia*, vol. 30 (January 1960), p. 345.
8 *Age*, 26 July 1966, p. 8.
9 'The Law and the Protection of the Investor', in Investment in Australia Symposium, *Proceedings*.
10 'The Profession's Attitude to Disclosure', *Chartered Accountant in Australia*, vol. 21 (October 1950), p. 201 and see similarly 'Principles or Profits', ibid., vol. 23 (May 1953), p. 645.
11 'Disclosure and the Annual Report', *Australian Accountant*, vol. 29 (September 1959), p. 507.
12 Op. cit.
13 *Analysis and Interpretation of Financial and Operating Statements*, 1st ed., p.18. A. A. Fitzgerald, together with G. E. Fitzgerald and later other collaborators, effectively carried out this process of inculcation through the various editions of *Form and Contents of Published Financial Statements*, 1948-.

References (Chapters 4-7)

14 R. K. Yorston, E. B. Smyth and R. S. Brown, *Advanced Accounting,* 1st ed., p. 9.
15 R. L. Kane (ed.), *C.P.A. Handbook,* chapter 18, p. 8.
16 'References to the Independent Accountant in Securities Registrations', *Statement on Auditing Procedure no. 22,* American Institute of Accountants, New York, May 1945.
17 M. Moonitz, *Accounting Research Study no. 1.*   18 Ibid., p. 48.
19 'Desirable Changes in the Form of Published Accounts and the Auditor's Statutory Report', *Chartered Accountant in Australia,* vol. 30 (June 1960), p. 588.
20 'What Investors Want from Company Accounts', *Accountant's Magazine,* vol. 69 (November 1965), pp. 952-69, pp. 1059-79.

5 THE FORMATIVE YEARS

1 What follows is based on Alex C. Castles' 'The Reception and Status of English Law in Australia', *Adelaide Law Review,* vol. 2 (1963), pp. 1-31.
2 Ibid., p. 28.
3 The first published balance sheets of these companies are reproduced in R. H. Goddard, 'An Historical Survey', *Chartered Accountant in Australia,* vol. 8 (April 1938), pp. 681-97.
4 'Among the Company Accounts', *Accountant's Magazine,* vol. 69 (May 1965), p. 420.
5 *The Australian Encyclopaedia,* (Sydney 1958), vol. 8, p. 220.
6 Western Australia, *Statutes,* The Joint Stock Companies Ordinance 1858, Act no. 6, 1858, table B, par. (70), and Tasmania, *Statutes,* The Joint Stock Companies Act 1859, Act no. 12, 1859, table B, par. (70).
7 *Parl. Deb.* (S.A.), 1859, vol. 3, col. 452.   8 Ibid., vol. 6, col. 112.
9 Ibid., col. 608.   10 *Parl. Deb.* (Vic.), vol. 9, p. 17.
11 Ibid., p. 1028.   12 Ibid., p. 284.
13 Ibid., p. 1054.   14 Ibid., p. 1240.
15 Ibid., p. 1290.
16 *Lee v. Neuchatel Asphalt Co.,* 1889, 41 Ch.D., p. 21.
17 L. C. B. Gower, *Modern Company Law,* p. 98.
18 2 Ch. (1894), p. 264.
19 R. K. Yorston, E. B. Smyth and S. R. Brown, *Advanced Accounting* (Sydney, 1959), vol. 2, pp. 244-57.
20 41 Ch.D., p. 26.   21 2 Ch., p. 240.
22 1 Ch., p. 286.   23 Gower, op. cit., p. 108.
24 Board of Trade (England), Company Law Amendment Committee, *Report* (1906), par. 33.
25 *Parl. Deb.* (Vic.), 1894, vol. 75, p. 161.   26 Ibid., p. 163.
27 Ibid., vol. 72, p. 440.

6 DEVELOPING CONCEPTS

1 Geoffrey Serle, *The Golden Age,* p. 369.
2 *Parl. Deb.* (S.A.), 1892, col. 535.

7 MR ISAACS'S BILL

1 M. Cannon, *The Land Boomers,* p. 16.   2 Ibid., p. 19.
3 Ibid., p. 20.   4 Ibid., p. 28.
5 Ibid., pp. 29-38.   6 *Sir Isaac Isaacs, A life of service,* p. 52.
7 The calendar of these events is also detailed by the Hon. H. Cuthbert in *Parl. Deb.* (Vic.), 1896, vol. 81, p. 1025.
8 Cannon, op. cit., p. 202.   9 *Parl. Deb.* (Vic.), vol. 67, p. 2160.
10 Ibid., vol. 69, p. 393.   11 Ibid., vol. 72, p. 428.
12 Ibid., p. 730.   13 Ibid., p. 729.

References (Chapters 7-10)

14 Cannon, op. cit., p. 198.
15 *Parl. Deb.* (Vic.), vol. 75, p. 159. 16 Ibid., p. 164.
17 Ibid., vol. 78, p. 2573. 18 Ibid., vol. 79, p. 3426.
19 Ibid., p. 4574. 20 Ibid., p. 4701.
21 Ibid., vol. 84, p. 4154. 22 *V. & P.* (L.C. Vic.), 1896, (D1).
23 *Parl. Deb.* (Vic.), vol. 84, p. 4918. 24 Ibid., p. 4155.
25 Ibid., vol. 82, p. 1237.
26 *V. & P.* (L.C. Vic.), op. cit., Minutes of evidence, par. 5.
27 Victoria, Act no. 1482, s. 24. 28 Forrest McDonald, *Insull*.
29 *Parl. Deb.* (Vic.), 1896, vol. 81, p. 135. 30 Ibid., pp. 190-207.

8 MR ISAACS'S BILL—POSTSCRIPT

1 *Parl. Deb.* (Vic.), 1910, vol. 124, p. 479. 2 Ibid., vol. 126, p. 2755.
3 Ibid., vol. 124, p. 479. 4 Ibid., pp. 480-1.
5 *V. & P.* (L.A. Vic.), 1910, 1 (D3).
6 *Parl. Deb.* (Vic.), 1910, vol. 125, p. 2197.
7 *V. & P.* (L.A. Vic.), 1910, 1 (D3), par. 92.
8 Ibid., par. 477. 9 *Parl. Deb.* (Vic.), 1910, vol. 126, p. 2758.
10 Ibid., pp. 2999-3005. 11 Ibid., p. 2757.
12 Ibid., p. 2758. 13 Ibid., p. 2755.
14 Ibid., p. 2756. 15 Ibid.
16 Ibid. 17 Ibid., p. 3797.
18 Ibid. 19 Ibid., p. 3224.
20 Ibid. where the letter is quoted by the Hon. J. D. Brown, Attorney-General.

9 DISCLOSURE AS A SAFEGUARD

1 Board of Trade (England), Company Law Amendment Committee, *Report* (1906), par. 25.
2 Ibid., par. 26. 3 Ibid. (1918), par. 46.
4 Ibid. (1906), par. 74. 5 Ibid. (1926), par. 28.
6 'Company Law Reform', *Accountant in Australia*, vol. 2 (March 1932), p. 117.

10 'TOWARDS UNIFORMITY'

1 *Parl. Deb.* (S.A.), vol. 1, p. 418.
2 Ibid. (N.S.W.), vol. 142, p. 4911. 3 Ibid. (Qld), vol. 159, p. 1024.
4 Ibid. (S.A.), vol. 1, p. 1314. 5 Ibid. (Qld), vol. 159, p. 1024.
6 Ibid. (S.A.), vol. 1, p. 1314. 7 Ibid., p. 1311.
8 *Parl. Deb.* (Qld), vol. 159, p. 671. 9 Ibid., p. 673.
10 *Parl. Deb.* (N.S.W.), vol. 142, p. 4914.
11 Board of Trade (England), Company Law Amendment Committee, *Report* (1926), par. 70.
12 'The Accountant's Duties to the Press and the Public in Relation to the Certification of Balance Sheets', p. 631.
13 *Parl. Deb.* (Qld), vol. 160, p. 2220.
14 President's address, *Commonwealth Journal of Accountancy*, vol. 11 (April 1932), p. 237.
15 Presidential address, ibid., vol. 14 (May 1935), p. 245.
16 Institute of Chartered Accountants in Australia, 'State Annual Meetings and Reports, Queensland', *Chartered Accountant in Australia*, vol. 7 (September 1936), p. 216.
17 *Commonwealth Journal of Accountancy*, vol. 5 (May 1926), p. 195.
18 *Parl. Deb.* (N.S.W.), vol. 142, p. 4912.

References (Chapters 10-13)

[19] 'New South Wales Company Law', *Chartered Accountant in Australia*, vol. 5 (October 1934), p. 151.
[20] *P.P.* (N.S.W.), 1934-5, vol. 3, p. 861.
[21] *Parl. Deb.* (N.S.W.), vol. 146, p. 1537.
[22] 'State Annual Meetings and Reports', *Chartered Accountant in Australia*, vol. 7 (September 1936), p. 213.
[23] A. G. H. Briskham, 'The Companies Act, 1934 (S.A.), as it relates to Auditors and Liquidators', ibid., vol. 6 (July 1935), p. 33.
[24] *Parl. Deb.* (S.A.), 1931, vol. 1, p. 1314.
[25] Vol. 5 (July 1931), p. 129.
[26] *V. & P.* (L.A. Vic.), 1928, 1(D3), p. 697.
[27] Ibid., 1929, 1(D3), pp. 435, 438.
[28] 'Is the Balance Sheet an Anachronism', *Australian Accountant*, vol. 1 (March 1936), p. 75.
[29] Board of Trade (England), Committee on Company Law Amendment, *Report* (1945), par. 96.
[30] Vol. 34 (January 1964), pp. 451-4.   [31] Op. cit., p. 76.

11 DISCLOSURE c.1928-1936

[1] 'Balance Sheet Reform', *Commonwealth Journal of Accountancy*, vol. 8 (June 1929), p. 292.
[2] E. V. Nixon and A. A. Fitzgerald, *Some Problems of Modern Accountancy*, p. 17.
[3] Ibid., pp. 19-20.
[4] 'The Reports and Accounts of Limited Companies', *Stock Exchange Official Record*, vol. 26 (May 1933), p. 151.
[5] 'Company Law and Secretarial Practice', *Australian Accountant*, vol. 3 (February 1937), p. 34.
[6] 'The Duties and Responsibilities of Auditors under the Queensland Companies Act, 1931', *Accountant in Australia*, vol. 2 (August 1932), p. 344.
[7] Institute of Chartered Accountants, op. cit.
[8] John Lloyd, 'Balance Sheets Under Companies Acts', *Australian Accountant*, vol. 18 (June 1948), p. 203.
[9] 'South Australian Companies Act', ibid., vol. 17 (May 1947), p. 184.

12 THE STOCK EXCHANGES

[1] A. H. Urquhart, 'The Stock Exchange in Focus'.
[2] G. E. Fitzgerald, 'Holding Companies', *Australian Accountant*, vol. 20 (December 1950), p. 462.
[3] 'Stock Exchange', *Australasian Insurance and Banking Record*, vol. 53 (August 1929), p. 681.
[4] 'Share Options', *Stock Exchange of Melbourne Official Record*, vol. 28 (December 1935), p. 606.
[5] 'Stock Exchange Conference', ibid., vol. 29 (March 1936), p. 109.
[6] 'Companies Interim Reports', ibid., vol. 32 (September 1939), p. 367.
[7] Stock Exchange of Melbourne, 'Official List Requirements' (September 1946), note 9.
[8] *Sydney Morning Herald*, 22 June 1962.   [9] *Age*, 19 June 1969.
[10] *Age*, 10 July 1969.

13 RESERVES AND PROVISIONS

[1] *Parl. Deb.* (Vic.), 1896, vol. 81, pp. 190-207.
[2] 'Principles of Accounting', *Australian Accountant*, vol. 5 (March 1938), p. 105.
[3] *Advanced Accounting*, 6th ed., p. 231.

4 *Book-Keeping and Accounts*, p. 54.
5 C. L. S. Hewitt, 'A Levy on Provisions for Depreciation', *Australian Accountant*, vol. 11 (November 1941), p. 541.
6 'Letters to the Editor', *Chartered Accountant in Australia*, vol. 17 (October 1946), p. 221.
7 'The Balance Sheet Audit and the Form and Content of Published Accounts', *Australian Accountant*, vol. 17 (April 1947), p. 132.
8 E. M. Jones et al., 'A Review of Published Accounts of 36 Selected Western Australian Companies', *Chartered Accountant in Australia*, vol. 28 (September 1957), p. 104.
9 *Statements on Accounting Principles and Recommendations on Accounting Practice*, 1965, p. 6, par. (7).
10 A. Sinclair, 'Reserves, Reserve Funds and Sinking Funds', *Commonwealth Journal of Accountancy*, vol. 3 (September 1923), p. 10.
11 Ibid. (March 1924), p. 164.
12 'The Criticism of Accounts', ibid. (April 1924), p. 184.
13 E. V. Nixon and A. A. Fitzgerald, *Some Problems of Modern Accountancy*, pp. 28-35.
14 Australasian Congress on Accounting, *Proceedings*, pp. 133-72.
15 Ibid., p. 144, Fitzgerald cites W. S. Krebs, *Outlines of Accounting* (New York, 1927), vol. 2, ch. 30.
16 *Australian Accountant*, vol. 4 (December 1937), p. 329.
17 Ibid., vol. 5 (March 1938), p. 109.
18 'Verification of Liabilities, Capital, and Reserves', *Chartered Accountant in Australia*, vol. 7 (November 1930), p. 343.
19 'Reserves and Provisions', *Australian Accountant*, vol. 14 (February 1944), p. 28.
20 'Prospective Improvements in Financial Statements of Companies', ibid., vol. 17 (November 1947), p. 457 and 'Accounting Doctrine and the 1947 English Companies Act', ibid., vol. 18 (September 1948), p. 305.
21 Ibid., vol. 17 (November 1947), p. 459.
22 'Form and Content of Company Financial Statements', ibid., vol. 18 (August 1948), p. 292.
23 'Some Comments on the New Recommendations on Accounting Principles', *Chartered Accountant in Australia*, vol. 34 (June 1964), p. 834.
24 R. R. Waddell et al., 'What Should we be Doing to Improve the Standard of Published Company Financial Reporting', ibid., vol. 29 (February 1959), p. 383.
25 'The Form and Content of Published Accounts of Public Companies', ibid., vol. 19 (May 1949), p. 764.
26 'Letter to the Editor', *Australian Accountant*, vol. 26 (December 1956), p. 520.
27 Jones, op. cit.
28 'An American View of Australian Financial Reports', *Chartered Accountant in Australia*, vol. 30 (January 1960), p. 347.

14 THE ROYAL MAIL CASE

1 Collin Brooks (ed.), *The Royal Mail Case*, p. xiii.   2 Ibid., p. 107.
3 Ibid., p. 39.   4 Ibid., p. 148.

15 VICTORIAN COMPANIES ACT 1938

1 'Accounting Doctrine and the 1947 English Companies Act', *Australian Accountant*, vol. 18 (September 1948), p. 298.
2 'Victorian Division, President's Address', *Commonwealth Journal of Accountancy*, vol. 10 (April 1931), p. 232.
3 'Presidential address', ibid., vol. 14 (May 1935), p. 248.

References (Chapters 15-17)   323

4 *Parl. Deb.* (Vic.), vol. 199, p. 219.
5 Ibid., p. 221 and vol. 204, p. 1000.   6 Ibid., vol. 204, p. 998.
7 'Companies Bill 1938 (Victoria)', *Accountant*, vol. 100 (May 1939), pp. 673-7.
8 'Victorian Companies Bill', *Australian Accountant*, vol. 2 (August 1936), p. 2.
9 'The Growing Significance of the Profit and Loss Account', ibid., vol. 3 (June 1937), p. 302.
10 *Parl. Deb.* (Vic.), 1938, vol. 205, p. 1938.
11 'Accounts and Audit under the Victorian Companies Act 1938', *Chartered Accountant in Australia*, vol. 10 (July 1939), pp. 30-47.
12 'Proprietary, Foreign, Holding and Investment Trust Companies under the Victorian Companies Act 1938', ibid., (August 1939), p. 117.
13 'Commonwealth Institute of Accountants', *Australian Accountant*, vol. 17 (July 1947), p. 280.
14 A. A. Fitzgerald, 'Company Law Amendment in the United Kingdom, Report of the Cohen Committee', ibid., vol. 15 (October 1945), p. 342.
15 Tait, op. cit., p. 132.

16 THE PROFIT AND LOSS STATEMENT

1 P. C. Spender & G. Wallace, *Company Law and Practice* (Sydney 1937), pp. 149, 730.
2 Board of Trade (England), Company Law Amendment Committee, *Report*, (1945), pars 5, 103.
3 'Company Law Amendment, Memorandum submitted by the Institute of Chartered Accountants in England and Wales', *Accountant*, vol. 110 (June 1944), p. 279.
4 'Current Developments in Corporate Accounting', *Australian Accountant*, vol. 18 (November 1948), p. 405.
5 'Democracy in the Corporation', ibid., vol. 33 (June 1963), p. 295.
6 'Items of an Abnormal Character', ibid., vol. 14 (March 1944), p. 82.
7 'Companies Bill 1938 (Victoria)', *Accountant*, vol. 100 (May 1939), pp. 673-7.
8 Fitzgerald, op. cit., p. 81.
9 John Lloyd, 'Balance Sheets Under Companies Act', *Australian Accountant*, vol. 18 (June 1948), p. 203.
10 'Current Developments in Corporate Accounting', ibid., (December 1948), p. 433.
11 E. M. Jones et al., 'A Review of Published Accounts of 36 Selected Western Australian Public Companies', *Chartered Accountant in Australia*, vol. 26 (September 1957), p. 112.
12 *V. & P.* (Vic.), 1954-5, vol. 1 (D1), p. 689.
13 'Amendments to Stock Exchange Listing Requirements', *Australian Accountant*, vol. 37 (November 1967), p. 649.

17 DIRECTORS' REMUNERATION

1 Board of Trade (England), Company Law Amendment Committee, *Report* (1926), par. 48.
2 G. C. Legertwood and C. L. Jessop, 'South Australia, The Companies Act 1934', *Chartered Accountant in Australia*, vol. 6 (May 1936), p. 627.
3 'Victorian Companies Act, Counsel's Opinion', ibid., vol. 10 (August 1939), p. 133.
4 The Victorian Companies Act 1938, pp. 109-10.
5 George J. Coles, *A Message from Mr. G. J. Coles*, p. 3.
6 Ibid., p. 5.   7 10 September 1935.
8 Coles, op. cit., p. 7.   9 1 September 1936.

References (Chapters 17-19)

10 *Age*, 28 September 1935.
11 'Company Law Amendment, Memorandum Submitted by the Institute of Chartered Accountants in England and Wales', *Accountant*, vol. 110 (May 1944), p. 253.
12 Board of Trade (England), Committee on Company Law Amendment, *Report*, (1945), pars 89, 90.
13 *V. & P.* (Vic.), 1954-5, vol. 1 (D2), p. 765.   14 Ibid., p. 813.
15 P. C. E. Cox, 'Company Law and Secretarial Section, Directors' Emoluments', *Chartered Accountant in Australia*, vol. 34 (August 1963), p. 125.
16 'A Series of Opinions on the Uniform Companies Acts', ibid., supplement to vol. 33 (November 1962).
17 'Significant Changes Proposed for Australian Company Law', *Australian Accountant*, vol. 38 (December 1968), p. 681.
18 M. C. Wells, 'Executive Stock Options—Again', ibid. (August 1968), pp. 461-6.

18 HOLDING COMPANIES

1 *Proceedings*, p. 48.
2 'The Audit of Parent and Subsidiary Companies', vol. 3 (January 1924), p. 111.
3 12 February 1964.   4 7 August 1934.
5 E. V. Nixon, 'Holding Companies', *Commonwealth Journal of Accountancy*, vol. 7 (August 1928), p. 364.
6 Ibid., p. 365.
7 *Holding Companies and their Published Accounts*, p. 58.
8 Board of Trade (England), Company Law Amendment Committee, *Report* (1926), par. 71.
9 'Holding and Subsidiary Companies', *Commonwealth Journal of Accountancy*, vol. 13 (December 1933), p. 94.
10 J. S. McInnes, 'Company Law and Secretarial Practice Section', *Australian Accountant*, vol. 3 (February 1937), p. 38.
11 'Questions at Dunlop Perdriau Meeting', *Argus*, 12 September 1936.
12 G. E. Fitzgerald, 'The Accounts of Holding Companies', vol. 5 (March 1938), pp. 137-59.
13 D. M. Ferguson, 'The Published Accounts of Holding Companies', vol. 1 (March, April 1931), pp. 152, 200-7.
14 'The Published Accounts of Holding Companies', vol. 18 (January 1948), pp. 483-6.
15 'Companies Bill 1938 (Victoria)', *Accountant*, vol. 100 (May 1939), p. 675.
16 'Australian Company Legislation', vol. 2 (September 1936), p. 99.
17 W. K. Fullagar, 'Counsel's Opinion', vol. 10 (August 1939), pp. 133-8 and Blake and Riggall and Hedderwick Fookes and Alston, 'Victorian Companies Act 1938, Holding and Subsidiary Companies', vol. 9 (June 1939), pp. 797-8.
18 Ewart, op. cit., p. 479.

19 VERIFICATION OF STOCK

1 65 L.J. Ch. 673 (1896).
2 'Duties of Auditors in Connection with Stock-in-Trade', vol. 5 (October 1925), p. 28.
3 'Valuation and Verification of Stock-in-Trade', vol. 14 (October 1935), pp. 409-11.
4 Charles Keats, *Magnificent Masquerade*.

References (Chapters 19-21)

⁵ T. C. Boehme, 'The McKesson and Robbins Case', *Chartered Accountant in Australia*, vol. 11 (July 1940), pp. 38-44; M. E. Peloubet, ibid., vol. 11 (February 1941), pp. 383-8, and L. W. Ferres, 'The McKesson Robbins Frauds', ibid., vol. 12 (May, June 1942), pp. 476-87, 521-32, and vol. 13 (July, August 1942), pp. 13-26, 48-59.
⁶ 'Stock in Trade', ibid., vol. 16 (November 1945), p. 199.
⁷ 'Auditing Procedures', ibid., vol. 21 (December 1950), p. 357.
⁸ L. O. H. Upjohn, 'Letters to the Editor', ibid., vol. 21 (February 1951), p. 470.
⁹ Australian Chartered Accountants Research and Service Foundation, *Bulletin no. 2*, p. 7.
¹⁰ Ibid., p. 22.
¹¹ *Auditing*, 2nd ed., pp. 125-33 and 3rd ed., pp. 161-80.

20 FORMAT OF STATEMENTS

¹ 'Why Do the Assets Appear on the Credit Side of the Balance Sheet', *Commonwealth Journal of Accountancy*, vol. 6 (July 1927), p. 351.
² R. K. Yorston, *Chartered Accountant in Australia*, vol. 17 (April 1947), p. 612.
³ 'The Form of the Balance-Sheet', vol. 4 (December 1933), p. 223.
⁴ 'Balance Sheet Problems III, The Form of the Balance Sheet', *Australian Accountant*, vol. 6 (September 1938), p. 165.
⁵ 'Balance Sheet Form', ibid., vol. 1 (June 1936), p. 401.
⁶ Chas. W. Lister, 'The Balance Sheet', *Accountant*, vol. 118 (March 1948), p. 206.
⁷ Fitzgerald, op. cit., p. 163.
⁸ *Australian Accountant*, vol. 12 (January 1942), p. 47.
⁹ 'Balance Sheets, Ancient and Modern', ibid., vol. 9 (March 1940), p. 136.
¹⁰ 'Clarity in Published Profit and Loss Statements', ibid., vol. 12 (September 1942), p. 451.
¹¹ 'Life Assurance Company Adopts Vertical Form', ibid., vol. 18 (July 1948), pp. 227-9.
¹² 'Current Developments in Corporate Accounting', ibid. (December 1948), p. 432.
¹³ 'Trends in Corporate Reporting', ibid., vol. 26 (December 1956), pp. 494-5.
¹⁴ E. M. Jones et al., 'A Review of Published Accounts of 36 Selected Western Australian Public Companies', *Chartered Accountant in Australia*, vol. 28 (September 1957), p. 102.
¹⁵ Op. cit., p. 495.
¹⁶ 'The Form of Balance Sheets', *Australian Accountant*, vol. 34 (September 1964), p. 488.

21 CLASSIFICATION IN THE BALANCE SHEET

¹ 'The Reports and Accounts of Limited Companies', *Stock Exchange Official Record*, vol. 26 (May 1933), pp. 151-2, and E. V. Nixon and A. A. Fitzgerald, *Some Problems of Modern Accountancy*, p. 19.
² 'The Criticism of Accounts', *Commonwealth Journal of Accountancy*, vol. 3 (April 1924), p. 183.
³ 'Fixed and Floating Assets', *Chartered Accountant in Australia*, vol. 16 (April 1946), p. 417.
⁴ 'The Form and Content of the Balance Sheet . . .', ibid., vol. 7 (December 1936), p. 427.
⁵ Ibid., pp. 431, 437.
⁶ 'Working Capital', *Australian Accountant*, vol. 5 (April 1938), p. 236.

326 References (Chapters 21-23)

7 Board of Trade (England), Committee on Company Law Amendment, *Report* (1945), par. 99, p. 58.
8 'Company Law Amendment in the United Kingdom . . .', *Australian Accountant*, vol. 15 (November 1945), p. 378.
9 'Annual Meeting of Members, South Australia', *Chartered Accountant in Australia*, vol. 19 (September 1948), p. 211.
10 M. S. Esau et al., 'The Form and Content of Published Accounts of Public Companies', ibid., (May 1949), p. 765.
11 'Stock-in-Trade', ibid., vol. 16 (November 1945), p. 200.
12 'Better Financial Statements, The Accountant Must Help', *Australian Accountant*, vol. 24 (March 1954), p. 112.
13 'Classification of Assets', *Accounting Research*, vol. 1 (July 1950), p. 371.

22 WESTERN AUSTRALIA

1 'Commonwealth Institute of Accountants, Annual Meetings of Divisions, Western Australian Division', *Commonwealth Journal of Accountancy*, vol. 14 (April 1935), p. 229.
2 'Company Legislation in Western Australia', *Australian Accountant*, vol. 1 (May 1936), pp. 257-61.
3 Ibid., where the Minister's letter is printed in full.
4 *Parl. Deb.* (W.A.), vol. 106, new series, p. 2213.
5 T. Macfarlane, 'W.A. Companies Act', *Chartered Accountant in Australia*, vol. 19 (September 1948), p. 173.

23 I.C.A.A. RECOMMENDATIONS

1 'General Council Meetings', *Chartered Accountant in Australia*, vol. 33 (June 1963), p. 788.
2 'Prospective Improvement in Financial Statements of Companies', *Australian Accountant*, vol. 17 (November 1947), p. 456.
3 'The Accounts of Holding Companies', ibid., vol. 15 (January 1945), p. 24.
4 'Accounting Doctrine and the 1947 English Companies Act', ibid., vol. 18 (September 1948), p. 303.
5 'The Form and Content of Published Accounts of Public Companies', *Chartered Accountant in Australia*, vol. 19 (May 1949), pp. 755-67.
6 'A Review of Published Accounts of 36 Selected Western Australian Public Companies', ibid., vol. 28 (September 1957), pp. 101-16.
7 F. E. Trigg, 'Shillings and Pence in Published Accounts', ibid., vol. 10 (June 1940), p. 818.
8 'Trends in Corporate Reporting', *Australian Accountant*, vol. 26 (December 1956), p. 497.
9 'Better Financial Statements, The Accountant Must Help', ibid., vol. 24 (March 1954), p. 112.
10 Op. cit., p. 103.
11 'Current Developments in Corporate Accounting', *Australian Accountant*, vol. 18 (December 1948), p. 433.
12 Op. cit., p. 496.   13 Op. cit.
14 Op. cit.
15 V. L. Gole, 'Trends in Published Accounts', *Australian Accountant*, vol. 25 (December 1955), p. 511.
16 'Auditor's Comments', *Commonwealth Journal of Accountancy*, vol. 8 (May 1929), p. 280.
17 Op. cit., p. 432.   18 Op. cit., p. 498.
19 Op. cit.   20 Op. cit., p. 103.
21 A. Donnelly, 'The Right Place for Comparative Figures', *Australian Accountant*, vol. 27 (January 1957), p. 51.

References (Chapters 23-26)

22 Board of Trade (England), Company Law Committee, *Report* (1962), p. 155.

24 THE VALUATION OF STOCK

1 J. S. McInnes, 'Balance Sheet Requirements of the N.S.W. Act', *Australian Accountant*, vol. 3 (February 1937), p. 38.
2 'The Spice of Accounting', ibid., vol. 19 (November 1949), p. 401.
3 'A Further Note on the Valuation of Trading Stocks', ibid., vol. 14 (December 1944), pp. 424-6.
4 'A Genealogy for "Cost or Market"', *Accounting Review*, vol. 16 (June 1941), p. 167.
5 'Valuation and Verification of Stock in Trade', *Commonwealth Journal of Accountancy*, vol. 14 (October 1935), p. 409.
6 Op. cit., p. 424. 7 Op. cit.
8 Op. cit., p. 162.
9 'Problems of Accounting Valuation of Stock in Trade', *Australian Accountant*, vol. 16 (July 1946), p. 263.
10 'Stock-in-Trade', *Chartered Accountant in Australia*, vol. 16 (November 1945), p. 199.
11 'Stock on hand in the Balance Sheets of Victorian Companies', *Australian Accountant*, vol. 21 (July 1951), p. 265.
12 'Prospective Improvements in Financial Statements of Companies', ibid., vol. 17 (November 1947), p. 460.

25 DEPRECIATION

1 *Concepts of Depreciation* and *Depreciation of Fixed Assets in Accountancy and Economics*.
2 'Should We Calculate Depreciation Accurately?', *Australian Accountant*, vol. 4 (October 1937), p. 242.
3 *V. & P.* (L.A. Vic.), 1910, 1(D3), p. 967, par. 119.
4 Ibid., p. 991, par. 477.
5 'Depreciation in Published Company Reports', *Accounting Research*, vol. 6 (1955), p. 163.
6 J. S. McInnes, 'Company Law and Secretarial Practice Section', *Australian Accountant*, vol. 3 (February 1937), p. 36.
7 Op. cit., p. 155.
8 V. L. Gole, 'Trends in Published Accounts', *Australian Accountant*, vol. 25 (December 1955), p. 511.
9 'Current Developments in Corporate Reporting', ibid., vol. 18 (December 1948), p. 432.
10 E. DeMaris and V. Zimmerman, 'An American View of Australian Financial Reports', *Chartered Accountant in Australia*, vol. 30 (January 1960), p. 346.
11 *Recommendations on Accounting Principles*, p. 55, par. (5).
12 C.S.R. advised its shareholders in 1963 that henceforth instead of providing for depreciation, the company would provide for replacement of assets.

26 A.I.M. AWARD AND REPORT PRODUCTION

1 *Management News* (June 1963), p. 15.
2 Australian Institute of Management [A.I.M.], Sydney Division, 'Panel of Adjudicators Annual Report Award', *1965 Report*, inside back cover.
3 'Trends in Corporate Reporting', *Australian Accountant*, vol. 26 (December 1956), p. 499.
4 A.I.M., *1964 Report*, p. 1.   5 A.I.M., *1961 Report*, p. 4.
6 A.I.M., *1964 Report*, p. 6.

7 E. S. Wolfenden, 'Criticism of a Company's Balance Sheet', vol. 7 (January 1928), p. 138.
8 'The Form and Content of the Balance Sheet, Profit and Loss Account and Auditor's Report', *Chartered Accountant in Australia,* vol. 7 (December 1936), p. 425.

27 OPERATING ACCOUNT DETAILS

1 'Financial Statement Presentation, What the Investing Public Needs (no. 1)', *Australian Accountant,* vol. 34 (November 1964), p. 626.
2 E. DeMaris and V. Zimmerman, 'An American View of Australian Financial Reports', *Chartered Accountant in Australia,* vol. 30 (January 1960), p. 345.
3 'Current Developments in Corporate Accounting', *Australian Accountant,* vol. 18 (December 1948), p. 428.
4 Board of Trade (England), Company Law Committee, *Report* (1962), pars 393-4.
5 'Significant Changes Proposed for Australian Company Law', *Australian Accountant,* vol. 38 (December 1968), p. 681, and *Australian Financial Review,* 10 March 1969.
6 'General Council Meetings', *Chartered Accountant in Australia,* vol. 30 (January 1960), p. 378.
7 'Pronouncement by General Council of the Institute on the Treatment of "Income Yet to Mature", in the Accounts of Finance and Other Companies', ibid., p. 380.
8 *Bulletin,* 2 September 1961.
9 'A Trap for Older Players, Too', *Sydney Morning Herald,* 6 July 1962.
10 'Pronouncement by the General Council of the Institute on the Principle and Methods of Apportioning "Income Yet to Mature"', *Chartered Accountant in Australia,* vol. 31 (June 1961), p. 615.
11 'Some Problems for Financiers', ibid., vol. 32 (October 1961), p. 218.
12 'Further Notes on Financiers', ibid. (January 1962), p. 401.
13 'General Council Meetings', ibid. (June 1962), p. 720.
14 'The Concept of Unearned Income', ibid., vol. 33 (October 1962), p. 229.
15 'Institute News', ibid. (January 1963), p. 459.
16 'Deferred Income in H.P. Contracts', ibid. (April 1963), p. 604.

28 TAXATION

1 'Criticism of a Company's Balance Sheet', *Commonwealth Journal of Accountancy,* vol. 7 (January 1928), p. 140.
2 Board of Trade (England), Committee on Company Law Amendment, *Report* (1945), p. 61.
3 V. L. Gole, 'Trends in Published Accounts', *Australian Accountant,* vol. 25 (December 1955), p. 511.
4 Committee appointed by the Western Australian Division of the Australian Society of Accountants, 'The Accounting and Taxation Concepts of Business Income', *A.S.A. Bulletin no. 9* (August 1962); Australian Society of Accountants, *Accounting Principles and Practices Discussed in Reports on Company Failures;* W. J. Kenley, 'Accounting Problems and Company Failures', *Australian Accountant,* vol. 35 (December 1965), p. 638.
5 J. A. L. Gunn, 'Special Initial Depreciation Allowance in respect of plant bought during five years ended June 30, 1950', *Australian Accountant,* vol. 16 (May 1946), p. 173 and 'Withdrawal of Initial Depreciation Allowance', ibid., vol. 22 (March 1952), p. 144.
6 'Inflation and Company Accounts', ibid., vol. 26 (February 1956), p. 65.
7 D. C. Wilkins, 'Investment Allowance for Manufacturing Plant', ibid., vol. 32 (March, July 1962), pp. 176, 362.

References (Chapters 28-30)

[8] J. D. Balmford, H. C. Clegg and J. A. Macdonald, 'Accounting for Investment Allowances', ibid., vol. 34 (September 1964), p. 531.
[9] 'Amendments to Stock Exchange Listing Requirements', ibid., vol. 37 (November 1967), p. 649.
[10] R. A. McInnes, *Reporting the Incidence of Company Income Tax, Society Bulletin no. 6* (February 1969), p. 23.
[11] R. J. Chambers, 'Tax Allocation and Financial Reporting', *Abacus*, vol. 4 (December 1968), pp. 99-123; Accounting Principles Board, American Institute of Certified Public Accountants, 'Accounting for the Investment Credit', *Journal of Accountancy*, vol. 115 (February 1963), pp. 70-2; H. Black, *Interperiod Allocation of Corporate Income Taxes*, A.I.C.P.A. Accounting Research Study no. 9 (New York 1966); and A. R. Wyatt, 'Case for Income Tax Allocation', *Financial Executive*, vol. 35 (September 1967), pp. 62-9.
[12] Op. cit., p. 25.
[13] Price Waterhouse & Co., 'Is Generally Accepted Accounting for Income Taxes Possibly Misleading Investors?', *Financial Executive*, vol. 35 (September 1967), pp. 70-4.
[14] S. Davidson, 'Accelerated Depreciation and the Allocation of Income Taxes', *Accounting Review*, vol. 33 (April 1958), pp. 173-80.
[15] Arthur Andersen & Co., *Accounting and Reporting Problems of the Accounting Profession* (2nd ed., Chicago 1962), p. 55.

29 GROUP ACCOUNTS

[1] 'Consolidated Statements', *Chartered Accountant in Australia*, vol. 17 (1947), pp. 510-14, 574-82, 643-7, 701-8 and vol. 18 (1947), pp. 22-9, 87-96, 147-56.
[2] 'The Accounts of Holding Companies', *Australian Accountant*, vol. 14 (1944), pp. 179-82 and vol. 15 (1945), pp. 20-4, 43-7, 138-43; 'The Consolidated Statement of Assets and Liabilities', ibid., pp. 20-5, 198-202, 245-9.
[3] *Holding Companies in Australia and New Zealand*.
[4] 'Examples of Holding Companies' Accounts', *Australian Accountant*, vol. 7 (June 1939), p. 306.
[5] *Holding Companies and their Published Accounts*, p. 63.
[6] V. & P. (L.A. Vic.), 1954-5, 1(D2), p. 764.
[7] Ibid., p. 747, par. 21(d).   [8] Ibid., p. 764.
[9] Ibid., p. 773.
[10] 'Amendments to Stock Exchange Listing Requirements', *Australian Accountant*, vol. 37 (November 1967), p. 649.
[11] *Age*, 22 July 1965.
[12] *Notes on the Preparation of Consolidated Statements, Society Bulletin no. 2* (March 1968), pp. 7-8.
[13] *Parl. Deb.* (Qld), 1963-4, vol. 237, p. 2074.

30 SUBSIDIARIES AND DIVISIONS

[1] Board of Trade (England), Company Law Amendment Committee, *Report* (1926), par. 87.
[2] Ibid. (1945), par. 53.   [3] Ibid. (1962), par. 63.
[4] *Age*, 23 December 1959.   [5] Ibid.
[6] Ibid. and *Herald*, 24 December 1959.
[7] *Parl. Deb.* (Vic.), vol. 258-60, part 4, p. 2804.
[8] Ibid. (Cwlth), vol. H. of R. 32, p. 1042.
[9] 'Financial Statement Presentation, What the Investing Public Needs, (no. 2)', *Australian Accountant*, vol. 34 (December 1964), p. 667.

31 VALUE IN THE BALANCE SHEET

1. John Thackray, 'Accounting for Inflation', *Dun's Review and Modern Industry*, vol. 84 (December 1964), p. 63.
2. 'Inflation and Company Accounts', *Australian Accountant*, vol. 26 (February 1956), p. 65.
3. D. M. Ferguson, 'Revaluation of Fixed Assets', *Chartered Accountant in Australia*, vol. 21 (June 1951), p. 697.
4. Op. cit., p. 61.   5. *V. & P.* (L.A. Vic.), 1964-5, 1(C1).
6. Board of Trade (England), Company Law Committee, *Report* (1962), par. 367.
7. *Statements on Accounting Principles and Recommendations on Accounting Practice* (1965), p. 9.
8. *Accounting for Leases*, A.S.A. Bulletin no. 13 (November 1965).

32 VICTORIA AND TASMANIA 1958

1. *Parl. Deb.* (Vic.), vol. 255-7, part 1, p. 333.
2. Board of Trade (England), Committee on Company Law Amendment, *Report* (1945), par. 99, p. 58.
3. See G. L. Allard, 'Victorian Companies Act 1958, Contents of Accounts, Comparison of Statutory Requirements', *Chartered Accountant in Australia*, vol. 29 (May 1959), p. 534.
4. P. M. Wood, 'Companies Act 1938—Filing of Private Balance Sheet', *Australian Accountant*, vol. 13 (September 1943), p. 339.
5. 'Private Balance Sheets', ibid., vol. 23 (November 1953), p. 463.
6. 'How do you Like the New Act', ibid., vol. 7 (March 1939), p. 106.
7. *V. & P.* (L.A. Vic.), 1954-5, 1(D1), p. 681.
8. *Parl. Deb.* (Vic.), vol. 255-7, part 1, p. 323.
9. Companies Act Amendment Act of 1954, Act no. 25 of 1954, s.2.
10. *V. & P.* (L.A. Vic.), 1954-5, 1(D1 and D2).
11. Victoria, *Statutes*, Act no. 5935, Companies Act, 1955, s.10 and Act no. 6047, Companies (Unit Trusts) Act, 1956, s.2.
12. Victoria, *Statutes*, Act no. 6455, Companies Act, 1958, s.63(8)(b).
13. *V. & P.* (L.A. Vic.), 1959-60, 1(D15), pp. 995-1001 and 1960-1, 1(C1), pp. 723-62.
14. *Parl. Deb.* (Vic.), vol. 255-7, part 1, p. 319-24.

33 THE UNIFORM ACTS

1. 'New South Wales Division Annual Report', *Commonwealth Journal of Accountancy*, vol. 6 (April 1927), p. 232.
2. *Parl. Deb.* (S.A.), 1931, vol. 1, p. 1556.
3. 'Commonwealth Institute of Accountants, Annual Meeting', *Commonwealth Journal of Accountancy*, vol. 5 (July 1926), p. 244, and 'New South Wales Division Annual Report', ibid., vol. 6 (April 1927), p. 230.
4. 'Stock Exchanges', *Australasian Insurance and Banking Record*, vol. 53 (August 1929), p. 681.
5. *Parl. Deb.* (N.S.W.), 1960, third series vol. 34, p. 1860.
6. 'General Council Meeting', *Australian Accountant*, vol. 19 (July 1949), p. 278.
7. 'General Council Meetings', *Chartered Accountant in Australia*, vol. 27 (June 1957), p. 727.
8. Ibid., vol. 30 (July 1959), p. 50.
9. *V. & P.* (L.A. Vic.), 1954-5, 1(D2), p. 755.
10. *Parl. Deb.* (Vic.), 1961-2, vols. 264-6, part 1, p. 603.
11. Ibid., p. 1001.   12. Ibid., p. 604.
13. 'General Council Meetings', *Chartered Accountant in Australia*, vol. 31 (January 1961), p. 359.

14 *Parl. Deb.* (Qld), vol. 228, p. 2148.   15 Ibid., p. 2149.
16 Ibid., vol. 229, p. 2256.   17 Ibid., vol. 230, p. 232.
18 'Institute News, New South Wales', *Chartered Accountant in Australia,* vol. 27 (April 1957), p. 611.
19 'Annual Meeting of Members', ibid., vol. 19 (September 1948), p. 207.
20 M. S. Esau *et al.,* 'The Form and Content of Published Accounts of Public Companies', ibid. (May 1949), p. 755.
21 Ibid., vol. 20 (October 1949), p. 257.
22 'Companies Bill for New Guinea', ibid., vol. 34 (September 1963), p. 178.

34 PUBLIC BORROWINGS ACTS

1 C. J. Thomas, 'The Borrowing Powers of Companies', *Commonwealth Journal of Accountancy,* vol. 12 (February 1933), p. 163.
2 A. A. Fitzgerald, 'Trends in Company Financing', in Investment in Australia Symposium, *Proceedings.*
3 *V. & P.* (L.A. Vic.), 1958-9, 1(D2), p. 803.
4 For a review of these events see R. J. Chambers, 'Company Losses—Safeguarding the Investor', *Current Affairs Bulletin,* vol. 34 (12 October 1964), and Australian Society of Accountants, *Accounting Principles and Practices Discussed in Reports on Company Failures.* The important reports by inspectors are *V. & P.* (L.A. Vic.), 1963-4, 1(C1, C2 and C3), 1964-5, 1(C1 and C2), 1965-6, 1(C2).
5 E. St John and P. Grogan, 'The Companies (Public Borrowings) Act 1963, of Victoria', *Chartered Accountant in Australia,* vol. 34 (February 1964), p. 516.
6 'Company Law and Secretarial Section, Companies (Public Borrowings) Bill of Victoria', ibid. (December 1963), p. 389.
7 Op. cit., p. 525.

35 INTERIM REPORTS

1 'Monthly Review of Current Events', *Australian Accountant,* vol. 26 (July 1956), p. 270.
2 'Amendments to Official Listing Requirements', *Stock Exchange of Melbourne Official Record,* vol. 51 (February 1958), p. 88.
3 Australian Associated Stock Exchanges, *Official List Requirements* (1964), p. 26.
4 Second Century Corporation Ltd and Automotive Components Ltd, discussed in *Age,* 17 September 1964.
5 *Parl. Deb.* (Qld), 1963-4, vol. 237, p. 2073.
6 Act no. 7281, Companies (Amendment) Act, 1965, s.4(1)(b).
7 G. L. Allard, 'The Impact of the Companies (Public Borrowings) Act 1963, on the Accountant and Auditor'.
8 Act no. 7281, Companies (Amendment) Act, 1965, s.4(1)(c).
9 'Amendments to Stock Exchange Listing Requirements', *Australian Accountant,* vol. 37 (November 1967), p. 649.
10 S. C. G. Macindoe, 'A Critical Look at Stockbroking and Underwriting' in Investment in Australia Symposium, *Proceedings.*

36 ADDITIONAL INFORMATION

1 'Where are the Profits', *Australian Accountant,* vol. 2 (December 1936), p. 453.
2 C. A. Martin, 'The Funds Statement—A Management Report', *A.I.C.A. Bulletin,* no. 2 (April 1967), pp. 7-12.
3 V. L. Gole, 'Trends in Published Accounts', *Australian Accountant,* vol. 25 (December 1955), p. 512.

[4] E. M. Jones et al., 'A Review of Published Accounts of 36 Selected Western Australian Public Companies', *Chartered Accountant in Australia*, vol. 28 (September 1957), p. 112.
[5] 'Trends in Corporate Reporting', *Australian Accountant*, vol. 26 (December 1956), p. 501.
[6] Ibid., p. 500.
[7] L. Goldberg and R. C. Clift, 'An Investigation into Shareholder Attitudes', ibid., vol. 38 (June 1968), p. 304.
[8] 'Significant Changes Proposed for Australian Company Law', ibid. (December 1968), p. 681.

37 CONCLUSION

[1] Cf. comments on segment reporting by R. K. Mautz, *Financial Reporting by Diversified Companies*, p. 66.

BIBLIOGRAPHY

OFFICIAL DOCUMENTS
Statutes

ENGLAND

An Act for the Registration, and Regulation of Joint Stock Companies, 1844, 7 & 8 Vic. c.110.
Companies Act 1862, 25 & 26 Vic. c.89.
Companies Act, 1900, 63 & 64 Vic. c.48.
Companies Act, 1907, 7 Ed. VII c.50.
Companies Act, 1928, 18 & 19 Geo. V c.45.
Companies Act, 1929, 19 & 20 Geo. V c.23.
Companies Act, 1947, 10 & 11 Geo. VI c.47.
Companies Act, 1948, 11 & 12 Geo. VI c.38.
Companies Act, 1967, 15 & 16 Eliz. II c.81.

NEW SOUTH WALES

Companies Act 1874, Act no. 19, 1874.
Companies Act 1906, Act no. 22, 1906.
Companies Act 1936, Act no. 33, 1936.
Companies Act 1961, Act no. 71, 1961.
Companies (Amendment) Act 1960, Act no. 31, 1960.
Companies (Amendment) Act 1964, Act no. 20, 1964.

QUEENSLAND

Companies Act 1863, Act no. 4, 1863.
Companies Act 1931, Act no. 53, 1931.
Companies Act 1961, Act no. 55, 1961.
Companies Act Amendment Act 1889, Act no. 18, 1889.
Companies Act Amendment Act of 1953, Act no. 15, 1953.
Companies Act Amendment Act of 1954, Act no. 25, 1954.
Companies Act Amendment Act of 1960, Act no. 24, 1960.
Companies Act Amendment Act of 1964, Act no. 10, 1964.

Bibliography

SOUTH AUSTRALIA

An Act to provide for the Registration of Joint Stock Companies, and for Limiting the Liability of Members thereof, Act no. 25, 1855.
Companies Act 1864, Act no. 13, 1864.
Companies Act 1892, Act no. 557.
Companies Act 1934, Act no. 2196.
Companies Act 1962, Act no. 56, 1962.
Companies Act Amendment Act 1886, Act no. 375.
Companies Act Amendment Act 1960, Act no. 31, 1960.
Companies Act Amendment Act 1964, Act no. 52, 1964.

TASMANIA

Companies Act, 1920, Act no. 66, 1920.
Companies Act, 1956, Act no. 29, 1956.
Companies Act, 1959, Act no. 29, 1959.
Companies Act, 1962, Act no. 66, 1962.
Companies Act, 1966, Act no. 28, 1966.
Joint Stock Companies Act 1859, Act no. 12, 1859.

VICTORIA

Companies Statute, 1864, Act no. 190.
Companies Act, 1896, Act no. 1482.
Companies Act, 1910, Act no. 2293.
Companies Act, 1938, Act no. 4602.
Companies Act, 1955, Act no. 5935.
Companies Act, 1958, Act no. 6455.
Companies Act 1961, Act no. 6839.
Companies (Amendment) Act, 1965, Act no. 7281.
Companies (Public Borrowings) Act, 1963, Act no. 7089.
Companies (Unit Trusts) Act, 1956, Act no. 6047.
Investment Companies Act 1938, Act no. 4621.

WESTERN AUSTRALIA

Companies Act 1893, Act no. 8, 1893.
Companies Act 1943, Act no. 36, 1943.
Companies Act 1961, Act no. 82, 1961.
Companies Act Amendment Act 1899, Act no. 54, 1899.
Companies Act Amendment Act (No. 2), 1960, Act no. 78, 1960.
Companies Act Amendment Act 1964, Act no. 69, 1964.
Joint Stock Companies Ordinance 1858, Act no. 6, 1858.

Reports

ENGLAND

Report of the Company Law Amendment Committee [Loreburn Committee, Chairman, Sir Robert Reed, later Lord Loreburn], Cd. 3052, House of Commons, Sessional Papers, 1906, vol. 97.

Bibliography 335

Report of the Company Law Amendment Committee [Wrenbury Committee], Cd. 9138, House of Commons, Sessional Papers, 1918, vol. 7.
Report of the Company Law Amendment Committee [Greene Committee], Cd. 2657, House of Commons, Sessional Papers, 1926, vol. 9.
Report of the Committee on Company Law Amendment [Cohen Committee], Cmd. 6659, House of Commons, Sessional Papers, 1945, vol. 4.
Report of the Company Law Committee [Jenkins Committee], Cmnd. 1749, House of Commons, Sessional Papers, 1962, vol. 12.

NEW SOUTH WALES

Report of the Royal Commission on Matters Concerning the Promotion and Operation of Certain Companies in New South Wales, P.P. (N.S.W.), (1934-5), vol. 3.

VICTORIA

Report of the Select Committee of the Legislative Council on the Companies Act 1890 Further Amendment Bill, V. & P. (L.C. Vic.), 1896.
Report of the Select Committee upon the Consolidation and Amendment of the Trading Companies Law, V. & P. (L.A. Vic.), 1910, vol. 1, D3, pp. 949-1006.
Report from the Joint Statute Law Revision Committee, V. & P. (L.A. Vic.), 1928, vol. 1, D3, pp. 653-707.
Progress Report from the Statute Law Revision Committee on Amendments of the Statute Law to Deal with Fraudulent Practices by Persons Interested in the Promotion and/or Direction of Companies and by Firms, V. & P. (L.A. Vic.), 1954-5, vol. 1, D1, pp. 657-734.
Report from the Statute Law Revision Committee on Amendments of the Statute Law to Deal with Fraudulent Practices by Persons Interested in the Promotion and/or Direction of Companies and by Firms, V. & P. (L.A. Vic.), 1954-5, vol. 1, D2, pp. 735-886.
Report from the Statute Law Revision Committee on the Law Relating to Invitations to the Public to Deposit Money with Companies, V. & P. (L.A. Vic.), 1958-9, vol. 1, D2, pp. 799-805.
Report from the Statute Law Revision Committee on Investments Offered by Vending Machine Companies, V. & P. (L.A. Vic.), 1959-60, vol. 1, D15, pp. 995-1004.
Report of the Inspector Appointed pursuant to the provisions of the Companies Act 1958 to investigate the Affairs of North American Vending Machine Co. Pty. Ltd. Vend-Rite Corporation Pty. Ltd. First Acceptance Corporation Ltd. General Vending Corporation Pty. Ltd. General Air-Conditioning and Refrigeration Co. Pty. Ltd. Halesmere United Corporation Pty. Ltd. Kempmore Industries Ltd. [by J. McI. Young], V. & P. (L.A. Vic.), 1960-1, vol. 1, C1, pp. 723-62.

Report of the Inspector Appointed pursuant to the Provisions of the Companies Act 1961 to investigate the Affairs of Testro Bros. Consolidated Ltd. Testro Print Proprietary Ltd. Testro Bros. Pty. Ltd. Suncoast Development Pty. Ltd. Surfers Paradise Land Development Corporation Pty. Ltd. [by J. B. Tait], V. & P. (L.A. Vic.), 1963-4, vol. 1, C2, pp. 779-806.

Interim Report of an Investigation under Division 4 of Part VI of the Companies Act 1961 into the Affairs of Reid Murray Holdings Limited and Certain of its Subsidiary Companies including Reid Murray Acceptance Limited [by B. L. Murray and B. J. Shaw], V. & P. (L.A. Vic.), 1963-4, vol. 1, C3, pp. 807-926.

Interim Report of an Investigation under Division 4 of Part VI of the Companies Act 1961 into the Affairs of Stanhill Development Finance Limited and Other Companies [by Peter Murphy], V. & P. (L.A. Vic.), 1964-5, C1, pp. 813-914.

Interim Report of an Investigation under Division 4 of Part VI of the Companies Act 1961 into the Affairs of Reid Murray Holdings Limited and certain other Companies and Final Report of an Investigation under Division 4 of Part VI of the Companies Act 1961 into the Affairs of Payne's Properties Pty. Ltd. and certain Subsidiary and Associated Companies [by B. L. Murray and B. J. Shaw], V. & P. (L.A. Vic.), 1964-5, vol. 1, C2, pp. 915-1092.

BOOKS

Australasian Congress on Accounting, *Proceedings*. Melbourne, 1936.

Australian Society of Accountants, *Proceedings of [Sydney] Convention*. Melbourne, 1958.

Brooks, Collin (ed.), *The Royal Mail Case*. London, 1933.

Burgess, E. H., 'The Audit of Group Accounts', in Chartered Accountants' Third Australian Congress, *Proceedings*, pp. 46-65.

Cannon, Michael, *The Land Boomers*. Melbourne, 1966.

Chambers, R. J., *The Function and Design of Company Annual Reports*. Sydney, 1955.

Chartered Accountants' Third Australian Congress, *Proceedings*. Adelaide, 1965.

Commonwealth Institute of Accountants, *The Victorian Companies Act 1938*. Melbourne, 1939.

Dicksee, Lawrence R., *Advanced Accounting*. 6th ed., London, 1921.

Fitzgerald, A. A., *Analysis and Interpretation of Financial and Operating Statements*. Sydney, 1947.

———, 'Accounting Terminology', in Australasian Congress on Accounting, *Proceedings*.

Fitzgerald, A. A. and Fitzgerald, G. E., *Form and Contents of Published Financial Statements*. Sydney, 1948.

Bibliography

Fitzgerald, G. E. and Speck, A. E., *Holding Companies in Australia and New Zealand*. Sydney, 1946.
Garnsey, G., *Holding Companies and their Published Accounts*. London, 1923.
Gibson, R. W., *An Introduction to the Theory of Financial Statements*. Melbourne, 1966.
Gilbert, Lewis D. and Gilbert, John J., *Annual Report of Stockholder Activities at Corporation Meetings*. New York, c. 1940-.
Gilman, S., *Accounting Concepts of Profit*. New York, 1939.
Goldberg, L., *Concepts of Depreciation*. Melbourne, 1960.
Gordon, Max, *Sir Isaac Isaacs, A life of service*. Melbourne, 1963.
Gower, L. C. B., *Modern Company Law*. 2nd ed., London, 1957.
Hall, A. R., 'The Annual Report and Accounts as a Source of Information to Economists', in Australian Society of Accountants, *Proceedings of [Sydney] Convention*, pp. 173-80.
Irish, R. A., *Auditing*. Sydney, 1957.
Kane, R. L. (ed.), *C.P.A. Handbook*. New York, 1953.
Keats, Charles, *Magnificent Masquerade: The strange case of Dr. Coster and Mr. Musica*. New York, 1964.
McDonald, Forrest, *Insull*. Chicago, 1962.
Mautz, R. K., *Financial Reporting by Diversified Companies*. New York, 1968.
Moonitz, M., *The Basic Postulates of Accounting, A.I.C.P.A. Accounting Research Study no. 1*. New York, 1961.
Nelson, C. Hewetson, 'The Accountant's Duties to the Press and the Public in Relation to the Certification of Balance Sheets', in International Congress on Accounting, *Proceedings*. New York, 1929.
Nixon, E. V. and Fitzgerald, A. A., *Some Problems of Modern Accountancy*. Melbourne, 1928.
Samuel, H. B., *Shareholders' Money—An Analysis of Certain Difficulties in Company Legislation, with Proposals for their Reform*. London, 1933.
Scambler, H. McE., 'The Annual Report and Accounts as a Source of Information to Bankers', in Australian Society of Accountants, *Proceedings of [Sydney] Convention*, pp. 183-90.
Serle, Geoffrey, *The Golden Age*. Melbourne, 1963.
Spicer, Ernest Evan and Pegler, Ernest C., *Book-Keeping and Accounts*. 6th ed., London, 1924.
Stahl, F. E., 'The Annual Report and Accounts as a Source of Information to Investing Institutions', in Australian Society of Accountants, *Proceedings of [Sydney] Convention*, pp. 191-7.
Tait, J. B., 'Opinion of Counsel on Following Matters . . .', in Commonwealth Institute of Accountants, *The Victorian Companies Act 1938*. Melbourne, 1939.
Webb, G. T., *Depreciation of Fixed Assets in Accountancy and Economics*. Melbourne, 1954.

Yorston, R. K. and Owens, S., *Annual Reports of Companies*. Sydney, 1958.

Yorston, R. K., Smyth, E. B. and Brown, R. S., *Advanced Accounting*. Sydney, 1947.

ARTICLES

Accountancy Research Foundation, 'What's Wrong with Financial Statements', *Australian Accountant*, vol. 38 (July 1968), pp. 385-96.

Accounting Principles Board, American Institute of Certified Public Accountants, 'Opinion No. 2 "Accounting for the Investment Credit" ', *Journal of Accountancy*, vol. 115 (February 1963), pp. 70-2.

Allard, G. L., 'Presentation of Accounts for Publication', *Chartered Accountant in Australia*, vol. 23 (May 1953), pp. 652-66.

————, 'Victorian Companies Act 1958', ibid., vol. 29 (May 1959), pp. 523-41.

'Amendments to Official Listing Requirements', *Stock Exchange of Melbourne Official Record*, vol. 51 (February 1958), p. 88.

'Amendments to Stock Exchange Listing Requirements', *Australian Accountant*, vol. 37 (November 1967), pp. 649-50.

'The Audit of Parent and Subsidiary Companies', *Commonwealth Journal of Accountancy*, vol. 3 (January 1924), pp. 111-12.

'Auditors Comments', ibid., vol. 8 (May 1929), p. 280.

'Australian Associated Stock Exchanges, Changes in Official List Requirements', *Australian Accountant*, vol. 31 (July 1961), p. 400.

Australian Hire Purchase Conference, 'Deferred Income in Hire Purchase Contracts', *Chartered Accountant in Australia*, vol. 33 (April 1963), pp. 603-14.

Australian Society of Accountants, 'Omission of Subsidiaries from Consolidated Financial Statements', *Australian Accountant*, vol. 39 (November 1969), pp. 487-90.

'Balance Sheet Reform', *Commonwealth Journal of Accountancy*, vol. 8 (June 1929), p. 292.

Balmford, J. D., Clegg, H. C. and Macdonald, J. A., 'Accounting for Investment Allowances', *Australian Accountant*, vol. 34 (September 1964), pp. 530-4.

Blake and Riggall, and Hedderwick Fookes and Alston, 'Victorian Companies Act 1938, Holding and Subsidiary Companies', *Chartered Accountant in Australia*, vol. 9 (June 1939), pp. 797-8.

Boehme, T. C., 'The McKesson and Robbins Case', ibid., vol. 11 (July 1940), pp. 38-44.

Briggs, D. H. and Parker, R. H., 'Some Comments on the New Recommendations on Accounting Principles', ibid., vol. 34 (June 1964), pp. 833-5.

Briskham, A. G. H., 'The Companies Act, 1934 (S.A.) as it Relates to Auditors and Liquidators', ibid., vol. 6 (July 1935), pp. 29-34.

Bibliography

Burt, W. O., 'Company Law Reform', *Accountant in Australia*, vol. 2 (March 1932), pp. 112-18.
Castles, Alex C., 'The Reception and Status of English Law in Australia', *Adelaide Law Review*, vol. 2, no. 1 (1963), pp. 1-31.
Chambers, R. J., 'The Spice of Accounting', ibid., vol. 19 (November 1949), pp. 398-401.
———, 'The Relationship Between Accounting and Financial Management', ibid., vol. 20 (September 1950), pp. 333-58.
———, 'Accounting and Business Finance', *Australian Accountant*, vol. 22 (July 1952), pp. 213-30.
———, 'Trends in Corporate Reporting', ibid., vol. 26 (December 1956), pp. 493-502.
———, 'Tax Allocation and Financial Reporting', *Abacus*, vol. 4 (December 1968), pp. 99-123.
[Cleveland, L. A.], 'Commonwealth Institute of Accountants, Annual Meeting, President's Address', *Commonwealth Journal of Accountancy*, vol. 5 (July 1926), pp. 243-5.
Clunies Ross, A., Correspondence, 'Balance Sheet Form', *Australian Accountant*, vol. 1 (June 1936), p. 401.
———, 'How do you Like the New Act?', ibid., vol. 7 (March 1939), pp. 102-9.
[Committee of the Victorian Research Society, The Institute of Chartered Accountants in Australia], 'Auditing Procedures', *Chartered Accountant in Australia*, vol. 21 (December 1950), pp. 357-9.
'Companies Bill for New Guinea', ibid., vol. 34 (September 1963), p. 178.
'Companies Interim Reports', *Stock Exchange of Melbourne Official Record*, vol. 32 (September 1939), p. 367.
Cox, P. C. E., 'Directors' Emoluments', *Chartered Accountant in Australia*, vol. 34 (August 1963), p. 125.
———, Company Law and Secretarial Section, 'Companies (Public Borrowings) Bill of Victoria', ibid. (December 1963), pp. 389-91.
Crowther, R. Calder, 'Company Legislation in Western Australia', *Australian Accountant*, vol. 1 (May 1936), pp. 257-61.
DeMaris, E. Joe and Zimmerman, V. K., 'An American View of Australian Financial Reports', *Chartered Accountant in Australia*, vol. 30 (January 1960), pp. 343-8.
Donnelly, A., 'The Right Place for Comparative Figures', *Australian Accountant*, vol. 27 (January 1957), pp. 51-2.
Elsworth, John, 'Financial Statement Presentation, What the Investing Public Needs (no. 2)', ibid., vol. 34 (December 1964), pp. 663-71.
Esau, M. S., 'The Form and Content of Published Accounts of Public Companies', *Chartered Accountant in Australia*, vol. 19 (May 1949), pp. 755-67.
Ewart, G. M., 'The Published Accounts of Holding Companies', ibid., vol. 18 (January 1948), pp. 463-88.

Ewens, L. T., 'The Modern Balance Sheet', ibid., vol. 5 (November 1934), pp. 180-4.

Ferguson, D. M., 'The Published Accounts of Holding Companies', *Accountant in Australia*, vol. 1 (March-April 1931), pp. 152-4, 200-7.

——, 'Revaluation of Fixed Assets', *Chartered Accountant in Australia*, vol. 21 (June 1951), pp. 697-711.

Ferres, L. W., 'The McKesson Robbins Frauds', ibid., vol. 12 (1942), pp. 476-87, 521-32 and vol. 13 (1942), pp. 13-26, 48-59.

[Fitzgerald, A. A.], 'Conventions of Accountancy', *Accountant in Australia*, vol. 1 (March 1931), pp. 133-4.

[——], 'Victorian Division Annual Meeting President's Address' [Commonwealth Institute of Accountants], *Commonwealth Journal of Accountancy*, vol. 10 (April 1931), pp. 230-6.

——, 'The Reports and Accounts of Limited Companies', *The Stock Exchange Official Record*, vol. 26 (May 1933), pp. 151-2.

[——], 'Is the Balance Sheet an Anachronism?', *Australian Accountant*, vol. 1 (March 1936), pp. 74-7.

[——], 'Victorian Companies Bill', ibid., vol. 2 (August 1936), pp. 1-2.

[——], 'Australian Company Legislation', ibid. (September 1936), pp. 98-9.

[——], 'The Growing Significance of the Profit and Loss Account', ibid., vol. 3 (June 1937), pp. 301-3.

[——], 'Should We Calculate Depreciation Accurately', ibid., vol. 4 (November 1937), pp. 241-3.

——, Review of 'Principles of Public Utility Depreciation' by Perry Mason, ibid. (December 1937), pp. 328-30.

——, 'Principles of Accounting', ibid., vol. 5 (March 1938), pp. 102-10.

——, 'Balance Sheet Problems, I, The Valuation of Stock on Hand', ibid., vol. 6 (August 1938), pp. 1-14.

——, 'Balance Sheet Problems, II, The Valuation of Fixed Assets', ibid. (September 1938), pp. 81-7.

——, 'Balance Sheet Problems, III, The Form of the Balance Sheet', ibid. (October 1938), pp. 161-9.

——, 'Published Accounts of Holding Companies under the Victorian Companies Act 1938', ibid., vol. 7 (March 1939), pp. 85-92.

——, 'Examples of Holding Companies', ibid. (June 1939), p. 306.

——, 'Refinements of Draughtsmanship', ibid., vol. 8 (November 1939), pp. 231-2.

[——], 'Clarity in Published Profit and Loss Statements', ibid., vol. 12 (September 1942), pp. 451-2.

[——], 'Reserves and Provisions', ibid., vol. 14 (February 1944), pp. 27-9.

―――, 'Items of an Abnormal Character', ibid. (March 1944), pp. 80-2.
[―――], 'Recommendations on Accounting Principles', ibid. (June 1944), pp. 179-82.
―――, 'A Further Note on the Valuation of Trading Stocks', ibid. (December 1944), pp. 424-6.
―――, 'The Valuation of Stock-in-Trade', ibid., vol. 15 (September 1945), pp. 301-6.
―――, 'Company Law Amendment in the United Kingdom, Report of the Cohen Committee, I, Recommendations Relating to Profit and Loss Accounts', ibid. (October 1945), pp. 339-42.
―――, 'Company Law Amendment in the United Kingdom, Report of the Cohen Committee, II, Recommendations Relating to Balance Sheets', ibid. (November 1945), pp. 377-80.
―――, 'Problems of Accounting Valuation of Stock in Trade', ibid., vol. 16 (July 1946), pp. 261-72.
―――, 'Prospective Improvements in Financial Statements of Companies', ibid., vol. 17 (November 1947), pp. 456-63.
[―――], 'Life Assurance Company Adopts Vertical Form', ibid., vol. 18 (July 1948), pp. 227-9.
―――, 'Accounting Doctrine and the 1947 English Companies Act', ibid. (September 1948), pp. 297-313.
―――, 'Accounting and Price Level Changes', ibid., vol. 20 (April 1950), pp. 129-47.
―――, 'Classification of Assets and Accounting Theory', *Accounting Research*, vol. 1 (July 1950), pp. 357-72.
[―――], 'Letter to the Editor', ibid., vol. 26 (December 1956), pp. 519-21.
Fitzgerald, G. E., 'The Accounts of Holding Companies', *Australian Accountant*, vol. 5 (March 1938), pp. 137-59.
―――, 'The Consolidated Statement of Assets and Liabilities', ibid., vol. 14 (January-July 1944), pp. 20-5, 198-202, 245-9.
―――, 'Holding Companies', ibid., vol. 20 (November-December 1950), pp. 409-19, 449-64 and vol. 21 (January 1951), pp. 1-9.
Fitzgerald, G. E. and Speck, A. E., 'The Accounts of Holding Companies', ibid., vol. 14 (1944), pp. 426-31 and vol. 15 (1945), pp. 20-4, 43-7, 138-43, 176-84.
Fitzgerald, T. M., 'Comments on "Should We Blame the Auditing Profession" by R. A. Irish', *Chartered Accountant in Australia*, vol. 34 (August 1963), pp. 90-1.
Fullager, W. K., 'Victorian Companies Act, Counsel's Opinion', ibid., vol. 10 (August 1939), pp. 133-8.
Gibson, R. W., 'Survey of Company Interim Reports—Are They Substantially Satisfactory?', *Australian Accountant*, vol. 36 (March 1966), pp. 133-6.

Gibson, R. W., 'Survey of Company Interim Reports', ibid. (December 1966), pp. 667-72.
———, 'Improvements in Company Interim Reports', ibid., vol. 39 (December 1969), pp. 557-60.
Goddard, R. H., 'An Historical Survey', *Chartered Accountant in Australia*, vol. 8 (April 1938), pp. 681-97.
Goldberg, L., 'Form and Content of Company Financial Statements', *Australian Accountant*, vol. 18 (August 1948), pp. 289-96.
———, 'Depreciation in Published Company Reports', *Accounting Research*, vol. 6 (1955), pp. 155-86.
——— and Clift, R. C., 'An Investigation into Shareholder Attitudes', *Australian Accountant*, vol. 38 (June 1968), pp. 297-305.
Gole, V. L., 'Trends in Published Accounts', ibid., vol. 25 (December 1955), pp. 507-12.
———, 'Democracy in the Corporation', ibid., vol. 33 (June 1963), pp. 291-6.
———, 'The Presentation of Financial Statements', ibid., vol. 34 (January 1964), pp. 13-20.
Grant, J. McB. and Mathews, R. L., 'Inflation and Company Accounts', ibid., vol. 26 (February 1956), pp. 61-6.
———, 'The Response of South Australian Companies to the Post War Inflation', ibid., vol. 27 (March 1957), pp. 143-59.
Gunn, J. A. L., 'Taxation Section, Special Initial Depreciation Allowance in Respect of Plant bought During five years ended June 30, 1950', ibid., vol. 16 (May 1946), pp. 173-4.
———, 'Withdrawal of Initial Depreciation Allowance', *Current Taxation* Supplement to *Australian Accountant*, vol. 22 (March 1952), p. 144.
Halkerston, K. W., 'Financial Statement Presentation, What the Investing Public Needs (no. 1)', *Australian Accountant*, vol. 34 (November 1964), pp. 625-31.
Hartland, W. R., 'Desirable Changes in the Form of Published Accounts and the Auditor's Statutory Report', *Chartered Accountant in Australia*, vol. 30 (June 1960), pp. 588-93.
Harvey, C. B., 'The Form and Content of the Balance Sheet Profit and Loss Account and Auditors Report', ibid., vol. 7 (December 1936), pp. 420-43.
Hewitt, C. L. S., 'A Levy on Provisions for Depreciation', *Australian Accountant*, vol. 11 (November 1941), p. 541.
Hill, B. J. and Desmarchelier, M. F., 'Some Problems for Financiers', *Chartered Accountant in Australia*, vol. 32 (October 1961), pp. 218-23.
———, 'Further Notes on Financiers' Problems', ibid. (January 1962), pp. 399-401.
Hungerford, C., 'Fixed and Floating Assets', ibid., vol. 16 (April 1946), pp. 417-26.

[Institute of Chartered Accountants in Australia], 'New South Wales Company Law', ibid., vol. 5 (October 1934), pp. 151-4.
[———], 'Pronouncement by General Council of the Institute on the Treatment of "Income Yet to Mature" in the Accounts of Finance and Other Companies', ibid., vol. 30 (January 1960), pp. 380-1.
[———], 'Pronouncement by the General Council of the Institute on the Principle and Methods of Apportioning "Income Yet to Mature" ', ibid., vol. 31 (June 1961), pp. 615-17.
[———], 'Memorandum by the Institute's Standing Committee on Company Legislation', ibid., vol. 33 (August 1962), pp. 87-96.
———, General Council Research Committee, 'Net Income, Prior Period Adjustments and the Disclosure of Extraordinary Items', ibid., vol. 40 (October 1969), pp. 4-7.
Irish, R. A., 'Holding Companies and their Subsidiaries', *Australian Accountant*, vol. 13 (September 1943), pp. 342-53.
———, 'Letters to the Editor, N.S.W. Companies Act', *Chartered Accountant in Australia*, vol. 17 (October 1946), pp. 221-2.
———, 'The Balance Sheet Audit and the Form and Content of Published Accounts', *Australian Accountant*, vol. 17 (April 1947), pp. 129-42.
———, 'The Evolution of Corporate Accounting', ibid. (November 1947), pp. 480-501.
———, 'Current Developments in Corporate Accounting', ibid., vol. 18 (November-December 1948), pp. 396-413, 427-36.
———, 'Fundamental Concepts of Corporate Accounting', ibid., vol. 20 (June 1950), pp. 214-29.
———, 'Should We Blame the Auditing Profession', *Chartered Accountant in Australia*, vol. 34 (August 1963), pp. 79-90.
Johnson, J. Campbell, 'The Stock Exchange Viewpoint on Company Annual Reports', *Australian Accountant*, vol. 25 (January 1955), pp. 555-8.
Johnston, T. R., 'The Role of Financial Reporting in a Partially Controlled Economy', ibid., vol. 31 (January 1961), pp. 21-35.
Joint Committee representing the Australasian Institute of Secretaries, Commonwealth Institute of Accountants, Federal Institute of Accountants, the Chartered Institute of Secretaries, 'Companies Bill 1938 (Victoria)', *Accountant*, vol. 100 (May 1939), pp. 673-7.
Joint Panel of Members of the Institute of Chartered Accountants in Australia and the Australian Society of Accountants, 'A Series of Opinions on the Uniform Companies Acts', Supplement to *Chartered Accountant in Australia*, vol. 33 (November 1962), and in *Australian Accountant*, vol. 33 (January 1963), pp. 29-36.
Jones, E. M. *et al.*, 'A Review of Published Accounts of 36 Selected Western Australian Public Companies', *Chartered Accountant in Australia*, vol. 28 (September 1957), pp. 101-16.

Kenley, W. J., 'The Form and Presentation of Company Financial Statements', *Australian Accountant*, vol. 34 (May 1964), pp. 229-37.
———, 'Accounting Problems and Company Failures', ibid., vol. 35 (December 1965), pp. 634-9.
Keown, K. C., 'Stock on hand in the Balance Sheets of Victorian Companies', ibid., vol. 21 (July 1951), pp. 265-6.
Ligertwood, G. C. and Jessop, C. L., 'South Australia, The Companies' Act, 1934', *Chartered Accountant in Australia*, vol. 6 (May 1936), pp. 627-9.
Lister, Chas. W., 'The Balance Sheet', *Accountant*, vol. 118 (March 1948), p. 206.
Littleton, A. C., 'A Genealogy for "Cost or Market"', *Accounting Review*, vol. 16 (1941), pp. 161-7.
Lloyd, John, 'Balance Sheets Under Companies Acts', *Australian Accountant*, vol. 18 (June 1948), pp. 203-4.
[Macbride, Wm. T.], 'Presidential Address' [Commonwealth Institute of Accountants], *Commonwealth Journal of Accountancy*, vol. 14 (May 1935), pp. 245-9.
[MacDonald, O. R.], 'Duties of Auditors in Connection with Stock-in-Trade', ibid., vol. 5 (October 1925), p. 28.
[———], 'Editorial', ibid., vol. 6 (September 1926), pp. 1-4.
[———], 'Valuation and Verification of Stock-in-Trade', ibid., vol. 14 (October 1935), pp. 409-11.
———, 'Where are the Profits?', *Australian Accountant*, vol. 2 (December 1936), pp. 453-7.
———, 'Working Capital', ibid., vol. 5 (April 1938), pp. 236-40.
Macfarlane, T., 'W.A. Companies Act', *Chartered Accountant in Australia*, vol. 19 (September 1948), pp. 173-92.
McInnes, J. S., 'Balance Sheet Requirements of the N.S.W. Act', in 'Company Law and Secretarial Practice', *Australian Accountant*, vol. 3 (February, March 1937), pp. 28-39, 82-93.
McInnes, R. A., 'Better Financial Statements, The Accountant Must Help', ibid., vol. 24 (March 1954), pp. 111-12.
'Monthly Review of Current Events', ibid., vol. 26 (July 1956), pp. 266-72.
Murray, A. F., 'What Investors Want from Company Accounts', *Accountant's Magazine*, vol. 69 (November 1965), pp. 952-69, 1059-79.
Nixon, E. V., 'The Criticism of Accounts', *Commonwealth Journal of Accountancy*, vol. 3 (April 1924), pp. 183-8.
———, 'Holding Companies', ibid., vol. 7 (August 1928), pp. 362-7.
———, 'The Shareholder's Right to Information', *Accountant in Australia*, vol. 2 (June 1932), pp. 264-8.
Outhwaite, A. H., 'Verification of Liabilities, Capital, and Reserves', *Chartered Accountant in Australia*, vol. 7 (November 1936), pp. 331-50.

Bibliography

―――, 'Accounts and Audit under the Victorian Companies Act 1938', ibid., vol. 10 (July 1939), pp. 30-47.
Runcie, N., 'The Concept of Unearned Income', ibid., vol. 33 (October 1962), pp. 229-34.
St John, E. and Grogan, P., 'The Companies (Public Borrowings) Act 1963 of Victoria', ibid., vol. 34 (February 1964), pp. 516-25.
Savage, W. E., 'The Duties and Responsibilities of Auditors under the Queensland Companies Act 1931', *Accountant in Australia*, vol. 2 (August 1932), pp. 341-5.
Saxon, O. Glenn, 'Annual Headache: The Stockholders' Meeting', *Harvard Business Review*, vol. 44 (January-February 1966), pp. 132-7.
Schumer, L. A., 'The Form of Balance Sheets', *Australian Accountant*, vol. 34 (September 1964), pp. 488-90.
'Significant Changes Proposed for Australian Company Law', ibid., vol. 38 (December 1968), p. 681.
Sinclair, A., 'Reserves, Reserve Funds, and Sinking Funds', *Commonwealth Journal of Accountancy*, vol. 3 (September 1923), pp. 10-11.
Slade, A. L., 'Presidential Address, Twelfth Annual Meeting of the Institute', ibid., vol. 14 (May 1935), pp. 245-9.
'South Australian Companies Act', *Chartered Accountant in Australia*, vol. 17 (March 1947), pp. 519-20.
Spackman, E. T., 'Private Balance Sheets', *Australian Accountant*, vol. 23 (November 1953), pp. 462-3.
'Stock Exchange Conference', *Stock Exchange Official Record*, vol. 29 (March 1936), p. 109.
'Stock Exchanges', *Australasian Insurance and Banking Record*, vol. 53 (August 1929), p. 681.
Stock Exchange of Melbourne, Committee of, 'Share Options', *Stock Exchange Official Record*, vol. 28 (December 1935), p. 606.
Sullivan, C. A. E., 'Balance Sheets, Ancient and Modern', *Australian Accountant*, vol. 9 (March 1940), pp. 136-8.
Tait, J. B., 'Reserves', *Commonwealth Journal of Accountancy*, vol. 3 (March 1924), p. 164.
―――, 'Proprietary, Foreign, Holding and Investment Trust Companies under the Victorian Companies Act 1938', *Chartered Accountant in Australia*, vol. 10 (August 1939), pp. 117-32.
Thackray, John, 'Accounting for Inflation', *Dun's Review and Modern Industry*, vol. 84 (December 1964), pp. 39-40, 63-4, 66.
Thomas, C. J., 'The Borrowing Powers of Companies', *Commonwealth Journal of Accountancy*, vol. 12 (February 1933), pp. 163-6.
Touche, G. L. C., 'The Form of the Balance Sheet', *Chartered Accountant in Australia*, vol. 4 (December 1933), pp. 206-23.
Trigg, F. E., 'Shillings and Pence in Published Accounts', ibid., vol. 10 (June 1940), pp. 818-25.
―――, 'Dual Balance Sheets', ibid., vol. 19 (May 1949), p. 714.

Trigg, F. E., 'The Profession's Attitude to Disclosure', ibid., vol. 21 (October 1950), pp. 201-19.

———, 'Principles or Profits', ibid., vol. 23 (May 1953), pp. 635-49.

Upjohn, L. O. H., 'Letters to the Editor, Auditing Procedure—Stock-on-hand', ibid., vol. 21 (February 1951), pp. 470-1.

Waddell, R. R. et al., 'What Should We Be Doing to Improve the Standard of Published Company Financial Reporting?', ibid., vol. 29 (February 1959), pp. 375-88.

Wells, M. C., 'Executive Stock Options—Again', *Australian Accountant*, vol. 38 (August 1968), pp. 461-6.

'Why Do the Assets Appear on the Credit Side of the Balance Sheet', *Commonwealth Journal of Accountancy*, vol. 6 (July 1927), pp. 351-2.

Wilkins, D. C., 'Investment Allowance for Manufacturing Plant', *Australian Accountant*, vol. 32 (March 1962), p. 176.

———, ibid. (July 1962), pp. 362-6.

Wolfenden, E. S., 'Criticism of a Company's Balance Sheet', *Commonwealth Journal of Accountancy*, vol. 7 (January 1928), pp. 137-47.

Wood, P. M., 'Companies Act 1938—Filing of Private Balance Sheet', *Australian Accountant*, vol. 13 (September 1943), pp. 339-40.

Wood, R. G. W., 'Letters to the Editor, Balance Sheets', *Chartered Accountant in Australia*, vol. 34 (January 1964), pp. 451-4.

Wright, G. G., 'Commonwealth Institute of Accountants [Tenth Annual Meeting], Queensland Division [President's Address]', *Commonwealth Journal of Accountancy*, vol. 11 (April 1932), pp. 236-8.

Wrigley, C. D., [President's Address], Commonwealth Institute of Accountants, *Australian Accountant*, vol. 17 (July 1947), pp. 275-81.

Wyon, Sir Albert W., 'Holding and Subsidiary Companies', *Commonwealth Journal of Accountancy*, vol. 13 (December 1933), pp. 85-7.

Yorston, R. K., 'Stock in Trade', *Chartered Accountant in Australia*, vol. 16 (November 1945), pp. 199-200.

———, 'Consolidated Statements', ibid., vol. 17 (1946-7), pp. 510-14, 574-82, 643-7, 701-8 and vol. 18 (1947-8), pp. 22-9, 87-96, 147-56.

———, 'Review of Elements of Accounting by L. Goldberg', ibid., vol. 17 (April 1947), p. 611.

———, 'Some Accounting Implications Arising from the Corporation Viewed as a Social Unit', *Australian Accountant*, vol. 22 (February-March 1952), pp. 41-54, 77-90.

———, 'Control in the Corporation', ibid., vol. 25 (July 1955), pp. 293-302.

———, 'Disclosure and the Annual Report', ibid., vol. 29 (September 1959), pp. 507-13.

———, 'Reporting Financial Information to Employees', ibid., vol. 30 (February 1960), pp. 80-8.

PAMPHLETS AND PAPERS

Allard, G. L., 'The Impact of the Companies (Public Borrowings) Act 1963 on the Accountant and Auditor', in *Combined Institutes Lecture Series, The Companies (Public Borrowings) Act 1963*. Melbourne, 1964.

Australian Associated Stock Exchanges, *Official List Requirements*. Melbourne, 1964.

Australian Chartered Accountants Research and Service Foundation, *Bulletin no. 2, The Audit of Stock-in-Trade for Limited Liability Companies*. Sydney, 1958.

Australian Institute of Management, Sydney Division, *Report of the Panel of Adjudicators, Annual Report Award*. Sydney, 1961- .

Australian Society of Accountants, *Accounting Principles and Practices Discussed in Reports on Company Failures*. Melbourne, 1966.

——, Committee appointed by Western Australian Division, *The Accounting and Taxation Concepts of Business Income, A.S.A. Bulletin no. 9*. Melbourne, 1962.

——, Consolidated Accounts Research Committee, New South Wales Division, *Notes on the Preparation of Consolidated Statements, Society Bulletin no. 2*. Melbourne, 1968.

——, State Research Committee, Victorian Divisional Council, *Accounting for Leases and the Associated Problems Relating to Decisions to Lease or Buy, A.S.A. Bulletin no. 13*. Melbourne, 1965.

[Chambers, R. J.], *Company Losses—Safeguarding the Investor, Current Affairs Bulletin*, vol. 34, no. 11, 1964.

Coles, George J., *A Message from Mr. G. J. Coles*. Toorak, 1936.

Fitzgerald, Sir Alexander A., 'Trends in Company Financing' in Investment in Australia Symposium, *Proceedings*.

Institute of Chartered Accountants in Australia, *Recommendations on Accounting Principles*. Sydney, 1946- .

——, *Statements on Accounting Principles and Recommendations on Accounting Practice*. Sydney, 1965- .

Institute of Chartered Accountants in England and Wales, *Recommendations on Accounting Principles*. London, 1944- .

——, *Statements on Auditing no. 2, Stock in Trade and Work in Progress*. London, 1962.

Investment in Australia Symposium, *Proceedings*. Melbourne, 1965.

McInnes, R. A., *Reporting the Incidence of Company Income Tax, Society Bulletin no. 6*. Melbourne, 1969.

Owens, E. S., *Report of the Panel of Adjudicators Annual Report Award*. Sydney, 1961- .

Rylah, A. G., 'The Law and the Protection of the Investor', in Investment in Australia Symposium, *Proceedings*.

Stevenson, T. A., 'Corporate Accounting—Subsidiary Companies versus

Divisions' in *A Survey of Recent Changes with an Emphasis on Practical Application of the Law*. Melbourne, 1966.

UNPUBLISHED MATERIAL

Australian Associated Stock Exchanges, 'Official List Requirements', 1960-1, 'Agreement to be made part of Application for Official Listing', 1946-60, 'Application Form A, 1949- '.

Stock Exchange of Melbourne, 'Official List Requirements', 1925-58, 'Agreement to be made part of Application for Official Listing'.

Urquhart, A. H., 'The Stock Exchange in Focus' [an Address to North Sydney Rotary, 22 July 1965].

Index

Abnormal items, 85, 117
Accounting principles: changes, 119
Aggregate statement of assets and liabilities, 76, 135
A.I.M. Award, see Australian Institute of Management Award
Allard, G. L., 11, 283
Amalgamated Wireless Australasia Ltd, 115, 121, 182, 191, 304, 313, 314
Ampol Ltd, 16, 182, 191, 238, 304, 313
Annual meeting notice, 205
Annual meeting proceedings report, 295
Ansett Transport Industries Ltd, 115, 159, 182, 191, 192, 213, 222, 233, 241, 254, 261, 292, 304, 312, 313
Associate companies, 234
Associated Pulp and Paper Mills Ltd, 182, 191, 214, 304, 313
Auditors' remuneration, 215, 273
Australasian Corporation of Public Accountants, 49, 192
Australian and Kandos Cement Ltd, 77, 182, 191, 272, 304, 313
Australian Associated Stock Exchanges: official listing requirements, (abnormal items) 123, (interim reports) 280, 283, (subsidiary losses) 239, (taxation) 229; see also Stock Exchanges
Australian Capital Territory, Companies Ordinance, 272
Australian Consolidated Industries Ltd, 121, 134, 182, 191, 253, 304, 312
Australian Finance Conference, 277
Australian Guarantee Corporation Ltd, 183, 191, 217, 219, 304, 313, 314

Australian Gypsum Ltd, 77, 160, 182, 191, 304, 313
Australian Hire Purchase Conference, 218-19
Australian Institute of Management Award, 95, 168, 178, 196, 223, 225, 292-3, 297
Australian Paper Manufacturers Ltd, 182, 191, 214, 304, 313, 314
Australian Society of Accountants: comments on Bills, 267, 270; pronouncement on bad debts, 256; submission to Victorian Statute Law Revision Committee, 128, 239; see also Commonwealth Institute of Accountants; Federal Institute of Accountants; Incorporated Institute of Accountants in Victoria

Balance sheet: classification, 64, 68, 108; form, 65, 173
Blue Metal Industries Ltd, 182, 191, 241, 254, 304, 313
Boral Ltd, 140, 177, 182, 191, 241, 304, 313, 314
Bradmill Industries Ltd, 90, 138, 182, 191, 234, 254, 304, 313
Brick and Pipe Industries Ltd, 149, 182, 191, 280, 304, 312
Brisbane Stock Exchange, 61, 270; see also Stock Exchanges
British Tobacco Company (Australia) Ltd, 121, 141, 160, 182, 191, 254, 304, 312
Broken Hill Proprietary Company Ltd, 16, 82, 114, 177, 182, 191, 192, 199, 203, 214, 221, 280, 304, 312

Calls to mining and forestry companies, 229
Capital expenditure, 258-60

349

350 Index

Carlton & United Breweries Ltd, 78, 182, 191, 222, 304, 312
Chambers, R. J., 17, 157-8, 175, 177, 179, 183, 185, 204, 292, 293
Chartered Institute of Secretaries, 61, 267, 270
Cleveland, L. A., 268
Clunies Ross, A., 154, 264
Cohen Committee: classification, 164; depreciation, 195; directors' remuneration, 128; effect on Australian law, 264, 269; fixed assets, 195; holding companies, 250; profit and loss statement, 111; proprietary companies, 250; recommendations, 109; taxation, 224; valuation of assets, 264
Coles, G. J. & Company Ltd, 126, 182, 191, 240, 296, 304, 313
Coles, George J., 126
Colonial Sugar Refining Company Ltd, 42, 182, 191, 214, 241, 280, 304, 313, 314
Commonwealth Industrial Gases Ltd, 182, 191, 304, 313, 314
Commonwealth Institute of Accountants: advocacy uniform law, 268; comments on Bills, 61-2, 105, 108, 169; consolidated statements, 143; interpretation of law, 63; *see also* Australian Society of Accountants
Companies Acts, *see* English Companies Acts; New South Wales Companies Acts; New South Wales Companies (Amendment) Acts; Queensland Companies Acts; Queensland Companies Act Amendment Acts; South Australian Companies Acts; South Australian Companies Act Amendment Acts; Tasmanian Companies Acts; Victorian Companies Acts; Western Australian Companies Acts; Western Australian Companies Act Amendment Acts
Comparative figures, 179, 273, 293
Conglomerates, 240
Consolidated statements, 79, 137, 140, 232-49, 273; *see also* Aggregate statement of assets and liabilities; Goodwill on consolidation; Minority interests; Reserve on consolidation; Subsidiary companies; Uniform group balance date
Containers Ltd, 121, 182, 191, 304, 313

Convertible securities, 278
Cost of annual report, 204
Currency conversion, 262
Current assets, 163, 256, 273
Custom Credit Corporation Ltd, 183, 191, 217, 304, 313

Debenture holders' needs, 12
Debentures, 275
Deferred taxes, 225
Deposits, 275
Depreciation, 65, 69, 106, 173
Directors' loans, 46, 65, 108, 124
Directors' remuneration, 64, 65, 72, 79, 85, 273
Discount on shares, 53
Discovered assets, 262
Diversification, 240
Dividend appropriations, 273
Divisional reports, 85, 240
Donations, 7
Drug Houses of Australia Ltd, 69, 76, 134, 182, 191, 253, 304, 312
Dunlop Australia Ltd, 127, 140, 160, 182, 191, 203, 254, 305, 312

Eggleston Committee, 130, 213, 236, 274, 297, 302
Electronic Industries Ltd, 182, 191, 238, 305, 313
Email Ltd, 76, 182, 191, 253, 305, 313
Employees: reporting to, 13; statistics, 296
English Companies Acts: 1900, 48, 58; 1907, 17, 54, 58; 1928 and 1929, (effect on Australian law) 18, 58, 194, (disclosure required) 60, (directors' loans) 124, (directors' remuneration) 125, (holding companies) 137; 1947 and 1948, (effect on Australian law) 171, 267, 269, (partial consolidation) 236, (profit and loss statement) 174, (taxation) 224, (uniform group balance dates) 248; 1967, (capital expenditure) 259, (classification) 167, (directors' remuneration) 130, (divisional reports) 242, (donations) 7, (employees) 466, (investments) 236, (non-listed investments) 258, (leases) 260, (liabilities schedule) 167, (nature of business) 206, (proprietary companies) 250, (taxation) 229, (turnover) 213, (unlimited companies) 250, (valuation of assets) 255

English Company Law Committees, see Cohen Committee; Greene Committee; Jenkins Committee; Loreburn Committee; Wrenbury Committee
Executives' details, 296
Export marketing allowances, 229
Extraordinary items, 85, 117

F. & T. Industries Ltd, 115, 138, 182, 191, 203, 253, 305, 313
Federal Institute of Accountants, 61, 63, 105, 169; see also Australian Society of Accountants
Fitzgerald, G. E., 117, 128, 142, 143, 173, 232, 239
Fitzgerald, Sir Alexander: abnormal items, 117; balance sheets, 66-8, 161; classification, 155, 164, 166; comments on law amendment, 104, 106, 170; consolidated statements, 143; depreciation, 190; disclosure, 21, 67; form of statements, 155; funds statement, 291; reserves and provisions, 86, 88, 92, 94, 96; stock valuation, 183, 185-6
Fixed assets, 273
Floating assets, 162
Funds statement, 291

Garnsey, Sir Gilbert, 137, 234
Gibson Kelite Industries Ltd, 10, 296
Goldberg, L., 94, 122, 190, 194-5
Goodwill on consolidation, 242
Greene Committee, 59, 124; holding companies, 137, 250; proprietary companies, 250; redeemable preference shares, 54

Half-yearly reports, 35, 81, 278, 280-90
Henry Jones (I.X.L.) Ltd, 134, 176, 182, 191, 203, 239, 305, 312
Herald and Weekly Times Ltd, 149, 156, 182, 191, 280, 281, 305, 313
Highlights page, 207
Holding companies, 64, 76, 173, 232; see also Aggregate statement of assets and liabilities; Consolidated statements; Goodwill on consolidation; Minority interests; Reserve on consolidation; Subsidiary companies; Uniform group balance date
Holmes, C. M., 44, 49, 192
Human assets, 262

Humes Ltd, 182, 191, 238, 261, 305, 312

I.A.C. (Holdings) Ltd, 121, 177, 183, 191, 217, 219, 277, 305, 312, 313
Imperial Chemical Industries of Australia and New Zealand Ltd, 182, 191, 261, 296, 305, 312
Income from investments, 215
Income yet to mature, 216
Incorporated Institute of Accountants in Victoria, 42, 44, 49, 50, 51, 193; see also Australian Society of Accountants
Initial depreciation allowances, 226
Institute of Chartered Accountants in England and Wales: audit of stock, 150; recommendations on accounting principles, (classification of balance sheet) 163, (form of statement) 154, (group accounts) 109, 232, (profit and loss statements) 109, 112, (reserves and provisions) 93, (stock valuation) 186
Institute of Chartered Accountants of Australia: advocates uniform law, 269; evidence submitted to, (Attorneys-General) 270, (Royal Commission) 62, (Victorian Statute Law Revision Committee) 129, 239; interpretation of Acts, 71, 106; opinions on disclosure, (audit of stock) 150, (auditors' remuneration) 215, (consolidated statements) 142, (recommendation on accounting principles, (capital expenditure) 259, (classification of balance sheet) 164, (depreciation) 190, 195, (form of statements) 154, (group accounts) 109, 232, (profit and loss statement) 103, 109, 112, (reserves and provisions) 93, 95-9, (stock) 186, 256, (taxation) 224, (unearned income on terms contracts) 216-19; see also Australasian Corporation of Public Accountants
Interest on expenditure on fixed assets, 54
Interest paid, 215
Investment allowances, 227
Investment companies, 109, 265
Investments in non-listed companies, 236
Investments in subsidiaries, see Holding companies

352 Index

Irish, Sir Ronald, 6, 18, 89, 112, 118, 150, 156, 177-9, 196
Isaacs, Sir Isaac, 32, 39-51, 87

Jenkins Committee, 180, 213, 259
Johns & Waygood Perry Engineering Ltd, 120, 182, 191, 305, 312
Johnston, Dr T. R., 7, 13, 23
Joint Committee of Accountancy Organizations, 105-8, 111, 117, 142
Jones, E. M., 90, 96, 118, 158, 174, 176, 180, 292
Jones, Henry (I.X.L.) Ltd, see Henry Jones (I.X.L.) Ltd

Kingston Cotton Mill case, 147-51

Larke Consolidated Industries Ltd, 204
Leases, 260
Liabilities schedule, 278
London Stock Exchange, 236
Loreburn Committee, 32, 53-4, 59

MacDonald, O. R., 17, 147, 163, 291
McInnes, R. A., 166, 176, 178, 180, 230
McKesson and Robbins, 148-52
Mackey, J. E., 48
McPhersons Ltd, 143, 182, 191, 237, 305, 312, 313
Materiality, 221
Melbourne Stock Exchange, see Stock Exchange of Melbourne
Minority interests, 247
Myer Emporium Ltd, 96, 182, 191, 217, 261, 312

Narrative format, 45, 153-9
Nature of the business, 206
National Consolidated Ltd, 115, 121, 182, 191, 222, 233, 292, 305, 313
New Guinea, 273
New South Wales Companies Acts: 1936, (classification of balance sheet) 162, (depreciation) 193, (directors' loans) 124, (directors' remuneration) 125, (history) 61-3, 102, (reserves) 46, (reserve fund) 87, (reserve and provision transfers) 219, (subsidiary companies) 137, 139, (underwriting commissions) 53; 1961, 81, 271; see also Uniform Acts

New South Wales Companies (Amendment) Acts, 1960, 1964; see Public Borrowings Acts; Sale of interests
Nixon, Sir Edwin, 18, 70, 92, 136, 161
No-liability companies, 36
No-liability trading companies, 50
Non-current assets, 166
Non-exempt proprietary company, 250, 273
Notes to report, 208
Notice of annual meeting, 205

Olympic Consolidated Industries Ltd, 155, 167, 182, 191, 254, 261, 305, 313
Options, 79, 108, 131
Outhwaite, A. H., 70, 93, 107, 143
Owens, E. S., 205-10

Papua, 273
Partial consolidation, 237
Petersville Australia Ltd, 149, 182, 191, 253, 305, 313
Private balance sheet, 46, 49, 264
Production quantities, 214
Products, 295
Profit and loss statement, 65, 103, 108, 173-4, 273
Proprietary companies, 43, 57, 250; see also Non-exempt proprietary company
Provisions, transfers, 219
Public Borrowings Acts, 3, 66, 167, 249, 281

Quarterly reports, 277, 280-90
Queensland Companies Acts: 1931, (classification of balance sheet) 162, (depreciation) 193, (directors' loans) 124, (directors' remuneration) 125, (history) 58-9, 61, 102, (reserve and provision transfers) 219, (subsidiary companies) 137, 139, (underwriting commissions) 53; 1961, 46, 270; see also Uniform Acts
Queensland Companies Act Amendment Acts: 1942, 265; 1953, 265; see also Public Borrowings Acts; Sale of interests

Redeemable preference shares, 54
Repco Ltd, 160, 183, 191, 305, 312
Reserve funds, 45, 55, 65
Reserve on consolidation, 242
Reserves, 65, 106, 174; transfers, 219

Index

Revaluation of assets, 256
Rothmans of Pall Mall (Australia) Ltd, 183, 191, 305, 313
Rylah, Sir Arthur, 19, 265, 267, 269

Sale of interests, 265
Share options, *see* Options
Share premiums, 55
Shareholders: statistics, 297; opinions on reporting, 9
Simplified financial statements, 298
Sleigh, H. C. Ltd, 121, 183, 191, 241, 254, 261, 305, 313
South Australian Companies Acts: 1934, (classification of balance sheet) 162, (directors' loans) 124, (directors' remuneration) 125, (history) 58, 63, 102, (reserves) 46, 87, (subsidiary companies) 137, 139, (underwriting commissions) 53; 1962, (depreciation) 193, (history) 272; *see also* Uniform Acts
South Australian Companies Act Amendment Acts, 1960, 1964, *see* Public Borrowings Acts; Sale of interests
Spackman, E. T., 265
Stock, valuation, 71, 119, 173, 256
Stock Exchange of Melbourne, 105, 127, 267; *see also* Stock Exchanges
Stock Exchange of Sydney, 62; *see also* Stock Exchanges
Stock Exchanges, 63, 202, 268; *see also* Australian Associated Stock Exchanges; Brisbane Stock Exchange; London Stock Exchange; Stock Exchange of Melbourne; Stock Exchange of Sydney
Subsidiary companies, 85, 106, 173, 273; losses by, 239; statements, 139, 143; *see also* Holding companies
Sydney Stock Exchange, *see* Stock Exchange of Sydney
Syndicates, 266

Tasmanian Companies Acts: 1920, 46, 53-5, 263; 1959, 124, 174, 193, 220; 1962, 272; *see also* Uniform Acts; Public Borrowings Acts
Tait, J. B., 91, 108, 127
Tax allocation, 225
Taxation, 85, 173, 273
Television Corporation Ltd, 183, 191, 238, 305, 313
Terms contracts, 216
Three-monthly report, 277, 280-90

Trigg, F. E., 11, 19, 234
Turnover, 212

Underwriting commissions, 53
Unearned income on terms contracts, 216
Uniform Acts, 3; auditors' remuneration, 215; capital expenditure, 259; classification of balance sheet, 167; comparative figures, 234; current assets, 152, 256; depreciation, 194; directors' loans, 125; directors' remuneration, 129; investments, 258; non-exempt proprietary company, 252; options, 131; profit and loss statement, 174; reserve and provision transfers, 220; sale of interests, 266; taxation, 224
Uniform group balance date, 248, 278; *see also* Aggregate statement of assets and liabilities; Consolidated statements
Unit trusts, 265
Unsecured notes, 275
Unusual events, 85, 117

Valuation bases, 68, 70, 255-8
Victorian Companies Acts: 1896, 43-7, 86, 154; 1910, 48-51, 53, 87, 154, 192; 1938, 64, 102, 171, (abnormal items) 117, (consolidated statements) 143, (depreciation) 193, (directors' loans) 124, (directors' remuneration) 125, (form of statement) 154, 163, (group definition) 234, (option) 131, (partial consolidation) 237, (profit and loss statement) 112, (reserves) 89, (reserve and provision transfers) 220; 1955, 119, 224; 1958, (abnormal items) 119, (auditors' remuneration) 215, (consolidated statements) 143 (currency conversion) 262, (deposits) 275, (history) 263-7, (interest paid) 215, (investment companies) 109, (non-exempt proprietary companies) 252, (sale of interests) 266; 1961, 271; Investment Companies Act 1938, 109; *see also* Public Borrowings Acts; Sale of interests; Uniform Acts
Victorian Companies Auditors Board, 265
Victorian Statute Law Revision Committee, 119, 128, 239, 265, 266, 275

354   Index

Western Australian Companies Acts: 1943, (abnormal items) 119, (depreciation) 193, (directors' loans) 124, (directors' remuneration) 125, (history) 169-71, (interest on capital expenditure) 54, (redeemable preference shares) 54, (reserve and provision transfers) 220, (reserve funds) 90, (reserves) 46; 1961, 271; *see also* Uniform Acts

Western Australian Companies Act Amendment Acts, (No. 2) 1960, 1964, *see* Public Borrowings Acts; Sale of interests

Whole pound/dollar statements, 175; *see also* Materiality

Woolworths Ltd, 76, 138, 177, 183, 191, 224, 260, 305, 313, 314

Wrenbury Committee, 53, 59

Yorston, Sir Keith, 9, 13, 19, 21, 149, 153, 166, 186, 232